Faulkner and Ideology

FAULKNER AND YOKNAPATAWPHA

1992

Faulkner and Ideology

FAULKNER AND YOKNAPATAWPHA, 1992

EDITED BY
DONALD M. KARTIGANER
AND
ANN J. ABADIE

UNIVERSITY PRESS OF MISSISSIPPI
JACKSON

98   97   96   95   4   3   2   1

The paper in this book meets the guidelines for permanence and durability of the
Committee on Production Guidelines for Book Longevity of the Council
on Library Resources.

Library of Congress Cataloging-in-Publication Data

Faulkner and Yoknapatawpha Conference (19th : 1992 : University of
Mississippi)
Faulkner and ideology / Faulkner and Yoknapatawpha 1992 ; edited
by Donald M. Kartiganer and Ann J. Abadie.
     p.   cm.
ISBN 0-87805-759-5 (alk. paper).—ISBN 0-87805-760-9 (pbk.: alk. paper)
1. Faulkner, William, 1897–1962—Political and social views—
Congresses.   2. Literature and society—Southern States—
History—20th century—Congresses.   I. Kartiganer, Donald M.,
1937–   .   II. Abadie, Ann J.   III. Title.
PS3511.A86Z7832113   1992
813\.52—dc20   94-35501
CIP

British Library Cataloging-in-Publication data available

Contents

Introduction

"An 'ideology' is like a god coming down to earth . . . like a spirit taking up its abode in a body."
—KENNETH BURKE

"[The writer] collects his material all his life from everything he reads, from everything he listens to, everything he sees, and he stores that away in sort of a filing cabinet . . . —in my case it's not anything near as neat as a filing case, it's more like a junk box—"
—WILLIAM FAULKNER

1

William Faulkner was not particularly inclined to attach great importance to the impact of the surrounding world on his fiction—whether that world consisted of the literary and intellectual traditions he knew or the socio/cultural milieu in which he grew up and lived all his life. His literary forebears he freely acknowledged, but less as what we usually mean by influences, insinuating themselves into his fictional vision, than as what he called "old friends,"[1] whose books he regularly and lovingly dropped into, as if for morning coffee—but whose power over his prose he would no more admit than he would the power of that person with whom morning coffee was not a metaphor. With contemporary writers he could be more cunning, claiming, for example, that he had not read *Ulysses* before writing *The Sound and the Fury*,[2] or, in the 1930s, that he had "never heard" of Thomas Mann.[3] At other times, however, he was as gracious with them as with the classics. Of Joyce and Mann he said simply: they were "the two great men in my time."[4]

With nonliterary influences he seldom felt the need for graciousness. "Everybody talked about Freud when I lived in

New Orleans, but I have never read him. Neither did Shake-speare. I doubt if Melville did either, and I'm sure Moby Dick didn't."[5] It was only in conversation with Joan Williams and later in an interview with a French graduate student—at a time when he had begun to feel a post-Nobel Prize obligation to represent his country as ambassador of good will—that he acknowledged the influence of Henri Bergson.[6]

As for "ideology," he may or may not have been familiar with Marx's use of the term, but his unwillingness to recognize its relevance to his work is clear enough. As he regarded the giants of literature and philosophy, so Faulkner seems to have regarded the social setting of his own life—and the ideas, attitudes, and habits implicit to that setting. They were nothing more or less than the material at hand: the "stuff" from which, like a meticulous carpenter, he would craft his fiction.

Such a stance may not be all that surprising, yet in Faulkner's case—given his fictional creation of an apocryphal world (loosely based on a real one) thick with the institutions of society and custom—the denial is noteworthy. Not that he ever suggested that his work was not thoroughly grounded in the matter and mores of the Deep South; rather, what he consistently played down was the *significance* of that fact, the power of his lifelong Southern experience to determine what his fiction would be-come: the forms it would take, the scenes it would single out, the meanings it would have. In the correspondence with Malcolm Cowley on the making of *The Portable Faulkner,* Faulkner wrote, "I'm inclined to think that my material, the South, is not very important to me. I just happen to know it, and don't have time in one life to learn another one and write at the same time."[7] The various institutional contexts of the South—what Louis Althusser calls the "apparatuses" of ideol-ogy—might be ones Faulkner held in contempt, such as the tendency to mob violence he describes in *Sanctuary, Light in August,* and *Intruder in the Dust,* or, like the books of older writers, ones he openly admired, such as the Christ story: "one of the best stories that man has invented, assuming that he did invent that story."[8] But what his references to those contexts makes clear is that it is the writer, not the ideology, that is the wellspring of writing. Asked once about the Christ symbolism of Joe Christmas in *Light in August,* Faulkner acknowledged its presence while denying any conscious symbolic intention, then wrapped up the whole subject in a typically offhand Faulknerian reduction: "that's a matter of reaching into the lumber room to get out something which seems to the writer the most effective way to tell what he is trying to tell."[9]

If there is ideology in Faulkner's fiction, it is absent, as far as he is concerned, of much of the comprehensive and subtle force that Marx and more recent commentators have attributed to it. For Faulkner, there may be a fatality in background—the place "I just happen to know"—as in culture: "Everyone that has had the story of Christ and the Passion as a part of his Christian background will in time draw from that."[10] But that fatality is no more than an imagery at hand, a set of manners, an inherited language, less the vital content of fiction than the tools with which the writer creates that content. Ideological context for Faulkner is virtually a constant, a universal which, when considering the significance of a writer's work, is almost beside the point. "(L)ife is a phenomenon but not a novelty," he wrote to Cowley, "the same frantic steeplechase toward nothing everywhere and man stinks the same stink no matter where in time."[11] That this life could somehow constitute a compelling argument of its own, could "speak" him as if he were nothing more than a passive vocabulary for predetermined values, is something he could not conceive of. Dependent upon a unique material experience narrower and more precisely defined than that of any other major American writer of his time, Faulkner nevertheless demonstrates a calm security as to the autonomy of his role as a creative artist. Whatever "made" him, he seems always to insist, is far less important than what he has made of it.

2

For recent literary critics the ideology of a social order harbors a pervasiveness, a power, and a purpose of which Faulkner's

casual commentary on his Southern context betrays little awareness. For such critics, ideology is deeply ingrained within
the social system, permeating every aspect from its modes of
production to its religious practices, from its forms of punishment to its popular arts and codes of fashion. As members of a
society, these critics claim, we do not select the ideology that
ultimately governs our thinking, as if picking it out from a
menu of possibilities, but rather it selects, situates, subjects us,
constituting our identities as its products—and its advocates.
According to Althusser, "ideology is the system of the ideas and
representations which dominate the mind of a man or a social
group," yet in a manner so subtle as to soften or disguise its
own systemic force. The representations of ideology "have
nothing to do with 'consciousness': they are usually images and
occasionally concepts, but it is above all as *structures* that they
impose on the vast majority of men . . . act[ing] functionally on
men via a process that escapes them."[12] Despite its disarming
delicacy, however, ideology—as Kenneth Burke suggests—
wields the power of a god taking hold of the rapt souls of
witnesses to a miraculous event.[13] We receive it as uncritically as
an experience of immanence, in the form of facts as confidently
assumed as the sun rising in the east, the sacredness of a human
being, the superiority of the democratic tradition.

In Althusser's terminology ideology exists as an action of
"hailing" us, of "interpellating" us as subjects so that we live
always already within the operative social system. The power of
this interpellation is such that we cannot help but regard our
social attitudes as not only inevitable and necessary, as we might
regard our sexual and racial identities, but as "natural" in
the sense of possessing an objective, common-sense, universal
value. These attitudes have a sanction beyond their prevalence
or practicality. They are "true"—true not only for ourselves but
for all others, whether they accept that fact or not.

The precise relationship between the ideology of a social
system and the actual lived experience of that system is debat-
able, ranging from Marx's notion of ideology as a false conscious-

ness, a set of illusory precepts and values that exist only to justify the dominant social class, to Althusser's claim that these precepts are a representation of "the imaginary relationship of individuals to their real conditions of existence."[14] While those real conditions remain concealed, ideology incorporates them into an imaginative form, as dreams in the Freudian economy secretly speak the repressed conditions that have generated them.[15] What remains uncontested, however, is that ideology is a form of fiction—an arbitrary ideational system implicit to a particular social system—that presents itself as self-evident truth. It is a set of "seeming universals" (Frederick Crews), a "strategy of containment" (Fredric Jameson), "the fictive . . . element in our discourse" (Hayden White).[16]

The combination of power over its subjects and its persuasive pretensions to truth lends ideology a decidedly sinister quality: it is something to be unmasked, exposed, interrogated. Its chief purpose, according to Marxist critics, is to ensure the survival of the system it undergirds, a system necessarily oppressive since it consists of a dominant class exerting power over another class or classes. Ideology, in other words, is inseparable from the arrangements of power within its social order. It implements, rationalizes, and sustains those arrangements; and it makes us, in all our beliefs and practices—including our art—accomplices in the oppression it sanctions.

Current critical emphasis on the nature and role of ideology has the dual effect of giving literary texts greater relevance while reducing their distinctiveness as privileged modes of utterance. On the one hand, by describing the ideology at work in a text critics restore that text to a material world, give it body by registering the actual social dynamics at work in it. On the other hand, by reading the text as crucially implicated by those dynamics, critics rid it of any unique power to transcend ideology, to speak timelessly and universally. Literature, like other, "lesser" forms of utterance, cannot help but repeat a specific historical moment's "interested" justifications of its mores.

Precisely *how* ideology exists in literary texts remains, however, a point of critical controversy. Does the text *reflect*, consciously or unconsciously, the ideology of its time, necessarily supporting that ruling class whose interests ideology represents? Or can the text *challenge* ideology?—and if so, how does it come to perform this act? Confined to the language of the existing social order (and how else can it be understood?), how can a text speak what that order does not "believe," what it has no means of articulating? To conceive of the text as capable of challenging the limits of its own language suggests an elitist stance: a mystification of the literary text and a New Critical heroization of the author. There is also the problem of the reader of such a text. Given the immersion in ideology of every member of the society, if a text *could* somehow speak beyond its own socially derived language, who but a reader as revolutionary (and as heroic) as the writer could read it?

In both cases—the text as reflection, the text as challenge—the great beneficiary, the new privileged being as it were, is the critic. One of the consequences of ideological analysis is that, while generally reducing writer and text to membership among the ideologically contained, it aggrandizes the critic, rendering him or her as the sole person capable of encountering, even mastering, ideology *as such:* exposing it in texts unconsciously pervaded by it, or giving voice to the nearly silent, marginal critique of ideology in those texts in which, somehow, critique has assumed verifiable form. The critic becomes the interrogator, unmasking the propaganda of the reflecting text; or the analyst, revealing the dangerous anti-ideological material of the challenging text, which the unaware reader (and sometimes the unaware writer) has been unable, or unwilling, to acknowledge.

Faulkner's texts can be particularly fruitful for ideological analysis because they belong so obviously to a particularized historical place and moment even as they convey the sense of a radical imagination at work, one that at least seems committed to the unmaking of any and all constructed visions. Does Faulkner's fiction "belong" to northern Mississippi in some partisan form (which his fellow citizens apparently missed entirely), or does it challenge that very world whose language it seems so fluently to speak?

These questions lead to larger ones pertaining to the very nature of writing and reading. Is literature confined to an expression of the social forces that generate it? Are we as readers doomed to learn from literature only what our own contexts permit? Was Kafka right, or only incurably Modernist, when, in a famous letter on the power of writing (and, by implication, of reading) he said:

> I think we ought to read only the kind of books that wound and stab us. If the book we're reading doesn't wake us up with a blow on the head, what are we reading it for? So that it will make us happy . . . ? Good Lord, we would be happy precisely if we had no books, and the kind of books that make us happy are the kind we could write ourselves if we had to. But we need the books that affect us like a disaster, that grieve us deeply, like the death of someone we loved more than ourselves, like being banished into forests far from everyone, like a suicide. A book must be the axe for the frozen sea inside us.[17]

3

The thirteen papers presented under the rubric "Faulkner and Ideology" range from a serious questioning of the whole project of ideological analysis to specific examples of such analysis, focusing either on individual Faulkner texts or on some of the particular socio/cultural contexts bearing on those texts.

In "Faulkner and the New Ideologues," André Bleikasten expresses a deep impatience with some of the directions that ideological criticism has taken in the study of Faulkner. Remarking on how, more than a decade earlier, he had in general welcomed the move from the "sanitary vacuum of the New Criticism" to a more "ideologically conscious approach," one attempting to address the anthropological, historical, social, and political dimensions of Faulkner's work, Bleikasten now regards that move as one that has gone awry. The problems, as he sees them, have to do with the general "ideological consensus" among critics—a seemingly hegemonic attraction to neo-Marxist, neo-Freudian (Lacanian), neo-feminist theory; the denigration of formal issues on behalf of a single-minded attention to content; and a simplistic binarism that forces Faulkner's texts into the service of a "Manichean morality of right and wrong." The result is an analysis and reevaluation of Faulkner's texts that leave little room for what Bleikasten considers to be the great strength of the novel form: "the sense of relativity and complexity, the spirit of doubt and questioning, what Milan Kundera calls 'the wisdom of uncertainty.' " Bleikasten sees not only a misplaced emphasis on some of Faulkner's lesser work but also, and more significantly, the possible misreading of the major work. The genius of that work is precisely its refusal to "serve ideological certitudes": its insistence on the "scandalous truth no one wants to hear, the truth that no single Truth is available."

Several papers in the collection repeat and attempt to address the problems Bleikasten raises. Frequently, however, they demonstrate less the tendentiousness Bleikasten fears than the discovery in Faulkner's texts of the signs of ideological conflict. That is, they trace the texts' enactment of struggle *within* ideology rather than identify either a dominant ideology or a revolutionary one.

Richard King points out Faulkner's general refusal to represent publicly any particular political position (or to do so inconsistently, as in the civil rights issue). He then focuses on the implicit ideological dimension of narrative, while warning that Faulkner may resist *all* ideological categorization. King addresses specifically Faulkner's narratives of "founding," with their attention to the exercise and often "abuse of power." He describes two modes of founding narrative in Faulkner: one is the "sublime" mode, epitomized in Thomas Sutpen and Carothers McCaslin; the other the "pastoral" mode, of the late essay "Mississippi" and the historical introductions of *Requiem for a Nun*. The first stresses a dynamic, self-creating yet brutal power, apparently doomed by the fathers' rejection of their black heirs; this mode of founding seems "originally," although perhaps retroactively, cursed. The second mode also traces a version of decline from some superior source, yet without "the tortured and agonized atmosphere" of the narratives of Sutpen and McCaslin. Indeed the violation and rapacity become absorbed into the elegiac, "a melancholic, though not bitter, vision of decline." Noting that the two narrative versions situate themselves rather neatly on either side of World War II, King infers a possible radical-conservative ideological split in Faulkner's work, yet also cautions against such a division, pointing out the danger of interpretations bent on finding only that Faulkner they can most easily live with. Instead, King suggests, we must recognize that his narratives may be refusing to be "domesticated" or normalized to suit any political camp; that he may be a writer exploring ideological issues in narrative rather than arguing for or against a particular ideology.

Like King, Richard Gray is more interested in describing conflicts in Faulkner's life and work than establishing any single ideologically informed theme. His particular concern is the tension between Faulkner's obsession with personal privacy and the complex social context in which he located his invariably isolated, often alienated characters. Gray establishes a link between Faulkner's own commitment to privacy—and the various personae that commitment may have led him to adopt—and the autonomy he insisted that his characters, once created, possessed: "any character that you write takes charge of his own behavior. You can't make him do things once he comes alive and stands up and casts his own shadow."

Gray relates these personal and professional convictions of Faulkner's to Mikhail Bakhtin's complex theory of the "full and equally valid voices" of character and author that constitute the novel: the paradoxical presence of autonomy and community as the essential novelistic condition. Gray summarizes that condition: "we exist *apart,* as autonomous subjects and authors of our own discourse, and as *part* of what Bakhtin called 'a speaking collective' from whom our words are derived and to whom, however implicitly, they are addressed." Faulkner's characters are "irrevocably private and yet implicated in history." The great drama of *Light in August,* for example, is Joe Christmas's attempt to "challenge the linguistic divisions" of his society. His life is "full of other people's words," yet the upshot of his death and castration is the possibility that "the linguistic and ideological divisions between black and white will be called into question and subverted"—that "the human subject still has the chance to alter the terms of his or her own culture."

One of the characteristics of ideological criticism—and a sign that it is being carried out comprehensively—is the abundance of nonliterary discussion it frequently gives rise to. Skepticism toward the New Critical separation of the literary work from the circumstances of the everyday world yields a willingness to investigate the particular cultural contexts that may be feeding into texts, although without necessarily determining their entire response to those contexts.

Robert Brinkmeyer addresses a specific ideological issue of the 1930s, the concern over emergent fascism in Europe and its possible American versions. For many in America, the strong regionalist identity of the South rendered it especially vulnerable to the radical nationalism of fascism, the essence of which was seen as "*the denial of universality* [:] The universality of truth, of value, of law, of human rights." Several Southern intellectuals, however, particularly the Agrarians, equally condemned fascism, but saw its incipient presence not in their own regionalism but in expanding industrialism and liberal democratic theory—in fact regarding radical democracy itself as a potential steppingstone to both fascism and communism. Brinkmeyer reveals how this ideological debate as to the sources of fascism and the nature of a genuine democratic tradition becomes a significant level of some of Faulkner's major texts, including *Go Down, Moses, Absalom, Absalom!,* and *The Hamlet.* The result, according to Brinkmeyer, is by no means a simplistic regionalism, upholding the Southern form of individualist democracy, but a characteristic complexity and comprehensiveness. While certainly providing powerful fictional representations of Southern traditionalism—as for example in the figure of Ike McCaslin—Faulkner also demonstrates the danger of fanatic defense of that traditionalism—as in the figure of Percy Grimm. Fascism, the texts seem to tell us, can lurk anywhere: in a democratic tradition verging on anarchy, or a narrow parochialism blindly committed to order.

Like Brinkmeyer's exploration of American attitudes toward fascism in the 1930s, Ted Ownby addresses the conflicting ideologies surrounding a single American cultural phenomenon: the birth of the consumer society in the first half of the twentieth century and Faulkner's fictional representation of it. Ownby identifies two attitudes toward the sudden availability and pursuit of consumer goods: one stresses the possible liberation from poverty and stultifying tradition, as well as the democratic move toward equality through the purchase of goods once reserved for a privileged class; the other recognizes a rising self-indulgence, a rejection of the past and a communal ethic based on a sense of collective responsibility rather than individual material acquisition. The complexity of Ownby's reading of Faulkner's several fictional accounts of these opposed attitudes is that while clearly recognizing Faulkner's deep interest in the past, he distinguishes him from such figures as William Alexander Percy and Richard Wright—both of whom attack modern consumerism, although according to vastly differing criteria. Faulkner for example treats with sympathy the efforts of people like Lena Grove, Joe Christmas, Anse and Cash Bundren, and the three "reivers" of his last novel to seek new pleasures and even economic equality through the purchase or appropriation of such consumer items as a box of sardines, a new suit, a phonograph, or, most significantly, an automobile. And yet in the Snopes trilogy Faulkner provides a devastating critique of both the pure consumerism of a family wholly without tradition, who seek wealth only in order to acquire more wealth, as well as the emptiness of the luxury consumer item that implies the pure isolation of individual self-indulgence.

Anne Goodwyn Jones's exploration of the ideology of "penetration" focuses largely on attitudes toward sexual intercourse current during Faulkner's most prolific period of writing. After a comprehensive and illuminating account of the different forms ideology may take in a particular historical period—and a reading of Faulkner's "Dry September" which demonstrates how even the apparent "truth" of a text may yet reflect an ideological position—Jones analyzes the ideological assumptions and biases of the very concept of "penetration." She contends that penetration is privileged over *being* penetrated, that it is a sign of social dominance and power: a mental construct (as opposed to a "natural" condition) that leads directly to the ambivalent attitudes toward sexual relations reflected in the popular sex manuals of Faulkner's time. The paradoxical gist of those manuals—in particular the seemingly revolutionary *Ideal Marriage*, by Theodore H. Van de Velde—is that they propose an equality in intercourse between the needs and pleasures of men and women, even as they subtly preserve the male's greater right to sexual satisfaction because of his need to experience sexual dominance. The effect is to legitimize female desire while "recuperating [it] . . . into patriarchal ideology." The ambivalence reflected here is even more complex in Faulkner's fiction, given his dual identifications as the male—the founder, the initiator, the hunter—and the female—the artist, the Southerner. That ambivalence surfaces in such texts as *The Sound and the Fury*, with Quentin's desire to be a man complicated by "his preference—albeit unconscious—for the feminine ideological position"; in *Light in August*, with Joe Christmas's uncertainties about gender as well as race; and in the repeated, classic Faulknerian scene of the outsider penetrating the door closed to him, a scene that is simultaneously of revolution and rape.

The focus of Martha Banta's "The Razor, the Pistol, and the Ideology of Race Etiquette" is the formation in post-Reconstruction America of an elaborate code of etiquette governing relations between blacks and whites, a code that extended from prescribed rules for common social interaction to rules for lynching and mob violence that emerged from the infraction of those rules. Using numerous examples from the original *Life,* a New York City weekly, Banta describes the shifting American attitudes toward race relations primarily in the years 1897–1907, as condescending sympathy toward blacks becomes fear, as amusement over an inferior race becomes dismay at the onset of the Other—which ultimately threatens the purity of white civilization with the danger of miscegenation. Some of Faulkner's most dramatic treatments of black-white engagement, in *Go Down, Moses* and *Light in August,* take on new meaning as Banta attends to the particular weapons blacks and whites take up in their anger and/or defense, as even here, in situations of seemingly uncivilized violence, ideologically informed codes of behavior govern "who is to kill whom and according to what rules of decorum." A significant contribution of the essay is the lines of connection it demonstrates between the popular magazine and the serious artist, its account of how social custom can affect both, even as the artist may be able to probe custom more deeply, may be able to imagine the individual whom convention cannot wholly determine or predict.

The subtlety of James Mellard's approach to *As I Lay Dying* lies in his assertion that the novel employs three different fictional aesthetic modes—realism, naturalism, modernism— each of which bears an implicit ideological freight. The presence and relative strength of these modes in the novel conform to the Marxist critic Raymond Williams's identification of any single cultural moment as a meeting ground of residual, dominant, and emergent forces. In place of a monolithic reading of an historical period, Williams insists on the existence of movement and change: one ideological force in decline, another paramount, a third ascending. By approaching *As I Lay Dying* through the critical discussion surrounding Faulkner in the 1930s, Mellard is able to demonstrate the dynamic relationship of the novel's conflicting fictional modes rather than, from the perspective of the present, simply assuming the supremacy of a modernism that only *became* dominant (in America at least) well after the novel was written. Anticipating, then, some of André Bleikasten's charges that ideological criticism has become tendentious and simplistic, Mellard reads several key scenes in the novel as demonstrations of one fictional mode first exerting dominance, then being challenged, "defamiliarized," by another—which is itself unable to become the novel's prevailing language. The result is a critical reading that tries to keep abreast of the ideological flux contemporary with its textual object rather than to impose a kind of anachronistic order from a remote and quite different vantage point.

The next three essays in the collection consist of detailed readings of specific Faulkner texts in the light of certain ideological concerns. As J. Hillis Miller has argued elsewhere, the close reading of texts must be the ultimate outcome of theory, and to neglect or dismiss such reading constitutes a "major treason against our profession."[18] Thadious M. Davis focuses on the ideological implications of Faulkner's 1945 "Appendix/The Compsons/1699–1945," which she reads not only as a summary of *The Sound and the Fury* but, even more, a revision of it: "At once an act of memory, the recollection of the novel, and an act of invention, the extension of the novel." The thrust of that revision is Faulkner's need to alter his own marginalization as a Southern writer in America (and in 1945 an apparently failed one at that) by emphasizing the Compson patriarchal line and diminishing the roles of women and blacks. The Appendix not only alters some of the central qualities of *The Sound and the Fury;* it is also testimony *as act* to the writer's quest for power "as creator and inventor." Its revisionary effect is the enhancement of the character of Jason—a "veiled celebratory attention paid to the entrepreneur"—and the drastic reduction of Caddy, now "static and voiceless," and the black Gibsons, all of whom are rendered as subjugated to various external restrictions. This subjugation extends even to Dilsey, who no longer can affect "either the world at war or Caddy in Europe or Melissa Meek in Jefferson."

For J. Hillis Miller, the different conceptions of ideology we find in Marx and two recent commentators, Althusser and Paul de Man, come together in their common recognition of ideology as "an erroneous relation between consciousness and material reality." The twofold question Miller raises is 1) does this assertion of the fundamental falsehood of ideology rest on a conviction of attainable truth lying behind that falsehood? and 2) to what extent is Faulkner's *Absalom, Absalom!* a novel about the imprisonment of human minds within ideology *and* an exploration of the possibility of moving beyond it? Miller demonstrates in detail the nearly overwhelming presence in the novel of the Southern ideologies surrounding class, gender, and race that at once command the belief of all the characters—and their victimization. Ideology, of course, exerts a control all the more powerful because of the characters' unawareness that their assumptions are in fact ideological rather than "natural," and because of the tendency—particularly vivid in Faulkner—towards generational repetition, "that most ineradicable of human habits: storytelling." Following his analysis of the ways in which individual characters unknowingly reenact their inherited ideological assumptions—which even readers are under enormous pressure to repeat as the very process of their reading—Miller suggests Faulkner's invocation of a material, "topographical" reality, as opposed to ideological reality. This is the reality of the body, of the land that concretizes ideology, that materializes memory, and thus offers to readers "a possible means of liberation": a new knowledge that conceivably might undo prevailing ideological constraints, might even issue as "right action."

Glenn Meeter reads *Go Down, Moses* in terms of the blend of Lost Cause ideology with the various biblical echoes that resonate throughout the book. Focusing primarily on "The Bear" and the somewhat neglected title story, Meeter identifies three typological frames of reference at work in *Go Down,*

Moses, each of which contributes a different ideological significance to the events. From the perspective of the Lost Cause,
the South is comparable to the Israelites of Exodus, wandering
in the wilderness and eventually to return to the Promised
Land; from the perspective of Ike McCaslin, the South is
the fallen Eden of Genesis, the redemption of which seems
hopelessly remote. The most interesting typology is that of
Molly Beauchamp of "Go Down, Moses," who identifies the
South with the Israelites—an identification which would seem
to link her with the defenders of the Lost Cause and its implicit
racism. The difference, Meeter points out, is that Molly is
thinking not of the Israelites of *Exodus* but the Israelites of
Genesis: "not as the defeated but still chosen Israel of Lost
Cause ideology but as the [inhabitants of] the promised land of
Canaan." Molly's allusions to her grandson Butch as a Benjamin
sold into Egypt, and to the McCaslin plantation as itself the
promised land, thus indicates a faith Ike McCaslin lacks as well
as an understanding of Southern inheritance far different from
that of the Lost Cause apologists.

The volume concludes—perhaps not surprisingly and even
properly so—with two further versions of André Bleikasten's
opening salvo against ideological analysis. Noel Polk does not
argue against such analysis, but he does point out what he
considers to be Faulkner's own dismay with ideology: his deeply
pessimistic conviction of the human need for the safety ideology
affords. Polk approaches the question of ideology in Faulkner
by attending to some of the apparent contradictions in his life
and work that emerge in the 1950s: between some of his public
and private statements, between a passion for privacy and a
willingness to present an ingratiating public self—ultimately the
more disturbing contradiction between the fiction of his later
years and the fiction between 1929 and 1942 that was primarily
responsible for the adulation and honor he was finally in the
process of receiving. Through readings of some late Faulkner
writings, all of them with autobiographical implications—an

essay on Sherwood Anderson, a short story, "Mr. Acarius," and the long essay "Mississippi"—as well as *A Fable*, Polk suggests a continuity between early and late Faulkner. That continuity is comprised of Faulkner's belief—reaching perhaps its most extreme expression in *A Fable*—that humanity's deepest need is its refusal to be free, to move beyond the boundaries of ideology. Inferring in Faulkner a recognition of the Cold War as a unified attack by contending ideologies against "the citizens of both persuasions," Polk reads *A Fable* as an epic battle between the old general, who would provide humanity with the comfort of ideological systems he believes it requires, and the corporal, who offers freedom from all ideology—a gift which arouses only fear and anger. The darkness of late Faulkner, Polk maintains, concealed behind his most notable public statements, is his conviction of the chronic, apparently necessary enslavement of people to their "ideological illusions."

Louis D. Rubin, while admitting that as readers we necessarily seek to organize our experience "into schematic categories," insists that ultimately we must bring those categories to bear on "the recalcitrance of the literary image itself, a recalcitrance that constitutes the source of its strength and authenticity." This is the crucial encounter for the reader, when he or she must finally confront the textual object itself: "the words on the printed page as written by William Faulkner." According to Rubin, the relevant ideological schemes are chosen consciously by the critic, as tools enabling us to make the reading experience both intelligible and useful. The problem emerges when those schemes seem to bypass or diminish the "literary image" itself, which, in the example of *Absalom, Absalom!* that Rubin uses, is essentially the "consciousness" of Quentin Compson: the process by which he comes to understand the Sutpen history he has been grappling with. For Rubin the critic's distinctive discipline is to encounter and sustain that "literary image": "the integrity and authenticity of the novel and the poem . . . are in our hands."

The issues Rubin raises exist, implicitly or explicitly, in all these essays: how does the "literary image" speak in the context of the ideological forces—belonging both to the reader and to the writer—that seem to surround it, that constitute its very language? Faulkner's texts, as these essays have tried to demonstrate, emerge from a rich network of socio/cultural materials whose impact seems beyond doubt; the question is the nature and degree of that impact. If the literary text can no more shed its material origins than expression the habiliments of language, is it also true that those origins ultimately forbid the revolutionary statement that would undo them? As I suggested earlier in this introduction, the essential question for ideological analysis is whether literature can ever violate its ideological context: can ever be *more and other* than what everything in its origins has determined it should be. How could such a literature be produced? How, for that matter, could a reader—equally "interpellated," equally constituted by ideology—be radical enough to recognize it? And yet what is the value of a literature that cannot commit such violation, or of a reading that cannot bear witness to it?

Donald M. Kartiganer
The University of Mississippi
Oxford, Mississippi

NOTES

1. *Lion in the Garden: Interviews with William Faulkner, 1926–1962*, ed. James B. Meriwether and Michael Millgate (New York: Random House, 1968), 251.
2. Ibid., 30.
3. Joseph Blotner, *Faulkner: A Biography* (New York: Random House, 1974), 1012.
4. *Lion in the Garden*, 250.
5. Ibid., 251.
6. Blotner, 1302; *Lion in the Garden*, 68–73.
7. *The Faulkner–Cowley File: Letters and Memories, 1944–1962*, ed. Malcolm Cowley (New York: The Viking Press, 1966), 14–15.
8. *Faulkner in the University: Class Conferences at the University of Virginia, 1957–1958*, ed. Frederick L. Gwynn and Joseph L. Blotner (Charlottesville: University of Virginia Press, 1959), 117.
9. Ibid.
10. Ibid.

11. *Faulkner–Cowley File*, 15.

12. Louis Althusser, *Lenin and Philosophy and Other Essays*, trans. Ben Brewster (New York: Monthly Review Press, 1971), 158; *For Marx*, trans. Ben Brewster (London: Verso Editions/NLB, 1977), 233.

13. Kenneth Burke, *Language as Symbolic Action: Essays on Life, Literature, and Method* (Berkeley: University of California Press, 1968), 6.

14. Althusser, *Lenin and Philosophy*, 162.

15. See Myra Jehlen's valuable discussion of Althusser, Marxism, and ideology in "Introduction: Beyond Transcendence," in *Ideology and Classic American Literature*, ed. Sacvan Bercovitch and Myra Jehlen (Cambridge: Cambridge University Press, 1986), 1–18.

16. See Frederick Crews, "Whose American Renaissance?" *New York Review of Books* 35 (October 27, 1988); 68; Fredric Jameson, *The Political Unconscious* (Ithaca: Cornell University Press, 1981), 53–54; Hayden White, *Tropics of Discourse: Essays in Cultural Criticism* (Baltimore: Johns Hopkins University Press, 1978), 99.

17. Franz Kafka, *Letters to Friends, Family, and Editors*, trans. Richard and Clara Winston (New York: Schocken Books, 1977), 16.

18. J. Hillis Miller, *Fiction and Repetition: Seven English Novels* (Cambridge: Harvard University Press, 1982), 21.

A Note on the Conference

The Nineteenth Annual Faulkner and Yoknapatawpha Conference sponsored by the University of Mississippi in Oxford took place August 2–7, 1992, with more than three hundred of the author's admirers from around the world in attendance. The six-day program on the theme "Faulkner and Ideology" centered on the lectures collected in this volume. Brief mention is made here of the numerous other activities that took place during the conference.

The program opened with *Voices from Yoknapatawpha*, readings of Faulkner passages selected and arranged by conference director Evans Harrington. Conference participants then gathered at Faulkner's home, Rowan Oak, for the announcement of winners of the third Faux Faulkner write-alike contest. On hand to introduce the first-place winner, Michael Crivello of Flower Mount, Texas, were author Barry Hannah, one of the judges, and Doug Crichton, editor of *American Way*, in-flight magazine of American Airlines. Cosponsoring the contest with *American Way* were Yoknapatawpha Press and its *Faulkner Newsletter* and the University. After a buffet supper, held on the lawn of Dr. and Mrs. M. B. Howorth, Jr., and sponsored by *American Way*, André Bleikasten delivered the opening lecture and Square Books hosted an autograph party.

Later in the week, four scholars from the Gorky Institute of World Literature—Nicolai Anastasiev, Sergei Chakovsky, Maya Koreneva, and Julia Palievsky—participated in a panel discussion titled "Views of Faulkner and Ideology from Moscow." Chester A. McLarty was moderator for "Oxford Women Remember Faulkner," a panel discussion featuring Mary McClain Hall, Minnie Ruth Little, Anna Kiersey McLean, and Bessie Sumners. Howard Duvall and M. C. Falkner served as panelists for sessions on "William Faulkner of Oxford." James B. Carothers, Robert W. Hamblin, Arlie Herron, and Charles A. Peek conducted "Teaching Faulkner" sessions. Other conference activities included a slide lecture by J. M. Faulkner, guided tours of North Mississippi, and the annual picnic at Faulkner's home, Rowan Oak.

The conference planners are grateful to all the individuals and organizations who support the Faulkner and Yoknapatawpha Conference annually. We offer special thanks to Mrs. Jack Cofield, Dr. and Mrs. M. B. Howorth, Jr., Dr. and Mrs. C. E. Noyes, Dr. William E. Strickland, Mr. Glennray Tutor, Ms. Patricia Young, Mr. Richard Howorth of Square Books, St. Peter's Episcopal Church, the City of Oxford, the Oxford Tourism Council, and *American Way*, the magazine of American Airlines.

Faulkner and Ideology

FAULKNER AND YOKNAPATAWPHA

1992

Faulkner and the New Ideologues

André Bleikasten

Qui chante en groupe mettra, quand on le lui demandera,
son frère en prison.
—Henri Michaux

Is "ideology" still a useful concept for literary criticism or does it only serve to stir up futile arguments? Does it help us to identify and clarify vital issues in a work of fiction which would otherwise remain unacknowledged and unintelligible or does it merely trivialize critical inquiry into pseudo-sociology and inept politicizing?

These were some of the questions I had in mind when, twelve years ago, at the first International Colloquium on Faulkner held in Paris, I delivered a paper entitled "For/Against an Ideological Reading of Faulkner's Novels."[1] Since the fifties, academic Faulkner criticism in America had been almost uniformly uncritical, and most of it was blandly ahistorical and apolitical. Faulkner's Southernness was of course too conspicuous to go unnoticed, but nearly everybody then assumed that with a genius of his magnitude regionalism could be little more than a contingent local inflection to his universal message. To read a Nobelized and canonized master of modern fiction without taking his humanistic credentials fully for granted would have been considered in poor taste. There was a clear need, then, to remove Faulkner's work from the sanitary vacuum of the New Criticism and to take a sharper look at its ideological implications. Yet, as the title of my paper was meant to suggest, I was of two minds about the issue, for as a close observer of the French intellectual scene, long dominated by the Sartrean

3

imperative of *engagement,* I was also uncomfortably aware of the ravages of ideological criticism, and too familiar with the crude aesthetics of most Marxist theorists not to fear a relapse into the leftist pieties and platitudes of the 1930s.

Despite my misgivings, however, my paper was indeed a call for a less reverent, less sentimental, and more ideologically conscious approach to Faulkner's fiction. My prayers, alas, were to be answered beyond my worst fears.

Not that Faulkner critics transferred allegiance from New Criticism to New Historicism overnight. Since the mid-1970s, when John T. Irwin's and Myra Jehlen's books on Faulkner appeared,[2] new areas of investigation have been charted, new methods put to use, and whenever there has been critical intelligence at play, the results have been provocative. Of the many studies on Faulkner published over the last two decades those still worth reading all depart in some significant way from the New Critical tradition, whether they focus on Faulkner's language from a Derridean perspective, as John T. Matthews[3] does, or whether they interrogate his fiction in broader cultural terms. Jehlen's discussion of class conflict in Faulkner's South as well as the later studies by Richard H. King, Carolyn Porter, Eric J. Sundquist, Thadious Davis, James A. Snead, Michael Grimwood, and Warwick Wadlington are interesting attempts to deal with the anthropological, historical, social, and political implications of his fiction.[4] But it is only over the past years, with the rise of cultural studies and the New Historicism, that ideology has become a central preoccupation of Faulkner criticism in America. In the wake of the challenging developments in literary theory since the late 1960s, one might have expected a fresh, more sophisticated approach to the topic. New questions have indeed been raised within seemingly new frameworks of analysis, new answers sometimes proposed, and the best books on Faulkner published in the late 1980s and early 1990s undeniably achieve a number of valid insights, yet it seems to me that those with the most obvious political concerns are too much trapped in their own ideology to help us rethink the relation of Faulkner's fiction to ideology in new terms.

What made me at once suspicious of these presumedly "revisionary" readings of Faulkner was that, notwithstanding their differences in scope, emphasis, and quality, they sound so much alike: they all use imported lexical kits (from Lacancan to Derridada), refer and defer all to the same authorities, and, with one or two exceptions, tend to make the same points over and over again about one text after another in the same kind of fuzzy prose.[5]

The accredited theorists are all there, no name connected with structuralism and poststructuralism is missing, and as a Frenchman I can hardly fail to be bemused by the massive presence of the French *maîtres* and *maîtresses à penser* from Claude Lévi-Strauss to Julia Kristeva. No one thinks alone, of course, least of all the literary critic. Criticism is parasitism, it has always sponged on other, more solidly established disciplines. But too much is too much. In *The Feminine and Faulkner*, Minrose C. Gwin admits to "flying uncharted courses under foggy conditions."[6] The courses, however, hold no surprise for anyone even remotely acquainted with the French feminism of the seventies, and what is most evident in Gwin's book is her fear of flying. In her rhapsodic "conversations" with Faulkner her own voice is seldom heard, and her own thinking never really takes flight. Like a fledgling venturing out of its nest, it flutters from Kristeva to Cixous, from Cixous to Irigaray, and from Irigaray on to some other triple-barreled feminist. There is scarcely a page in her book that is not thickly strewn with all these by now slightly shopworn names, scarcely an argument that is not bolstered with copious quotations from their work, and the same ritual invocation of authorities, the same compulsive name-dropping, the same citational intemperance, can be observed in most recent Faulkner studies with "postmodern" theoretical claims.

What this frantic flurry of intertextuality points to is the highly syncretic and scholastic nature of the greater part of the new Faulkner criticism. Syncretic, because its guiding concepts are wrenched from various systems of thought with minimal regard for the differential structures in which they operate, and then jumbled together with heedless abandon;[7] scholastic, because, while pretending to dismiss authoritative paradigms, it submits meekly to the authority of the new Church fathers or the new Church mothers. So it is wrong to say that current Faulkner criticism is more rigorously grounded in theory than it was previously. What unifies it is not theory, that is, a serviceable set of working assumptions, but a new ideological consensus, another *doxa*, a gaudy bundle of received ideas and fashionable clichés ultimately just as arbitrary and just as constraining as those of the New Criticism of the 1950s.

This new orthodoxy has its saints and its sinners, its articles of faith, its fetishes and taboos, all borrowed from neo-Marxism, neo-Freudianism (especially in its Lacanian version), neo-feminism, and, in spite of glaring incompatibilities, Deconstruction. What holds it together is a notion that has been around for a very long time: the old Marxist tenet that all writing is "social practice" determined by its historical moment, and that therefore all texts carry a more or less heavy ideological freight. Commonplaces are of course not all collective lies, and this one obviously has some truth in it. Literary discourse does have political components, and once you have decided to read it politically, everything in it becomes political, just as everything in it becomes rhetorical once you have decided to read it rhetorically. Any object of investigation is a function of the concerns one brings to it. The New Historicist critics, however, not only insist that Faulkner's texts are conditioned by their sociohistorical context, they claim that the relationship of text to context is all that matters.

It would seem, then, that those who thought that Faulkner's novels were about many things were mistaken. Despite Faulkner's own disclaimers,[8] we are now requested to admit that his undertaking was informed by one design, one large design: to write about the South. Sundquist's book was already dedicated to the single proposition that racial conflict in the South is the crux of Faulkner's major fiction. Similarly, for Richard C. Moreland, the exposure of Southern myth and Southern reality is the main objective of Faulkner's "ongoing critical project";[9] for Wesley and Barbara Morris it is his "primary goal."[10] And since more than a passing interest in language and craftsmanship would make their historicizing, ideologizing, and politicizing more difficult, these new critics all tend to focus on content— content determined in advance, regardless of the text at hand, by issues of power, exploitation, oppression, and resistance, invariably discussed in terms of class, race, and gender, the new holy trinity of American critics.

Granted, structuralism and poststructuralism have sensitized them to the primacy of the textual, the discursive, the symbolic. Most of them have read some Foucault, and the Morrises, for instance, at once remind their readers that Faulkner's South is not the "real" South, but "a South realized, articulated in discursive practice."[11] Yet if the Foucauldian phrase "discursive practice" turns up on nearly every page of their book, it is nonetheless the "real" South that Faulkner's novels are presumed eventually to reveal, and their "representational" power (what in earlier days would have been praised as the compelling strength of their "realism") is emphasized over and over again. "To ignore this representational force," the Morrises observe apropos of *Absalom, Absalom!*, "vitiates the novel's power, for it is presence that must be faced in the South not absence. It is the enduring fact of racism, classism, and sexism that *Absalom, Absalom!* reveals."[12]

The referent—not so long ago ridiculed as an obsolete mirage for the naive—has come back with a vengeance. But not any referent. The barely hidden assumption of the Morrises and like-minded critics is that literature is valuable only insofar as it represents the larger conflicts of society, and that it is the more valuable as it does so in the politically correct way, that is, contributes to the emancipation of the downtrodden minorities and to the attainment of the hallowed goals of "social transforma-

tion." Novelists must make themselves useful in the revolutionary battle against injustice and oppression, they must point and
pave the way to a fairer and better world. To be any good, their
work has to fit into the master narrative of what Fredric Jameson
calls in his Marxian lingo mankind's "collective struggle to wrest
a realm of Freedom from a realm of Necessity."[13]

The task of the Faulkner critic, then, is to find out to what
extent Faulkner's novels measure up or fail to measure up to
these grand expectations, to what extent they conform or fail to
conform to a specific political agenda. For, unlike the skeptical
deconstructionists, the new ideologues are people with strong
convictions. They do not merely see themselves as members of
a theoretical avant-garde, they not only claim to occupy a
superior standpoint from which all literary texts can be "unmasked" and "demystified"; they consider themselves distinctly
"progressive" in every field, firmly believing that their political,
cultural, moral, and philosophical views are truer—more "advanced"—than those of their predecessors. They know more,
they know better. They alone stand on the rock of truth, and
there is no truth but the latest truth. Hence a smug sense of
superiority not only over earlier critics but also over the be-
nighted writers before their own time whom they condescend
to discuss. "Writers of the earlier part of this century," John N.
Duvall pityingly notes, "seem hopelessly backward in their
sense of women and men, so much so that calls for moratoriums
on reading their texts almost seem correct."[14]

Correct: an ugly word. And from moratorium it is only a short
step to censorship. Whether progressive or conservative, critics
with a heavy moralistic bias have always been potential inquisi-
tors. Indeed, in their missionary zeal some of these anti-New-
Critical critics take us back to the worst forms of self-righteous
sermonizing—a disease literary criticism has been sporadically
afflicted with since its beginnings. Their cultural relativism
barely conceals a Manichaean morality of right and wrong:
whatever the case may be, innovation is right, tradition is
wrong, equality is right, hierarchy is wrong, femininity and

bisexuality are right, masculinity is wrong, etc. Faulkner's novels are hence investigated on the basis of a rigidly binary code, and the more readily approved of as they can be shown to serve the noble cause of liberation.

Even for the perfectly legitimate purposes of ideological analysis, such a utilitarian and normative approach seems to me old-fashioned and crushingly reductive. In *Le degré zéro de l'écriture*,[15] his first book-length essay, Roland Barthes, then still flirting with Marxism, showed splendidly how, through the very choice of a conventional "literary" style, the "proletarian" novels of the communist Roger Garaudy conveyed a trivial petit-bourgeois ideology, and he argued that the relationship between fiction and ideology depended less on content than on structure and form. Indeed, paying close attention to a text's immanent formal properties is, I think, a prerequisite for a valid analysis of its ideology. But focusing on form is now frowned upon as a deplorable concession to formalism. And to some, even "close reading" of the text has become suspicious. Thus the Morrises contend that "out of respect for the text" one should "refuse to read it closely,"[16] which is like saying that out of respect for a Haydn quartet one should refuse to listen to it, or that out of respect for the beloved one should refuse to make love.

To find the reasons for these absurd suspicions and rejections, we need only reconstitute the chain of guilt. Formalism and close reading are associated with New Criticism, New Criticism grew out of Southern Agrarianism, and since the Southern Agrarians were reactionaries, consideration of a literary text as such, of its internal structure and of its texture of ironies, ambiguities, and paradoxes, must be denounced as a reactionary practice. And yet irony, ambiguity, and paradox were not invented and monopolized by the New Critics; they are notions literary criticism cannot dispense with, especially when it attempts to analyse the tortuous workings of ideology. So why throw out the baby with the bathwater? True, close reading can easily become closed reading, but there is no need for the critic to choose between close reading and distant commentary, and for a comprehensive and balanced understanding of a writer's work we definitely need both.

There can be no fair criticism without a keen sense of nuance and proper acknowledgment of textual complexity. One would have expected the new concern with political reference not to preclude all awareness of the problematic nature of linguistic artifacts and the hazards and limits of their interpretation. Yet, instead of facing these embarrassing questions, many of the new Faulkner critics prefer to go for easy targets or construct straw men to knock down bravely. Though some of them express timid reservations about Deconstruction, the old New Criticism is in fact their sole enemy in the critical field, and they devote all their polemical ardor to exorcising its haunting specter. You would think, reading some of these pieces, that the New Critics still hold the center stage of Faulkner studies and that until yesterday everyone was swearing by Cleanth Brooks and his Agrarian acolytes.

To relate Faulkner's work to its various intertextual and extraliterary contexts, to reread it against the background of its reception and its successive interpretations, to reexamine the cultural and historical circumstances under which it was written and to scrutinize the ways in which they reinscribe themselves in his texts, is assuredly a worthwhile enterprise, yet for such an enterprise to succeed, the evidence must be scrupulously checked and all inferences and judgments seriously pondered. Blanket assumptions and glib extrapolations will not do. All too often current Faulkner criticism combines a narrowly selective and a priori oriented reading of Faulkner's texts with wholesale indictments of American and Western culture which hardly bear close scrutiny. No doubt the troubled and often tragic history of the South may be read as an epitome of the many sins of Western civilization. Indeed, no one has contributed more effectively to make us envision it as such than Faulkner, and that much is by now acknowledged by everybody, so that there is no real need to remind us once again that his "representation of the South contains its own critique of the South."[17] Yet racism, sexism, classism, capitalism, colonialism, and imperial-ism—words bandied about in current criticism as agreed refer-ence points for the root of all ills—clearly do not tell the whole story, and the concept of oppression, to which all these -isms refer, should not be used in such an exclusive and undifferenti-ated way as to cover everything from slavery to marriage.

Catchall categories and sweeping statements are the meat of political propaganda and ideological discourse. In literary criticism they should be energetically resisted. Unfortunately, the new Faulkner critics hardly take account of the complexity of Western culture and literature, nor do they give proper attention to the many-faceted and extremely ambiguous issue of modernity, as can be seen from the simplistic way in which they deal with modernism. Moreland's *Faulkner and Modernism,* for instance, rests on a discomfitingly parochial view of the modern-ist movement. Modernism, in his book, is seen throughout as an exclusively Anglo-American phenomenon, "predominantly middle class, white, and male."[18] T. S. Eliot and Joyce are occasionally referred to, but such important figures of modern-ism as Gertrude Stein and Virginia Woolf are never mentioned, nor are Proust, Valéry, Kafka, Rilke, Musil, Broch, or Gadda. Continental modernists don't count. And, even though modern-ism involved a wide spectrum of ideological affiliations, from Brecht's communism to Pound's fascism, it is taken for granted that, in political terms, it was monolithically right if not ultra-right. For Moreland, modernism was just a cultural version of Freudian melancholia, testifying to the failure of Western bourgeoisie to come to terms with loss and do the work of mourning, and all it has to offer is nostalgia for a golden past and an equally retrograde self-protective irony.

Reducing modernism to a syndrome of male bourgeois ma-laise, both Moreland and the Morrises relate it to the regressive and repressive forces of twentieth century Western culture. Modernism both denies and confesses what it springs from. Modernism is formalism. Modernism is aestheticism. Modern-ism is subjectivism. Modernism is monologic, oedipal, individualistic, sentimentally nostalgic and/or nihilistically ironic, and hence out of touch with the emancipatory forces at work in History.[19] Such grievances have been voiced before, in almost identical phrasings, by the propagandists of "socialist realism," and they remind one of nothing so much as Georg Lukács's doctrinaire diatribes against the "degenerate art" of Joyce, Kafka, Beckett, and . . . Faulkner.

*   *   *

Given their low opinion of (what they take to be) modernism, one might have expected Moreland and the Morrises to mount a full-scale assault on Faulkner's work. Faulkner was a modernist, after all, or at the very least assumed by most readers to be one. However, he still looms large, he is still an intimidating figure, the time has not come yet to expel him from the canon. So these critics deploy their sophistry to rescue him at all costs from modernism, to demonstrate that, all considered, he is less of a modernist than he is generally thought to be, and that his best works are altogether immune to modernism.

But which are the best? One noteworthy consequence of this rescue operation is a growing tendency to revaluate Faulkner's career and revise the Faulkner canon. While the late novels— from *Intruder in the Dust* to *The Reivers*—are reexamined with extreme benevolence, the early masterpieces are now downgraded because of their all too private "oedipal" concerns and their "formalistic" experimentalism. *The Sound and the Fury,* in particular, tends to shrink in current estimation to what Sundquist already called "a literary curiosity."[20] Taking one of Faulkner's statements literally so as to ascribe to him their own prejudices, the Morrises argue that "Faulkner considered the novel a failure precisely because of its modernist aesthetics," and fault it specifically for "the subjectivism, the monologic style of modernist stream-of-consciousness" and "the antinarrative effects of its oedipal symbolism."[21] Moreland, though less openly critical of *The Sound and the Fury,* likewise signals repeatedly "the contradictions and inadequacies" he finds in the "Southern, modernist mode"[22] of Faulkner's novels before *Absalom, Absalom!,* and his book's whole argument revolves around the idea that Faulkner freed himself in midcareer from modernism and spent his later years revising his prior work. Through "revisionary repetition," Moreland contends, Faulkner came to abandon the sterile moods of his modernist phase and to extend his sympathy to the oppressed—poor whites in "Barn Burning" and *The Hamlet,* blacks in *Go Down, Moses,* women in *Requiem for a Nun* and *The Reivers.*

That Faulkner's writing came to be more and more deeply involved in social and historical issues, and that this later fiction revises his early work and rearticulates his critique of Southern mythmaking, is beyond dispute, and Faulkner's "revisionary strategies" clearly deserve the meticulous consideration they are given by Moreland and the Morrises. Yes, Faulkner's restless mind was capable of growth, and as his career advanced, his social and historical understanding—or rather the social and historical understanding embodied in his fiction (his post-Nobel public statements and essays are rather evidence to the contrary)—expanded. Yet from this one should not automatically infer that it also gained in depth and made Faulkner a better writer. Nor should one ignore the fact that the willingness to listen to the voices of the defenseless was there almost from the start. *Light in August,* a novel of the early 1930s strangely neglected in most recent Faulkner studies, is as radical in its critique of exploitation and repression, as vehement in its denunciation of Southern racism and Southern sexism as anything Faulkner wrote later on, and even *The Sound and the Fury,* if Quentin's and Jason's monologues are properly read through each other, turns out to be an admirably perceptive diagnosis of Southern ideology. Faulkner's later novels reconsider these issues from other angles, through other arrangements and procedures, and allow other voices to be heard. They do not go further, they go elsewhere; and they are not necessarily more significant for dealing more explicitly and more self-consciously with class, race, and gender. Let us give them full credit for what they achieve, but let us not be ruled by narrow preconceptions about thematic priorities.

The trouble with the New Historicists is precisely that they are bent on forcing all of Faulkner's novels into their ideological straightjacket. *"The Sound and the Fury,"* say the Morrises, "only grudgingly gives way to the master theme of Faulkner's most moving narrations: the South. It distorts and digresses from the powerful thematics of race, class, and gender which become central to Faulkner's career for the next two decades."[23] In other words, *The Sound and the Fury* is a failure because it is not Southern enough and does not give sufficient attention to the mandatory triple theme. Conversely, *Requiem for a Nun* is given a high rating because it is thought to meet these requirements. As Moreland puts it in his grimly fussy style, "in recasting an abortion again as an infanticide, Faulkner bypasses the reductive terms of the supposedly biological issue of live baby vs. not-yet-fully-alive foetus, in order to raise instead the more clearly and broadly social issue of the necessity of radical breaks in certain habits of thought and practice surrounding sexual and gender issues in particular, but extending as well to issues of race and class."[24] Neo-feminism likewise reads its own program into Faulkner's novels, so that "Rosa's text" in *Absalom, Absalom!* becomes "a feminist discourse which questions and challenges patriarchy,"[25] and Joseph R. Urgo transforms all the texts into a vast heretic cryptogram, which gives him full license to interpret *A Fable* and the Snopes trilogy as eloquent calls for permanent revolution.[26]

Faulkner must not only be shown to have swerved ever further from modernism and to have moved ever more daringly into the public domain of historical and social discourse; to gain the new postmodern generation's respect and admiration, he must be reclaimed for all the good causes and turned into a writer with strong political commitments on the left. On the dust jacket of *Reading Faulkner,* he is presented as "a fully engaged *political* writer." Duvall finds his novels "potentially liberating, not repressive."[27] Urgo ranks him "among the most politically radical of all those whom America's literary establishment privileges as its major authors,"[28] and even makes the extravagant claim that Faulkner proposed "a political and ideological alternative to . . . the totalitarianism of modern society."[29] And what the author cannot accomplish himself, his characters will do in his stead: "Faulkner," writes Gwin, "becomes in his greatest work the creator of female subjects who, in powerful and creative ways, disrupt and sometimes destroy patriarchal structures."[30]

There was a time when Faulkner was taken to task for being a misogynist, a racist, an arch-conservative Southerner, or was even suspected of being a crypto-fascist. Then, after the Nobel Prize, came the time when he was celebrated as a Christian traditionalist or a liberal humanist. Now we have moved into a third phase, a spectacular reversal of the first and second: Faulkner, we are told, was neither a conservative nor a liberal; he was (at least "potentially" and perhaps *malgré lui*) a radical, a champion of the wretched of the earth, a protofeminist, a scourge of racism, or even an anarchist apostle of rebellion against all forms of authority.

Whether meant to condemn or to praise, these labels are all largely irrelevant. Sticking labels on Faulkner is to fix his fiction around a set of stable, reassuring signifiers, and thus foreclose critical debate—the ideological gesture par excellence. To reject all easy categorizations, as I think we should, does not mean, however, that all inquiry into Faulkner's treatment of social and political matters must be abandoned. But we have to investigate them within Faulkner's own field of competence: that of the novelist.

A novelist, at any rate a novelist worth his or her salt, is not just a man or a woman writing about events that never happened and people that never existed. A novel is not merely an "object of knowledge" for the professional critic to dissect, as the Morrises, following Macherey, seem to assume.[31] In one sense, it is also a subject of knowledge or at least a deposit, an inscription of knowledge. Yet Moreland is just as mistaken in assuming that the serious novelist provides "analyses" of the social world he represents in his fiction.[32] Philosophy, science, and art, as Gilles Deleuze and Félix Guattari have recently argued, are all ways of thinking and knowing about the world, but what sets artists, and hence novelists, apart, is that they think with affects and percepts rather than concepts.[33] And novelists try to think what philosophers and scientists exclude from their speculations and inquiries as the unthinkable: the particular, the singular, the non-identical, the contingent, that which cannot be fitted into the systems of society and the patterns of orderly conceptual thinking. Not all novelists, of course: ninety percent of all novels merely cater to their readers' yearning for clichéd romance; most published fiction is ideological trash. But this has never been the case with the novelists I persist in calling great. For them, to imagine is not to regurgitate the collective imaginary but to decompose it so as to expose its many lures. Testing the generality of ideas and of language itself against singular and complex representations of human beings and human events, their fictions are indeed experiments, and such testing is bound to estrange the familiar, to blur customary distinctions, to unhinge common categories and question common assumptions, and so to leave us at a loss.

As Milan Kundera, a passionate apologist for the Western novelistic tradition, points out: "Man desires a world where good and evil can be clearly distinguished, for he has an innate and irrepressible desire to judge before he understands. Religions and ideologies are founded on this desire. They can cope with the novel only by translating its language of relativity and ambiguity into their own apodictic and dogmatic discourse. They require that someone be right: either Anna Karenina is the victim of a narrow-minded tyrant, or Karenin is the victim of an immoral woman; either K. is an innocent man crushed by an unjust Court, or the Court represents divine justice and K. is guilty."[34] In the same way, many Faulkner critics require that "someone be right": either Joanna Burden is a neurotic spinster turned nyphomaniac, or, as feminist readers will claim, she is, like nearly all women in Faulkner, the helpless victim of Southern patriarchy; either Joe Christmas is an innocent man crushed by a racist community, or, as Brooks suggested, the community stands for rightful law and order, and Christmas is guilty.

But no one, in *Light in August* or any other Faulkner novel, is absolutely right. The language of Faulkner's fiction is never the exclusionary language of either/or. It keeps faith to what has been most valuable in the great tradition of the novel since Cervantes: the sense of relativity and complexity, the spirit of doubt and questioning, what Kundera calls "the wisdom of uncertainty."[35] Admittedly, in invoking this tradition I expose myself in turn to the charge of ideologizing. Whether championed by F. R. Leavis or by Kundera, "great traditions," it might be objected, are themselves ideological constructs. We also know that the novel rose with the bourgeoisie, served its interests, and over the past two hundred years has been an insidiously powerful instrument of social control. From Sterne to Joyce, from Diderot to Proust, however, the novel has revealed itself over and over again as a remarkably open, self-conscious and self-questioning genre, and among "discursive practices" it is perhaps the only one capable of countering ideology with some chance of success, because it is the most preoccupied with the particular and the least concerned with abstract and final truths. Good novelists not only alert us to the confounding complexity of human affairs and to the irreducible ambiguities of human behavior; they point to their entanglement in language and make us aware of how language works, of how it mediates our relationship to reality, of how it degrades and distorts the singularity of experience. By rendering language visible and reality opaque, the novel offers nothing in the way of positive affirmation. It does not add to our stock of useful knowledge, nor does it sustain our creeds or foster our hopes. And yet, by thwarting our need to believe and by robbing us of our private fantasies and common illusions, it brings us closer to what might well be truth, the scandalous truth no one wants to hear, the truth that no single Truth is available.

This paradoxical truth is also at the dark core of Faulkner's work. His great novels all attempt to dismantle the language of the tribe, to break through the myths by which the white South legitimized and sustained its iniquitous order, and to bring to light the disorder beneath. In breaking through these fictions, Faulkner discovered their horrendous costs, the waste, the madness, the injustice, the suffering, and came to listen to the marginalized voices of the dispossessed. As for the reader, he may respond to Faulkner's fiction in aesthetic detachment or with moral outrage, and if he wishes to draw pragmatic political lessons from it, he is free to do so. The beginning of political consciousness is awareness, not illusion, and the lack of final truths is no alibi for resignation. But there is no reason to ask for more than what we are offered. To think that the failure to find "an alternative utopian reality" was Faulkner's "personal tragedy"[36] is to misconceive the very nature of his enterprise and to misunderstand what, from *Don Quixote* to *Ulysses*, has been the novel's disenchanting function. Utopias are by definition unreal. Arising out of a sentimental nostalgia for a paradisiacal future, they turn inevitably into nightmares when tested against reality, and novelists have known all along that they are the most dangerous fictions of all. So why should we expect Faulkner to sweeten the pill by providing idyllic models of alternative communities? Why can we not accept his novels in their savage honesty? Blueprints for the future have never been the novelist's business. Some of Faulkner's later books like *Intruder in the Dust* carry a progressive message; they testify to the aging novelist's desire to become "articulate in the national voice"[37] but are too well-meaning and too garrulous to be counted among his best. Faulkner's finest novels are his fiercest, and they all refuse to serve ideological certitudes. They believe neither in possible arrangements nor in necessary overturnings, promote neither myths of restoration nor utopias of progress. Interrupting all communal discourse, inscribing themselves in the exposed space of its interruption, they keep reminding us that most communities are built on murderous lies, that history is seldom more than sound and fury, that to be *in* the world is not to be *of* the world, and all they deeply, cruelly, tenderly care about are the singular conditions and singular becomings of singular beings, which only a novelist's voice—the attentive and vulnerable voice of unbelonging—can relay and convey.

NOTES

1. *Faulkner and Idealism: Perspectives from Paris*, ed. Michel Gresset and Patrick Samway (Jackson: University Press of Mississippi, 1983), 27–50. The conference was held in March 1980 at the Sorbonne and the University of Paris VII.

2. John T. Irwin, *Doubling and Incest/Repetition and Revenge: A Speculative Reading of Faulkner* (Baltimore: Johns Hopkins University Press, 1975); Myra Jehlen, *Class and Character in Faulkner's South* (New York: Columbia University Press), 1976.

3. *The Play of Faulkner's Language* (Ithaca, N.Y.: Cornell University Press, 1982).

4. *Seeing and Being* (Middletown: Wesleyan University Press, 1981); Richard H. King, *A Southern Renaissance: The Cultural Awakening of the American South, 1930–1955* (New York: Oxford University Press, 1980); Eric J. Sundquist, *Faulkner: The House Divided* (Baltimore: The Johns Hopkins University Press, 1983); Thadious Davis, *Faulkner's "Negro": Art and the Southern Context* (Baton Rouge: Louisiana State University Press, 1983); James A. Snead, *Figures of Division* (New York: Methuen, 1986); Michael Grimwood, *Heart in Conflict: Faulkner's Struggle with Vocation* (Athens: University of Georgia Press, 1987); Warwick Wadlington, *Reading Faulknerian Tragedy* (Ithaca: Cornell University Press, 1987).

5. Among recent books on Faulkner, Stephen M. Ross's *Fiction's Inexhaustible Voice: Speech and Writing in Faulkner* (Athens: University of Georgia Press, 1989), is one of the very few that combine theoretical awareness with rigor of method, and focus with sustained critical intelligence upon a major aspect of Faulkner's work.

6. *The Feminine and Faulkner: Reading (Beyond) Sexual Difference* (Knoxville: The University of Tennessee Press, 1990), 8.

7. Psychoanalytical concepts, in particular, are handled in an annoyingly loose and confusing way. In *Reading Faulkner* (Madison: The University of Wisconsin Press, 1989), for instance, when Wesley Morris and Barbara Alverson Morris equate Thomas Sutpen with the "Symbolic Father," then with "Michael Rogin's imaginary father" (213), one must assume that the two phrases are equivalent. If they are, the Morrises confuse the Imaginary with the Symbolic; if they are not, one would like it to be made clear how Sutpen can be at once or in turns a "Symbolic Father," an "imaginary father," and (as is suggested elsewhere) a Freudian oedipal father. There is nothing wrong with drawing on different psychonalytical theories, but the differences should be properly acknowledged. Another, even more flagrant case of muddled thinking is Minrose Gwin's treatment of the "feminine." Over and over again, page after page, she reminds us that the feminine is both a disruptive force and an irrepressibly creative process. Yet her insistence on the feminine as power and process does not prevent her from referring to Caddy Compson's "essence as a female subject" (*The Feminine and Faulkner*, 56). Here she insists on the uniqueness of woman's body and woman's experience, and is not far from subscribing to an essentialist, even biologistic notion of femininity; there, following Kristeva, she uses the feminine beyond sexual difference as a mere trope of whatever has been marginalized, repressed and silenced by the patriarchal order. And while

blaming phallocentric culture for having relegated femininity to "otherness," she asks us to acknowledge its "strangeness" (77), identifies it with the unbounded, the unstructured, the unrepresentable (that is, all those blind, chaotic forces that patriarchal culture has invented to define itself against them), and devalues reason and order as hopelessly male, thus reinstating standard sexual stereotypes in an inverted form and resurrecting the primitive mythology of the *ewig Weibliche*.

8. "I'm inclined to think that my material, the South, is not very important to me. I just happen to know it, and don't have time in one life to learn another one and write at the same time." Letter to Malcolm Cowley in *The Faulkner–Cowley File: Letters and Memories, 1944–1962* (New York: The Viking Press, 1966), 14–15.

9. *Faulkner and Modernism: Rereading and Rewriting* (Madison: The University of Wisconsin Press, 1990), 4.

10. *Reading Faulkner*, 10.

11. Ibid., 3.

12. Ibid., 194.

13. Fredric Jameson, *The Political Unconscious: Narrative as a Socially Symbolic Act* (Ithaca, N.Y.: Cornell University Press, 1981), 19.

14. *Faulkner's Marginal Couple: Invisible, Outlaw, and Unspeakable Communities* (Austin: University of Texas Press, 1990), 16.

15. Paris: Editions du Seuil, 1953.

16. *Reading Faulkner*, 7.

17. Ibid., 6.

18. *Faulkner and Modernism*, 21.

19. Moreland's animosity toward irony is particularly shrill and tenacious. He does not seem to be aware that in the course of literary history irony has manifested itself in many modes, and that, far from being "an alibi and a consolation" (*Faulkner and Modernism*, 25), it has been since Swift and Voltaire one of the most redoubted weapons against dominant ideologies. In his discussion of *Absalom, Absalom!* he rightly stresses the complacencies of Mr. Compson's practice of irony, but fails to demonstrate how the novel itself exemplifies "the failure of irony" (*Faulkner and Modernism*, 33). In its demystification of historical discourse, *Absalom, Absalom!* seems to me the supreme triumph of Faulknerian irony.

20. *The House Divided*, 3.

21. *Reading Faulkner*, 133. I wish the Morrises had told us why "oedipal symbolism" has "antinarrative effects." To me the assumption is by no means self-evident, nor was it to Roland Barthes, who wondered whether all narratives did not come down to a retelling of the Oedipus story. See *Le Plaisir du texte* (Paris: Editions du Seuil, 1973), 75.

22. *Faulkner and Modernism*, 194.

23. *Reading Faulkner*, 82.

24. *Faulkner and Modernism*, 238.

25. *The Feminine and Faulkner*, 70.

26. See *Faulkner's Apocrypha: A Fable, Snopes, and the Spirit of Human Rebellion* (Jackson: University Press of Mississippi, 1989).

27. *Faulkner's Marginal Couple*, xi.

28. *Faulkner's Apocrypha*, 83.

29. Ibid., 4. What the alternative might be is never made clear. When it comes to defining the political content of Faulkner's assumed radicalism, current criticism withdraws into embarrassed silence or evasive rhetoric, and more often than not politics turns out to be an empty word. Thus Urgo, while emphasizing the subversive charge of Faulkner's "apocrypha," contends that he "is no institutionalist, no social elitist, no believer in party politics or *political panacea of any kind*" (*Faulkner's Apocrypha*, 209, italics added). So all that is left is individual rebellion in a political vacuum.

30. *The Feminine and Faulkner*, 4.

31. *Reading Faulkner*, 7.

32. See *Faulkner and Modernism*, 10, 29.

33. *Qu'est-ce que la philosophie?* (Paris: Les Editions de Minuit, 1991).

34. *The Art of the Novel*, trans. Linda Asher (London: Faber and Faber, 1990), 7. First published in French as *L'Art du roman* in 1986 by Gallimard.

35. Ibid., 7.

36. *Reading Faulkner*, 132.

37. The phrase occurs in a letter to Malcolm Franklin, dated December 5, 1942. See *Selected Letters of William Faulkner*, ed. Joseph Blotner (New York: Random House, 1977), 166.

Faulkner, Ideology, and Narrative

RICHARD H. KING

In every work of genius we recognize our own rejected thoughts; they come back to us with a certain alienated majesty.

—RALPH WALDO EMERSON

Cain slew Abel, and Romulus slew Remus; violence was the beginning and, by the same token, no beginning could be made without using violence, without violating. . . . Whatever brotherhood human beings may be capable of has grown out of fratricide, whatever political organization men may have achieved has its origin in crime.

—HANNAH ARENDT

Though an Enlightenment concept, ideology is most closely associated with Karl Marx and the history of Marxist thought. Within Marxism, the meanings of ideology have been various; but the core Marxist understanding equates ideology with "false consciousness," the tendency to see (our) particular values and beliefs as universal or universalizable. Ideology in this sense implies, however, that there is a truth about the nature of human arrangements to be discovered. A second meaning gives ideology an interpretive (as opposed to a critical) spin. Ideology refers in this second sense to any more or less coherent worldview such as Christianity or psychoanalysis or Marxism or nationalist–ethnic faith. There is finally a third meaning, according to which ideology refers to a shared belief system that not only interprets the world but enjoins us to act in it, either to defend or overthrow the current arrangements. Most interpretive ideologies are also ideologies of action and all ideologies of action carry an interpretive component. Indeed, most ideologies combine these critical, interpretive, and political moments and imply that knowledge claims and imaginative representations have some crucial relationship to power and action.[1]

At our historical moment, ideology as false consciousness has a distinctly old-fashioned, patronizing ring to it. But the interpretive and political meanings of ideology are still worth retaining in some form or the other. That said, the concept of ideology can often be replaced by "narrative" or "story"; in certain contemporary accounts, the way we orient ourselves and justify our actions, the ways we talk about who we are and what we want, is by telling stories or constructing narratives. From this perspective, Marxism, for instance, tells one kind of story about the human enterprise, while psychoanalysis tells another. Further, the use of story or narrative in this broad sense has the advantage of not attributing privileged, "scientistic" status to various forms of *Ideologiekritik*. Moreover, to talk of narratives rather than ideologies is to place temporality at the heart of individual and collective self-understanding.[2]

This substitution of narrative or story for ideology is particularly appropriate in connection with William Faulkner, who was far from being a formal philosopher or social theorist. Faulkner was a committed or consistent public spokesman for no particular cause. Though he was known to attend the local Episcopal church in Oxford, a careful reader would find it hard to detect the good news of Christianity in his oeuvre. Though he was a Jeffersonian Democrat who voted for Adlai Stevenson in 1956 (but for Eisenhower in 1952), he had little time for professional politicians or politics. Indeed, Faulkner tended to equate the term "politician" with the Vardamans and Bilbos and political action with mob rule of the sort favored by the Klan. On race and civil rights, Faulkner was all over the place, sometimes speaking out courageously and at other times sounding like the worst sort of Southern patriot. He was certainly no apologist for "the Lost Cause," yet loved the dash and romance of the Confederacy at war. His overseas travels during the 1950s reveal Faulkner, the American patriot, but he had nothing but contempt for the sinister depredations of Senator Joseph McCarthy. This is not to say that Faulkner was totally detached from his historical moment or that he never took sides. But it does suggest that Faulkner did not see himself as a public position-taker or as a spokesman for any cause very often or very readily or very convincingly.[3]

Faulkner was, however, passionately devoted to understanding the world and his world in terms of stories. One of his favorite ways of passing the time was listening to, rather than telling, stories; and, as a novelist, one of his great gifts lay in his storytelling ability. Besides being a great storyteller in the straightforward sense, Faulkner's fictional narratives are themselves often arranged around the telling and retelling of stories, simulacra of what Freud referred to as "repetition, recollection and working through."

But Faulkner's stories were more than just evocative tales of man against the wilderness or explorations of interior, intensely personal dilemmas. They were "about" the exercise and often, even usually, the abuse of power. Though I do not think we have exhausted the meaning of politics when we focus on the play of power and interests, one central concern of politics is certainly with acquiring and exercising power. If that is the case, then Faulkner's distaste for "real world" politics was belied by his fictional concerns. Certainly no novelist as obsessed as Faulkner with creating a fictional world could ignore the nature of the power relations holding that world together or causing it to disintegrate. Suffusing every version of the family romance in Faulkner's work—that of Ike and Sam, Henry, Bon and Judith, even Quentin and Caddy—are the intricacies of class, race, and gender relationships and of familial, technological, and regional political power. Those positive virtues which Faulkner so often evokes, such as courage and honor, are profoundly social, other-regarding virtues, incomprehensible apart from the structures of power at the heart of his fictional and historical South.[4] Generally, Faulkner's great theme was not just the representation of the South in conflict with the modern world; it was also the fictional evocation, dramatization, and questioning of the received master narratives, of the dominant ideologies, of both Southern history and of modern progress.

Needless to say, political/ideological readings of Faulkner did not begin in the 1980s. For instance, one influential early reading of Faulkner stressed his role as the chronicler of the tragedy of Southern modernity as expressed in the fictional conflict between the Sartorises and the Snopeses.[5] Whatever the merits of this reading, it is manifestly a political/ideological reading *of* Faulkner *as* an essentially political writer. This suggests that, contrary to his stated intentions and to the way his greatness has often been understood, Faulkner's work, as Carolyn Porter has emphasized, is not only about the "flight from society" but also about "penetrating to history and social reality."[6] Certainly much, even most, Faulkner criticism over the last decade or so has sought to demonstrate the aptness of Porter's judgment.

There are many ways to understand the historical and ideological realities that Faulkner addresses. Most historically oriented studies have assumed that Faulkner's fiction implies a master narrative of decline and fall, loss and grief, mourning and melancholy. Of course there is a prominent element in his work which is suffused with mourning not only for *what* has been lost—coherence and meaning, heroism and courage—but also *that* it has been lost: "its not even time until it was."[7] Furthermore, memory lies at the heart of the dilemma it seeks to overcome. It is not that time creates memory but that memory creates and then tries to defeat time.

Of less concern in Faulkner criticism has been Faulkner's treatment of narratives of foundings. To be sure, Richard Moreland's recent *Faulkner and Modernism* is organized around the "primal scene" of Sutpen's fall into social (self)consciousness.[8] And Thomas Sutpen and Carothers McCaslin are often recognized as founders of family dynasties. But wider questions such as—What does it mean to found an order? and how does Faulkner narrate those founding stories?—also need to be

raised. These questions seem to me of great moment in understanding the theme of "Faulkner and Ideology."

Narrating Foundings

It is customary to assert that American culture has been historically oriented toward the future, while the South, always already
in decline, has been obsessed with the past. Yet the fact that
America has identifiable historical origins and lays claim to
historical uniqueness has created a general American obsession
with decline as expressed in narratives of declension and jeremi-
ads.[9] The Reagan era's obsessive concern with restoring American "greatness" is only the latest in a tradition which began
with the Puritans' sense of betrayal of their "errand into the
wilderness"; continued with the fear of having abandoned the
first principles of the Founding Fathers' new republic and its
recreation in the cauldron of the Civil War (Lincoln's "new birth
of freedom"); echoed in the loss of democratic virtues associated
with the frontier apotheosized in Frederick Jackson Turner's
"The Significance of the Frontier in American History" (1893);
and was expressed more recently in John Kennedy's call to recreate a "New Frontier" in the early 1960s. The crucial point is
that a revolutionary culture created *within* historical memory
and dedicated to one or several propositions will be obsessed
with decline from origins. It will literally be reactionary even in
its utopian dreams: *America is back—where/there?*

Similarly, Faulkner's great project, obsessed with decline and
fall, with last things, implies a concern with foundings. At first
glance, Faulkner's fictional world seems to be constructed upon
a binary opposition between origins and endings. Corruption
implies an original innocence; weakness and confusion suggest
an earlier strength and clarity of purpose; exploitation and
oppression signify a falling off from harmony and cooperation;
and community gives way to an atomized society of possessive
individuals. In sum, as the conservative reading of Faulkner has
it, where Sartoris once was, there Snopes will be.

But if we look—and read—more closely, it is very difficult to find these neat dichotomies in Faulkner's work. For one part of Faulkner's imagination undermined, deconstructed as it were, the binary opposition between an ideal past and a corrupt present. Innocence and corruption are often represented in Faulkner's work through feminine sexuality. But although Faulkner spoke movingly of Caddy as the "sister he never had," we never see her in *The Sound and the Fury* as anything but already "fallen," the muddy drawers becoming the synecdoche for that state. Temple Drake is no innocent besmirched but a flirt who "asks for it." The Sartorises are hardly exemplars of high seriousness and *gravitas,* while Gail Hightower's heroic grandfather is killed while engaged in the pointless act of stealing a chicken. Nor for that matter are all Snopeses "Snopeses" and Jason Compson can give Flem Snopes a run for his money any day. The Indians were, on Faulkner's account, hardly noble beings ruthlessly dispossessed of their land, but property owners quite willing to sell the land and to adopt slavery. And though the wilderness itself often functions as a fixed point of moral reference, it already contains the seeds of its own destruction. Old Ben's most salient qualities are those identified with Carothers McCaslin: an indomitable will, heedless and ruthless of opposition. Other examples could be cited, but I think the point is clear.

It is this "realism" about the Southern past, this ambivalence about decline narratives, that so distinguishes Faulkner from Southern conservatives such as the Vanderbilt Agrarians. Because of his ambiguous self-location among received regional and national narratives of collective origins, Faulkner found it difficult, at least in the period of his greatest achievement, to believe unequivocally the accepted narrative of regional decline—Southern humiliation caused by the power of the Union army and the ethos of Yankee (read "modern") capitalism—or the civic republican story of the foundation of a democratic republic. (The new county seat is named Jefferson, not after Thomas Jefferson but after Thomas Jefferson Pettigrew, who delivered the mail from Nashville in those early years of settlement.) Faulkner's narratives of foundings recount the formation of a society based on families rather than a polity based on citizenship: it is Roman not Greek in ethos. Thus we might say that Faulkner's Old South was hardly a political order at all, i.e., a social order raised to self-conscious, self-regulation through laws and public institutions, until the Civil War.[10]

That having been said, it is important to note that Faulkner constructs narratives of founding in two different, though never neatly distinguishable, ways. Roughly the same in "content," the tonality and focus of the two modes are significantly different. In the terms set by Edward Said, we might say that Faulkner attempts in the first mode to represent "origins," while in the second he represents "beginnings;" or in Hayden White's terminology, Faulkner's first mode is "sublime" and the second is "pastoral."[11] The first sort of founding narrative can be seen most clearly in *Absalom, Absalom!* and "The Bear," while the second can be seen in the "Appendix" (1945) to *The Sound and the Fury,* Faulkner's long essay "Mississippi" (1954), and the historical sketches introducing the three acts of *Requiem for a Nun* (1951).

In reference to the first mode, I want to examine the stories of Thomas Sutpen and Carothers McCaslin. What is it that links these two founders? What does it mean to be a founder? First, they are self-created, founders of themselves. Referring to Lucas Beauchamp and through him to Carothers McCaslin, Faulkner writes:

> by himself composed, himself self-progenitive and nominate, by himself ancestored, as, for all the old ledgers recorded to the contrary, old Carothers was.[12]

Sutpen, of course, struggles to escape his original poor white identity in western Virginia and then shucks off his second West Indies self after discovering his wife and hence his son have black blood. Sutpen "abrupts" onto the scene in Jefferson, apparently without a past. It is one of the "points" of the novel to try to reconstruct the reasons for Sutpen's life-long task of self-recreation.

Second, and related to this, the dominant position of Sutpen and Carothers derives not from gradual accretions of influence or cultivation of contacts within the community. Rather they are interlopers, usurpers, and violators, exemplifications of what Orlando Patterson has called "sovereignal freedom,"[13] They are Hegelian "masters" and Freudian primal patriarchs. Such founders in Faulkner's world are not so much the first as they are the most powerful; not literal priority but the will to dominate defines the nature of the founder and his founding action: *In the beginning was the deed.* Sutpen's peremptory creation of a new order foreshadows the violations to be revealed in "The Bear": Carothers's originary act of founding a dynasty is grounded in a social transgression (miscegenation) compounded by an outrage (incest) that leads to the suicide of his black daughter.

Carothers always remains shadowy, referred to rather than heard or seen directly, and thus all the more mysterious, even ominous. Because Faulkner presents us with more of Sutpen, Sutpen tends to lose in heroic or demonic proportion as his background is fleshed in. At the public level, Sutpen's scandalous behavior is more stylistic than substantive—his force of will and brazenness, his sheer ambition, rub the community the wrong way by, among other things, revealing the hypocrisy of its most upright citizen, Mr. Coldfield. But Sutpen's impersonal, brutal side is revealed in the real site of founding sovereignity, the "primal" scene in the barn where, gratuitously, Sutpen battles hand to hand with his slaves, as the townsmen— and his two young children—look on in voyeuristic fascination. Thus Sutpen represents a return of what Jefferson has repressed as a community. He is the truth of the apparently settled and relatively benign community; it is not that he corrupts but that he confirms its essential nature. As Moreland writes: "when he first arrived, he was already there."[14] *In every work of genius we recognize our own rejected thoughts; they come back to us with a certain alienated majesty*. Sutpen's story, whether he is figured as the "demon" or a hero or a pathetic old man, reveals what lies at the origin of that community—ruthlessness and domination: *"Given the occasion and the need, this man can and will do anything."*[15] Sutpen lacks the sheer force of Ahab's intelligence but Faulkner on Sutpen's design echoes Melville on Ahab's obsessive search for the white whale: *"If he was mad, it was only his compelling dream which was insane and not his methods."*[16] Women are of secondary importance in this patriarchal order. They are exchange objects, linking families together to form societies and producers of heirs. The real conflict arises between males—insiders versus outsiders, white versus black. At stake are social prestige, the control of life and death of the other, and sexual access to women of both races.

If the Oedipal struggles within the family and among the males for control of women echo Freud's primal horde story of the origin of society based upon murder and guilt, then another founding vision of social hierarchy based upon the struggle to death for recognition—Hegel's philosophical drama in the "Lordship and Bondage" section of *Phenomenology of the Spirit*—illuminates the problem of succession and the transmission of power in a patriarchal, biracial (or triracial) society. Both Sutpen and Carothers refuse to recognize or acknowledge their male heirs, a refusal which implicates class, gender, and race. Sutpen *just doesn't get it*. He fails to recognize the nature of his own design; fails to recognize women (Rosa and Milly) as more than breeders for the male heir he desires; fails to recognize himself (or his father) in the person of Wash Jones, who by murdering Sutpen represents the return of the white social repressed; and fails, most dramatically, to recognize Bon as his legitimate heir or even as his son. This failure of acknowledgment is summed up in Ike McCaslin's horrified realization that the entire Southern order rests on Carothers's (and Sutpen's) refusal to say *"My son to a nigger . . . Even if My son wasn't but just two words."*[17] The effect of this failure of recognition is a curse upon the society and upon the families for their exploitation of nature and of other human beings.

The closest Faulkner comes to presenting a narrative of origins comes in the fourth section of "The Bear." Readers have been dizzied, not to mention confused, by the dialectic between Ike and his cousin McCaslin Edmonds in which the two exchange proposals and counterproposals in an attempt to "master" the meaning of Ike's abnegation, repudiation, relinquishment, or whatever they (or we) want to call it. Arguments shift and slide, are taken up and modulated, and then passed over. Part of the difficulty lies in Faulkner's deliberate elision of the differences between the two. This suggests that the positions of Ike and Cass are two warring aspects of Faulkner's own agonized thinking on the subject. He can wholeheartedly accept neither position fully. On the one hand if

> He [God, the Arbiter, the Umpire] created man to be His overseer on the earth and to hold suzerainty over the earth and the animals on it in His name . . . [and] hold the earth mutual and intact in the communal anonymity of brotherhood[18]

then Ike's repudiation or relinquishment is justified. Only this way can the curse of ownership and exploitation be transcended. And yet Ike has already located the origin of the curse prior to its purchase by the Sutpens, the Compsons, and the McCaslins

> because on the instant when Ikkemotubbe discovered, realised, that he could sell it for money, on that instant it ceased ever to have been his forever, father to father to father, and the man who bought it bought nothing.[19]

There are several lines of thought here worth pursuing. First, these passages seem to suggest that the New World innocence, the Edenic condition, never existed in the first place:

> He saw the land already accursed even as Ikkemotubbe and Ikkemotubbe's father old Issetibbeha and old Issetibbeha's fathers too held it, already tainted even before any white man owned it.[20]

Though this would seem to exonerate the white man, it doesn't exactly. Ike will go on to suggest that "He" used the white man's specific violations to work out the curse, to bring it to an end. Thus Ike's relinquishment—and John Brown's action—are moments in the political theodicy of the region and the nation.

If we shift from the moral-theological dimension to the formal and structural properties of founding narratives, we run up against the conceptual paradoxes, internal incoherence, and infinite regress that always mark accounts of the founding of a social order from pre-social (even pre-human) unity and innocence. The essential paradox is prefigured in Faulkner's discussion of the loss of virginity and his dilations on time in *The Sound and the Fury:* no original condition (female virginity or nature's innocence) or pre-temporal state (an absolute origin or present) can be conceptualized unless and until it no longer exists. From a wider perspective, Faulkner's attempt to think/ represent origins suggests that we cannot think or represent origins—from the Eden story down to "state of nature" stories (in Hobbes, Locke or Rousseau, Freud or Hegel)—without presupposing what is to be explained.

Put more simply: Faulkner's state of nature story in "The Bear," the culmination of his "sublime" founding stories, reveals what all these stories of absolute origins inadvertently reveal: that there is no state of nature, no Eden before the Fall, no first time, no human life without power and hierarchy. In conceptual terms, there is no point of origin, only infinite regress. It is impossible to represent such a state so that the transition from it to recognizable human society, however defined, makes logical or psychological sense. Even the author(s) of Genesis had to insert the serpent into Eden as the instrument of Adam and Eve's fall. Without the serpent, God's beneficence is called into question; yet with the serpent, his omniscience and omnipotence seem distinctly shaky. Finally, it is the function of founding stories, as Paul Ricoeur has noted, "to account for this transition [from original to actual, essence to existence] by means of narration." The time of myth is not "the time of history" nor are "mythical places" to be identified with "geographical space."[21] Faulkner's confusion about the origins of the curse results not from his failure to think the issue through sufficiently. Rather, in trying to do so, he ran up against the limitations of our capacity to do so without falling into incoherence.

The other set of founding narratives tell much the same story, but in a quite different mode. Whereas the foundings initiated by Sutpen and Old Carothers are narrated in what Erich Auerbach called the "Hebraic" mode, the later founding stories resemble that produced by the "Greek" sensibility.[22] The heroic myths of origins are mysterious and angular, replete with chiaroscuro and obscurity, and narrated with obsessiveness and bewilderment. The latter, pastoral ones are told from a more detached, often ironic and bemused, point of view. They present the long view—from the foundation of Jefferson by largely Anglo-Saxon pioneers through the emergence of the Sutpen, Compson, Sartoris, and McCaslin families to the Civil War and Reconstruction, and then the rise of the Snopeses and the coming of modern society. They are decline narratives, but lack the tortured and agonized atmosphere of the founding stories told in *Absalom* or "The Bear." Differences are smoothed out and injustice becomes normalized as part of history as a kind of pageant.

Indeed, the founding stories in the "Appendix" to *The Sound and the Fury*, "Mississippi," and *Requiem* present Faulkner's version of the frontier thesis, the specifically American story of the origins of society. Contrary to the high tradition's canonical stories of foundings in Hobbes, Locke, Rousseau, Freud, and Hegel, Turner's frontier thesis traces the collision of fragments of European, primarily British, society with the state of nature. (Faulkner, more than Turner, emphasizes the presence of the Indians.) On the frontier, the patina of civilization is stripped away and Europeans are reduced to a "natural" condition from which they build a new society, whose progress is paradoxically a form of decline from that imaginary, still point of uniqueness. As Faulkner writes in *Requiem*: "Because these were the frontier, pioneer times, when personal liberty and freedom were almost a physical condition like fire or flood."[23]

With this freedom come moments of collective, self-conscious foundings, involving both white and black (though Faulkner's characterization in *Requiem* of slaves as having "the simple child's mind" is a regression in his thinking):

> because it was theirs, bigger than any because it was the sum of all and, being the sum of all, it must raise all of their hopes and aspirations level with its own aspirant and soaring cupola . . . as if they were realising, or were for a moment at least capable of believing, that men, all men, including themselves, were a little better, purer maybe even, than they thought, expected, or even needed to be.[24]

This is one of the few moments in Faulkner where the aspiration to community is represented in a positive, literally constructive way. This contrasts with the less sunny, more ominous account of Sutpen and his slaves as they build his plantation house. The community "looked on" as the house goes up: "it had watched him as with that grim and unflagging fury he had erected that shell of a house."[25]

Yet the high, inspiriting rhetoric of communal founding is modulated, though not exactly undercut, by an ironic, God's eye view of the "progress" brought by (white) civilization. In describing the entrance of the original Anglo-Saxon pioneers— the "tall men"—onto the scene, Faulkner shifts into the rhetoric of the tall-tale of Southwestern humor:

> roaring with Protestant scripture and boiled whiskey, Bible and jug in one hand and (like as not) a native tomahawk in the other . . . uxorious and polygamous: a married invincible bachelor, dragging his gravid wife and most of his mother-in-law's family behind him . . . and at the same time scattering his ebullient seed in a hundred dusky bellies through a thousand miles of wilderness . . . changing the face of the earth: felling a tree which took two hundred years to grow, in order to extract from it a bear or a capful of wild honey.[26]

This passage is a "comic" retelling, without the agonized mediation of Ike, of the process by which men such as Carothers

McCaslin and Thomas Sutpen established their orders. Faulkner's narrative voice is under control, relatively undivided and working within generic conventions. His prose is idling, providing a gloss on his own world. The narrative is not so much immoral as amoral, a retrospective chronicling of founding and settlement. Similarly, Faulkner takes approximately a page to retell Sutpen's story without the intrusion of Rosa's obsessive demonizing, Mr. Compson's melancholy reflections, or Quentin's and Shreve's insistent questioning. Sutpen becomes a token in a series which constitutes a type: the first generation of family dynasties. Dispossessed and dispossessers (Indian and white), master and slave (white and black), husband and wife (though women get little mention), founders and latecomers (Compsons et. al. and Snopeses)—they all act out their appointed roles in wresting a society from the wilderness. The result is a kind of American/Southern realistic pastoral, replete with high aspiration and low dealings, community spirit and exploitative hierarchy. It's how the West was won.

Among these accounts of Jefferson's, Yoknapatawpha's, and Mississippi's beginnings, only Faulkner's "Mississippi" essay allows an intermittent reentry of the personal voice of judgment and explicit comment. In that essay the focus falls upon a Faulkner surrogate—"the boy," the "youth," the "middle aging" man—who functions as a kind of narrative relay to personalize the Olympian perspective. The essay is deeply elegaic, an attempt, perhaps, at reconciliation with all those he had outraged with his earlier work. The note of historical change, which in Faulkner tends to be equated with decline, is certainly there. But the conflict is represented not so much as one of Sartoris versus Snopes as one between the wilderness and the forces represented by the Snopeses:

> the boy a man now and in his hierarchial turn Master of the camp and coping, having to cope, not with the diminishing wilderness where there was less and less game, but with the Snopeses who were destroying that little which did remain.[27]

Still, the note of inevitability sounds: in the beginning the end was already present. What Faulkner writes of the Indians' first confrontation with the Europeans reveals a form of ironic historical consciousness, not so much critical as accepting of the process with neither great hope nor disillusionment: "In the beginning, the obsolescent, dispossessed tomorrow by the already obsolete,"[28] a passage that reminds us of, by undermining it, the opening phrase of the essay's second paragraph: "In the beginning it was virgin . . ."[29] Here Faulkner comes close to suggesting a primal innocence, but it is one that only existed before man (humans) and before men (sexual beings) possessed the V (the unspoiled Delta wilderness and the presexual female), the V being, as Richard Godden notes, "an explicitly female figure" which "designates an almost exclusively male space."[30] It is finally the unstable relationship between innocence and a kind of fallenness, figured in the wilderness and the depredations visited upon it, to which Faulkner refers, with regret but without anger, when he writes near the end of the essay: "Home again, his native land: he was born of it and his bones will sleep in it; loving it while hating some of it."[31]

Thus in the second mode of historical narration, the violation and rapaciousness, even the outrage, are integrated into a melancholic, though not bitter, vision of decline: a process balanced, or countered, by human endurance, courage, and honor. *That's the way it was*.

Ideological Implications

What are the ideological implications of Faulkner's two modes of narrating foundings and beginnings? The first thing to observe is that the two modes fall respectively into the pre- and post-World War II periods, thus coinciding roughly with the great and the not-so-great periods of Faulkner's literary career. The ironic, pastoral mode in particular is a variant, I think, upon the stoic humanism which emerges with full force in Faulkner's 1950 Nobel Prize address ("man will not only endure he will prevail"). Notoriously, the Cold War years were not a period of public questioning and radical dissent in American life, particularly when contrasted with the 1930s. And though Faulkner's work never directly addressed the pressing political and social issues of the 1930s, his agonized vision comported better with the mood of questioning of that decade than it did with the "age of conformity" of the 1950s. While these historicizing generalizations are crude, they do reflect (on) Faulkner's shift, as Lawrence Schwartz has put it, from a "prewar nihilist" to a "postwar moralist," from a writer whose work was out of print in the early 1940s to a writer who was awarded the Nobel Prize in 1950.[32]

The question then becomes: was this a shift in Faulkner's own vision or was it a shift in the way he was read? Not surprisingly, I think it was some of both. Whether the shift represents the completion of the process by which Faulkner came to terms with his personal and spiritual demons or whether it is an example of a writer who had depleted his energies and abilities beyond renewal, there is no doubt that the later Faulkner, including the Faulkner of "The Appendix," of "Mississippi," and of *Requiem*, was not only a writer of less power than earlier but also a writer attempting to eke out some "positive" vision of the human condition. Indeed, his attempt to write about "the human condition," about "Man," was itself a symptom of his decline.[33]

On the other hand, Faulkner's critics began to read him differently after World War II. The contrast between Alfred Kazin's ambivalent treatment of Faulkner in *On Native Grounds* (1942) and his admiring and powerful essay "The Stillness of *Light in August*" (1958) illustrates this point well. But Faulkner was also championed by Southern critics of Agrarian-New Critical provenance, to which I have already alluded. Central in the postwar readings of Faulkner were those offered by Robert Penn Warren, who saw Faulkner as creating "a legend of our general plight and problem. The modern world is in moral confusion"; and by Cleanth Brooks, who contended that "The community is the circumambient atmosphere, the essential ether of Faulkner's fiction . . . the field of man's action and the norm by which his action is judged and regulated." Faulkner's work, wrote Brooks in 1978, presents "a coherent ethical and moral position that is traditional and conservative."[34] Although Warren stressed Faulkner's universality and his tragic vision, while Brooks emphasized Faulkner's grounding in the Southern ethos and his essentially comic vision, both critics saw him as a diagnostician of the modern world's moral incoherence. All this, it should be added, was a far cry from the 1930s when some critics, particularly on the Left, saw Faulkner as a nihilist who flirted with a fascist vision of reality.

The conservative, not to say, apologetic dimension of Brooks's reading of Faulkner can be seen precisely in his treatment of Sutpen. As presented by Brooks, Sutpen is geographically and socially an outsider to Jefferson and ethically at odds with its essential values. His story is not an exemplification of the tragedy of the Old South but of the flaw inherent in the American dream. Similarly, Percy Grimm's lynching of Joe Christmas is an horrific act taken against, not in the name of, the community. When Brooks comes to "The Bear," he fails to deal with Carothers McCaslin's violations at all.[35] Thus in Brooks's reading of Faulkner, evil and disruption are external to, not inherent in, the traditional Southern order and the values attendant to it.

The other ideologically charged dimension of the first generation of Faulkner critics, one which still persists today in many quarters, is the moral abuse heaped upon the Snopeses. They become, not without Faulkner's encouragement, the all-purpose villains in the decline narrative of Southern modernization. It is a decline narrative which both Right and Left can share, since both consider capitalism as the villain. Here Richard Moreland's reference to a kind of "structural anti-Semitism" in connection with the Snopeses is relevant.[36] For the Snopeses serve, in Faulkner's world and in many critics' interpretation of that world, as a placeholder for everything that is rapacious, greedy, and rootless about the modern South. This is not to claim that all those who dislike that bizarre clan are closet anti-Semites; but it does suggest that there is a certain ritualistic quality about the condemnation of the Snopeses. Indeed, such a reaction calls to mind the Jewish joke set at a Nazi rally where the speaker is lambasting the Jews as responsible for all the evils besetting Germany. A Jew on the fringes of the crowd turns to a bystander and whispers, "It's not the Jews but the bicycle riders who are at the root of our problems." The bystander is taken aback and asks, "Why the bicycle riders?" The Jewish man retorts, "Why the Jews?" *Why the Snopeses?*

My point here is that Brooks's dissociation of Sutpen from what he sees as essential Southern values, along with the easy moralizing about the Snopeses, allows the Southern tradition to escape a certain scrutiny. But as Elizabeth Spencer wrote in the paper she delivered at the 1981 Faulkner and Yoknapatawpha Conference:

> If you are trying to deal with business matters in Mississippi, you should not confine your wariness to the Snopeses. While you are busy watching out for spotted horses, somebody with the bluest blood between the Alabama state line and the Mississippi River will sneak up behind you and take everything you've got to call your own.[37]

Just to be evenhanded here, I should also add that the Faulkner critics on the contemporary, more theoretically inclined Left, among whom I count myself, have understandably wanted to claim Faulkner for their camp as a radical critic of racism and of the individualistic ethos so central to the development of capitalism.[38] According to this view, Sutpen's and Carothers McCaslin's overweening ambition and disregard for others are causally linked with and epitomize both racism and capitalism.

But if we are going to be "historical," then there are complications to be noted. Whatever its aetiology in the New World, racism can exist independently of capitalist development or of slavery; and for both Marx and Weber, slavery and capitalism are at odds with one another. (Not to mention the fact that to be anti-slavery or even hostile to capitalism was—and is—no guarantee against holding racist views.) Moreover, laying slavery and racism at the foot of capitalism explains too much—and thus too little. Capitalism in reality is not one but many things. And there are a multitude of capitalisms or stages of capitalism in Faulkner's world. Mr. Coldfield is a petty bourgeois merchant; the yeoman are small-scale producer capitalists or sometimes even pre-capitalists; while the large planters, however seigneurial their aspirations, are also involved in the rationalization of production for profit in the national and world market. Finally, of course, capitalists in the North and in Britain were among the leaders of the anti-slavery movements beginning in the first quarter of the nineteenth century and one major economic/capitalist argument against slavery was its inefficiency as a form of labor.

My point here is that, although Faulkner may provide the reader the raw materials for a critique linking capitalism, slavery, racism, and individualism, we should neither automatically accept that linkage or assume that Faulkner did so. As any reading of Faulkner should reveal, Faulkner's attitude toward the Sutpens and the Carothers McCaslins of his world was decidedly ambivalent, as was his attitude toward the virtues of Southern slave society. The horrors of patriarchy and a racist order are amply dissected in Faulkner's great work; but it is just the point that he makes no generalizations from that and fails, rightly or wrongly, to move from a moral to a social and political analysis. No one, including Faulkner, could figure out how to get rid of slavery and transcend the curse of racism, yet forestall the process of modernization.

A final reason for focussing on the two types of founding stories in Faulkner is to suggest that Faulkner's vision of history fits comfortably into neither the traditionalist nor the progressive ideology/story of Southern history. In his great period, and after, he shocked and outraged conservatives and liberals. I have encountered no explicit evidence that Faulkner's delineations of

Sutpen and Old Carothers were in any way responses to, or reflections on, triumphant fascism in Italy, Germany, Spain, and Eastern Europe. But it deserves noting that several Southern writers and intellectuals of the 1930s and 1940s were preoccupied with disruptive, transgressive, and rootless figures who threatened the given order and, indirectly, with comparing and contrasting the South with Nazi Germany or Mussolini's Italy. Both W. J. Cash in *The Mind of the South* (1941) and the liberal-tending Warren in *All the King's Men* (1946) explored such issues. Allen Tate in *The Fathers* (1938) dissected the helplessness shown by the traditional South in the face of challenges from a figure of amoral energy and will such as George Posey, while Will Percy in *Lanterns on the Levee* (1941) explicitly linked the Nazis with the end of civilization. It only remained for a second generation Agrarian, Richard Weaver, to acknowledge the similarities between traditional Southern values and the Nazi emphasis upon *Blut und Boden*, before then explaining why they were so different.[39]

If we place Faulkner in this historical and regional context, his fascination with the Sutpens and Carothers McCaslins assumes a different aspect. This is not to impute to him conscious intention, just as it would be absurd to suggest that Melville knowingly anticipated the totalitarian leader in the figure of Ahab (though Melville may have had John C. Calhoun more relevantly in mind). But there was something in Faulkner that was obsessed with, and drawn toward, violence, sex, and death, which make up the poisonous brew from which generic fascism emerges. To violate and be violated; to assert hard individuality and to desire one's eradication or engulfment; to create an imperishable order and to bring it down in a kind of *Götterdämmerung;* to desire to dominate but without regard or acknowledgment; to racialize sexuality and to sexualize racism—Faulkner was engaged with these themes and obsessions in his great work. But it is not always clear that he fought clear of their seductive power.

Thus, Faulkner was playing for very large stakes, one definition of dangerous literature. We misread Faulkner when we fail to recognize or obscure his "dangerous" qualities. Like Sutpen and Carothers, he was ruthless and heedless and he paid the cost. What this also suggests for current debates about the ideological function of literary canons is that perhaps we have got it the wrong way around. The conventional wisdom is that canonized writers are those who reenforce the dominant order of "Dead White Bourgeois Males." No doubt there are plenty of figures so canonized. But with Faulkner—and perhaps others—it may work the other way around: the process of canonization itself creates safe writers and conformist readings. In the case of Faulkner, we need to reread him, continually and constantly, against all efforts to domesticate or normalize him for any particular ideological position—which is not the same thing as saying he transcends ideology. But Elizabeth Spencer put it best when she wrote:

> let's not ever get folksy and cozy about our great writer. Let's not ever make it pure and simple. Let's keep it pure and difficult—complicated, wild, passionate, dark and dangerous—the real thing.[40]

NOTES

1. In *Warrant for Genocide: The Myth of the Jewish World-Conspiracy and the Protocols of the Elders of Zion* (New York and Evanston: Harper Torchbooks, 1969), 16, Norman Cohn notes that "myth" generally has three meanings or dimensions which coincide with those I have suggested encompass the meanings of ideology. See also Karl Marx, "The German Ideology," in *Marx and Engels: Basic Writings on Politics and Philosophy* ed. by Lewis Feuer (Garden City: Doubleday Anchor, 1959), 246–51; Daniel Bell, "The End of Ideology in the West," in *The End of Ideology* (New York: Collier Books, 1962), 393–404; and George Lichtheim, *The Concept of Ideology* (New York: Vintage, 1967), 3–46. It should be noted that there is an ambiguity in the Marxist notion of ideology which sees ideology either as a straightforward reflection of social reality or an inversion of social reality. Ultimately, the ideology/truth opposition derives from the appearance/reality opposition so fundamental to Platonism.

2. The term "master narrative" *(grand recit)*, as used by Jean-François Lyotard in *The Postmodern Condition* (Manchester: Manchester University Press, 1984), refers generally to Christianity, Liberalism, and Marxism and is roughly synonymous with ideology as philosophy of history. For further discussions of the centrality of narrative in human self-description, see the work of Alasdair MacIntyre, Richard Rorty, Charles Taylor, Hayden White, and Paul Ricoeur.

3. Frederick Karl in *William Faulkner: American Writer* (London: Faber, 1989) writes that in the 1930s Faulkner "lacked an acute sense of what was occurring in the

larger world" and that his "image of America was basically apolitical in any committed sense" (595–96). Later, this would change to a degree.

4. See for instance Bertram Wyatt-Brown, *Southern Honor* (New York: Oxford University Press, 1982).

5. George Marion O'Donnell, "Faulkner's Mythology," in *William Faulkner: Three Decades of Criticism*, ed., Frederick J. Hoffman and Olga Vickery (East Lansing: Michigan State University Press, 1960), 82–93.

6. Carolyn Porter, *Seeing and Being* (Middletown: Wesleyan University Press, 1981), xvii. See also my *A Southern Renaissance* (New York: Oxford University Press, 1980) for a reading of Faulkner as being "about" the historical crisis in Southern culture, a political reading in the broadest sense.

7. William Faulkner, *The Sound and the Fury* (New York: Vintage, 1954), 222.

8. Richard C. Moreland, *Faulkner and Modernism: Rereading and Rewriting* (Madison: University of Wisconsin Press, 1990).

9. See Sacvan Bercovitch, *American Jeremiad* (Madison: University of Wisconsin Press, 1978).

10. In *William Faulkner* Karl notes that "the political, in Faulkner, is assimilated into the social." (82).

11. Edward Said, *Beginnings: Intention and Method* (New York: Basic Books, 1975); and Hayden White, "The Politics of Historical Interpretation: Discipline and De-Sublimation," in *The Content of the Form* (Baltimore: Johns Hopkins University Press, 1987).

12. William Faulkner, "The Bear," *Go Down, Moses* (New York: Modern Library, 1942), 281.

13. Orlando Patterson, *Freedom: Freedom in the Making of Western Culture* (New York: Basic Books, 1991), 3–4.

14. Moreland, *Faulkner and Modernism*, 39.

15. William Faulkner, *Absalom, Absalom!* (New York: Modern Library, 1951), 46.

16. Ibid., 166.

17. "The Bear," 269–70.

18. Ibid., 257.

19. Ibid. Howard C. Horsford, "Faulkner's (Mostly) Unreal Indians in Early Mississippi History," *American Literature*, 64, 2 (June 1992): 311–30, suggests that no chief could have disposed of land in this manner and that more generally Faulkner had "very little familiarity with early Mississippi history or with the Choctaws and Chickasaws who were its victims" (311).

20. Ibid., 259.

21. Paul Ricoeur, *The Symbolism of Evil* (Boston, MA.: Beacon Press, 1969), 162; 5. A few instances: Hobbes must presuppose a certain authority in the state of nature in order for institutional authority to be produced; Locke, contrarily, must assume a flaw of some sort in the state of nature, which has been represented as flawless. Rousseau's state of nature, immune to artifice and corruption, generates inequality of property. Similarly, the sons who, according to Freud, kill the patriarch and establish society grounded in guilt over this action must already have a rudimentary capacity for guilt in order to establish this society, while Hegel's combatants for recognition already are aware of their freedom, itself to be generated in the struggle for recognition.

22. Erich Auerbach, *Mimesis* (Garden City, N.Y.: Doubleday Anchor, 1957), chapter 1 ("Odysseus' Scar").

23. William Faulkner, *Requiem for a Nun* (Harmondsworth, U.K.: Penguin, 1960), 10.

24. Ibid., 40.

25. *Absalom, Absalom!*, 38, 42.

26. *Requiem for a Nun*, 89–90.

27. William Faulkner, "Mississippi," in *Essays, Speeches and Public Letters*, ed. by James B. Meriwether (London: Chatto and Windus, 1967), 13. See also James Cobb,

"The South's South: The Enigma of Creativity in the Mississippi Delta," *The Southern Review*, 25, 1 (January 1989): 72–85.

28. "Mississippi," 13.

29. Ibid., 11.

30. Richard Godden, *Fictions of Capital* (Cambridge: Cambridge University Press, 1990), 155.

31. "Mississippi," 36.

32. Lawrence Schwartz, *Creating Faulkner's Reputation: The Politics of Modern Literary Criticism* (Knoxville: University of Tennessee Press, 1988).

33. Though Frederick Karl's massive biography has any number of flaws, it does particularly valuable work in exposing the many symptoms and causes of Faulkner's decline, most saliently the sheer expense of time and energy in Hollywood and the long–term effects of alcohol.

34. Robert Penn Warren, "William Faulkner," in *Three Decades of Criticism*, 112; Cleanth Brooks, *William Faulkner: The Yoknapatawpha Country* (New Haven: Yale University Press, 1963), 52; *Toward Yoknapatawpha and Beyond* (New Haven: Yale University Press, 1978), 275.

35. See Brooks, *William Faulkner*, chapters 4, 12, and 14.

36. Moreland, 145.

37. Elizabeth Spencer, "Emerging as a Writer in Faulkner's Mississippi," in *Faulkner and the Southern Renaissance*, ed. by Doreen Fowler and Ann J. Abadie (Jackson: University Press of Mississippi, 1982), 136.

38. Besides King, Porter, and Moreland, see also Eric Sundquist, *The House Divided* (Baltimore: The Johns Hopkins University Press, 1983).

39. See Richard H. King, "Anti-Modernists All!," *The Mississippi Quarterly*, 44,2 (Spring 1991): 193–201 for a discussion of Weaver's analysis of the similarities between the fascist and Southern ideology.

40. Elizabeth Spencer, "Emerging as a Writer . . . ," 137.

On Privacy:
William Faulkner and the Human Subject

RICHARD GRAY

In 1949, when he was finally beginning to receive the kind of public recognition he deserved, William Faulkner wrote this to the critic Malcolm Cowley:

> It is my ambition to be, as a private individual, abolished and voided from history, leaving it markless, no refuse save the printed books; I wish I had had enough sense to see ahead thirty years ago and, like some of the Elizabethans, not signed them. It is my aim, and every effort bent, that the sum and history of my life, which in the same sentence is my obit and epitaph too, shall be them both: He made the books and he died.[1]

There are several ways of reading this. One, and the simplest perhaps, is simply to see it as a pose. Faulkner's claim that he either was or wanted to be "the last private individual on earth" could be seen as simply that: a claim, with little or no foundation in perceptible experience. Faulkner played many roles in his life—the effete, bohemian aristocrat, the wounded war hero, the farmer unkempt in body and in mind, the red-coated, stiff-backed huntsman on horseback—and maybe it could be argued that this obsessive, widely proclaimed pursuit of privacy was simply another change of clothes, a further way of allowing Faulkner to enact his identity, to turn his experiencing self into a performing self. The Faulkner clan, their neighbours often felt, were a "showy," histrionic group of people: one had only to look at the eight-foot likeness of Faulkner's great-grandfather, Colonel William Clark Falkner, that towered above his grave in

Ripley, Mississippi, to appreciate that. And if many of Faulkner's family liked to play a part, including Faulkner himself, then possibly they were only carrying a local tendency to extremes. An aristocratic culture, the historian J. M. Huizinga has observed, is one in which people imitate some idea of aristocracy, an "illusion of heroic being, full of dignity and honour, of wisdom and, at all events, of courtesy."[2] The South, both before and after the Civil War, wanted desperately to see itself as aristocratic; and, to this extent, many white Southerners were ready to turn themselves into actors: to adopt the aristocratic pose and so reinvent themselves as gentlemen and ladies. Part of this pose could and did involve aloofness, a *hauteur* that at once invited admiring attention and discouraged curiosity: approval, or even wonder, was what was required rather than intimacy. "Privacy," as invoked by the person laying claim to special, aristocratic status, became, in effect, a strategy for transmuting personality into performance; the actor was not literally to be left alone but viewed from a respectful distance, as he or she carried out a series of masterly, and mainly evasive, gestures.

To stop there, however, or to suggest, as one commentator has, that Faulkner's pursuit of inaccessibility was simply a ruse, a device for making himself more mysterious, more desirable, is hardly to do justice to the fierceness of his devotion to his own company. At his most polemical, Faulkner was even inclined to identify the entire project of America with the idea of privacy. His essay "On Privacy," for example, is sub-titled "(The American Dream: What Happened to It?)"; and it fluctuates between fierce denunciations of institutional forces that seem bent on violating "individualness" and simpler, but no less heartfelt complaints about the inquisitiveness and insensitivity of journalists. Without "individual privacy," Faulkner testily argued, there was no "individuality," and without individuality there was "not anything at all worth the having and keeping"; so privacy, in a sense, becomes the significant basis of life. "The qualities of individualism whose possession we boast since they

alone differ us from animals—gratitude for kindness, fidelity to
friendship, chivalry toward women and the capacity for love":[3]
these, he insisted, depend on a respect for distance, an absolute
refusal to "strip" the individual "naked of the privacy" that
alone saved him from degenerating into "one more identityless
anonymous unprivacied mass which seems to be our goal." The
violence of the language perhaps alerts us to the extremity of
the commitment: a respect for privacy becomes a ritual of
deference, with sexual overtones ("chivalry toward women"),
and, conversely, the lack of respect is associated with an act of
violation. To preserve privacy is to keep the body of the subject
intact, inviolate; to deny it is to turn subject into object, to
ignore or resist the otherness of the other person in the belief
that no corner of the personality is unavailable for immediate
conquest and appropriation.

Faulkner's rejection of the kind of moral imperialism that, as
he saw it, the failure of privacy entails carried certain significant
consequences. In his life, it led to the assumption of personae,
formulaic answers to interviewers, and the reinvention of his
own past history. The roles, already referred to, permitted him
to express specific aspects of his character and impulses but
through a glass darkly, as it were, shaded by or distorted in the
flamboyant details of the performance. The aristocratic dandy
of his adolescence, for instance, was a convenient means of
dramatizing his uneasy, ambiguous relationship to his home-
place. Like many others in Oxford, Mississippi, and in the
South, he was at home and yet not at home in the modern
world: compelled to inhabit a bourgeois, utilitarian culture that
only minimally answered his emotional needs. Unlike most of
them, however, he responded to this compulsion by exaggerat-
ing his difference from *everyone*, including those who shared
his uncertainties: in his clothes, the arts he favored, and in his
air of almost aggressive indolence. A pose like this at once
expressed a part of his personality and kept the rest hidden: it
was, simultaneously, a form of self-exposure and of concealment.
It allowed communication, even revelation, but it also preserved

a measure of anonymity: the audience, observing such a performance, could learn something about the performer but were made aware that, in the final analysis, he remained apart, separate and private.

Similar strategies were at work in Faulkner's behavior towards interviewers. Very early on in his career, he adopted what one interviewer in 1931 termed a "barrier" to protect "the sensitive part of him." He was capable of what a later interviewer was to call "the most exquisite but the most obdurate politeness" as a weapon for fending off unwelcome inquiries. "That famous wall" of exquisite *politesse* was only one of many maneuvers, though. Simple "shyness and defensiveness" was another, a nervousness that as one observer saw it, "places an interviewer on his honor not to probe forbidden areas." Alternatively, Faulkner would fall back on obduracy and irony, claiming "I prefer silence to sound" or that "an artist shouldn't talk too much." "He is not a great talker," one perplexed and clearly defeated interviewer opined, "in fact he is not a talker at all."[4] This comment would have surprised some of those closest to Faulkner, familiar as they were with his skill at storytelling or willingness to quote poetry at the drop of a hat. And, in any event, it sat uneasily with Faulkner's own claim that Southerners "love to talk" because, as he put it, "oratory is our heritage." Sometimes, disingenuousness of the kind Faulkner reserved for certain interviewers would spin off into tall tales and comic *bravura*. In 1931, for instance, in an interview with a Memphis reporter, the writer made wry fun of his own reluctance to reveal too much about himself by offering this brief autobiographical sketch:

> I was born male and single at an early age in Mississippi. I am still alive but not single. I was born of a Negro slave and an alligator, both named Gladys Rock. I had two brothers, one Dr. Walter E. Traprock and the other Eagle Rock, an airplane.[5]

In response to persistent questioning about his books Faulkner would frequently insist that he was a farmer, not a literary man.

Or he would declare that there were many things he would rather be than a professional writer: a tramp perhaps, the landlord of a brothel (with plenty of free time in the day and plenty of company and conversation in the evening), or even a buzzard. "Nothing hates him or envies him or wants him or needs him," he said of the buzzard. "He is never bothered or in danger, and he can eat everything."[6] Finally, if such deadpan evasiveness did not work, and the interviewer seemed determined to go home with something apparently substantial in his notebook, Faulkner would be ready to fall back on set-piece answers and formulaic phrases: about man enduring and prevailing, about a writer's responsibility to tell the truth and the difference between "facts" and "truth," about the books that were "old friends" (*Don Quixote, Moby Dick, Huckleberry Finn, Madam Bovary*, and *The Brothers Karamazov* were invariably included in this catalogue) and the great writers whom he believed were his "masters." In terms of their empirical details, none of these answers was untrue: even the weariest catalogue or the most clichéd formula was rooted, in the end, in a fiercely held opinion or commitment, just as the tallest tale or wildest *jeu d'esprit* had its ultimate source in some significant part of Faulkner's dreams, his fantasy life. It was just that, as with the role-playing, Faulkner was withholding as much as he was giving away; he was willing to surrender only on terms that enabled him to retreat with dignity—with a sense of his own privacy intact.

And then there was the lying. The legends nurtured by Faulkner about his piloting experiences are perhaps the most memorable instance of this. Anxious to be a pilot, Faulkner joined the Royal Air Force in Canada and was posted to Toronto to be trained. This was an important moment for him, since he believed in both the courage and the sexuality of flight: the pilot figured for him—as it did for many of his contemporaries—simultaneous and, to some extent, self-contradictory notions of military honour, individual daring, mastery of machinery and death, limitless freedom, and erotic conquest. Unfortunately,

the dream was never realized; the war was over before he had
completed his training; he may never even have had a flight in
a plane, let alone served in action. Unimpeded by the facts,
however, Faulkner proceeded to construct a personal myth. He
wrote home about the stimulation of soloing and "joy rides" and
about crashing his plane upside down in the rafters of a hangar.
Discharged as a cadet, he nevertheless purchased an officer's
uniform before returning to Mississippi, complete with swagger
stick; he then wore this on the train home despite the fact that,
even if he had been entitled to wear it, regulations restricted its
use to military occasions; and he arrived at Oxford railway
station limping, having acquired a mythical war wound to
complete his identity as hero of the air. By the time Faulkner
moved to New Orleans, in 1925, he had even adopted a second
wound, in the evident belief that no hero could have too many.
His brother Jack had been injured by shrapnel while in France
and severely wounded in the head; among his friends in New
Orleans, Faulkner claimed a similar injury. Some of those
friends, including the writer Sherwood Anderson, even believed
that the young man from Mississippi had had a steel plate
inserted in his skull. As the years passed, the legend grew: he
had crashed *two* planes during the war, costing the British
government four thousand pounds; he had been dragged out
more dead than alive from the wreck of his plane with not one
but *both* legs broken. It was almost thirty years, in fact, before
Faulkner felt inclined to trim the fantasy. In 1946, when Malcolm Cowley was preparing the introduction to *The Portable
Faulkner*, Faulkner began to renege on his reinvention of his
own history. "If you mention military experience at all," he told
Cowley, who was planning to include some biographical notes,
"say 'belonged to RAF 1918.'" "I could have invented a few
failed RAF airmen," he added ominously, in parentheses, "as
easily I did Confeds." He would not disclose the truth, however,
that he had lied consistently and magnificently. The closest he
would come to candor, in response to Cowley's repeated desire

to incorporate tales of military daring into the story, was this angry and desperate plea:

> You're going to bugger up a fine dignified distinguished book with that war business. . . . If, because of some later reference back to it in the piece, you cant omit all European war reference, say only what Who's Who says, and no more:
> Was a member of the RAF in 1918.[7]

Faulkner was, as usual, willing to go only so far in the name of self-revelation, even when he felt, as he evidently did in this case, that he was standing in the tribunal of history. His lies were important to him, not only because they were inseparably linked to the fictive impulse that helped him create, among other things, all the young pilots of his stories, but because they too were a means of strictly partial disclosure. In rehearsing his life as an air ace, Faulkner was telling and not telling; he was offering lies like truth in order to expose a deeper truth—about the desires and anxieties provoked in him by what he saw as the male role. "A book is the writer's secret life," declares a character in *Mosquitoes*, "the dark twin of a man";[8] the terms could just as easily be reversed, under the pressure of Faulkner's tendency simultaneously to reveal and to conceal. For him, life frequently became a book in which he inscribed his secret struggle with a darker, more potent and dangerous, twin whom he both longed and feared to embrace.

"I think that a writer is a perfect case of split personality," Faulkner remarked once; and, with Faulkner himself, that split was not only demonstrable in his life but in his writing.[9] He enacted an urge simultaneously to expose and to hide in his books as much as in his behavior in Oxford and elsewhere. One crucial way he did this brings us right back to the issue of privacy, as he addressed that issue with reference to his characters and their voices. "Just talk to people," Faulkner gave as his advice to the aspiring writer in one early interview.[10] "I listen to the voices," he said elsewhere, "and when I put down what the voices say, it's right."[11] This was the initial and seminal moment in the act of creation for him: hearing the voice of

another, separate if imagined, person trying to explain, and
then reproducing that speech as writing, whether that speech
might be public or private, conversation or talking to oneself.
An act of possession or appropriation was implicit here, of
course: Faulkner was not above declaring of his characters,
"These people . . . belong to me" in the belief that, since he
had given them voice and imaginative identity, he owned them,
they were his. But more often than not, he took what might
seem a curiously, even naïvely, detached attitude to what, after
all, were the products of his own imaginings. "Any character that
you write takes charge of his own behavior," he declared. "You
can't make him do things once he comes alive and stands up and
casts his shadow."[12] "In general he has a very objective attitude
toward his writings," one commentator observed in 1932, "and
seems to take them as facts of nature, like the rain, about which
one does not feel impelled to pass judgment, good or bad."[13]

This observation is, perhaps, not quite right. Faulkner was
perfectly willing to offer judgments of his books and characters.
The point was not so much that he did not offer judgments but
rather that they were offered in a decidedly unauthoritative and
detached way: as if they carried no more weight than the
opinions of any other "simple private individual." "I don't
remember the books," Faulkner insisted. "Once I have written
them they no longer belong to me." It was the book and its
characters that mattered, he argued time and again, not the
author; or, as he put it, "The artist is of no importance. Only
what he creates is important."[14] So, if he offered opinions on
characters like Jason Compson (the character he disliked most,
he admitted) or Dilsey Gibson and V. K. Ratliff (his favorites,
he declared) he did so only in the same spirit as he ventured
comments on other characters in other books written by other
people. If he wished to pass an observation on one of his novels
he did so in the spirit of a reader who, somehow, possessed a
separate identity from the writer: *The Sound and the Fury*, he
wrote to his aunt, was "the damndest book I ever read"—almost
as if this came to him as a surprise. Receiving an essay from

a professor of English on "William Faulkner and the Social Conscience," Faulkner wrote back to him referring to the subject in the third person: "I agree with it," he confided, "I mean, re Faulkner's aim."[15] Asked if Charles Bon, in *Absalom, Absalom!*, ever suspected who his father was, he responded much more speculatively than most critics of the novel have. "I think he knew," Faulkner said, "I don't know whether he—his mother probably told him. I think he knew."[16] In effect, Faulkner was denying the authority of authorship: once the characters "grew up" and "escaped the nest" (as he put it once), they assumed their own status as independent subjects.

At times, Faulkner was willing to push this insistence on the private nature and independent voice of his characters to extremes. In a very early interview, for example, he argued that the best way to keep character separate from the author was more or less to eliminate the author altogether. "Mr. Faulkner had the very interesting idea," recalled the interviewer, "centering about the thesis that Dostoevski could have written the *Brothers* in one third the space had he let the characters tell their own stories instead of filling page after page with exposition"[17] "The character, the rhythm of the speech, compels its own dialect," Faulkner insisted elsewhere; self-revelation, with all its strange mixture of intimacy and secrecy was perhaps best left as the responsibility of each individual voice. This was, as so often with Faulkner, a partial truth, concealing as much as it revealed. In the first place, remarks about how Dostoevski might have written *The Brothers Karamazov* so as to compress and improve it sound like pure mischief, another example of Faulkner's delight in deadpan irony, when it is recalled that the book was always listed among his four or five favorites: into which, he said, he would dip again and again, "just as you'd meet and talk to a friend for a few minutes."[18] In the second, a recommendation that "characters tell their own stories" tends to play down the significance of *inner* speech for Faulkner: "talk" for him was a matter not just of the subtle maneuvers and rituals of everyday conversation but also of the voices a person hears within him as he struggles to emerge into identity through words. And in the third place nothing that Faulkner might say about the "dead weight" of the author—and the need to eliminate him in the interests of the "objective presentation" of something like "play technique"—can hide the fact that the authorial voice is there in his narratives: not, usually, as an authoritative discourse but as one voice among many.

Faulkner's reference to Dostoevski, in this context, is especially and oddly relevant; for all his occasional, disparaging references to "page after page" of exposition, his practice was very similar to that of the author of *The Brothers Karamazov*. Faulkner has frequently been described as "the Dostoevski of the South": but this, more often than not, has been taken to imply a shared interest in themes of alienation and dispossession. There is another side to this connection, however, this "spiritual kinship" (to borrow a phrase Faulkner himself used) and it has to do with the fundamentals of the two writers' imaginative projects.[19] In his book, *Problems of Dostoevsky's Poetics*, Mikhail Bakhtin argued that Dostoevski was the creator of a new form, "the polyphonic novel." What distinguishes this form, Bakhtin suggested, is that "a character's word about himself and his world is just as fully weighted as the author's word usually is." The voice or word of the character is not subordinated to the voice or word of the author; on the contrary, it "sounds, as it were, *alongside* the author's word" combining "both with it and with the full and equally valid voices of the other characters."[20] "A world of autonomous subjects, not objects" is consequently created: a dialogue of voices that engage on an equal basis with each other. There is no privileging of the author: each character realized in terms of speech is allowed the fundamental right of being active and apart—in Faulkner's own special terms, his privacy.

Several things need to be emphasized about Bakhtin's notion of the polyphonic novel, and its relationship to Faulkner's creative practice. A crucial one, perhaps the most crucial, is that, as Bakhtin perceives it and Faulkner practices it, dialogue does not just occur *between* voices, but also *within* them. "Our speech is full of other people's words,"[21] Bakhtin argued. We can therefore no more escape from dialogue, even in conversation with ourselves, than a character like Quentin Compson can forget the voice of his father. This point about the dialogic nature of even interior discourse is another way of saying that language is social—and that, in turn, human life, which is constituted by language, is inseparable from historical life. The paradox is that we exist *apart*, as autonomous subjects and authors of our own discourse, and as *part* of what Bakhtin called "a speaking collective" from whom our words are derived and to whom, however implicitly, they are addressed. "Two voices are the minimum for life," to put it in Bakhtin's terms;[22] or "it takes two to make the book, the poem," to use Faulkner's.[23] Even Benjy Compson, in order to "be," has to engage in "trying to say" (as Benjy himself puts it): he has to exist in a dialogue that he cannot literally have, because without words he cannot be there, not only for author and readers but for himself. As with all Faulkner's so-called "interior monologues," the supposed monologist is actually engaged in a dialogue because (to quote Bakhtin again), "No member of a verbal community can ever find words in the language that are neutral, exempt from the aspirations and evaluations of the other, uninhabited by the other's voice."[24]

Not only simultaneously inner and outer, personal and social, language is, according to these definitions, an open system, a "mobile medium" that resists closure. "Each individual utterance," Bakhtin observed, "is a link in the chain of speech communication"; and, by its very nature, that chain is of indefinite length or duration, it can have no beginning or end. The possibility of a final, finalizing discourse is consequently excluded, along with the claims of an authoritative one. Even questions of personal identity, "Who am I?" or "Who are *you*?" are drawn into "a continuous and open-ended dialogue," a chain of speech communication that is a process rather than a product.[25] Even the vast sprawl of the Yoknapatawpha series is no more, and no less, than what Bakhtin would call a "great dialogue" or "open dialogue": in which "the object is precisely the passing of a theme through many and various voices"—rather, that is, than any terminal or even tentative conclusion.[26]

The relevance in detail of all this to the fiction must be left for the moment, however; all that can be mentioned for now is the broader implications of these notions of voice both to the literature and to the life. As far as the literature is concerned, some of these implications have been hinted at already. In Faulkner's narratives, set in Yoknapatawpha or elsewhere, character is irrevocably private and yet implicated in history, a complex web of *social* relations: a paradox that is registered in the rhythms and inner dynamics of each individual voice. And the narratives themselves operate within an equally complex web of *intertextual* relations, as a result of which each book or story, while constituting its own system of languages, exists in dialogic contact with other systems, other books in the series. Each of Faulkner's texts, in these respects, enacts his special notion of "privacy," as a mode or activity of simultaneous disclosure and concealment. The voices *within* the text and the voices *of* the text assert, by their very nature, both connection (I can only speak to you by inhabiting the same "speaking collective" as you) and withdrawal (I can only speak to you by being other than you). They remind us, as Faulkner constantly reminded his interlocutors, that "a speaking human being" is at once situated in a common verbal culture and set apart in his own verbal space: he is, as it were, a member of a club with certain tacit rules of linguistic exchange—but a member with his own private membership card, his own ticket of entry inscribing his difference.

It is perhaps worth observing, in passing, that these notions, as they inhabit Bakhtin's thought and Faulkner's practice, are inseparable from the idea of historical change. "Language, discourse," Bakhtin observed, "is almost the totality of human life";[27] it is constitutive of human existence. And "language," he added, "is something that is historically real";[28] "the entire part of human existence," as he put it once, "does not belong to the individual but to his *social group* (his social environment)."[29] Faulkner almost certainly would have resisted the particular verbal formulations Bakhtin favored. He was, after all, a member of a quite separate "speaking collective"; he entered into history on radically different terms. Nevertheless, it is not difficult to see how much he shares similar priorities: how much for him, too, meaning or communication is a matter of active, communal use. Communication, in Faulkner's work, implies community. Concretely, one always uses a language inhabited by the voice of another and addressed to another (actual or imagined) who does not assume a purely passive role but participates in the formation of meaning. Different voices—heard in the courthouse square perhaps or heard in the head—create identification, struggle for power, collude, collaborate, and conflict in the process of understanding and explanation. They engage actively in what Bakhtin called "the *social* dynamics" of speech; and, in doing so, they themselves and "the whole complex *social* situation" in which this engagement occurs are crucially and irrevocably altered.

Faulkner was, as it happened, acutely (if intuitively) aware of the dialogic nature of his involvement with language and culture: just how much his understanding of speech and habits of behavior were a matter of reciprocity and exchange. He was, as he never tired of saying, "present yet detached" in his culture.[30] This was not merely a love of paradox on his part, nor just a product of the situation of crisis that he shared with others of his generation—particularly writers, and especially Southern ones. It was related, crucially, to his sense that he was carrying on a conversation with systems of speech and value that were important to him: a conversation in which he had to play the part of double agent, a person whose collaboration was a form of subversion—who engaged with a system in a critical, even alienated, way but always, as it happened, from within. "By Southern Rhetoric out of Solitude" was one of his formulations for explaining the nature of his style: by which he meant, he explained, that the style was "the result of solitude, and . . . was further complicated by an inherited regional or geographical (Hawthorne would say, racial) curse." "You might say," he added, "studbook style: 'by . . . Oratory out of Solitude.'"[31] Such a formulation did two things at once: it laid claim to privacy and it also paid off a debt to his public situation. It acknowledged the fact that, as he saw it, his writing project was personal and social at the same time. And it did so, ultimately, by finding the definitive human activity in speech: the interchange between separate yet mutually involved voices.

The significance of voices for Faulkner can hardly be exaggerated. When he thought about it, in fact, he tended to associate speech with the fall into history. "All evil and grief of this world stems from the fact that mankind talks," he declared; "speech is mankind's curse," he added, "just too goddam many of the human race . . . talk too much." Remarks like this came naturally to a man who could insist, with apparently perfect candor, that he liked "peace and quiet" or who could claim, "I've spent almost fifty years trying to cure myself of the curse of human speech."[32] But they need to be set in the context of his reluctance to talk about his work to interviewers and critics: his books, he felt, did his talking for him and anything he might say about them would simply add one more meddling and distinctly unauthoritative voice. And they need to be set beside his admissions of his compulsive "need to talk." His voice, and other human voices, could perhaps produce "evil," but that was because it was the voice that made human beings distinctively human: it was through it that men and women entered into consciousness of self and community and so into the potentiality of deliberate, moral action. "I achieve consciousness," Bakhtin remarked, "I become myself only by revealing myself to another and with another's help. . . . To be means to be for the other, and through him, for oneself."[33]

As Bakhtin saw it, and as Faulkner sensed it, the Biblical Fall was a fall into speech: into the articulation of self and other, the ability to speak the words "I" and "thou." Identity, history, and the need to talk became, in this context, coextensive; as long as human beings survived, they would retain their voices and therefore their capacity for doing evil and good. "When the last ding-dong of doom has clanged and faded," Faulkner declared in his Nobel Prize acceptance speech, "from the last worthless rock hanging tideless in the last red and dying evening then there will still be one more sound: that of his puny inexhaustible voice, still talking."[34] Or, as he put it in less grandiose terms elsewhere: "The last sound on the worthless earth will be two human beings trying to launch a homemade space ship and already quarreling about where they are going next."[35]

Voices within and voices without, talking that occurs inside human beings and talking that happens between them: the entire process of a life history assumes, in these terms, a special character—as a seamless pattern of dialogue. The individual human being enters into a conversation, active and reactive, with the whole complex web of relations that constitute his moment in space and time. The figure of the web, or pattern, is chosen advisedly because it was one favored by both Faulkner and Bakhtin when they were trying to explain what, as they saw it, was the status of the individual utterance within the labyrinth of conflicting voices that constitute human history. Here, first, is Bakhtin: "The living utterance, having taken its meaning and shape at a particular historical moment in a socially specific environment, cannot fail to brush up against thousands of living dialogic threads . . . it cannot fail to become an active participant in social dialogue."[36] And here, for comparison, is a relevant passage from *Absalom, Absalom!* It is attributed to one of the characters, Judith Sutpen, and, like all of the voices in Faulkner's novels, it is hardly authoritative. Nevertheless, it signals one possible response to the plurality of voices that define the book's structure; and, in that sense, it is closer to the heart of the matter, the crux of the argument, than most remarks of this kind are:

> you are born at the same time with a lot of other people, all mixed
> up with them . . . all trying to make a rug on the same loom only

each one wants to weave his own pattern into the rug: and it cant matter, you know that, or the Ones that set up the loom would have arranged things a little better, and yet it must matter because you keep on trying or having to keep on trying.[37]

Clearly, the Faulkner passage offers us a more passionate perception, partly because the voice that speaks here turns what Bakhtin describes as a participative process into a devouringly destructive one, to be resisted or, at the very least, feared. But what both voices engage with here is seen as an historical inevitability—human experience as a kind of feverish debate in which each participant, eagerly or otherwise, struggles to make himself heard. The struggle is particularly difficult because the terms in which he speaks are themselves mediated by others. The voice that fights for a private identity is, in sum, for all that it searches for privacy, a public one; it is inextricably interwoven with the speech that surrounds it, shaped by voices talking before and after.

*   *   *

"I listen to the voices, and when I put down what the voices say, it's right." There's perhaps not too much time to show just how Faulkner's preoccupation with what "the voices say" was realized, fired into life in specific books. But take this passage, by way of example, from *Light in August*, in which talk seems to take on a distinctive, active and malleable, personality of its own:

> Through the long afternoon they clotted about the square and before the jail—the clerks, the countrymen in overalls; the talk. It went here and there about the town, dying and borning again like a wind or fire until in the lengthening shadows the country people began to depart in wagons and dusty cars and the townspeople began to move supperward. Then the talk flared again, momentarily revived. . . . And on the next day, the slow, pleasant country Sunday while they squatted in their clean shirts and decorated suspenders, with peaceful pipes about country churches or about the shady dooryards of houses where the visiting teams and cars

were tethered and parked along the fence and the womenfolks were in the kitchen, getting dinner, they told it again: "He dont look any more like a nigger than I do. But it must have been the nigger blood in him."[38]

The distinction of a passage like this, and what follows it, is that it shows a community trying to come to terms with an unexpected event by absorbing it within a familiar—and, in this case, racist—vocabulary: Joe Christmas's murder of Joanna Burden is to be defined and determined, it seems, in terms of what is called "the nigger blood in him." Two points need to be emphasized, I think. In the first place, Faulkner's interest here clearly lies in the process whereby different groups come together to try to explain what is for them the inexplicable: to accommodate an awkward historical reality to the language that supports and authenticates their way of life—that serves and confirms their own interests. And in the second place, Faulkner's concern in the book as a whole is, I believe, to show how that language—and, with it, social relationships and systems of belief—can begin to change when faced with the assault of history, the particular stories *Light in August* has to tell.

In the passage I have just quoted, speech is personified. More often, though, in *Light in August* Faulkner shows an acute ear for the way intimate and rhetorical levels of language interact. The moment, for instance, when Joanna Burden learns from her father about the so-called "curse" visited by the black race on the white, and then tries to explain how this changed her attitude towards black people—this, I think, is a good illustration of how words can act as a personal *and* a social agent: to manipulate, to exclude, and to suppress. "I had seen and known negroes since I could remember," Joanna says, "I just looked at them as I did at rain, or furniture, or food or sleep. But after that I seemed to see them for the first time not as people, but as a thing, a shadow in which I lived, we lived, all white people, all other people" (253).

The irony of this passage stems from the fact that Joanna does not really see or know the black people around her at any moment in her life. Far from progressing from simple seeing to deeper vision—which, of course, is her notion of the change effected by her father's lesson—all she does is move from one form of blindness to another. Like so many of Faulkner's characters, in fact (for example the deputy in the story, "Pantaloon in Black"), she uses her eyes and idiom to perform an act of exclusion. To be more exact, she begins by regarding black people as an unremarkable part of life's furniture, something not to be noticed or noted; and then subsequently she turns them into an object of fear, a tactic that seems to dematerialize them, in a way, and certainly serves to dehumanize them. A further irony lies in the relationship this speech implies between Joanna and the people of Jefferson, and between their respective vocabularies. Joanna may feel distanced from the community by her abolitionist forebears and her supposedly progressive views about what she terms "a shadow." The community, in turn, may feel distanced from and suspicious of her. The significant point, however, is that both use speech to deny substance. Joanna may appear to be talking about black people and so by implication acknowledging their existence, understanding them by bringing them within the confines of speech. But what she is really doing is what the townsfolk do: relegating individual black men and women, and the black race as a whole, to silence—a shadowy area (circumscribed by words like "thing" or "nigger") where they must remain anonymous and unknown.

So the silences, the gaps or spaces in between the speeches and conversations of the people of Yoknapatawpha are, perhaps, just as important as the actual talk. What their vocabularies omit or suppress is just as significant, just as revelatory, as what they get around to saying. Joanna Burden's speech in *Light in August* illustrates a paradoxical situation, in which an apparent acknowledgment of presence is actually a revelation of absence. And the speech of many of the other white inhabitants of Yoknapatawpha also places the black on the margins of language: denies him or her the dignity of an adequate definition. Constitutive absence in *Light in August* may assume one of several forms. A screen of words may provide a mode of concealment, as perhaps it does in Joanna Burden's case. Or the gap between word and object may be widened to the point at which it becomes an unbridgeable abyss. Whatever the form it assumes, though, language acts in such cases to exclude and suppress: to "unsay," as it were, what is "unsayable." It serves to deny the personally unacceptable and the socially unmanageable or intolerable. In *Light in August*, the primary act of exclusion is performed by that one word: "nigger."

As used in Mississippi during the 1930s, the word "nigger" meant, evidently, any person having more than one eighth black blood. The fraction is arbitrary, and blood is, of course, not black. Yet that arbitrary fraction and the metaphor add up to that elaborate system of ideas concerning racial superiority and social station with which the word "nigger" is charged. Racial demarcation, in turn, supports and is supported by all manner of social categories, so that the term "nigger" becomes part of a network of linguistic divisions—black/white, male/female, elect/damned, rich/poor, and so on—through which the system defines and perpetuates itself. *Light in August* could, in fact, be read as a thriller, in which the villain of the piece is the word "nigger"; and the key to the plot and fate of Joe Christmas, in particular, can be found in the use of that word. The reason for this is simple. In Joe's case, the black/white opposition, which gives the word its substance and turns black people into a peculiarly absent presence, is nonoperative. The question of his racial status cannot be answered. Joe, in effect, can be a catalyst for conflicting social forces, the site of a peculiarly painful verbal struggle, because he is neither black nor white: or, rather, because he can be either. The choice is his. And by manipulating a white skin and a black word, he can challenge the linguistic divisions of the people of Yoknapatawpha. He can undermine their confidence in the distribution of meaning. Joe's presence, on his own kind of neutral ground, throws the dualistic categories of his society against one another. Standing between extremes, between divisive definitions or terms, he calls the bluff on *all* terms. Language distributes and allocates power even as it pretends to be innocent communication. Joe senses this, perhaps. Certainly, a passage like the following, fairly early in the novel, seems to suggest so:

> Then it seemed to him, sitting on the cot in the dark room, that he was hearing a myriad sounds of no greater volume—voices, murmurs, whispers: of trees, darkness, earth; people; his own voice; other voices evocative of names and times and places—which he had been conscious of all his life without knowing it, which *were* his life (105, my emphasis).

Voices may be, or constitute, Joe's life: but almost from the first (or, at least, from the moment when the dietician calls him "You little nigger bastard!"), Joe tries to resist them. There is a constant struggle in the book between the linguistic community that Joe inhabits—and which demands that a man should act "like a nigger or a white man"—and the sheer indeterminacy of Joe himself, the fact that he is (to quote one critic of the novel) the sign of resistance to fixed signs. The struggle is complicated, of course, because it occurs *in* Joe as well. Of necessity, his speech and thoughts are, as Bakhtin would have put it, full of other people's words. He cannot escape from the terms of his verbal culture or the word "nigger," even in conversations with himself. So the dialogue, the debate (or, to be more accurate, the fight for survival) occurs not just *between* but *within*: its arena is not just the courthouse square, "about country churches or the shady dooryards of houses," it is also in Joe's interior speech, inside his head.

Once Joe is captured, a fresh attempt is made to call him "nigger," to pin him down to a particular (and particularly demeaning) name and identity. This comes out, in the first instance, among the people of Mottstown, many of whom demand that Joe should be lynched. The demand is a horrifying one, certainly, but it is, perhaps, not so unexpected, given its source. For lynching, too, can be seen as part of the communal language: a tribal ritual accepted, it seems, even beyond the borders of Yoknapatawpha. Not just an act of violence, it is an

act of collaboration: meant to underpin a whole series of categories (and so reassure the community) by putting a so-called
"nigger murderer" in his place. This time the language fails,
however; the collaborative ritual is botched. What happens to
Joe, when he is taken back to Jefferson, cannot be accommodated within the traditional vocabulary of crime and punishment. Admittedly, Joe's eventual death has a grimly ritualistic
quality to it that seems to reflect (or, at least, relate to) primitive
notions of scapegoating and sacrifice: as the killer and (so the
rumor goes) possible violator of a white woman, he is killed and
also castrated. Admittedly, too, Joe's killer, Percy Grimm—
while an aberrant figure—could be said to be responding to the
hidden impulses of his community. Like so many of Faulkner's
outsiders, in fact, Grimm is perhaps alienated from the group
by the very ferocity with which he embraces its beliefs. Having
admitted all that, though, it has to be added that what Grimm
does is perceived by the people around him (his neighbors in
Jefferson) as nothing other than a "murder": that is, an act of
violence deprived of even unofficial communal sanction. And
for this perception it is surely right to say that it is Grimm's
victim, Joe Christmas himself, who is primarily responsible. For
Joe (as I've tried to suggest already) is a subversive agent: an
indeterminate figure, whose indeterminacy (and whose willingness to press that indeterminacy home) calls into question the
fixities and definites—and the exclusions—of the communal
language. Confronting everyone he meets with the inadequate,
arbitrary nature of the black/white division, running at the
wrong time, and dying on the awkward margins of the town's
consciousness, he (above all) ensures that what happens to him
in the end is something to which the language of rough justice
does not apply. "It is human history alone," argues Roland
Barthes in *Mythologies,* "which converts reality into speech,
and it alone rules the life and death of a language."[39] And the
description of Joe's death makes it sound like one of those
moments when history is beginning, specifically, to rule the
death of a language: when the vocabularies evolved by a group

to enable them to conceive of—and manage—the world begin
to disintegrate, dissolve into irrelevance. Here is just part of the
passage in question:

> When the others reached the kitchen . . . they saw that the man
> was not dead yet, and when they saw what Grimm was doing one of
> the men gave a choked cry and stumbled back into the wall and
> began to vomit. . . . But the man on the floor had not moved. For a
> long moment he looked up at them with peaceful and unfathomable
> and unbearable eyes. Then his face, body, all, seemed to collapse
> . . . and from out the slashed garments about his hips and loins the
> pent black blood seemed to rush like a released breath. It seemed
> to rush out of his pale body like the rush of sparks from a rising
> rocket; upon that black blast the man seemed to rise soaring into
> their memories forever and ever. They are not to lose it, in
> whatever peaceful valleys, beside whatever placid and reassuring
> streams of old age, in the mirroring faces of whatever children
> they will contemplate old disasters and newer hopes. It will be
> there . . . (464–65)

"It"—the memory of Joe Christmas killed and castrated—it
will be there, we are told: suggesting a very different reading of
experience from the one predicated in the word "nigger." The
choked cry that one of the observers utters here is one of those
moments of absolute inarticulateness that punctuate Faulkner's
narratives—like, say, Benjy Compson's howling in *The Sound
and the Fury*—and that seem to define the limits of speech acts,
any attempt to turn experience into a communal language, by
seeking deliverance and redress in a nonverbal world. In turn,
the vomiting that follows this cry—as a clear gesture of horror
and denial—is one of the things that helps us take the measure
of this act of violence: that helps us to locate it, in fact, as a
possible act of transformation. As the image of Joe Christmas
solidifies in memory, the suggestion is that perhaps the verbal
and moral *apartheid* practiced in the use of the word "nigger"
will begin to be dismantled; the linguistic and ideological divisions between black and white will be called into question and
subverted. The reference to "peaceful valleys" and "placid and
reassuring streams" is, in this context of violence, sharply ironic:

this is not Arcadia, a world of simple, pastoral romance. Nor, for that matter, can any place situated in history ever be. But the reference that follows this, to "old disasters and newer hopes," does surely prevent a response of horror freezing into a reflex of despair: does allow, in effect, for the possibility of improvement. More to the point, perhaps, the passage as a whole—and the story of Joe Christmas that it concludes—does anticipate the possibility that history may generate new directions in language, voice, and vision: new habits of meaning and action.

*　　*　　*

Faulkner was well aware of the difficulties of language: difficulties that would prompt him to claim that all he really liked was, as he put it, ". . . silence. Silence and horses. And trees." "Sometimes," he said once, "I think of doing what Rimbaud did." But then he added hastily, "I will certainly keep on writing as long as I live."[40] One reason he kept on writing, I believe (and not the least important one, at that), was his feeling for words as double agents—that is, as enablers simultaneously of intimacy and withdrawal: his sense that speech is a dual currency, a matter of public exchange *and* private property, minted out of what Bakhtin once called "*a plurality of independent and unmerged voices.*"[41] "We need to talk," Faulkner said of himself and other Southerners, and in particular Southern writers, "we need to tell." And Faulkner, quite simply, was a writer who not only talked but listened to talk and, through listening, developed an extraordinary ear for tone, and understanding of the possibilities as well as the problems of speech. Through listening, he also began to realize how voices, working together, argue about, protect, ignore, invent, and, above all, alter the world to which they belong. Much of the excitement of his fiction (of a book like *Light in August,* for instance) comes, I think precisely from this: the author's experience of language, which he then communicates to us as a field of contention, an area of debate where different voices dispute meanings and distribute power. And much of it also comes from his sense that, since it *is* a field of contention, language can change: that the human subject still has the chance to alter the terms of his or her own culture—and that, more specifically, different, less polarized and less exclusive, systems of speech and habits of social exchange are not only necessary but perfectly possible.

NOTES

1. *The Faulkner–Cowley File: Letters and Memories, 1944–1962,* ed. Malcolm Cowley (New York: The Viking Press, 1966), 126. See also *Selected Letters of William Faulkner,* ed. Joseph Blotner (New York: Random House, 1977), 276. I am indebted to Maggie Brown, Mary McLain Hall, Minnie Ruth Little, and Bessie Sumners and others for comments on Faulkner's family, and other advice given to me during my visit to Oxford, Mississippi in July–August, 1988.

2. J. M. Huizinga, *The Waning of the Middle Ages* (New York: Anchor Books, 1954), 39.

3. *Essays, Speeches, and Public Letters,* ed. James B. Meriwether (New York: Random House, 1966), 70–71. See also Frederick R. Karl, *William Faulkner: American Writer* (New York: Ballantine Books, 1989), 17–18.

4. *Lion in the Garden: Interviews with William Faulkner, 1926–1962,* ed. James B. Meriwether and Michael Millgate (New York: Random House, 1968), 9, 229, 216, 248, 219, 273.

5. Ibid., 9.

6. Ibid., 243.

7. *Faulkner–Cowley File,* 77, 82.

8. William Faulkner, *Mosquitoes* (New York: Boni & Liveright, 1927), 209. For details of Faulkner's service record and his subsequent stories about it, see Joseph Blotner, *Faulkner: A Biography* (New York: Random House, 1974), 205ff; David Minter, *William Faulkner: His Life and Work* (Baltimore: The Johns Hopkins University Press, 1980), 30ff.; Judith Wittenberg, *Faulkner: The Transfiguration of Biography* (Lincoln: University of Nebraska Press, 1979), 32ff.

9. *Faulkner in the University: Class Conferences at The University of Virginia, 1957–1958,* ed. Frederick L. Gwynn and Joseph L. Blotner (New York: University of Virginia Press, 1959), 268.

10. *Lion in the Garden,* 57.

11. *Faulkner–Cowley File,* 114.

12. *Faulkner in the University,* 79, 263.

13. *Lion in the Garden,* 32.

14. Ibid., 284, 238.

15. *Selected Letters,* 41, 296.

16. *Faulkner in the University,* 79.

17. *Lion in the Garden,* 18.

18. Ibid., 128, 251.

19. *Selected Letters,* 413.

20. Mikhail Bakhtin, *Problems of Dostoevsky's Poetics,* ed. and trans. Caryl Emerson (Minneapolis: University of Minnesota Press, 1984), 7. See also Bakhtin, *The Dialogic Imagination: Four Essays,* trans. Caryl Emerson and Michael Holquist (Austin: University of Texas Press, 1981), 332.

21. *The Dialogic Imagination*, 195.

22. *Problems of Dostoevsky's Poetics*, 212, 282.

23. *Lion in the Garden*, 116.

24. *Problems of Dostoevsky's Poetics*, trans. W. W. Rostel (Ann Arbor: Ardis Press, 1973), 131.

25. Bakhtin, *Speech Genres and Other Late Essays*, trans. Vern W. McGee (Austin: University of Texas Press, 1986), 84. While, for the sake of convenience, attributing the works associated with Bakhtin's name to him, I am aware of the problems involved and, in particular, of the possibility that Medevedev and Volosinov were at least partly responsible for, respectively, *The Formal Method in Literary Scholarship* and *Marxism and the Philosophy of Language*. Since my aim is simply to enter into dialogue with the ideas developed in these books, I can only refer the reader interested in the problem of their authorship to the relevant introductions to the translations and to chapter 1 of Tzvetan Todorov, *Mikhail Bakhtin: The Dialogical Principle*, trans. Wlad Goldzich (Minneapolis: University of Minnesota Press, 1984).

26. *Problems of Dostoevsky's Poetics*, trans. Caryl Emerson, 75, 265.

27. *The Dialogical Principle*, 24.

28. *The Dialogic Imagination*, 356.

29. Bakhtin, *Freudianism: A Marxist Critique*, trans. I. R. Titunik (New York: 1976), 128.

30. *Essays, Speeches, and Public Letters*, 87.

31. *Faulkner–Cowley File*, 78.

32. *Selected Letters*, 424, 263, 234.

33. *Problems of Dostoevsky's Poetics*, 287.

34. *Essays, Speeches, and Public Letters*, 120, 124.

35. Ibid., 167.

36. *The Dialogic Imagination*, 276.

37. William Faulkner, *Absalom, Absalom!* (London: Chatto and Windus, 1937), 127.

38. William Faulkner, *Light in August* (New York: Vintage International Edition, 1990), 348–49. Further references will be cited in the text.

39. Roland Barthes, *Mythologies*, trans. Annette Lavers (New York: Hill and Wang, 1972), 110.

40. *Lion in the Garden*, 71.

41. *Problems of Dostoevsky's Poetics*, 6.

Faulkner and the Democratic Crisis

ROBERT H. BRINKMEYER, JR.

During the 1930s and early 1940s, Faulkner's critical reception was by and large harsh and unfavorable. Much of the commentary followed the lead of Alan Reynolds Thompson's influential 1932 essay, "The Cult of Cruelty," that argued, as the title indicates, that Faulkner was one of a modern cult of writers who embraced "a pessimistic skepticism, to which morals and aspirations are merely customs and dreams, and the world is an inhuman mechanism."[1] Leftist critics, espousing social realism and literature's role in the class struggle, were decidedly hard on Faulkner. Particularly disturbing to these critics were what they saw as Faulkner's heavy use of the grotesque and his failure to underscore clearly the social and economic causes for the suffering and violence of his fictional world. In *The Great Tradition*, Granville Hicks wrote that although Faulkner certainly understood well the people of the South,

> he will not write simply and realistically of Southern life. He is not primarily interested in representative men and women; certainly he is not interested in the forces that have shaped them. . . . The ordinary affairs of this life are not enough for Faulkner; even the misery and disease born of generations of poverty and ignorance are not adequate themes for the expression of his horror and disgust. Nothing but crime and insanity will satisfy him. If he tried to see why life is horrible, he might be willing to give a more representative description of life, might be willing to occupy himself with the kind of suffering that he can see on every hand, the kind of crime that is committed every day, and the kind of corruption that gnaws at every human being in this rotten society. As it is, he can only pile violence upon violence in order to convey a mood that he will not or cannot analyze.[2]

70

Philip Rahv, in his 1936 review of *Absalom, Absalom!*, found Faulkner so locked within his brooding and suffering consciousness that he remained blind to the workings of history and followed instead what Rahv called "an ideological dream" that is "always in danger of degenerating into mystification . . . [and] is ever on the brink of the dilettantism of horror."[3] In his essay on Faulkner following the 1946 publication of Malcolm Cowley's *The Portable Faulkner*, Robert Penn Warren summed up Faulkner's critical reception in the 1930s and 1940s by arguing that, with a few exceptions, Faulkner had up until Cowley's book been characterized as "a combination of Thomas Nelson Page, a fascist and a psychopath, gnawing at his nails. Of course, this picture is usually accompanied by a grudging remark about genius."[4]

In his comment on the critical perception of Faulkner as "a combination of Thomas Nelson Page, a fascist and a psychopath," Warren may have had in mind Maxwell Geismar's analysis of Faulkner in *Writers in Crisis* (1942). Geismar here argues that Faulkner vents his blinding hatred for the social and economic forces that were transforming the South upon two scapegoats—blacks and women. "And what better images, after all, could the artist have found to express his discontent—this great hatred of the entire complex of modern northern industrial society—than the Negro and the Female?" Geismar writes. "The emancipated negro who to the southern writer is the cause of the destruction of all he held dear. And now showing this negro as Joe Christmas, as Jim Bond, as the inhuman criminal, the degenerate who will dominate the civilization which freed him, Faulkner proclaims at once his anger and his revenge upon those who have destroyed his home." Equally appropriate, Geismar adds, is the way Faulkner manipulates the traditional image of the Southern woman. "How shall the artist better show the universal debasement of modern times than to turn the pure Lady into the contemporary Female, now wanton, graceless, and degraded?" he writes.[5] Geismar proceeds to compare what he sees as Faulkner's abuse of his scapegoats with the Fascists' mistreatment of Jews, arguing that "the using of the one object that is certainly not responsible for our woes as being the single creator of them (so the Fascists use the Jew)—this is an inversion all too familiar to us today in other areas, another symptom of the confused emotions of our time. What genuine ills can be ignored by this again infantile preoccupation with scapegoats (so the child blames its mother), the infatuation with chimeras, what terrible ills can be created by it." Extending his disturbing suggestion that Faulkner's imagination flirts with fascist tendencies, Geismar argues that Faulkner's fiction is best understood as an expression of the antimodern revolt he sees underpinning fascist ideology. "I have used the title of Maurice Samuel's penetrating study of the Fascist superstitions, 'The Great Hatred,' to best describe Faulkner's work as a whole. For it is in the larger tradition of reversionary, neo-pagan, and neurotic discontent (from which Fascism stems) that much of Faulkner's writing must be placed—the anticivilizational revolt which has caught so many modern mystics, the revolt rising out of modern social evils, nourished by ignorance of their true nature, and which succumbs to malice as their solution."[6]

There's no evidence I know of that Faulkner ever read Geismar's *Writers in Crisis*, although Cowley did point the book out to him in a 1944 letter, saying that while Geismar was "not so dumb for a professor"—actually he wasn't a professor— "when he comes to Faulkner, you might as well have written your novels in Minoan or Hittite for all the sense he makes of them."[7] If Faulkner did read Geismar's chapter on his work, he no doubt was stung by the accusation of protofascism, as he certainly was when other leftist critics accused him of fascist tendencies. Blotner points out that years later Faulkner still rankled at being called "a Gothic fascist" during the 1930s and 1940s.[8]

Such accusations must have been particularly galling to a man who—though for the most part staying free of active politics—nonetheless in his own way took his stand against fascist regimes. In 1938 Faulkner contributed his typescript of *Absalom, Absalom!* (and offered others) to a relief fund for the

Spanish loyalists and signed (and perhaps drafted) the following statement for the League of American Writers: "I most sincerely wish to go on record as being unalterably opposed to Franco and fascism, to all violations of the legal government and outrages against the people of Republican Spain."[9] Once America entered the Second World War in 1941, Faulkner spent a great deal of time and energy concocting various schemes for joining the war effort, though in the end he remained a civilian. His letters during the war reflect both his wholehearted support of the nation's war policy and his awareness that the fight for freedom and liberty at home would be a battle that would be waged for a long time after the fighting was over in Europe and the Pacific. In a letter to his nephew Malcolm Franklin, dated 5 December 1942, Faulkner wrote that "we must see that the old Laodicean smell doesn't rise again after this one. But we must preserve what liberty and freedom we already have to do that. We will have to make the liberty sure first, in the field. It will take the young men to do that. Then perhaps the time of the older men will come, the ones like me who are articulate in the national voice, who are too old to be soldiers, but are old enough and have been vocal long enough to be listened to, yet are not so old that we too have become another batch of decrepit old men looking stubbornly backward at a point 25 or 50 years in the past."[10]

The irony that plagued many blacks about the nation's war against Nazi Germany—that blacks were being sent overseas to fight a racist regime when they themselves faced stifling racism at home—was also not lost on Faulkner. In another letter to his nephew, dated 4 July 1943, Faulkner wrote about the troubling chronological juxtaposition that had recently occurred: on the same day that a squadron of black fighter pilots had performed heroically in the skies over Africa, white mobs in Detroit had murdered 20 blacks. Faulkner commented on the situation by describing a scenario involving himself and his nephew in Africa where blacks were the dominant race:

Suppose you and me and a few others of us lived in the Congo, freed seventy-seven years ago by ukase; of course we cant live in the same apartment hut with the black folks, nor always ride in the same car nor eat in the same restaurant, but we are free because the Great Black Father says so. Then the Congo is engaged in War with the Cameroon. At last we persuade the Great Black Father to let us fight too. You and Jim say are flyers. You have just spent the day trying to live long enough to learn how to do your part in saving the Congo. Then you come back down and are told that 20 of your people have just been killed by a mixed mob of civilians and cops at Little Poo Poo. What would you think?

A change will come out of this war. If it doesn't, if the politicians and the people who run this country are not forced to make good the shibboleth they glibly talk about freedom, liberty, human rights, then you young men who live through it will have wasted your precious time, and those who don't live through it will have died in vain.[11]

If many blacks at this time were embracing the logic of the "double V" campaign—victory abroad *and* at home—so, too, was Faulkner, as his letter to his nephew suggests. Whatever critics were finding in his fiction to suggest his fascist propensities, it's clear that Faulkner was anything but a supporter of fascist ideology and that his patriotic support of the war in all likelihood deepened his understanding of the South's—and America's—racial inequities rather than blinding him to them.

*   *   *

As surprising as Geismar's and other critics' accusations of Faulkner's incipient, Southern-style fascism appear to us today, for their day such critiques were anything but startling. Indeed, such analyses fall right into place in the larger cultural critique of the South by the rest of America (and by some Southerners) that took place from the mid-1930s through World War II—a critique that centered on issues involving the meaning and value of democratic ideology. As Morton Sosna has shown, during the years leading up to and then into the Second World War Americans rallied patriotically around a national identity that was rooted first and foremost in democratic ideology. Termed by historians "the democratic revival," this surge in democratic fervor swept through both popular and intellectual culture, in large part in response to the rise of European dictatorships, particularly the Nazis. "Not since Tocqueville (whose own revival was part of the phenomenon)," Sosna writes, "had there been such an extended inquiry into the nature of American democracy."[12]

Typifying the thinking engendered by the democratic revival is anthropologist's Margaret Mead's study of America, *And Keep Your Powder Dry* (1942). Here Mead argues that a person's attitudes and behavior are not determined by racial characteristics but by the "character structure" of that person's culture—that is, by the pattern of life that pervades a culture's everyday order and functioning. For American culture, argues Mead, this defining structure is democratic ideology, which she asserts is "a type of behavior and an attitude of mind which runs through our whole culture" and which accommodates and melds together America's diverse ethnic populations. Not all cultures, and not surprisingly she points her finger most sharply at Germany, are underpinned by a democratic character structure; and she argues that it is thus absurd to expect such antidemocratic cultures suddenly to change their ways and act as a truly democratic culture would, as much of the world expected Germany to do after World War I. Mead writes: "The Germans lacked democratic machinery because their way of life lacked those emphases and attitudes on which democratic machinery can flourish. Democratic procedures are not something that people have, like automobiles or hot-dog stands or a way of building roads. Democracy is not something which can be added or subtracted; it is not one of an array of items found on closet shelves, in stores or text-books, not just one more detail in a hodgepodge of furniture models, written laws, and grammar books."[13]

If America during the late 1930s and early 1940s was rallying around a democratic vision of itself, using fascist and communist

dictatorships as alternative ideologies to establish its own difference, the nation faced a disturbing "other" closer to home that
threatened its unsullied vision of itself: the South. This is a
footnote in *And Keep Your Powder Dry* in which Mead clarified
her use of the designation "American culture":

> Statements about the culture of the United States have to be
> qualified in many cases, if they are to apply both to the North and
> the South. The introduction in the South of the bi-racial classifica-
> tion of humanity means that caste is sometimes a directly formative
> element in developing standards of behavior. The generalizations in
> this book should be regarded as based primarily on the North,
> Middle West, and West, and should not be called into question
> because certain elements of Southern culture differ from them, as
> this is inevitable. A discussion which overrode the very considerable
> differences between North and South would often be too abstract to
> be fruitful.[14]

And this is Mead in a letter after a trip in 1942 to Georgia and
Alabama: "This was my first trip to the South, and nothing that
I had read had prepared me for the extent to which the South
differed from the North, nor for the degree to which the South
resembled a colonial country like New Guinea or South Africa
in which no white person ever dares to [forget?] their racial
status for a moment."[15] Clearly, Mead saw the South as having
its own "character structure," one established along racial,
not democratic, ideology; and by making this claim, as Sosna
observes, Mead essentially banishes the South from the American experience.

Of course, in many ways the South had from its very beginnings been outside the American mainstream, and particularly
ever since the 1830s when the Southern states began to establish
their own regional identity and history. But perhaps at no time
save the years leading up to the Civil War had the region
appeared so radically different and threatening to the rest of
America. During the 1930s aspects of Southern society deemed
abuses of the democratic system came under intense scrutiny
by the rest of America: Jim Crow laws, lynching, sharecropping,

prison conditions, demagoguery. President Roosevelt said in 1937 that the South was the nation's number one economic problem, but for many Americans economics was merely one aspect of Southern society that needed correcting.   *regionalism*

Besides scrutinizing specific cultural codes of the South, American criticism of Dixie called into question the very concept of regionalism. As Sosna has shown, regionalism during the years of the democratic revival quickly became associated in the American mind with dangerous antidemocratic parochialism. If democracy came to represent universal values transcending national and regional interests, regionalism came to be seen as a version of the fanatical nationalism embraced by fascist countries. In his 1939 study of fascism and its challenges to democracy, *No Compromise: The Conflict Between Two Worlds*, Melvin Rader writes that the essence of fascism is "*the denial of universality*. The universality of truth, of value, of law, of human rights—in other words, the solidarity of mankind—is rejected in favor of the partisanship of race, nation, and class."[16] Rader does not discuss American sectionalism here, but his argument's implications for interpreting Southern regionalism as a threat to the universal impulse of democratic ideology can easily be deduced—and indeed such deductions were being made during the period.

The extremes to which regionalism was associated with antidemocratic ideology is perhaps most obviously seen in the utter dismantling of the regionalist movement in painting that occurred in the late 1930s and early 1940s—a dismantling so ruthless that a number of artists, including John Stewart Curry, Thomas Hart Benton, and Grant Wood were branded fascists merely because their art celebrated indigenous rather than international subject matter.[17] Not atypical were the 1946 comments of H. W. Janson, who proclaimed that "almost every one of the ideas constituting the regionalist credo could be matched more or less verbatim with the writings of Nazi experts on art."[18] "Many of the paintings officially approved by the Nazis," Janson added, "recall the works of the regionalists in this country." Abstract art, on the other hand, was understood to transcend national biases and interests, its perceived universality seen as an expression of the democratic spirit. Even though nonrepresentational art, as Cecile Whiting points out, generally "spoke to an elite audience," it nonetheless represented "the notion of pure art as an indicator of the existence of freedom under democracy."[19]

The pressures of the democratic revival in its interpretation of the South and its denigration of regionalism had an equally profound, if not always so visible, impact on Southern writers, including Faulkner. We've already seen that Faulkner during the 1930s and 1940s was accused of fascist tendencies, and recently Lawrence H. Schwartz has convincingly argued that Faulkner's stunning rise in critical recognition occurred only after 1946 when critics reinterpreted him as a writer dealing less with regional matters than with universal ones.[20] Faulkner's difficult and tortuous prose, once typically considered as decadent as his subject matter, now came to be seen, like abstract art, as embodying the artist's heroic quest for self-expression in a democratic society that encouraged such endeavor. The protofascist artist before the war became the democratic hero after, global hero and Nobel laureate.

The impact of the democratic revival, however, extended far beyond merely the critical reception and perception of Southern writing. During the 1930s and 1940s, many Southern writers, in their explorations of the region and their relationships with it, openly addressed issues of the democratic crisis and their impact on Southern matters, literary and otherwise. From the left, writers such as Erskine Caldwell, Lillian Smith, Richard Wright, and Katherine DuPre Lumpkin examined in their work various manifestations of Southern injustice, frequently making connections between Southern culture and fascist ideology and practice. In her 1941 review of William Alexander Percy's *Lanterns on the Levee*, for instance, Lillian Smith bemoaned what she identified as Percy's "lyrical longing to be a gentleman," saying that such longing expressed white Southerners' overwhelming desire "to blow ourselves up from miniature dimensions to the magnificent proportions of a super race and a super class."[21] W. J. Cash specifically linked the South's violent character with that of totalitarian Europe, writing that the South had established "the savage ideal as it had not been established in any Western people since the decay of medieval feudalism, and almost as truly as it is established today in Fascist Italy, in Nazi Germany, and in Soviet Russia—and so paralyzed Southern culture at the root."[22] Katherine DuPre Lumpkin makes the fascist connection even more explicit in her analysis of Southern life, *The South in Progress* (1940). She entitles one section "The Role of Fascist-Like Groups" and concludes that the rhetoric of the Ku Klux Klan "sound[s] exactly like the hideous racism of Nazi Germany" and that antiunion vigilantes in the South employ techniques which were "used by Mussolini and perfected by Hitler Germany."[23]

At the other end of the spectrum, writers from the right (most notably the Agrarians) embraced an unyielding Southern traditionalism during the period of the democratic revival, seeing the stability and order of Southern society as a check to the devouring onslaught of industrialism and progress that they linked to the democratic political system. One need only turn to the table of contents of the Agrarians' second symposium, *Who Owns America?* (1936) to see how significant issues of democratic ideology were to these writers. Subtitled "A New Declaration of Independence," the symposium contains essays entitled "The Foundations of Democracy," "Notes on Liberty and Property," "That This Nation May Endure—The Need for Political Regionalism," "Liberty Under the Old Deal." Although Southern traditionalists almost uniformly condemned European fascism, they typically were extremely critical of liberal democratic theory. William Alexander Percy's declaration in *Lanterns on the Levee* forcefully underscores the antidemocratic sentiments of Southern traditionalists: "In time we are all good democrats; in the manger we look the same and in the grave. But at this particular time and place, viewed not from a peak in eternity but from the ephemeral now, I rejoice to be of a caste which, though shaken and scattered, refuses to call itself Demos."[24]

In condemning European fascism during the democratic revival, most Americans accepted the rigid opposition between fascism and democracy, between authoritarian absolutism and democratic pragmatism. Southern traditionalists, in contrast, saw things otherwise, arguing that fascism (together with communism) was not diametrically opposed to democracy but actually was its logical conclusion. The opposition established in their arguments set Southern paternalism against radical democracy, the order and stability of traditional society against the disorder and violent upheaval of unchecked democracy and its terrifying political ends—fascism and communism.

Nowhere is this line of analysis more forcefully put than in the work of Richard Weaver, particularly his wartime essay, "The South and the Revolution of Nihilism" (1944). Here Weaver attempts to explain why the South, of all the American regions, was the most interventionist and anti-Hitler. Weaver begins by acknowledging the apparent similarities between fascist ideology and Southern traditionalism, writing that in

> open debate the South would have been hard put to it to distinguish between some of the slogans of the New Order and the tenets of its own faith, sealed with Confederate blood and affirmed in many a post-bellum oration. That the Southern whites considered themselves *Herrenvolk* in relation to the Negro is one of the obvious features of our sociological landscape, and belief in the influence of blood and soil is powerful with them, as with any agrarian people. The glorification of the martial spirit, the distrust of urban liberalism, the hatred of money economy are pages that might be found in the book of any unreconstructed Southerner.

But Weaver then argues that the South recognized the terror of fascist ideology because, despite fascism's promise "to restore the ancient virtues," its ideology was actually a form of "extreme equalitarianism," a "new and extreme proletarian nihilism," "the kind of usurpation toward which radical democracy always tends"—in other words, a form of radical democracy which the South had always resisted. Weaver locates the roots of fascism in the turmoil of the French Revolution and its aftermath in the nineteenth century, an era he describes as terrifying, when "society was changed from a hierarchy, from a state with a corporate form, held together by traditions, bonds of sentiment, a vision of the whole, into the undifferentiated democratic mass, with free competition regarded as the sole means of measuring position and power." After the devastating crises of World War I and the Great Depression, fascism emerged in full force, primed for what Weaver writes was "a final assault upon society as that term has been understood in Western civilization." Southerners did not fall prey to the lure of fascism because, according to Weaver, the South never underwent the radical democratization unleashed by the French Revolution and instead clung steadfastly to the ideals of traditional society. And so, writes Weaver, "in the ideological conflict between the South and Fascist Europe the world before the French Revolution looks at the world after the French Revolution and finds it hateful."[25] In an essay on his guiding light, Albert Taylor Bledsoe, Weaver makes it clear that he sees America under the grip of the same sort of "pragmatic liberalism" that was unleashed by the French Revolution and that has brought the world "totter[ing] uneasily between fascism and communism."[26]

*   *   *

Now, on to Faulkner. Even though Faulkner did not see his fiction as a weapon in the ideological struggles of his day, as many other writers of the era did, it's nevertheless clear that his imaginative vision was shaped by the democratic crisis and that his fiction speaks crucially, if at times obliquely, about this upheaval. Several of Faulkner's short stories from this period explicitly address issues of the crisis. In "The Tall Men," "Two Soldiers," and "Shall Not Perish," Faulkner writes primarily as a straightforward Southern traditionalist, praising the simple virtues of courage and valor possessed by the folk of the Southern countryside. If some Southerners have fallen prey to the ills of modern liberalism and meddling big government, such as the government investigator in "The Tall Men," those of the rural South still act with dignity and righteousness. In _Democracy and Poetry,_ Robert Penn Warren argues that the motion of American democracy has been and continues to be toward the diminishment of the self. "Effective action in our world seems to imply more and more the denial of any central self," Warren writes, and he adds that because of the relativist and pragmatic basis of democracy (democracies tell us what we cannot do, not what we should do), "fluidity of selves replaces the integrity of self as the source of effectiveness, and identity is conceived in terms of mere action, with action determined completely by the fluctuating contingencies of the environment."[27] But as the title "The Tall Men" suggests, Faulkner's rural folk, living for the most part outside the political system, suffer no such diminishment. These are the men who willingly go to war to fight the fascist enemy; they almost instinctively recognize the threat of fascism to their way of life. These young men are the backbone and fitting embodiments of America, as strong and virtuous as the forefathers and foremothers who founded and built the nation—and much stronger than piddling moderns. Faulkner's rural heroes embody the South of Richard Weaver—a world essentially free from the polluting effects of democratic ideology—and are the forerunners of folk hero Buford Pusser, who, as portrayed in the "Walking Tall" movies, takes the law into his own hands with a baseball bat to clean up and knock sense into a Tennessee town grown soft on crime, punishment, and morality.

None of these stories represents Faulkner's best work; all are too pat in their straightforward dichotomy of rural independence and modern diminishment. More compelling and complex is Faulkner's great work of the 1940s, Go Down, Moses, particularly those chapters focusing on the trials of Isaac McCaslin, trials shaped profoundly by the issues of the democratic crisis, though not so obviously as the situations of "The Tall Men," "Two Soldiers," and "Shall Not Perish." The place to start our analysis is the conversation in "Delta Autumn" between Ike and his companions about the fascist threat to America. Roth Edmonds brings the topic up after Ike asks him why he has bitterly announced that this hunting trip will be his last:

> "After Hitler gets through with it? Or Smith or Jones or Roosevelt or Willkie or whatever he will call himself in this country?"
> "We'll stop him in this country," Legate said. "Even if he calls himself George Washington."
> "How?" Edmonds said. "By singing God bless America in bars at midnight and wearing dime-store flags in our lapels?"
> "So that's what's worrying you," the old man said. "I aint noticed this country being short of defenders yet, when it needed them. You did some of it yourself twenty-odd years ago, before you were a grown man even. This country is a little mite stronger than any one man or group of men, outside of it or even inside of it either. I reckon, when the time comes and some of you have done got tired of hollering we are whipped if we dont go to war and some more are hollering we are whipped if we do, it will cope with one Austrian paper-hanger, no matter what he will be calling himself. My pappy and some other better men than any of them you named tried once to tear it in two with a war, and they failed."
> "And what have you got left?" the other said. "Half the people without jobs and half the factories closed by strikes. Half the people on public dole that wont work and half that couldn't work even if they would. Too much cotton and corn and hogs, and not enough for people to eat and wear. The country full of people to tell a man how he cant raise his own cotton whether he will or wont, and Sally Rand with a sergeant's stripes and not even the fan couldn't fill the army rolls. Too much not-butter and not even the guns—"[28]

The conversation between Isaac and Roth encapsulates much of the cultural discussion about democracy and freedom of the era. Ike's argument is essentially that of the Southern traditionalist, of the voice that dominates in Faulkner's three stories of World War II mentioned above. His basic line of thought is that despite whatever social and political problems the American government has engendered in its rampant and unchecked democracy (Ike doesn't challenge Roth's description of a society in chaos), Southerners are still true of mind and purpose and represent the best check to the fascist threat. This threat, as Roth suggests (again unchallenged by Ike), apparently comes as much from politicians at home as from the Nazis abroad—fascism, in other words, is presented as an extension of, or at least made possible by, democracy. Roth of course rejects Ike's idealism; he cynically attacks Ike's view of Southern heroism and suggests that the infection of democracy has so weakened the nation that it now lies open to fascist takeover, its will and commitment reduced to empty patriotic chants.

The wartime interplay between Southern idealist and cynic calls to mind the scene in "Shall Not Perish" when Mrs. Grier goes to Major de Spain's house to pay her respects to his son who has been killed in the war. De Spain launches into a ferocious tirade against the war effort, saying that he repudiates his country because it is run by men no better than thieves. His son, he says, "died for an illusion. In the interests of usury, by the folly and repacity of politicians, for the glory and aggrandize-ment of organized labor! . . . The fear of elective servants for their incumbencies!" While Major de Spain argues that the ideals of the South were lost with the Civil War—"ravaged and polluted and destroyed eighty years ago"—Mrs. Grier suggests otherwise, that amidst a fallen world "all men are capable of courage and honor and sacrifice."[29] Her stoic fortitude in facing the death of her own son in the war deeply impresses Major de Spain; her strength mirrors the courage and valor of the fallen soldiers, both her son's and Major de Spain's. The story ends with Mrs. Grier inspiring her remaining son to envision an undiminished line of conquering American heroes; significantly, the boy describes his vision as a wheel, with its hub in French-man's Bend and its spokes reaching out to the heroes past and present. Those simple folk like Mrs. Grier and her two sons, together with the other people of their village, live by the heroic virtues on which the country was founded. In his vision, the boy recognizes the heroes whose stature, the story makes clear, he and his people share: "I knew them too: the men and women still powerful seventy-five years and twice that and twice that again afterward, still powerful and still dangerous and still coming, North and South and East and West, until the name of what they did and what they died for became just one simple word, louder than any thunder. It was America, and it covered all the western earth."[30]

Things are not so upbeat in Ike's and Roth's conversation, for despite the vigor with which Ike speaks here and the disdain we hold for Roth, it is Roth's voice that speaks with authority, not Ike's. Ike's argument is essentially that of Mrs. Grier: that present-day Southerners are every bit as heroic and honorable as the Southerners who fought during the Civil War, are just as tall as those who fought seventy-five years before. While Mrs. Grier's heroic vision overwhelms the cynicism of Major de Spain, Ike's words in contrast fall powerlessly before Roth's. Everywhere about them in the hunting camp lies abundant evidence of the truth of Roth's vision of a depleted nation and the sham of Ike's celebration of ongoing Southern heroism. The debasement of the hunt points clearly to the decline in stature of Southern men. No longer sharing the commitment of the hunting rituals once held by their ancestors, the present hunters do not live by the previously honored rules of the hunt, seen most obviously when Roth shoots a doe. Theirs is a much different hunt from the one in "The Bear," described as "the ancient and unremitting contest according to the ancient and immitigable rules which voided all regrets and brooked no quarter;—the best game of all, the best of all breathing and forever the best of all listening" (184). The present hunters' incessant bickering, much of it meanspirited, suggests their failure to hold a common ethic which would join them together in a harmonious community, and that lack suggests the larger lack of an ideological foundation in the Southern society at large.

Ike's dream of timeless, unsullied Southern heroism is thus precisely that—a dream, and a dream as false as his vision of a timeless, uncut wilderness with a continuous immortal hunt.

While Ike dreams of "the faces of the old men he had known
and loved and for a little while outlived, moving again among
the shades of tall unaxed trees and sightless brakes where the
wild strong immortal game ran forever before the tireless belling
immortal hounds, falling and rising phoenix-like to the soundless
guns" (337–38), the loggers are cutting progressively more trees,
sealing the wilderness's doom. Likewise, as Ike boasts about
unchanging Southern heroism, Southern men move further
down the road toward the nihilism which Richard Weaver
argues is the final destination of those who turn aside from "the
traditions of self-restraint" (170).

   Go Down, Moses, indeed, focuses on the depletion of Southern society and history. Despite Ike's efforts to alter its direction, the South moves progressively toward not the immortal
world of Ike's dreams but the chaos of radical democracy. If
Roth Edmonds reenacts Old Carothers's sin, Southern society
seems destined to return to the chaos that marked Reconstruction, a world, as described in "The Bear," overrun by a "nameless horde of speculators in human misery, manipulators of
money and politics and land, who follow catastrophe and are
their own protection as grasshoppers are and need no blessing
and sweat no plow or axe-helve and batten and vanish and leave
no bones, just as they derived apparently from no ancestry, no
mortal flesh, no act even of passion or even of lust" (278). As
unscrupulous carpetbaggers tore apart the post-Civil War
South, now the undisciplined masses of bourgeois civilization,
"men myriad and nameless even to one another" (185), gnaw
away at both the flank of the wilderness and the flank of the
body politic. Their progress on both marks the decline of
traditional life.

   Most crucially signalling the decline of Southern society is
the void that lies at its ideological center. There's neither a
shared ethic nor a recognized leader who embodies a unified
community ideal. The men of Ike's generation, at least for a
while, had both—the ethic of the hunt and Old Ben. If not a
true leader of men, Old Ben nonetheless stood as the figurehead

of the life of the hunt and thus by extension of the ordered world of traditional Southern life. Sam Fathers says of him, "He's the head bear. He's the man" (190). For the hunters, he's a legendary force, "indomitable and invincible out of an old dead time, a phantom, epitome and apotheosis of the old wild life which the little puny humans swarmed and hacked at in a fury of abhorrence and fear like pygmies about the ankles of a drowsing elephant;—the old bear, solitary, indomitable, and alone; widowered childless and absolved of mortality—old Priam reft of his old wife and outlived all his sons" (185–86). As these words suggest, Old Ben stands in opposition to the spreading and unchecked masses of modern life; and so, not surprisingly, as his tenure draws closer to an end with each passing year, more and more of the settlers around the forest come to witness the annual hunt. These are the people who will make up the new order when Old Ben is gone; they sense that their time is coming.

The freedom and liberty that Old Ben represents are quite different from that of the coming new order. Although Old Ben lives alone in the wilderness, his freedom is less individual than social, for he always acts according to the well-defined codes and rituals that exist between hunter and hunted. Opposed to this freedom, a freedom to be part of a community, to have one's identity established within a society, is the radical freedom of modern democracies, the subjective and personal freedom of the individual. Such is the freedom of which Fonsiba's husband speaks when he tells Ike, with the "sonorous imbecility of the boundless folly and the baseless hope," that "we are seeing a new era, an era dedicated, as our founders intended it, to freedom, liberty and equality for all, to which this country will be the new Canaan—" (266–67). Ike is perfectly aware of the atomizing and alienating effects of such freedom, and he fires back: "Freedom from what? From work? Canaan?" (267).

Old Ben's death signals the defeat of the old order. Not long afterwards Major de Spain sells the timber rights to a lumber company and cutting begins apace. The annual hunt disbands.

"The Bear" ends with the ritual and order of the hunt reduced to Boon Hoggenback's mindless pounding of his dismantled rifle against a tree filled with squirrels which he claims are his. "Get out of here!" he shouts at Ike. "Don't touch them! Don't touch a one of them! They're mine!" (315). The camaraderie of the old hunt has given way to the rapacity of consumerism and individual greed—to the ways of the fragmented society that now rules over the forest—rules over it, that is, until all the resources have been depleted and sold.

As the order and stability that have heretofore maintained his family, society, and hunting grounds come undone, Ike McCaslin takes a bold step in an effort to halt the process: he relinquishes his inheritance so to free his family and the South from the curse he sees haunting them. As much as Ike's repudiation seems a shirking of responsibility, his surprising act is actually, as I've argued elsewhere, a strategy of empowerment, a move that he hopes will establish him as a leader of his community.[31] As Old Ben was, he hopes to be "the man." Ike's strategy emulates that of the Desert Fathers, who in their ascetic withdrawal from society paradoxically became society's leaders. Perceived as the embodiments of divine presence, the ascetics were consulted by and passed judgments upon the villages neighboring their retreats. "Above everything, the holy man is a man of power," Peter Brown writes in *The Body and Society*,[32] and so too would Ike like to be—a spiritual leader and arbiter of a Southern society held fast in time, free from the taints of past sins and resistant to the threats of dissolution posed by the modern liberal state.

Ike, of course, fails in his quest for power, unable to fill the void and provide the leadership that his family and society so sorely need. His community sees him as an anachronism and interprets his relinquishment as an act of weakness, a shirking not an assuming of responsibility. And so while he does wield some influence, being "uncle to half a county" (3), it is actually the influence of a more powerful uncle—Uncle Sam and the democratic society he embodies—who determines the direction

and shape of Ike's community and more generally that of the
South. That his society wanders directionless and fragmented—a collection of isolated individuals lacking a coherent
sense of community and purpose—makes it vulnerable to the
Moses of the modern state: the fascist dictator. This breakdown
of the South suffering under the atomizing influence of liberal
democracy looms behind Roth's fear of the coming dictator—
"Hitler . . . Or Smith or Jones or Roosevelt or Willkie or
whatever he will call himself in this country" (322)—and indeed
the action of the entire novel.

*   *   *

In his 1935 novel, *It Can't Happen Here*, Sinclair Lewis presented a scenario that suggested that it most certainly could—
that a fascist dictator could come to power in America. Lewis's
fascist leader is Berzelius Windrip, who wins the 1936 election
and then immediately establishes a ruthless dictatorship. Windrip's most zealous supporters are menial workers and those of
the underclass, who look to him for immediate empowerment
and reward in a newly organized society. One of Windrip's
most fanatic supporters and vindictive henchmen is a former
yardman, Shad Ledue, described at one point as "the kind of
vindictive peasant who sets fire to barns."[33] Lewis's fear of the
masses galvanized behind a mesmerizing leader was apparently
shared by Faulkner, who created his own vindictive barn burner
in Ab Snopes; and *The Hamlet*, depicting the rise to power of
Flem Snopes, Ab's son, is perhaps best understood as Faulkner's
It Can't Happen Here. Flem may represent, too, the type of
American dictator Roth Edmonds in "Delta Autumn" most
feared. While Flem is of course no fascist ideologue, his unscrupulous power plays that end with the transfer of social and
economic power into his hands call to mind the similar, if much
grander, actions by European dictators. (In a 1938 letter to
Robert Haas, Faulkner briefly outlined the action of the novel
that was to become *The Hamlet*, saying that Flem "gradually

consumes a small village until there is nothing left in it for him to eat."[34]

As Michael Grimwood has suggested, Faulkner admired poor whites as long as they passively endured and stayed in their place, like those he depicted in the wartime stories previously discussed; he recoiled in horror when such people strove upward and displaced the traditional elite of Southern society through cunning and demagoguery.[35] Faulkner's views were not atypical for their day. William Alexander Percy in *Lanterns on the Levee*, for instance, blames the demise of traditional life in the Delta on the political power of the poor whites and their demagogues. After his father's defeat in the 1912 Senate race by James K. Vardaman, Percy sums up the situation by the comment of an old man, "Wal, the bottom rail's on top and it's gwiner stay thar."[36] For Percy—and a good many other Southerners, too—the enfranchised poor whites and their rabble-rousing leaders were leading the country toward a version of fascist rule. Faulkner, too, apparently came close to seeing things this way.

But if Faulkner scorned Flem and his brood for undermining the foundation of traditional Southern society, he at the same time saw Flem as a victim of a society so hidebound in its traditionalism that it refused to acknowledge the contradictions and injustices on which it was structured—the violent origins that Richard King speaks of in his essay in this volume. Flem rises to power because he masters the skills by which Southern society operates; his unabashed manipulation of land, money, and people foregrounds his society's dark underside—the underside to which traditional Southerners would just as soon not admit. And so, rather than examining themselves and their ways in light of Flem's activities, the people of Frenchman's Bend divorce themselves from him. They react, as Richard C. Moreland suggests, to the disturbing "suspicion [Flem] cast[s] upon the system itself, in the all too common twentieth-century style of popular fascist anti-Semitism: they . . . identify Flem with (and vilify him in place of) their entire system of commodity fetishism (in money) and bureaucratic depersonalization (in law) of social exchange." Flem functions, in the words of Moreland, as the "'structural' Jew."[37] Faulkner underscores Flem's connections with, rather than divorcement from, the workings of traditional Southern society by ending the novel with Ratliff, Armstid, and Bookwright unsuccessfully trying to outwit Flem, driven by motives of greed and vengeance at their heart every bit as conniving as Flem's own.

Thomas Sutpen in *Absalom, Absalom!* likewise foregrounds Southern society's violent origins in his furious efforts to build a plantation dynasty. As with Flem, Faulkner apparently remained deeply ambivalent about his efforts. From one perspective, Sutpen is another, grander version of Snopes, the poor white usurper. Sutpen sets about building his little empire, Sutpen's Hundred, with a ruthless efficiency and a determination to succeed at all costs—echoes of the popular conception of the fascist dictator, and Quentin's fascination with and horror for Sutpen may just be on some level an expression of America's—and Faulkner's—own ambivalence toward the fascist experiment. (It was not until after Mussolini's invasion of Ethiopia in 1935 that American public opinion turned decidedly against fascist dictatorships.) And yet, from another perspective, Sutpen is less the destroyer of Southern traditionalism than its defiant embodiment. As they did with Flem, the local folk ostracize Sutpen, even taunting and tossing vegetables at him at his wedding, in their efforts to keep from viewing the disturbing image of themselves that Sutpen's presence holds up to them. Like Flem, Sutpen becomes at once the thematic fascist and the structural Jew—an ironic conflation that is perhaps Faulkner's commentary on the South's efforts to disassociate itself from accusations and interpretations of fascism.

This is not the place to present extensive discussions of *The Hamlet* and *Absalom, Absalom!*, and I bring them up here merely to suggest the thickened context that exists when Faulkner's fiction is read in light of the ideological conflict between democracy and fascism that permeated American society during

the 1930s and 1940s. As we have seen, Faulkner addressed the
democratic crisis both explicitly and implicitly, exploring issues
of class, race, and demagoguery that were crucial elements in
the cultural dialogue then taking place concerning democracy's
weaknesses and strengths. In most of his fiction Faulkner wrote
with the underlying assumptions of the Southern traditionalist—
that Southern society was a check to the radical experiment of
democracy and its terrifying offspring, fascism. These assumptions, of course, ran counter to those of the prevailing democratic revival that saw regionalism, not democracy, as the seed-
bed of fascism. Thus, Faulkner left himself open to the charge
of fascism, despite the fact of his strong interventionist stance—a
fate the South in general also suffered.

Rarely, however, did Faulkner write as a traditionalist without at the same time challenging traditionalist assumptions,
undercutting the types of visions presented by Ike McCaslin
and Mrs. Grier and her son. If he on the one hand was
sympathetic to the traditionalist logic put forth by Richard
Weaver and other conservatives, he also understood the potential dangers of such thinking, particularly those involved in
blindly defending the traditional order without recognizing the
system's injustices and in defending the social order with unjust
means. Faulkner had precisely these dangers in mind when, in
a 1945 letter to Malcolm Cowley, he wrote of Percy Grimm's
brutal emasculation of Joe Christmas in *Light in August:* "If I
recall him aright, he was the Fascist galahad who saved the
white race by murdering Christmas. I invented him in 1931. I
didn't realise until after Hitler got into the newspapers that I
had created a Nazi before he did."[38] Grimm is another manifes-
tation of the fearful modern Moses—the avenging Southern
knight, the fascist Galahad, the dark shadow of those vengeful
heroes, like Buford Pusser, who walk tall and carry a big stick
but fail to see that they tread on the ideals and values of the
very tradition they seek to preserve.

It is this awareness of the dangers of extremist regionalist
thinking that separates Faulkner from most Southern tradition-

alists, who forthrightly stood by their logic that linked democ-racy—not the South—with fascism. Faulkner made this anti-democratic connection, but he also understood that such regionalist thinking had dark undercurrents—undercurrents every bit as dangerous to the traditional order and every bit as potentially fascist as the abuses of democracy that Faulkner recognized in the political landscape of the South and America. His evocation and examination of these issues in his fiction of the 1930s and 1940s place Faulkner as a central figure, if not so obvious a one as Erskine Caldwell or William Alexander Percy, in the cultural dialogue involving democracy, fascism, and the South.

NOTES

1. Alan Reynolds Thompson, "The Cult of Cruelty," quoted in *William Faulkner: Three Decades of Criticism*, ed. Frederick J. Hoffman and Olga W. Vickery (East Lansing: Michigan State University Press, 1960), 2.

2. Granville Hicks, *The Great Tradition: An Interpretation of American Literature Since the Civil War* (New York: Macmillan, 1933), 266.

3. Philip Rahv, Review of *Absalom, Absalom!*, in *William Faulkner: The Critical Heritage*, ed. John Bassett (London: Routledge and Kegan Paul, 1975), 210.

4. Robert Penn Warren, "Cowley's Faulkner," in *William Faulkner: The Critical Heritage*, 328.

5. Maxwell Geismar, *Writers in Crisis: The American Novel Between Two Wars* (Boston: Houghton Mifflin, 1942), 179, 180.

6. Ibid., 182.

7. *The Faulkner–Cowley File: Letters and Memories, 1944–1962*, ed. Malcolm Cowley (New York: Viking, 1966), 10.

8. Joseph Blotner, *Faulkner: A Biography* (New York: Random House, 1974), 2:1030.

9. Blotner, 2:1030.

10. William Faulkner, *Selected Letters of William Faulkner*, ed. Joseph Blotner (New York: Random House, 1977), 166.

11. Ibid., 175–76.

12. Morton Sosna, "Democratic Discourse: Implications for the South," paper presented at Southern Historical Association Meeting, 1987.

13. Margaret Mead, *And Keep Your Powder Dry: An Anthropologist Looks at America* (New York: William Morrow, 1942), 20.

14. Ibid., 24.

15. Margaret Mead, letter to M. L. Wilson dated 5 April 1942, quoted in Sosna.

16. Melvin Rader, *No Compromise: The Conflict Between Two Worlds* (New York: Macmillan, 1939), 337.

17. For a good overview of the decline of regionalist art, see Cécile Whiting, *Antifascism in American Art* (New Haven: Yale University Press, 1989), particularly chapter 4.

18. Quoted in Whiting, 99.

19. Whiting, 197.

20. Lawrence H. Schwartz, *Creating Faulkner's Reputation: The Politics of Modern Literary Criticism* (Knoxville: University of Tennessee Press, 1988).

21. Lillian Smith, Review of *Lanterns on the Levee*, in *From the Mountain*, ed. Helen White and Redding S. Sugg, Jr. (Memphis: Memphis State University Press, 1972), 16.

22. W. J. Cash, *The Mind of the South* (New York: Vintage, 1991), 134.

23. Katherine DuPre Lumpkin, *The South in Progress* (New York: International Publishers, 1940), 115, 116.

24. William Alexander Percy, *Lanterns on the Levee: Recollections of a Planter's Son* (New York: Knopf, 1941), 60.

25. Richard M. Weaver, "The South and the Revolution of Nihilism," in *The Southern Essays of Richard M. Weaver*, ed. George M. Curtis, III and James J. Thompson, Jr. (Indianapolis: Liberty Press, 1987), 183, 187, 184, 186, 184.

26. Weaver, "Albert Taylor Bledsoe," in *The Southern Essays of Richard M. Weaver*," 158.

27. Robert Penn Warren, *Democracy and Poetry* (Cambridge: Harvard University Press, 1975), 58–59.

28. William Faulkner, *Go Down, Moses* (New York: Vintage International, 1990), 322–23. Further references are cited parenthetically in the text.

29. William Faulkner, "Shall Not Perish," in *Collected Stories of William Faulkner* (New York: Random House, 1977), 108.

30. Ibid., 114–15.

31. Robert H. Brinkmeyer, Jr., "*Go Down, Moses* and the Ascetic Imperative," in *Faulkner and the Short Story*, ed. Evans Harrington and Ann J. Abadie (Jackson: University Press of Mississippi, 1992), 206–28.

32. Peter Brown, *The Body and Society: Men, Women, and Sexual Renunciation in Early Christianity* (New York: Columbia University Press, 1988), 87.

33. Sinclair Lewis, *It Can't Happen Here* (Garden City, N.Y.: Doubleday, Doran, 1935), 46.

34. Faulkner, *Selected Letters*, 107.

35. Michael Grimwood, *Heart in Conflict: Faulkner's Struggles with Vocation* (Athens: University of Georgia Press, 1987), 163–64.

36. Percy, *Lanterns on the Levee*, 153.

37. Richard C. Moreland, *Faulkner and Modernism: Rereading and Rewriting* (Madison: University of Wisconsin Press, 1990), 144, 145.

38. Faulkner, *Selected Letters*, 202.

The Snopes Trilogy and the Emergence of Consumer Culture

TED OWNBY

Automobiles play important roles in Faulkner's last two works. In *The Mansion* Linda Snopes Kohl has a pre-ordered British Jaguar delivered the day after Flem Snopes is killed with her assistance. To pay for it, she uses the money she will receive from Flem's insurance policy. For this worker for the goal of human equality to indulge in a luxury that belies any notions of equality seems to suggest either that Faulkner was condemning his only radical character for her hypocrisy or that he was condemning the consumer society for its ability to entice even its most serious critics. In his last book, *The Reivers*, an automobile becomes a vehicle not of destructiveness or self-indulgence but of democracy. An automobile unites a wealthy white boy, a poor black man and a poor white man in the pleasures of a buoyant democracy that come not only with sharing the same experience but also with escaping from a rural community in which everyone knows what to expect from each other and themselves. This essay explores the tension in Faulkner's work between those two perspectives on the meanings Mississippians in the twentieth century have given to consumer goods. The positive meaning stresses escape from rural poverty and the confining aspects of Southern traditions, while offering a form of democracy that reveals itself in appearances. The negative meaning stresses the indulgence of the self at the expense of responsibility for other people and communication with them.

The issue has to do with why people want money—ultimately,

the nature of economic success and its rewards—which leads ultimately to the nature of the American Dream itself. The twentieth-century dream of the consumer society, evoked by advertisers, corporate leaders, therapists, and politicians, has not merely held that wealth should be available to anyone; it has promised that everyone can enjoy the fruits of American abundance in a new culture based on excitement, novelty, and the pleasures of an ever changing series of consumer goods. The dream of the consumer society has promised an America that will be classless in appearance if not reality and, as a teenaged New Yorker said after an afternoon at Macy's in 1907, "more fun than a barrel of monkeys."[1]

Scholars, at least until recently, have tended to set up consumer culture as an insidious opponent of older value systems—a system of achieving self-worth through work and possibly creativity, or an agricultural system in which people resist spending out of fears of losing their farms, or a system of rural or small town and often ethnic loyalties in which people's identities are rooted in families and communities. Scholarly writing about American consumers dates from Thorstein Veblen's 1899 *Theory of the Leisure Class,* which harshly attacked professions and businessmen for caring less about their work and their workers than about the selfish and private pleasures of consumer goods. It continued in 1929 with the publication of *Middletown* by Robert S. Lynd and Helen Merrell Lynd, which viewed workers' fascination with the pursuit and enjoyment of consumer goods, especially automobiles, as an ultimately empty substitute for any degree of control over their work lives. Scholars from the left have tended to interpret advertising, the lure of goods, and the fascination of shopping as traps to lure the poor into long hours of work without protest and to compensate women for their economic powerlessness. Frequently scholars have viewed the culture of the consumer as the enemy, a great corruptor in some kind of Eden. And scholars of literature have often viewed the need to publish for a mass market as an obstacle to the production of great art.[2]

To understand the meanings of consumer goods, we should suspend at least momentarily the judgments we make of our own society and its power relations. A growing body of scholars, rather than focusing on the forms of capitalism or patriarchy that may lie behind consumer behavior, have begun to analyze the appeal of consumer goods and the everyday ideals of people in a consumer society. At the center of the consumer ideal is the importance of choice—the ability to express oneself by choosing goods. A model for the modern consumer society, with both its goals and its economic practices, rests on four main points:

1. Modern consumers have the financial ability to buy goods not exclusively in order to survive, and they have the opportunity to choose among different goods.

2. They want some of the more expensive goods, especially goods of a quality approaching those owned by the wealthy.

3. They find pleasure and even adventure in shopping, either in stores or from catalogues and in seeing or hearing advertisements.

4. They maintain a romantic, unquenchable thirst for the new experiences promised not just by modern consumer goods but by the constant novelty of the whole progression from one product to the next.

All of those points might be useful in studying parts of Faulkner's work, but it is the fourth point that is especially important in thinking about the work of someone who placed so much emphasis on the past and on the community. The experience of the modern consumer is the intense individualism of the romantic. As Colin Campbell and Jean-Christophe Agnew have argued, attaching personal fulfillment to the next product one can buy, and then the next and the next, places consumers in the position of the nineteenth-century romantic, hoping for "something evermore about to be."[3] At its extreme the consumer society offers the individual the life of the child in the toy store, saying, "I want that one, and that one, and that one, and that one." It is a life that both demands novelty and celebrates it, a life that says today should always be better than yesterday and that tomorrow should be even better. It is the economic system and the cultural ideal of what Martha Wolfenstein calls fun morality, a morality that turns the child's fascination with every new color, shape, smell, and taste into a model of behavior for all ages.[4]

It would be easy to stress the manipulative sides of the consumer economy and especially the advertising industry, but the twentieth-century spokesmen for the consumer society claim that it offers a new and special meaning of democracy. It is democratic, they say, in the sense that traditional material expressions of elitism become so widely available that they lose their attachment to any traditional values of aristocracy or paternalism or peculiarly upper-class manners. In a consumer society, none of those traditional expressions of elitism can last very long. They return on occasion as styles change, but they lose their connotations of timeless virtues. Consumer culture can be democratic in the sense that almost all groups share the experience of shopping, often in the same stores. It can be democratic in the sense that the American poor are constantly urged to dress and drive and decorate their homes in ways that resemble the appearance of the wealthy; if they cannot afford the best goods, advertisers urge them to wait for the goods to go on sale, or to buy goods that at least look like those of the wealthy. And, finally, consumer culture offers a democratic ideal in its lines of communication between rich and poor.[5]

Consumer culture has generally involved a middle-class, city and town, forward-looking, homogenizing ideology, and the history of Mississippi has generally been none of those things. In some significant ways, what was becoming a dominant ideology outside the South posed a particular challenge in the Deep South. Faulkner's work is so rooted in everyday experience that it seems useful to discuss him in the context of Mississippi contemporaries who addressed the same issues. One Mississippi conservative and one Mississippi radical both came to condemn the growing importance of consumer goods.

Will Percy was the conservative. Percy articulated the conser-

vative perspective with particular clarity by discussing its decline and impending death. In *Lanterns on the Levee,* he saw
the rise of the consumer as one of the many signs of the
inevitable decline of humane values and the rise of empty forms
of democracy. Percy's perspective was unique among aristocrats
because he did not celebrate the glories of a luxurious past when
people truly understood how to use their goods to convey
leadership and hospitality and perhaps graceful ease. He had no
time or sentiment for blathering over mansions burned or hoop
skirts no longer worn. The Greenville of his family's past, he
wrote, never had "those roomy old residences, full of fine
woodwork and furniture and drapery" that had graced Natchez
and Charleston. At one point he doubted if any twosome "ever
looked less aristocratic" than he and his grandfather, the latter
"in his neat but well-worn and out-of-style sack suit, I barefooted
and hatless." A favorite aunt could make calls on Virginia high
society "from her mule-drawn, ancient vehicle in a homemade
print dress" without attracting derision of any kind. If material
goods mattered little, what did matter? In his eyes, the Percy
family and their kind upheld timeless virtues of manners,
charm—especially in women—kindness, good conversation and
hospitality, a broad range of duties he called honorable, respect
for intellect and fantasy, and a paternalistic care for the poor
and weak. They concentrated "not on those virtues which make
surviving possible, but on those which make it worth while."[6]

Like many social critics, Percy was more specific about what
was objectionable in the present than what was valuable about
the past. Americans in the twentieth century, for Percy, were
too concerned with physical comfort and, above all, with appearances. Anyone could take on the look of the elite without
knowing the values people with power should inherit; even
James K. Vardaman was "immaculately overdressed." The life
of the wealthy in Greenville in the 1930s was no longer dedicated to the pursuit of timeless virtues but to economic progress
and the immediate and hollow rewards available for purchase.
He complained about the prominence of nightly mass entertain-

ment that came with the railroads and then the trucks and busses and telephones and electric lights. "The river town has a White Way, picture shows, many radios, a Chamber of Commerce, and numerous service clubs. We have gone forward, our progress is ever so evident." The movies represented the frivolous frolicking of an urban upper class; the radio represented a simple numbing of the mind through repetition and the avoidance of thought. He sneered at the values of comfort and appearance in modern America in one memorable passage: "I'm unhappily convinced that our exteriors have increased in importance while our interiors have deteriorated: it is a good paint job, but the lighting and sanitation are execrable. A good world, I acknowledge, an excellent world, but poor in spirit and common as hell. Vulgarity, a contagious disease like the itch, unlike it is not a disease of the surface, but eats to the marrow."[7]

If the wealthy were losing their traditional understanding of the things that mattered more than appearances and economic progress, what of the rest of society? Percy had no patience for the notion that the consumer society offered new dignity to the poor. Freedoms, yes, but those freedoms represented no progress or dignity. Will Percy believed that the poor were better off enjoying contented leisure than pursuing better paying work. He respected the talent he thought Afro-Mississippians possessed for enjoying their time away from work. That talent was only possible in an economic system in which the poor had security but not expectations for more pay or more responsibilities or more outlets for skills. Sharecropping, for him, continued the ability of earlier labor systems to provide workers a contented subsistence without tempting them with higher ambitions or exhausting them through constant toil. "Our plantation system seems to me to offer as humane, just, self-respecting, and cheerful a method of earning a living as human beings are likely to devise. I watch the limber-jointed, oily-black, well-fed, decently clothed peasants on Trail Lake and feel sorry for the telephone girls, the clerks in chain stores, the office help, the unskilled laborers everywhere—not only for their poor and fixed wage but for their slave routine, their joyless habits of work, and their insecurity."[8] That the sharecroppers were *well* fed but only *decently* clothed shows what he found most important for workers. And that he included chain stores in his litany of modern failures suggests that he was thinking of the numbing effects of consumption as well as menial labor.

Such impassioned remarks become even stronger when Percy described what happened to a favorite servant who left the South and its supposed protections. Ford, who called himself Fode, was in Percy's description content in Mississippi. When Fode moved to Detroit, he frequently called Percy asking for money from the room he shared with four roommates with "a single window to keep out the cold and a gas burner for cooking and heat."[9] The idea was an old one that the poor did not understand what to do with spending money and were better off in a system that provided security rather than choices. Percy was new in his open despair about the hopelessness of what happened when the old forms of security were lost. With an upper class without manners or a sense of paternalistic responsibility, all that remained was a democratic pursuit of cheap pleasures which might not even materialize.

The radical Mississippian was Richard Wright. With a childhood with few of the novel stimulations the consumer society tries to recapture and with no respect for the virtues of independent farm life, Wright described in *Black Boy* his futile effort to take satisfaction in the choices available in stores. When he was able to make some money, "the boys would now examine some new article of clothing I had bought; none of us allowed a week to pass without buying something new." Wright ultimately used such stories to display the hollowness of the small victories available to African-Americans in the South whose daily lives were "bound up with trivial objectives."[10]

He used the same adjective in one of the harshest condemnations of consumer culture written by an American. Early in *American Hunger*, Wright described his disappointment with the empty pleasures pursued by two white waitresses in Chicago. He had hoped life outside the South offered the possibility for new forms of freedom, but "all their lives they had done nothing but strive for petty goals, the trivial prizes of American life." He listed those trivial prizes, believing it was "the daily values that give meaning to life" that "stood between me and those white girls with whom I worked. Their constant outward-looking, their mania for radios, cars, and a thousand other trinkets that made them dream and fix their lives upon the trash of life, made it impossible for them to learn a language which could have taught them to speak of what was in their or others' hearts. The words of their souls were the syllables of popular songs."[11]

Wright criticized consumer culture on two closely related levels. One was that of the individual. Throughout his life he sought a self-understanding he believed most people lacked and did not even want. The goal Wright set for himself and which he wanted for all individuals was a combination of education and self-analysis that could bring out all possibilities for genius, creativity, and self-expression. The "outward-looking" nature of consumer culture, the desire to identify oneself with a series of new things, prohibited the pursuit or even the beginning of that introspection.

On the level of the group, Wright as a maturing Marxist believed that the American fascination with goods hindered the development of a revolutionary working class. Those goods served the hegemonic purpose of encouraging popular support for capitalism, diverting the attention of workers and the unemployed from their lack of real power over their lives. Instead, most Americans had "a lust for trash" and "the basest goals in the world." In his lament Wright did not merely agonize over the empty goals of the dominant white culture. He was even more troubled that American capitalism and consumer culture had been able to convince a great many African-Americans of its essential worth. They too, he said, were consumers, or at least they wanted to be. "The most valued pleasure of the people I knew," he wrote of his Chicago acquaintances, "was a car." A revolution would come, he said, not from those who tried but could not share in those pleasures but from "those who do not dream of the prizes that the nation holds forth."[12] Only then would blacks and whites struggle together as fellow workers, because only then could they identify themselves with something other than the search for immediate pleasure.

For all of their differences, Wright and Percy shared the belief—almost as old as Americans' ideas about themselves— that America was selling its soul for pleasures that were meaningless and temporary. For Percy, that soul lay in the past of the South and of Western civilization. For Wright, it lay in the possibilities of a future international working class. But both believed that too much immediate enjoyment of consumer pleasures stood in the way of higher values. William Faulkner would seem to have held a similar attitude. Faulkner often has V. K. Ratliff make categorical statements about Flem Snopes's single-minded greed. "To Flem Snopes," he says, "there aint a man breathing that cant be bought for something."[13] The notion that anything, including people, can be bought would seem to suggest that Faulkner shared with Percy and Wright a belief that consumer culture represented a new form of slavery or self-enslavement. And in *Intruder in the Dust* Faulkner has Gavin Stevens make an almost blandly conventional critique of the ways American males in the twentieth century have misused their abundance. "The American really loves nothing but his automobile: not his wife his child nor even his bank-account first (in fact he doesn't love that bank-account nearly as much as foreigners like to think because he will spend about any or all of it for almost anything provided it is valueless enough) but his motor-car. Because the automobile has become our national sex symbol."[14] By condemning the practice of spending on anything without value, and by linking that practice to automobiles and the pursuit of sexual pleasure, Faulkner would seem to be just another critic of the fun morality of twentieth-century America. Finally, Faulkner would seem to have had little patience for the ways consumer culture tends to deny both pain and the past,

because without pain and the past, he really would not have had
much to write about.

Despite the apparent clarity of his criticisms first of capitalism
and second of the consumer society, Faulkner falls into no
easy categories. He could condemn greed easily enough, but
criticizing consumer pleasures was much more difficult. Unlike
Will Percy, Faulkner did not look back or show sympathy for
characters who look back to a hierarchical golden age when
people recognized the ultimate irrelevance of goods. Unlike
Richard Wright, he did not condemn goods for their part in the
false consciousness of the poor. Instead, Faulkner displays
people in conflict with themselves, and in those conflicts lie
part of Faulkner's perspective on the meaning of twentieth-
century America.

In his own life Faulkner lived out many of the primary
tensions in consumer society. Some of his ancestors could afford
the luxury of the big house that marked them as Southern
aristocrats, but the financial problems of his father made visible
the differences between upper-class ideals and financial realities. As a teenager, William Faulkner occasionally put on silk
ties and expensive suits, bought for him by his grandfather, in
an effort to live up to a traditional ideal.[15]

As an adult, he was constantly and sometimes deeply in debt,
partly because he insisted on keeping up a home clearly beyond
his means and partly because of the spending habits of Estelle
Faulkner. One of the many reasons for their running battles was
an almost stereotypical dispute between the woman who wanted
expensive clothes and the man who maintained interests in
large investments but could be frugal to the point of cheapness
on smaller expenses. It is surely important that when Faulkner
ran a notice in Mississippi newspapers denying responsibility
for Estelle's debts, he was thinking not just about the future of
their marriage but also about those debts themselves. The
distinction between spending for a home and spending for
clothing was important, because it suggests that Faulkner believed that his own purchases helped create and sustain perma-

nence and respect in the community, whereas Estelle's were selfish, flighty, and insignificant. By identifying expenses for personal pleasure as something female even as he went into debt for automobiles and an airplane, Faulkner was also sharing with much of American culture the idea that spending on personal goods was a frailty of women.[16]

As if these tensions were not enough to give Faulkner a personal understanding of the importance of consumer goods and their conflicting meanings, consider the tensions between his life in small-town Mississippi and the time he spent in Hollywood. In Mississippi he not only tried to keep up Rowan Oak as a sign of continuity with upper-class family traditions, he also owned a farm and talked frequently about the need to stay independent and out of debt, just as farmers did. Hollywood, on the other hand, always represented impermanence, economic necessity for him and greed in almost everyone else, and standards for personal and artistic life so low he hardly considered them standards. Hollywood was the place where cheap and passing pleasures were made for the rest of the country. As much as Madison Avenue and probably more, Hollywood was the center of the culture of the consumer.[17]

In his own life, then, Faulkner was partly attracted to consumer culture and partly troubled by it. In his work, he was able to combine his well-known respect for the past with sympathy for rebels in order to explore some of the challenges consumer society presented both to upper-class and agricultural traditions. And it is especially important that he presents this challenge with some characters and scenes that were fairly positive. Colonel Sartoris stands as a pretty ridiculous spokesman for traditional upper-class uses of goods. Like Will Percy, Sartoris deplores the idea of a democracy of appearances. Unlike Percy, Sartoris takes steps to restore the appearances that accompany class hierarchy. First, he proposes a law "that no Negro woman should appear on the streets without an apron."[18] Then, Faulkner uses him to demonstrate the traditionalist's rejection of modern goods in *The Town*. When his carriage—a symbol of elitism dating not just to the antebellum South but to early modern England—has a confrontation with Jefferson's first automobile, Mayor Sartoris authors a law banning automobiles from the streets. Faulkner may have had personal reasons for seeing the rise of the automobile as a revolution. Automobiles made obsolete the livery stable his father had to give up in 1912,[19] and it seems possible that a teenager who heard his father bemoaning the influence of automobiles might have seen opposition to them as the height of closed-minded conservatism.

What Faulkner called the "destiny of America" would not be denied. Manfred de Spain initiates a new generation of both political and cultural leadership simply by opposing the ban on automobiles. Faulkner turned sociologist in discussing the basis for opposition to Sartoris. First, the opponents were young. The automobile ban "was the opportunity which that whole contemporary generation of young people had been waiting for, not just in Jefferson but everywhere." Second, they were part of an ambitious, nonagricultural middle class. They were "the clerks and bookkeepers in the stores and gins and offices." De Spain and his automobile loving followers turn the defeat of Sartoris into a defeat of elitist traditions in the South. When they hang the automobile law in the courthouse and laugh about it along with the automobile generation from all over the country, they are celebrating the entry of Jefferson into a twentieth-century America that stresses the pursuit of pleasure, easy mobility, and widespread involvement in cosmopolitan culture. De Spain buys the first automobile, a red one in contrast with many of the black and less flashy cars that followed. Even more important, de Spain starts the first automobile dealership in town and from his position in the bank gladly lends money to anyone wanting to buy a car. So he embodies not only the excitement of consumer culture but also its goal of spreading its availability far beyond the wealthy.[20]

On the appeal of the automobile as a challenge to traditional forms of hierarchy, Faulkner was not just a sociologist but a good sociologist. The coming automobile age, he said, celebrated a particular kind of sexual pleasure. The red car was "alien and debonair, as irrevocably polygamous and bachelor as de Spain himself."[21] Part of this sexual freedom came simply with the settings the automobile provided for couples to escape public view. From a broader perspective, the car itself was a consumer product of real importance. As with Faulkner himself, whose first car was a yellow Model T Ford with a modified racer body, owners took pleasure in their cars' appearance and capacity for speed. By producing new models every year, auto manufacturers tried to stimulate the desire for new appearances and new driving experiences.[22] And cars also promised pleasures that were open-ended in their ability to take people farther and more quickly than previous forms of transportation. The automobile offered the constant expectation of new cars, new places to go, new pleasures of many kinds—pursuits that led ultimately to the constant sexual enticement of mass culture. De Spain foreshadowed what Faulkner called "that new national religious cult of Cheesecake as it translated still alive the Harlows and Grables and Monroes into the hierarchy of American cherubim." The imagery that untouchable, sexually alluring women were part of America's most sacred figures suggested that constant desire—sexual desire—had become the way to honor the country's highest ideals.[23]

Faulkner also took on a sociological tone in detailing the change in the consumer habits of farmers in the early twentieth century. In *Intruder in the Dust,* he draws a distinction between the long-time rural visitors who come to Jefferson on Mondays and those who have only recently started visiting on Saturdays. Monday visitors are men. They come to do their trading, make their purchases, and then take part in the slow-moving whittling and spitting and storytelling culture that Faulkner found so intriguing. Trading for such men often takes the form of barter, and in Faulkner's world, barter matters mostly for the horse trading, slick-talking public skill of doing it well rather than the private pleasure of enjoying the horse or milk separator or whatever the fruits of the barter may have been. The long stories of trading and tricking stress the significance of oral communication and the pride and shame of winning and losing. When Ab Snopes seeks revenge for a public horse trading humiliation at the hands of Pat Stamper, "Ab wasn't trying to beat Pat bad. He just wanted to recover that eight dollars worth of honor and pride of Yoknapatawpha County horse-trading, doing it not for profit but for honor." If the goal of the Monday crowd is not profit, it obviously is not the pleasure of a good product to take home.[24]

The new, Saturday visitors fill the streets with more women, more teenagers and children of both sexes. This is the crowd of the automobile age who go shopping every Saturday for the excitement of the throngs and the possibility of new experiences of many kinds. They are buying "staples and delicacies like bananas and twenty-five cent sardines and machine-made cakes and pies and clothes and stockings and feed and fertilizer and plough gear."[25] In other words, they are mixing functional goods with pleasure goods. And rather than sitting and spitting and drinking like the Monday crowd, the Saturday visitors turn up the volume on their cars and cruise the square.

Faulkner portrays the perspective of the Saturday crowd as a legitimate alternative to the rural perspectives of most of his characters. The possibilities for new kinds of excitement very often lurk as troubling temptations for his characters, but they can also offer forms of individual liberation. Faulkner understood the perspective of the poor who stayed outside the consumer society and resisted its allure. Until late in the nineteenth century, most Southern farmers had what economic historians call a "safety-first orientation" toward feeding their families first and only then entering the marketplace, with all of its risks and possibilities.[26] By the twentieth century, most subsistence farming had given way to market production, either by choice or force. But even if safety first agriculture was fast on the decline, the beliefs and values that accompanied it remained strong, leaving people in doubt over whether to feel and think like independent farmers cautious about the economic dangers

of consumer spending or like modern consumers who saw
economic life as a series of small adventures available for purchase. The three prevailing reasons not to make purchases were
debt and the fear of the threat that debt posed to personal
independence, the commitment to self-denial demanded by
evangelical religion, and an agricultural life that sought contin-
ual renewal rather than new pleasures. All of these appear with
clarity and some sympathy in Faulkner's work, but, significantly, his characters very often find these principles restrictive
and try to overturn them.

Two of the perspectives of traditional agricultural folk appear
in *Light in August*. Faulkner portrays Lena Grove as a woman
of nature and, for her, it is a struggle to buy things. She fears
that being improvident might cost her the independence that
allowed her to travel in her effort to unite her household. At
one country store, "she is waging a mild battle with that
providential caution of the old earth of and with and by which
she lives." Earth people, then, are born with a literally natural
reluctance to become consumers. In Faulkner's perspective, a
primary principle of the earth is that of renewal, of repeating
things in order to survive. Within that renewal, there is little
room for the desire for the novelty of consumer goods. But
Faulkner continues the scene. "This time she conquers. She
rises and walking a little awkwardly, a little carefully, she
traverses the ranked battery of maneyes and enters the store,
the clerk following." This picture of a woman running a male
gauntlet to enter a country store shows that in Yoknapatawpha
County, the so-called feminization of consumer spending has
not occurred, and it takes some courage to go against both the
conventions of the genders and the traditions of the old earth to
make a purchase. "'I'm a-going to do it,' she thinks, even while
ordering the cheese and crackers; 'I'm a going to do it,' saying
aloud: 'And a box of sardines.' She calls them *sourdeens*. 'A
nickel box.'" By splurging on what is to her a luxury, if a small
luxury, Lena is violating one of the characteristics that make her
an earth woman.[27]

Another character in the same book attempts to avoid consumer spending for religious reasons. The Presbyterian McEachern gives a heavy sigh every time he has to leave his responsibilities on the farm and face the temptations and degradations of the town. Visiting town, he cautions Joe Christmas, "is no good habit for a man who has yet to make his way." The danger lies in anything that tempts people not to fulfill their responsibilities. Specifically, McEachern sees luxury goods as signs of indulgence. When Joe sells his cow to buy a suit, his stepfather challenges him for the reason. "What else would you want with a new suit if you were not whoring." Of course it is McEachern who has given Joe the cow, with the clear goal of testing his ability to overcome temptation. For Joe to buy the suit, largely for the reason McEachern thought, is a way to break free from the confining morality of his step-father and the expectations for self-denial that accompany agricultural life.[28] Once again, then, Faulkner is showing a degree of respect for a character who uses the ability to consume as a way to escape the confinements of agricultural tradition.

A third scene, addressing several reasons for reluctance to spend money, occurs at the conclusion of As I Lay Dying. Here two of Faulkner's most exasperating characters, Anse and Cash Bundren, find common and actually sympathetic ground in the appeals of consumer pleasures. Both characters exemplify the farmer's traditional reluctance to spend money. Anse is a poor farmer, head of a large family, husband of a woman who believes the purpose of life is to prepare for death. As a farmer, his life centers on renewing the earth and economizing in order not to lose the farm. He lives in real fear of debt, four times in the book stating, "we would be beholden to no man."[29] As a member of a family that is in part religious, he has heard about the dangers of temptation, and his home is clearly not a setting for the pleasures of new experiences. As a rural Mississippian a good distance from Jefferson, he has little contact with the fashion and novelty of mass culture. In the tradition of agricultural republicanism, he resents not only the power of merchants in Jefferson but also their enjoyment of the wealth they receive through his work. He makes, with what is for Faulkner unusual clarity, a farmer's criticism of the locals who control the cash economy. "Nowhere in this sinful world can a honest, hardworking man profit. It takes them that runs the stores in the towns, doing no sweating, living off of them that sweats. It aint the hardworking man, the farmer. Sometimes I wonder why we keep at it. It's because there is a reward for us above, where they cant take their autos and such. Every man will be equal there and it will be taken from them that have and give to them that have not by the Lord." The sentiment was commonplace among rural Protestants that people who did not use their muscles made money unfairly by manipulating those who did, and that the merchants used their corrupt gains for showy pleasures like "autos and such." The sentiment is also commonplace that farm work represents earthly duty that will have its heavenly reward. As usual, however, Faulkner's characters use conventions only to defy them. After detailing the virtues of work and austerity, Anse thinks, "it's a long wait, seems like," and he repeats a desire that occurred to him when Addie died. "But now I can get them teeth. That will be a comfort."[30]

Anse's son Cash seems to be a stereotypical hard worker. He fears the temptations of consumer goods because they could interfere with his commitment to work. He wonders what a record player might cost on installment, and he imagines the pleasure recorded music might give to the evenings after days of hard work. But he decides, "I reckon it's a good thing we aint got ere a one of them. I reckon I wouldn't never get no work done a-tall for listening to it."[31]

The many objections the Bundren father and son raise to consumer goods indicate that they have given them considerable thought. By the end of the book, however, they finally take refuge from their troubles in the pleasures of consumer goods. First, Anse starts asking his children to lend him money for reasons he does not make clear. After all he has done for them, he says, a few dollars are not much to ask. This obviously shows a willingness to violate his often-stated fear of indebtedness in order to pursue new pleasures. When he buys his new teeth and when he shows up with a new Mrs. Bundren, he is looking to a better future—not to a renewal of the work and limited expectations of his past. When the new Mrs. Bundren meets the family, she is carrying a record player, and this inspires Cash, too, to look to a future in which work will no longer dominate. "Everytime a new record would come from the mail order and us setting in the house in the winter, listening to it, I would think what a shame Darl couldn't be to enjoy it too."[32] He is not merely looking forward to leisure and pleasure at home—things that as far as we know he has never had—he is looking forward to novelties that will come several times a year through catalogues. Cash has become the modern consumer, looking not for any kind of redemption or personal character improvement or ties to tradition but for what will come through the next mail.

To this point this paper has argued that Faulkner could be sympathetic and sometimes even positive about the potential for consumer culture to offer individual liberation from traditional forms of confinement. De Spain lets loose the pleasures of the automobile age as liberation from the ideals of planter hierarchy, Lena Grove overcomes the tendency of the old earth to do nothing more than renew itself, Joe Christmas overcomes the pleasure-denying evangelicalism of his step-father, and Cash and Anse Bundren overcome the joyless economizing that independent farm life have demanded. Finally, in *The Reivers*, the trio of Boon Hogganbeck, Ned McCaslin, and Lucius Priest set off in an automobile on a trip that defines freedom as the experience of classlessness. In all of those cases, the enjoyment of consumer goods undercuts traditions associated with a pantheon of white Southern ideals—aristocracy, paternalism, life close to the soil, the independence of the rural household, evangelical religion, and white supremacy. From this evidence it seems that Faulkner might even have been a defender of consumer culture, at least in its ability to offer choices that allow people to escape, even if only momentarily, the constraints into which they have been born. It is this sense of personal liberation that most clearly distinguishes Faulkner from Richard Wright. For Wright, being a consumer meant giving in to the existing system of power relations. For Faulkner, it could mean breaking free from it.

Faulkner's attitude toward consumer society is complex, given that the liberation consumer spending celebrates is ultimately a liberation from whatever people have experienced in their pasts. The question is, how does Faulkner reconcile his deep concern for the past as an influence worthy of our attention with his apparent sympathy for those characters like de Spain, Lena Grove, Joe Christmas, and Cash Bundren who gain new freedoms through the fulfillment of consumer desire? The goal of consumer society is always some new fascination, a new pleasure to replace whatever pleasures have lost their fascination. The issue then becomes not liberation from particular grievances but a whole new perspective on life that pursues no ultimate goals and has no absolute values but that promises a constant pursuit of something new. What kind of life, then, is one that stresses an almost constant liberation, and in which the main definition of freedom is freedom from any goals and experiences of the past?

The groups for whom this sense of constant novelty is most meaningful are groups who have few ties to the past, who have risen from poverty to some degree of wealth, and who have no reason to save their money. In Faulkner's work, that group is preeminently the Snopes family. As David Minter has argued, the Snopeses are unique among Faulkner characters in that no ghosts of past generations haunt them, either with the ideals of the ages or the sins of the fathers.[33] On the second point, some of the Snopeses are newly wealthy and are thus in a position to spend money for pleasure without old notions of leadership, display, or charity. Just as important, all of the Snopeses who make economic progress do so outside agriculture, believing as Flem says, "aint no benefit in farming."[34] Thus they do not feel the need farmers have long felt to deny themselves goods in order to keep the farm.

To investigate how Faulkner examines consumer issues in the trilogy, this paper concentrates on five Snopeses, Ab and Mink, Montgomery Ward, Flem, and Linda. Fellow sharecroppers Ab and Mink are not consumers, but they belong in a different category from the independent farm families such as the Bundrens and the McEacherns. The sharecropping system forces them to limit their purchases by keeping them without cash for long stretches during the year and by encouraging them to try anything to escape the debt that controls their lives.

The first Yoknapatawpha Snopes, Ab, first appears as a barn-burner, a man for whom issues of justice outweigh any concerns about economic gain. He sneers at the hierarchical pretensions of de Spain, tracks manure on the hundred-dollar rug in the front hall and says, "If I had thought that much of a rug I dont know as I would keep it where folks coming in would have to tromp on it." Ab's two daughters, at work every time we see them, do not spend much, nor does anyone seem to spend money on them. One of the daughters wears a sunbonnet that is, significantly, faded, suggesting that she spends considerable time in the sun and that she does not wear new clothes. The other daughter wears "a shapeless hat which at one time must have belonged to the man."[35] So she receives hand-me-downs—a sign of economic necessity and of not being a consumer—and she wears a man's hat and is therefore outside the process that had turned fashions for women into one of the most frequently and dramatically changing parts of the consumer economy.

Faulkner's picture of the sharecropping Snopeses indicates neither agrarian respect for farm life nor any particular excitement over or desire for the consumer goods that threaten it. Time after time they embody the approach of the agricultural poor to material goods. Goods serve utilitarian purposes rather than emotional satisfactions. Mink's home is like the cabins most sharecroppers rent, a run-down two-room dogtrot with nothing to distinguish it from the homes of the other poor families in the area. It is not comfortable; the roof leaks and the weatherstripping is rotting away. It is not attractive; it has no paint and apparently no decoration. As a young man, Mink stands outside a theater but does not bother to enter. He watches young people in city clothes in the drug store, but expects never to taste the soft drinks that are displayed there like jewelry. He is curious to see an automobile but he cannot even dream about the kind of money that will allow him to buy one. Eventually— and most significantly—he grows accustomed to the material side of prison life, where the clothes and food are no worse than he has had outside Parchman. He has never expected economic progress, and he has no problems with a lack of opportunity for novel experiences. In fact, parts of prison life offer real relief. "No more now to go to a commissary store every Saturday morning to battle with the landlord for every gram of the cheap bad meat and meal and molasses and the tumbler of snuff which was his and his wife's one spendthrift orgy."[36] So here is another reason not to become a consumer. Trying to become one has put him at the mercy of a landlord, and in prison he has found he can accept life without the daily conflicts that go with trying to survive.

The Snopes sharecroppers have not turned the need to economize into a virtue that later Snopeses can use or to which they can look back. As dependent laborers who expect to stay dependent, they proclaim no love of the independence of farm life. Their hope for the future is based on a sense of personal honor that the system should work with enough fairness to allow them to survive with less struggle and worry.[37] Ab and Mink are not people of the earth, with any kind of attachment to the regenerative virtues of the soil. Mink knows the soil is "his sworn foe and mortal enemy."[38] Moreover, they show no signs of a religious rejection of self-indulgence. Thus they leave no legacy of economic thinking to the other Snopeses that might hinder their development as consumers. When other Snopeses have the chance to make money, they have no traditions that keep them from spending it with a clear conscience—or no conscience at all.

It is the Snopes generation that leaves the farm that represents a changed attitude about goods. Most obvious is the extravagantly named Montgomery Ward Snopes, a character who presents rare opportunities for the historian of consumer culture. The not so simple fact of his name stands in comic contrast to that of his father, I. O. Snopes. Debt was the primary economic reality for poor Southerners. For a Snopes to be saddled with the name I. O. suggests that his entire identity is wrapped up in the poor man's condition and in the consequent need to economize. And for I. O. Snopes to father Montgomery Ward Snopes signals a dramatic break in that tradition. Montgomery Ward was a large department store that began in the 1870s to distribute the nation's first mail-order catalogue, offering to rural people a variety of goods never before available outside urban areas and exposing rural folk to affordable versions of cosmopolitan styles.

In Montgomery Ward Snopes, Faulkner portrays some of the most unsavory aspects of consumer culture and gives us his view of consumption at its worst. Montgomery Ward Snopes begins his business career as a storekeeper in France in World War I. While running a canteen for soldiers, he builds a room in the back and hires a French woman to work as a prostitute. When he returns to Jefferson, he opens Atelier Monty, an erstwhile photography studio that does most and then all of its business displaying French postcards in the dark room.

Faulkner had already drawn the connection between consumer goods and sexual pleasure when he described de Spain's introduction of the automobile into Jefferson as a precursor of Hollywood cheesecake and when he had Gavin Stevens call the automobile the national sex symbol. What Montgomery Ward offers is sexual excitement without responsibility or even physical contact. By portraying untouchable forms one after another on his wall, he offers the men of Jefferson pleasures without consequences. In modern consumer culture, sexuality carries few of the burdens it carried in the agricultural South—burdens of personal identity, religious identity, racial identity, ties to the family, and ties between the family and the economy. The fact that the women in the pictures are French can only make them seem more untouchable and more removed from conventional rural and agricultural and Protestant meanings of sexual experience. The pleasures are brief, they can be experienced repeatedly, and they leave the customer wanting more.

For a time Montgomery Ward Snopes is able to cast sexual excitement in a respectable light. He opens Atelier Monty with a tea for Jefferson society and then displays pictures of weddings and graduations in his front window. Such an attempt to make self-indulgence into a mainstream, respectable form of morality represents a crucial element of the consumer society of the twentieth century. The power of mass culture has rested on the ability of media like the motion picture, recorded popular music, and eventually television to make acceptable and even commonplace behavior, or at least representations of behavior, that has long been considered indulgent.

Montgomery Ward Snopes comes to represent the principle that anything—especially immediate gratification—is available for purchase. He ends up in the cradle of consumer pleasures—Hollywood—in what Faulkner calls a "quite lucrative adjunct or correlative to the motion-picture industry or anyway colony."[39] We can confidently assume that Montgomery Ward Snopes has become connected to the business of pornographic films. So Faulkner takes the commodification of immediate pleasure and turns it into one of the uglier sides of mass culture in what has to be a slap at the crassness he endured in Hollywood.

For all that the historian of consumer behavior might love to dwell on a character named Montgomery Ward, Flem Snopes and Linda Snopes Kohl ultimately represent the culmination of Faulkner's thinking about the meanings of economic success. The story of Flem is a rags-to-riches tragedy, and part of the reason it is tragic is that he never finds enjoyment in the benefits of the economic system he helps bring to Yoknapatawpha.

Flem is the leading figure in converting Yoknapatawphans into consumers. The changes he makes in marketing at Varner's store were changes taking place throughout the rural South in the early twentieth century as cash replaced credit as the means of payment. After he takes over Varner's store, Flem's major innovation is to deny store credit to customers who have learned to expect it. The shift from credit to cash purchases is far more important than it may appear, and indeed in today's age of the credit card it might seem a step away from the modern economy rather than toward it. But the Varners have traditionally offered credit at the store as part of the control they exercised over local farmers. The store has operated in an economic system in which little really matters except land and labor. The customers themselves, mostly farmers with debts to the Varners, shopped mostly for subsistence goods and they have more incentives to limit their purchases than to enjoy them. With the Varners foreclosing on one farm after another, farmers have good reason to buy as little as they can. Varner records customers' purchases in a ledger, and customers who cannot pay at the end of the year face the possibility of losing their land. Thus the form of storekeeping that the Varners practice hardly encourages farmers to seek excitement in their goods or in the process of shopping.[40]

In this financial setting, Varner's general store remains a sleepy setting for male recreation. Almost ninety percent of the visitors to general stores in the nineteenth-century South were male,[41] and in Faulkner's work they do much more talking than shopping. All of the men at Varner's store wear the overalls that were physical signs of the unity between work and personal identity. In both the lack of interest in new appearances and the lack of women at the store, Varner's store stands outside the modern consumer economy. The modern alternative would be the department store, described by historians as a palace for selling, which involves consumers in the excitement of shopping for luxury goods and which caters more to women than men.[42]

Flem Snopes has no interest in turning the store into a palace for selling or encouraging people to attach a sense of romance to their goods. However, the fact that he converts the store from credit to cash, disdains the trust that has accompanied the Varners' notions of paternalism, and has no time for male small talk all signify that he is trying to revolutionize the general store to make profits by selling rather than simply using the store to support the Varners' hold over the land. A key scene occurs when he brings a plug of tobacco to Will Varner and stays around until Varner pays for it in cash—a sign that Flem has successfully taken aim at the economic customs of planter domination.

One of the clearest examples of Flem's enticing Yoknapatawpha into a consumer economy is the episode of the spotted horses. One of Flem's employees whips the horse-trading crowd into a frenzy of consuming excitement that the consumers themselves find surprising. The selling of the wild horses represents, as Cleanth Brooks argues, "the world of advertising and Madison Avenue, in this instance set down in a little backwater of a community. . . . The people of Frenchmen's Bend are stirred up to buy what they do not want and cannot afford and will not be able to use." The horses represent something novel and exciting and above all extravagant. As John T. Matthews writes, "they are mainly indistinguishable from each other, and so might as well be mass produced, but they swirl with color like exotic parrots." Not only are the horses not work animals, they represent a dramatic repudiation of the association of animals with work by offering instead the possibility of an outlandish form of play.[43]

What makes Flem Snopes remarkable in a discussion of the meanings of goods is that he believes in neither traditional nor modern views on what goods can do for the individual. He is more unknowable and more mysterious than depictions of materialistic Americans from George Babbitt to Thomas Sutpen to Gordon Gecko because he has no goals in mind for his money and he derives no enjoyment from it. As Donald Kartiganer writes, he embodies "pure acquisitiveness but (is) indifferent to acquisitions."[44] Flem has none of the conventional reasons for wanting money. He does not adopt a traditional upper-class view of goods that sees them as ways to earn the respect of the community. Nor does he adopt a modern view that consumer goods are part of a constant search for new pleasures. And he does not have the Puritan insecurities that, in the interpretation of Max Weber, made accumulation of wealth a sign of God's blessing on those who were doing well in pursuit of their divinely appointed duties.[45] For Flem, what matters is not the uses of wealth but the wealth itself. He uses his goods to try to earn the economic trust of people who can make him more money.

Particularly intriguing here is the attention Faulkner gave to the relation Flem should have with the homes of Jefferson. In the original plan for the Snopes trilogy, Flem in the final volume was to bulldoze the largest homes in Jefferson and replace them with subdivisions.[46] Faulkner decided that instead of having Flem become a real estate mogul he should instead move into a mansion but take no pleasure from it. By leaving out the overtly destructive side, Faulkner emphatically portrays Snopes as a character who cares about nothing but making money and keeping it. Were Flem to become a bulldozing realtor, he would be an active opponent of Jefferson's old upper class and its aristocratic values. He would represent a wealthy and much more menacing culmination of the goals of the first Snopes, who by burning barns and destroying carpets sneered at the goods that either sustained or symbolized wealth and leadership.

Instead of having the destruction of homes as a prominent metaphor and story line, Faulkner made the mansion itself a central feature of the book and the conclusion of the trilogy. When Flem becomes president of the bank, he buys and moves into de Spain's two-story mansion. The importance of its two stories lies in the traditional connection between the big house and leadership. He has columns, two stories high, added to the front of the house to make it conform more clearly to an antebellum version of a classical image.[47]

There are at least three meanings one can express with a large and luxurious home. The traditional meaning of a mansion, rejected by Flem, is the expression of hospitality and paternalism conveyed by a large home that is occasionally open to the public. The traditional upper-class way to express leadership stressed that a mansion should if possible be located on a hill between God and the common folk and that it should have a large room or two where the nonwealthy should occasionally be welcome. Flem has no interest in this traditional form of paternalism. His home is completely private. He leaves some rooms just as de Spain had left them, and Eula hires a Memphis decorator to furnish others, but neither he nor anyone else ever goes into the decorated parts of the house.

The second way to use a large house is the contemporary way—to turn it into a setting for a never-ending series of private ways for the family to amuse itself, with a family room designed for the enjoyment of new technology and a yard with a barbecue and a plastic pool for the kids. The freedom of the modern home supposedly represents a denial of the discipline demanded in the workplace.[48]

If Faulkner had carried out his plan to have Flem destroy the old homes and replace them with suburban houses, Flem would have emerged as a supporter of the modern home. In *Intruder in the Dust*, Faulkner describes modern suburbs in a way that makes clear the challenge they pose to the South of people like Colonel Sartoris and Will Percy. The new homes were

> small new one-storey houses designed in Florida and California set with matching garages in their neat plots of clipped grass and tedious flowerbeds, three and four of them now, a subdivision now in what twenty-five years ago had been considered a little small for one decent front lawn, where the prosperous young married couples lived with two children each and (as soon as they could afford it) an automobile each and the memberships in the country club and the bridge clubs and the junior rotary and chamber of commerce and the patented electric gadgets for cooking and freezing and cleaning and the neat trim colored maids in frilled caps to run them and talk to one another over the telephone from house to house while the

wives in sandals and pants and painted toenails puffed lipstick-
stained cigarettes over shopping bags in the chain groceries and
drugstores. [49]

In short, a large house could provide a great deal of pleasure,
when used by people who seek the constant novelty of the
consumer society. But Flem has no taste for pleasure and
certainly not for novelty. He uses only the dining room and a
bedroom, "except that one room at the back where when he
wasn't in the bed sleeping he was setting in another swivel chair
like the one in the bank, with his feet propped against the side
of the fireplace: not reading, not doing nothing: jest setting with
his hat on, chewing that same little mouth-sized chunk of air he
had been chewing ever since he quit tobacco." Flem makes
only one addition to the house to suit his own tastes: "a little
wood ledge, not even painted, nailed to the front of that hand-
carved hand-painted Mount Vernon mantelpiece at the exact
height for Flem to prop his feet on it."[50] It is that little wood
ledge that distinguishes Flem from so many other materialistic
characters in American fiction, because it shows that he wants
neither modern novelty nor traditional upper-class respectability in using his wealth.

The meaning of Flem's home is mercenary. As a son of the
poor, he intends the mansion and the columns he adds to it to
earn the trust of people who have good reason not to trust him,
simply because people with money in his bank or money they
are thinking about putting into his bank will know that he does
not need to cheat them.

And finally, Linda Snopes Kohl. As Faulkner's only radical
character, she assumes considerable importance in addressing
issues of ideology. Linda's most significant action is her rebellion
against conventions governing, among other things, small-town
life, family life, sexuality, race relations, the class system,
relations between Jews and Gentiles, and international politics.
And she does not merely believe in radical causes; her identity
is defined by very active and often courageous forms of commitment.

One of her many rebellions against convention concerns her indifference to the products of American capitalism. Until the end of the trilogy, Linda shows little interest in consumer products or shopping or expressing herself through goods. Faulkner provides no descriptions of her toys as a child or clothing as a teenager. In a Pascagoula defense community during World War II she feels at ease wearing Rosie the Riveter overalls not just at work but also outside the workplace, and she leaves Jefferson at the end of the trilogy wearing khaki coveralls. Thus, Faulkner clothes his only radical in the genderless garb of a communist worker and has her drive a functionally black automobile not to pursue new pleasures but to buy alcohol in quantities that numb the mind.

The conclusion of the trilogy, in which Flem's murder allows Linda to buy one of the most extravagant consumer goods imaginable, has structural similarities to the end of *As I Lay Dying*. Like Cash and Anse Bundren, Linda is escaping the confinements imposed by her family, and like the Bundrens she marks her escape with a consumer purchase that differs from anything in her past. In each conclusion the characters gain their liberation through the elimination of another character— Anse has Darl sent to an asylum, and of course Linda has Flem murdered. But in Linda the consumer pleasure is much more tragic, because of who she has been. The Jaguar represents the end of her idealism. It is very private, not a group pleasure that a record player can provide. The Jaguar is very fast, not the slow experience the Bundrens can enjoy on the porch after work. Rather than using a consumer product to overturn the confining aspects of life in Yoknapatawpha, Linda uses one to escape the county and its people altogether, with the clear intention of not coming back.

The logic of consumer culture ultimately includes a major contradiction. One side emphasizes the democracy of appearances and the irrelevance of inherited class traditions. Anyone with the money can purchase whatever he or she wants, and the process of choosing helps to link the consumer to other consumers. The other side of consumer culture emphasizes the never-ending search for new experiences. This side is by necessity individualistic, leading eventually to indulgence of the self and even obsession with the self. No matter how fully the consumer is linked to fellow consumers through a shared system of meanings, the desire for novelty ultimately drives the consumer to search for the best goods, the most exciting, the most colorful, the most powerful, the goods that offer the greatest sense of individual satisfaction. A fast car is not good enough, nor is a colorful one, or one with a good stereo or interior. When Linda buys a Jaguar to get the hell out of Yoknapatawpha, she represents Faulkner's suggestion that this primary contradiction of twentieth-century American ideology cannot be reconciled.

Montgomery Ward Snopes, Flem Snopes, and Linda Snopes Kohl take consumer culture to three of its ugliest culminations. Montgomery Ward represents an extreme form of an ultimately empty self-indulgence that can be purchased again and again. In that way the pornography industry becomes the culmination of the promise of the Montgomery Ward catalogue. Flem embodies something close to the opposite. Uninterested in sexual experience or pleasures of any kind, Flem takes the desire to accumulate money to its culmination by refusing to spend it except in ways that will allow him to make more. And Linda embodies the ability of consumer culture to cut people off from shared interests with other people or unity with them.

To summarize, Faulkner seems torn between the personal liberation some of his characters find in becoming consumers and the ultimately destructive uses these three Snopeses make of consumer culture. We are left with the notion of ambivalence—a notion that is unsatisfying largely because it is so unsurprising. If we look to Faulkner's other characters in search of hints of the author's perspective, the watchers and opponents of the Snopeses provide clear critiques of consumer culture. Gavin Stevens sees the liberating power of consumer goods and at one point announces that he feels so good he plans to buy a red necktie. But he cannot come to terms with what he calls the national sex symbol—the automobile. First, he has surrogates lay tacks in the road to blow up a tire on Manfred de Spain's sportscar. Later, he buys a Cadillac but puts it on blocks—a good image of a man torn between old and new and unable to operate in either. V. K. Ratliff is clearly Faulkner's favorite opponent of the Snopeses. And as a sewing machine salesman, he might seem to represent the emerging consumer culture, convincing people, as Cleanth Brooks said of Flem, to buy things they do not need and cannot afford. But sewing machines were unusual consumer goods that encouraged people to stay out of the consumer economy by making their own clothes, as Ratliff himself did. Ratliff's confusion about goods shows itself most clearly when he is baffled to the point of giggling about a seventy-five dollar designer necktie in New York. He initially finds the idea of paying so much money out of the question, but he keeps going back until he finally buys it.

To draw a conclusion about Faulkner's treatment of the issue of consumer culture, we should consider the well known importance Faulkner saw and felt in the past. The postwar America in which Faulkner wrote *The Town* and *The Mansion* showed a remarkable respect for youth and for things that were new. This was the time when Peter Pan was a popular show and Walt Disney built Disneyland, the time when Benjamin Spock wrote about the virtues of the baby exploring his universe, the time when teenagers with guitars were becoming cultural heroes and spokesmen. Faulkner's characters almost always feel the weight of the past, for bad or good. For all his respect for the power of the past, however, he obviously believed that any tradition could produce the need for people to free themselves from it. Had he been able to identify any tradition as the right one, he would not have experienced and fictionally embodied so many of the powerful ambivalences so many Faulkner scholars have analyzed. Faulkner could treat with real respect characters who used the attractions of consumer culture to free themselves from the confining aspects of their own traditions. But

Faulkner was hardly ready to give up on traditions. Traditions have their problems—and their tragedies—but traditions are better than nothing. In the Snopeses he created characters who had no traditions, and when he turned them loose to face the opportunities and contradictions of the consumer society, they ended in destructiveness and self-obsession.

NOTES

1. William Leach, "Transformations in a Culture of Consumption: Women and Department Stores, 1890–1925," *Journal of American History*, 71–72 (September 1984), 319.

2. Thorstein Veblen, *The Theory of the Leisure Class: An Economic Study of Institutions* (New York: New American Library, 1953, orig. pub. 1899); Robert S. Lynd and Helen Merrill Lynd, *Middletown: A Study in Modern American Culture* (New York: A Harvest/HBJ Book, 1956, orig. pub. 1929). For examples of the rapidly growing field of consumer history, see Richard Wightman Fox and T. J. Jackson Lears, eds., *The Culture of Consumption: Critical Essays in American History, 1880–1990* (New York: Pantheon Books, 1983); Simon J. Bronner, ed., *Consuming Visions: Accumulation and Display of Goods in America, 1880–1920* (New York: W. W. Norton, for the Winterthur Museum, 1989); Daniel Horowitz, *The Morality of Spending: Attitudes toward the Consumer Society in America, 1875–1940* (Baltimore: Johns Hopkins University Press, 1985); Roland Marchand, *Advertising the American Dream: Making Way for Modernity, 1920–1940* (Berkeley: University of California Press, 1985); Lawrence Veysey, "A Postmortem on Daniel Bell's Postindustrialism," *American Quarterly* (Spring 1982); Andrew J. Heinze, *Adapting to Abundance: Jewish Immigrants, Mass Consumption, and the Search for American Identity* (New York: Columbia University Press, 1990); Lizabeth A. Cohen, *Making a New Deal: Industrial Workers in Chicago, 1919–1939* (Cambridge: Cambridge University Press, 1990), 99–158; Neil McKendrick, John Brewer, and J. H. Plumb, *The Birth of a Consumer Society: The Commercialization of Eighteenth-Century England* (Bloomington: Indiana University Press, 1982); Colin Campbell, *The Romantic Ethic and the Spirit of Modern Consumerism* (Oxford: Basil Blackwell, 1987).

3. Campbell, *Romantic Ethic:* Jean-Christophe Agnew, "A House of Fiction: Domestic Interiors and the Commodity Aesthetic," in Bronner, ed., *Consuming Visions*.

4. Martha Wolfenstein, "The Emergence of Fun Morality," *Journal of Social Issues*, 7 (1951), 15–25.

5. See Cohen, *Making a New Deal*, 99–158; Lois W. Banner, *American Beauty* (Chicago: University of Chicago Press, 1983), 66–85; John Fiske, *Understanding Popular Culture* (Winchester: Unwin Hyman, 1989), 1–22.

6. William Alexander Percy, *Lanterns on the Levee: Recollections of a Planter's Son* (Baton Rouge: Louisiana State University Press, 1973), 7, 41, 61, 62.

7. Ibid., 143, 13, 62.

8. Ibid., 280.

9. Ibid., 296.

10. Richard Wright, *Black Boy, a Record of Childhood and Youth* (New York: Harper & Row, 1966, orig. pub. 1945), 166, 251.

11. Wright, *American Hunger* (New York: Harper & Row, 1944), 12–13, 14.

12. Ibid., 13, 21, 45.

13. William Faulkner, *The Town* (New York: Vintage Books, 1961, orig. pub. 1957), 171.

14. Faulkner, *Intruder in the Dust* (New York: Random House, 1948), 238–39.

15. See Joseph Blotner, *Faulkner, A Biography*, 1-volume edition (New York: Random House, 1984), 53; David Minter, *William Faulkner, His Life and Work* (Baltimore: Johns Hopkins University Press, 1980), 19.

16. See Minter, *William Faulkner*, 113–164. On the so-called feminization of consumer spending, see Marchand, *Advertising the American Dream*; Leach, "Transformations;" Rachel Bowlby, *Just Looking: Consumer Culture in Dreiser, Gissing and Zola* (New York: Methuen, 1985); Elaine S. Abelson, *When Ladies Go A-Thieving: Middle-Class Shoplifters in the Victorian Department Store* (New York: Oxford University Press, 1989).

17. Minter, *William Faulkner*, 137–164.

18. Faulkner, "A Rose for Emily," in *Collected Stories of William Faulkner* (New York: Random House, 1950), 119–120.

19. Blotner, *Faulkner*, 40.

20. Faulkner, *The Town*, 11, 13.

21. Ibid., 14.

22. John Faulkner, *My Brother Bill, An Affectionate Reminiscence* (New York: Trident Press, 1963), 145.

23. Faulkner, *The Town*, 14. On automobiles as ultimate consumer goods, see Ronald W. Edsforth, *Class Conflict and Cultural Consensus: The Making of a Mass Consumer Society in Flint, Michigan* (New Brunswick: Rutgers University Press, 1967); James Flink, *The Car Culture* (Cambridge: MIT Press, 1975).

24. Faulkner, *The Hamlet* (New York: Vintage Books, 1958, orig. pub. 1940), 36. For a discussion of the "trade ethic," see Donald M. Kartiganer, *The Fragile Thread: The Meaning of Form in Faulkner's Novels* (Amherst: University of Massachusetts Press, 1979), 115–116. For a recent description, see William Ferris, *"You Live and Learn, Then You Die and Forget it All": Ray Lum's Tales of Horses, Mules, and Men*, with a foreword by Eudora Welty (New York: Anchor Books, 1992).

25. Faulkner, *Intruder in the Dust*, 235.

26. See Gavin Wright, *Old South, New South: Revolutions in the Southern Economy Since the Civil War* (New York: Basic Books, 1986).

27. Faulkner, *Light in August* (New York: Vintage Books, 1968, orig. pub. 1932), 23–24.

28. Ibid., 171, 154.

29. Faulkner, *As I Lay Dying* (New York: Vintage Books, 1964, orig. pub. 1930), 19, 110, 111, 218.

30. Ibid., 104–5.

31. Ibid., 247–48.

32. Ibid., 249–50.

33. Minter, *William Faulkner*, 83. See also Margaret M. Dunn, "The Illusion of Freedom in *The Hamlet* and *Go Down, Moses*," in Louis J. Budd and Edwin H. Cody, ed., *On Faulkner: The Best from American Literature* (Durham: Duke University Press, 1989), 235–251.

34. Faulkner, *The Hamlet*, 23.

35. Ibid., 15, 20.

36. Faulkner, *The Mansion* (New York: Random House, 1959), 92. On the distance between Mink and cosmopolitan culture, see Michael Millgate, *The Achievement of William Faulkner* (New York: Random House, 1963), 295; Warren Beck, *Man in Motion: Faulkner's Trilogy* (Madison: University of Wisconsin Press, 1963), 175.

37. On Mink and ideas of honor, see Beck, *Faulkner* (Madison: University of Wisconsin Press, 1976), 649–651; Cleanth Brooks, *William Faulkner, The Yoknapatawpha Country* (New Haven: Yale University Press, 1963), 221; Kartiganer, *Fragile Thread*, 119–120; James Gray Watson, *The Snopes Dilemma: Faulkner's Trilogy* (Coral Gables, FL: University of Miami Press, 1968), 152–160.

38. Faulkner, *The Mansion*, 90.

39. Ibid., 368.

40. See Richard Moreland, *Faulkner and Modernism: Rereading and Rewriting* (Madison: University of Wisconsin Press, 1990), 137.

41. Ted Ownby, "Sewing, The Household Economy, and Notions of Women's Responsibilities in Nineteenth-Century Mississippi," presented at the Arkansas Women's History Institute, Bismarck, AR, October 1991.

42. Gunther Barth, *City People: The Rise of Modern City Culture in Nineteenth-Century America* (New York: Oxford University Press, 1980); Susan Porter Benson, *Counter Cultures: Saleswomen, Managers, and Customers in American Department Stores, 1890–1940* (Urbana: University of Illinois Press, 1988); Leach, "Transformations;" Heinze, *Adapting to Abundance.*

43. Brooks, *William Faulkner*, 185–186; John T. Matthews, "Shortened Stories: Faulkner and the Market," in *Faulkner and the Short Story, Faulkner and Yoknapatawpha, 1990*, ed. Evans Harrington and Ann J. Abadie (Jackson: University Press of Mississippi, 1992), 18. See also Kartiganer, *Fragile Thread*, 115; Watson, *The Snopes Dilemma*, 60–65.

44. Kartiganer, *Fragile Thread*, 119.

45. Max Weber, *The Puritan Ethic and the Spirit of Capitalism*, trans. Talcott Parsons (New York: Charles Scribner's Sons, 1958).

46. Minter, *William Faulkner*, 177.

47. My understanding of the significance of housing in the Snopes trilogy draws on William T. Ruzicka, *Faulkner's Fictive Architecture: The Meaning of Place in the Yoknapatawpha Novels* (Ann Arbor: UMI Research Press, 1987), 69–82.

48. See Clifford E. Clark, Jr., *The American Family Home, 1800–1960* (Chapel Hill: University of North Carolina Press, 1986), 217–244; Kenneth T. Jackson, *Crabgrass Frontier: The Suburbanization of the United States* (New York: Oxford University, 1985).

49. Faulkner, *Intruder in the Dust*, 119–120.

50. Faulkner, *The Mansion*, 155, 156.

Desire and Dismemberment: Faulkner
and the Ideology of Penetration

ANNE GOODWYN JONES

This essay—true to its title, perhaps—falls into parts, whose connection to one another may seem initially obscure, but which will, I hope, become evident as the argument unfolds. The parts appear in something like a chrono-logic. I began the project with the observation that body parts litter the Faulkner corpus. My initial hypothesis was that Faulkner's membered and dis-membered bodies represent and critique the ideology of the stable, unified subject, the coherent self.

I then saw the need to consider first the more general question of ideology itself before focussing on a particular ideol-ogy, much less a critique of it. To illustrate my uses of "ideol-ogy," I chose to read "Dry September" in a new way: as a sophisticated representation of ideology in process.

Meanwhile, back on the dismemberment front, I began to suspect that Faulkner was representing and critiquing another ideology, related to and supporting that of the unified subject but different from it in crucial ways. This ideology had to do with gender, but not with the more familiar notions of the possession and/or loss of the phallus; it had to do with what men *do* with the phallus, with masculine performance. In brief, this ideology linked (male) power with male sexuality—phallus and penis—in a single overdetermined act: the act of entering an "other." I called it the ideology of penetration,[1] and looked for research that might confirm or reject my new hypothesis: that Faulkner's dismembered bodies worked as a critique of the ideology of penetration. No one whose work I read focused specifically on penetration, or called it an "ideology," yet the narrative of penetration became increasingly visible as I read more about (in the words of one title) *The Cultural Construction of Sexuality*,[2] looked more closely at Faulkner criticism, and thought about Faulkner's work in the more general context of Southern literature.

What you read here is preliminary and speculative. My most general argument, or perhaps I should say hunch, is that the "ideology of penetration" (along with resistances and challenges to it) pulls together several "discourses" within Faulkner's work that many critics have commented on separately: gender and sexuality, hunting, art, Southern race and class, power and dominance, and the unified or disseminated self, to name several. Further, it helps us to understand something about the relations between the construction of desire, the construction of sexuality, and the dismemberment of bodies in the Faulkner corpus.

We have several parts to make our way through before we can begin to put the pieces together again with a brief look at Faulkner texts. Those parts concern theories of dismemberment; ideology; "Dry September"; and the ideology of penetration. We will start by remembering Faulkner's dismemberments.

1. Body Parts

Faulkner's bodies have a tendency to fall—or be taken—to pieces.

The split narrator in "Carcassonne" imagines a severed horse whose "several halves [went] thundering on . . . wrapped still in the fury and pride of the charge, not knowing that it was dead."[3] Quentin thinks about cutting off his genitals in *The Sound and the Fury*, and in the short stories "The Leg" and "Crevasse" dismembered parts turn into horrific agents of destruction.

Sometimes people supplement their bodies with more parts,

spare parts: Quentin buys his flatiron fins or gills, Drusilla offers her pistols, Popeye uses his cob. André Bleikasten writes about *Sanctuary*'s bodies that "bodies do not know how to contain and control themselves. . . . Sweat, spittle, vomit, blood—through all those oozings and flowings and outpourings flesh bespeaks its incontinence and inconsistency, announces its carrion future."[4] Faulkner's bodies are either insufficient or excessive, then; they will not stay in their place, bounded by a single simple skin. They fall to pieces, or supplement themselves.

But we must add to this rendering of the individual body a social dimension. For not only does the body not control itself, as Bleikasten has it, but others will assist at its decomposition, whether gladly or no. Addie Bundren has holes drilled into her and otherwise decomposes; Mink Snopes's victim Houston "comes to pieces on him" in *The Hamlet*.[5] In *Mosquitoes*, Gordon makes a statue of an ideal woman who has no legs, no arms, and no head; in *Light in August*, Joe severs Joanna's head, and Percy Grimm Joe's genitals; Linda Snopes Kohl loses her vocal chords in *The Town*, Grumby loses his hand in *The Unvanquished*, Charlotte Rittenmeyer is cut open in *The Wild Palms*. In the original version of *Sanctuary*, a black woman's head is severed on the first page and in the narrative's representation of Temple Drake at the trial, as André Bleikasten has noticed, she is "taken apart, her body disassembled: her hair, her face, her hands, her legs . . . become *membra disjecta*."[6]

How are we to understand these indecorous Faulknerian bodies, these bodies that refuse or are refused their proper bounds? Several interpretive models might tempt us.

2. Discarded Dismemberment Theories

We might take a cue from Carolyn Dean's observation that "images of decapitation, corporal dismemberment, and mutilation, have been common metaphors used by Derrida and Kristeva to disarticulate the Enlightenment concept of the rational, stable self" and to "represent an alternative concept of a subjectivity in flux."[7] Such a reading would see Faulkner's decomposing bodies as representations of the failure of the self to be identical with itself, and thus of Faulkner's challenge to the dominant bourgeois ideology of a "rational, stable self." It might look at "Carcassonne," for example, as a scene of ideological construction: in his imagination, the protagonist reunifies his own dismembered identity by representing the severed horse as whole and living.

Or we might move to psychoanalysis. We could begin with the notion of castration, work with Freud's connection between castration and decapitation in "Medusa's Head," and turn to *Light in August,* which gives us both. Then perhaps we could move to Helene Cixous' revision of Freud in "Castration or Decapitation?" and Luce Irigaray's critique in *This Sex Which Is Not One*.[8] Such a reading would have the advantage of introducing the ideology of gender, the absence of which has been a problem with discussion of the genderless "rational, stable self."

A third possibility might begin by locating dismemberment within the history of racism. Trudier Harris argues that in the black literary tradition of representations of lynchings and burnings, "a castration or some other mutilation usually accompanies the killing in addition to a gathering of trophies from the charred body. . . . Sometimes the crowd lingers to have its picture taken with the victim."[9] One such photograph appears in a volume called *The Black Book:* it shows a group of white men smiling for the photographer, surrounding the remains of a fire in which, barely distinguishable from the logs, lies the charred and broken body of a black man."[10] Such a photograph does ideological labor by representing white people to themselves as whole, living, whitefleshed bodies, constituted as such by their opposition to dismembered, dead, black—insistently black, burnt black—bodies. Still more, those individually unified white bodies are gathered together in a representation of social unity, even identity; the single, or two or three, black bodies are isolated from a black community in order to form the center of this white one, Southern white community constituting itself by dismembering black community. As Trudier Harris puts it, lynchings served powerful ideological purposes by allowing whites to "consolidate themselves against all possible encroachments upon their territory by Blacks."[11] A fascinating inversion of this sort of dismemberment appears in a polemic written by a minister, W. S. Armistead, and published in Tifton, Georgia, in 1903. *The Negro Is a Man, a Reply to Professor Charles Carroll's Book "The Negro Is a Beast, or, In the Image of God"* devotes over 200 pages to human body parts, detailing in each instance—skin, hair, bones, muscles, urinary organs, "organs of generation," and so forth—the lack of difference between black and white bodies. Armistead in effect stitches together these body parts as he dismembers them, to construct out of them a unified, presumably postracial human body.[12]

Interestingly, the shift in Faulkner's reputation that Lawrence Schwartz locates in *Creating Faulkner's Reputation,* a shift that transformed him from obscurity into fame as an "emblem of the freedom of the individual under capitalism," arguably turns upon the issue of dismemberment as well, allowing us to add a fourth, and political, reading of Faulkner's bodies. Schwartz notes that before the Second World War, critics like Bernard De Voto had attacked Faulkner's "fondness for 'rape, mutilation, castration, incest, patricide, lynching, and necrophilia'"; other critics saw his work as "lacking values," and Faulkner feared that he would be remembered only as the "corncob man." Yet after the war, Faulkner was praised for his "steadiness of vision"; in Robert Penn Warren's words, "Faulkner gave his readers a sense of a 'moral reality beneath the crust of history.'"[13] This shift in critical ideology—from Faulkner the debased modern to Faulkner the moral hero—paralleled a shift in the focus of Faulkner's critics, from seeing literary images of dismemberment to seeing literary coherence and unity, the basis for New Critical formal analysis.

The New Critical aesthetic (and its politics) shares with the ideologies of the "rational, stable self," of essentialist gender, and of racial purity, certain assumptions about coherence and radical independence. To this way of thinking (or ideology), the work of art, like the moral system, the "individual," and the gendered and raced man or woman, has a unified and noncontradictory identity that is independent of context and history, and that persists over time. Clearly, then, these readings would overlap: all are preoccupied with ideologies of unity and continuity. In writing that resists such ideologies, we might expect contradiction, incoherence, process, and change. Perhaps these are the meanings of Faulkner's dismembered bodies.

In Part 5, I want to offer another reading of dismemberment and desire, as an alternative to these perhaps predictable readings. At this point I want to shift the focus to what I believe is another related but distinguishable ideological network, which I call the ideology of penetration. I speculate that this ideology, though powerfully disseminated on both sides of the Atlantic culture during Faulkner's lifetime, found a particularly receptive site in the American South, for reasons that I will briefly suggest. If we read Faulkner's work as located within (and at times resisting) this ideological position, we can find some fascinating and perhaps unexpected networks of meaning and representation in the writing of dismemberment. For penetration ideology marshals the organization of a single, directed subject and sees as its goal the (dis)semination of the object—yet carries out this project at the very moment of the most risk to its own coherence. Thus dismemberment comes to represent the origin, goal, and risk of penetration: it represents, in short, the feminine.

Before elaborating, however, on what may now seem a rather odd notion, this "ideology of penetration," I would like to comment briefly on the history and meanings of the more general term "ideology" itself.

3. Detour through Ideology

In their introduction to the collection of papers first presented in Paris at a conference called *Faulkner and Idealism*, Michel

Gresset and Patrick Samway remark that early in the conference, it became clear that widely varying definitions of "ideal" were being assumed, ranging from "utopian" to "ideological."[14] I suspect that may be the case with "ideology" as well. In fact, Terry Eagleton calls it not a word but a "text" because of its multiple, contradictory meanings.[15]

Traditionally understood, ideology is, to quote James Kavanagh, a pejorative term describing an "especially coherent and rigidly held system of political ideas."[16] By this definition, you might be ideological, but I have common sense. In one of the best introductions to the term I have come across, Myra Jehlen wittily describes the conventional (and pejorative) use of "ideology" by literary critics as "a trace of incomplete combustion [in a given literary text] in the transformation of the material of history into the spirit of literature. [Thus] to call a writer 'ideological' was to mean that he or she was less accomplished."[17]

Rather than a system of consciously held ideas, recent literary critics argue that whatever seems common sensical—or rational, or natural, or normal—in a given setting is most likely to be "ideological." Sacvan Bercovitch says it succinctly: "I mean by ideology the . . . system of interlinked ideas, symbols, and beliefs by which a culture—any culture—seeks to justify and perpetuate itself; the web of rhetoric, ritual, and assumption through which society coerces, persuades, and coheres." This "system" or "web" works because it feels like common sense.[18] Two lines of intellectual descent have given birth to this understanding, one from Karl Marx and one from Max Weber.

Marx saw ideology as, in effect, a lie: for him, common sense was false consciousness. For ideology emerged from and sustained an economic base which benefitted the few at the cost of the many by convincing people to believe illusions. Ideology as false consciousness mystified economic reality and thus kept the people docile and even satisfied.[19] Weber, according to Jehlen, viewed ideology in a more positive light. Whereas the Marxist tradition sees ideology as "negative" in its emphasis on the ways ideology misleads and oppresses the already powerless, the other or "positive" tradition, extending from Weber through Karl Mannheim to Clifford Geertz, sees ideology as a productive force, not necessarily oppressive or illusory, and more fundamental than any material base.[20] In a parallel distinction, Sacvan Bercovitch distinguishes the two lines by their capacity to generate, respectively, what he calls "extrinsic" and "intrinsic" critical perspectives.[21] The Marxist tradition is "extrinsic" in that critics presumably stand outside ideology in order to deconstruct it, while the Weber tradition is "intrinsic" in that no critic can speak "outside" ideology; every utterance is by definition ideological, and one's perspective is inevitably "intrinsic." Such a view downplays dominance; nevertheless, it can generate critiques of dominant ideology, or explain their emergence, by arguing that alternative ideologies can develop and can mobilize resistance to a dominant ideology.

Gramsci and Althusser have revised Marx's understanding. Whereas for Marx, ideology consisted of "morality, religion, metaphysics,"[22] and other more or less organized structures of ideas, Antonio Gramsci understood ideology, for the first time, according to Terry Eagleton, as "lived, habitual social practice," practice that evolves from consent as much as, perhaps more than, from state coercion. "Hegemony" is thus a more subtle concept than Marx's "ideology."[23] Gramsci was particularly intrigued with how people could consent to their own oppression. His notion of hegemony—ideology—is "consent" created through social practice and supported by coercion. Louis Althusser moved into still more particularity by locating ideology in the individual's unconscious. Althusser argued that people are "interpellated" (Althusser's coinage) by ideology; in "naming" people, ideology addresses the individual's very sense of identity in an interested manner.

Both hegemony and interpellation are represented in a scene from W. J. Cash's *Mind of the South*. Cash gives us this scene, set in the antebellum South: "There would always be a fine gentleman to lay a familiar hand on the [common white man's] shoulder, to inquire by name after the members of his family, maybe to buy him a drink . . . and to come around eventually to confiding in a hushed voice that that damned nigger-loving Garrison, in Boston— . . . in short . . . to send him home glowing with the sense of participation in the common brotherhood of white men."[24] In this scene of hegemony, of social practice that creates consent to racism, the lower class white man is addressed—interpellated—by the fine gentleman in terms that give him a sense of identity which pleases him at the same time that it obscures the conflict of interest between the two men. Further, the scene both calls upon and perpetuates Southern ideologies beyond the obvious racism: ideologies of personal uniqueness, family cohesion, and masculine solidarity.

Finally, Michel Foucault has refused the concept of ideology altogether. Foucault argues that the notion of ideology depends on three concepts which he calls into question: first, a notion of truth (as opposed to falsehood); second, "something of the order of a subject"; and third, a determining infrastructure. The "ideology" Foucault critiques thus seems to belong to a fairly early moment in the Marxist line of descent. Foucault continues: "I believe that the problem does not consist in drawing the line between that in a discourse which falls under the category of scientificity or truth, and that which comes under some other category, but in seeing historically how effects of truth are produced within discourses which in themselves are neither true nor false."[25] When Foucault turned to examine the history of sexuality, it is in precisely these terms: his interest is in the production and proliferation of the discourses of sexuality, rather than in the question of their accuracy. At moments he sees sexuality itself as an effect of discourse, not something outside it to which discourse refers. "Sexuality must not be thought of as a kind of natural given which power tries to hold in check, or as an obscure domain which knowledge tries gradually to uncover," he writes, but as a product of discourse, a construction of power.[26] We might even, for our purposes, call it an ideology.

However, Foucault perhaps inevitably invokes a distinction

between representation (or discourse or ideology, loosely speaking) and reality when he calls for an alternative to the discourse of sexuality. To "counter the grips of power" he calls upon "the claims of bodies, pleasures, and knowledges, in their multiplicity and their possibility of resistance. The rallying point for the counterattack against the deployment of sexuality ought not to be sex-desire," he writes (sex-desire is already within the discourse of sexuality), but "bodies and pleasures."[27] For our purposes, we can say that Foucault here calls for a new ideology (of bodies and pleasures) to resist the ideology of sexuality. Yet in this passage, Foucault subtly shifts from speaking of discourse ("claims of") to speaking of something like reality ("bodies and pleasures"), which sounds quite like the very "natural given" he earlier rejects. Thus he implies the possibility of truth, a subject, and a (biological) infrastructure.

This issue—reality vs. representation—will become important to the effort to define "ideology of penetration," for if ideology disappears in favor of discourse, and if discourse and only discourse constitutes "reality" (or if reality exists but is unrelated to discourse), then penetration loses its comprehensibility as an ideology that privileges the biological realities of the male body: the phallus is unhinged from the penis.

What then are the meanings of "ideology" that work best for understanding Faulkner and the ideology of penetration? From the earlier Marxists, we can retain the conviction that there is a reality, however understood, and however screened, "outside" a given ideology, to which ideology is an interested and sometimes contradictory response, a response that articulates reality in terms of power. From Gramsci and Althusser, we can retain the focus on social practice and unconscious internalization. From Weber and the sociological tradition, we can retain the possibility of generating multiple (including resisting) ideologies. And from Faulkner, we can retain the focus on the power of discourse and hence the dissemination of power across multiple and local discursive formations, without agreeing that discourse is all there is. Finally, while we can retain the possibility of carrying out a critique of ideology from the Marxists, from the sociologists we can also retain the awareness that no critique is ever "extrinsic," that every critique is itself ideologically based.

Let me suggest a few more characteristics of ideology that will, I hope, prove useful. If ideology consists of a set of shared assumptions, "common sense," a discourse, then this discourse typically fills the space of representability concerning its subject. What cannot be spoken in its terms does not exist. Thus it constructs a sense of fullness or plentitude. Secondly, ideology typically organizes itself by thinking in terms of oppositions—black/white, male/female, inside/outside. Thirdly, those ideological assumptions frequently claim a basis in biology, and thus appear to be natural, possibly permanent and universal, and certainly scientifically verifiable. And finally, ideology has a tendency to mystify or simply ignore its own contradictions.

4. A Story of Ideology

Faulkner's story "Dry September" takes ideology as its very subject. (In the following discussion, "ideology" takes on at times its traditional meaning as a predictable, rigid set of beliefs, and at other times its more complicated meanings spelled out briefly in part 3; I hope these shifts are clear.)

Let us read "Dry September," then, by foregrounding its exposure of the very process of ideological practice. You remember the hot weather, the barbershop, the "rumor, the story, whatever it was . . . about Miss Minnie Cooper and a Negro"; the resisting barber Hawkshaw, the war hero McLendon, the black man Will Mayes, and the white woman Minnie Cooper. The story tends to produce readings that are themselves ideological (in the traditional sense of the term); some don't like it because it "stereotypes spinsters"; some like it because it shows the power and injustice of racism in the South. But such readings of the story (as sexist, or as an attack on racism), however appealing, are hardly more complex than the clichés mouthed by characters in the story. So if we read the story not as a mouthpiece for sexist or anti-racist ideology but as a meditation on and a textual staging of ideology, we will find ourselves in a more complicated space.

A fruitful starting point for analyzing Faulkner's staging of ideology might be André Bleikasten's suggestion twelve years ago that we first "identify the deposits of ideology on the text's surface . . . [that is,] blatantly ideological statements" attributed to major characters.[28] These statements make general, simplifying claims about groups of people and call them common sense; in "Dry September," they are legion. Perhaps the most powerful, because it exposes itself as such pure ideology, is McLendon's "Are you going to let the black sons get away with it until one really does it?"[29] This apparently nonsensical statement—a statement that ignores its own contradictions— makes sense if we consider that McLendon may be quite aware that the referent for "it" is not a material fact (a rape) but instead a discursive reality (a story about rape), and that this awareness is precisely the source of his concern. That is, now that the story is circulating, it is for McLendon and for the community "real"; the "black sons" can't get away with the *story* of a black man's uncontested power. If so, then McLendon understands the process of ideology perfectly. For him to refuse to enter the story's ideological plot and play his part would be tantamount to refusing to punish a "real" rape: it would abrogate his discursive, or ideological, power, which is at least as important as the power of the law, or of his body. Put differently, McLendon chooses to respond to ideological narrative not by testing it against "truth," as Hawkshaw claims to do, but by entering the story and shaping it to his own ends. To use Gramsci's terms, a bit of coercion, whatever the "reason," will produce a lot of consent.

A more careful look at Henry Hawkshaw's appeal to truth as the heroic alternative to McLendon's appeal to ideology, however, exposes its own internal contradictions and conflicts with other, less visible ideologies. Hawkshaw's resistance to McLendon and company is grounded in a repeated sentence: "I know

Will Mayes" (169, 170). This sentence seems to be anti-ideological, both because it makes a truth claim (unlike McLendon's blatantly ideological "who cares?"), and because it makes a particular rather than a general claim. Indeed, this sentence constitutes what seems initially to the reader to be the stable basis for knowledge in the story—where all else is only "rumor," to "know" a person is to know the "truth." On its basis, we like and admire Henry, suspect Minnie, despise McLendon, and see the story as antiracist: Henry shows integrity, loyalty, and courage, we think, in sticking to personal knowledge as far as he is able.

But in fact Henry's claim is no less ideological than McLendon's "black sons." How so? White people's "personal knowledge" of black people—"I know Will Mayes"—is at the heart of Southern paternalism: Zora Neale Hurston makes this clear in "The 'Pet' Negro System," and Quentin suggests it in his racial insights at Harvard in *The Sound and the Fury*.[30] That is, what a white person actually "knows" of any black person—still more what he or she claims to know in a given social context—is a complicated function of masks and silences that serves not "truth" but ideological peace.

In case we missed it, though, Faulkner makes the point explicit when Henry Hawkshaw claims he also "knows" Minnie Cooper. To back up *this* claim, Hawkshaw says, "She's about forty, I reckon. She aint married. That's why I dont believe . . ." and he goes on: "I leave it to you fellows if them ladies that get old without getting married dont have notions. . . . I just know and you fellows know how a woman that never—" and so forth. Hawkshaw proves his "personal knowledge," in short, by backing it up not with personal details but with ideological generalizations, here about women. This is Southern paternalism in its gender rather than its racial mode. And as far as I can tell, we have no reason to assume that Hawkshaw's claims do not represent his own more private thinking as well. We seem to be, with Foucault, in a world where there is no truth, but only claims of truth, only discourse.

In "Dry September" Faulkner shows further how ideology simultaneously simplifies reality and creates contradictory beliefs. Two moments of gender ideology appear in the story. One is the simplifying claim that a woman's word cannot be trusted, and the other is the equally simplifying claim that a woman's word must be believed. Within a sexual context, Minnie's voice is discounted—even by her "friends"—as a spinster's hysterical fantasies; within a racial context, her voice counts, for it tells the "truth" about black men's stepping out of place. Separately, these assumptions work; together they create a contradiction. Separately, both assumptions privilege white men, as opposed to, first, women, and then blacks; together, they construct an incoherent and self-contradictory subject position for the white woman, the person both assumptions address, or interpellate. Minnie's laughter thus may be registering the conflict between the success of her voice in its racial context (where she seems to have initiated a social narrative starring herself), and the failure of her voice in its gendered context where, as a spinster, she is silenced outside the only story of femininity, that of marriage and motherhood. Thus paternalistic ideology has produced the contradiction that a woman's word both cannot and must be trusted.

But there is no ideological context at all here within which Will Mayes's speech can be believed. Instead, he can only try to mimic and thus to exploit the dominant Southern ideologies of personal knowledge and racial superiority for his own resisting purposes. Looking from face to face, calling upon their commitment to "personal knowledge" by using their first names, Will Mayes at the very same moment appeals to the ideology of black inferiority by interpellating them as "white folks" and "captains," and by preceding every first name with a "Mr." Failing at the manipulation of "consent," he whirls and curses and slashes with his "manacles" and fails just as terribly to fight coercion with coercion.

Ideology is about words, representations, naming. In this story of ideological battle the question is, whose word to take:

"Won't you take a white woman's word before a nigger's?"
(169) asks an incredulous youth. At the end of the story, John
McLendon is angry at his wife's refusal to follow his words:
"Haven't I *told* *you* [my emphasis] about sitting up like
this. . . ." he says, and repeats it twice: "Didn't I tell you? . . .
[and again] Didn't I tell you?" (182). Failing at language, he
turns to physical violence, striking his wife and flinging her
across the chair. This sequence pairs him with Will Mayes. It
also pairs gender with racial ideology: he behaves to his wife as
Mayes did to him and his men. And though he seems obviously
the most powerful of the three (in controlling coercion if not
consent), the irony of the juxtaposition exposes him too as a
victim of Southern ideology, in this case the ideology of gender.
Like Mayes but in the register of gender, he fails to control both
consent and coercion, ideology and force. We last see John
McLendon naked, sweating and panting, pressed not against his
wife (which within the ideology would be a sign of success) but,
impotent, against a dusty screen on a dark porch.

But what about the question of truth? Does Faulkner leave
us with Foucault in a world of competing discursive formations,
a world where power is everything and there is no check to it
from the real, perhaps no reality at all? Characters in "Dry
September" seem obsessed with whether "anything happened,"
(170), whether he "really done it to her" (173) whether "anything
really happened" (182). This desire assumes a dichotomy between the "true" facts (what is "real," what "happens") and the
"false" story. And this dichotomy is, of course, what McLendon
challenges when he demands "Are you going to let the black
sons get away with it until one really does it?" Conversely,
Hawkshaw appeals to this dichotomy when he says "I know Will
Mayes; I know Minnie Cooper." Because Hawkshaw is its
advocate, the dichotomy can easily be read as one the text
itself endorses. Even if we are convinced of the inadequacy of
Hawkshaw's "personal knowledge" as a way of finding the facts,
we remain convinced that they can be known, and that they will
vindicate Will Mayes.

Yet a reading that is attentive to ideology might turn the question back to the text, to wonder instead whether the dichotomy serves a purpose within the community. What could the gap between fact and story produce that would benefit whom? Let us observe that the uncertainty itself—the gap— titillates the community. When the women ask if "anything really happened" their eyes are "darkly aglitter, secret and passionate" (182). Their pleasure arguably depends not on knowledge or certainty, but on the tension between "truth" and a lie, on the undetermined space between reality and representation. That is the "space" that prevents narrative closure and thus ensures the continuation of the story. Their pleasure depends, then, on the gap because it depends on the perpetuation of narrative itself. Lack of narrative closure, lack of a clear boundary between discourse and "what really happened," itself produces excitement. The narrator describes the movie theater as a "fairyland," a "*screen*" where—on the other hand—"*life* began to unfold, beautiful and passionate and sad," a "silver *dream*" where "*life* [is] caught in its terrible and beautiful mutations" (181, my emphasis). Even if there is a reality that is separable from discourse, these people don't want to know about it.

But what is the narrator's stake in the question of ideology? Indeed, the narrator's own representations at times foreground his (or her) own simultaneous location within and awareness of ideological construction, a location both "extrinsic" and "intrinsic." For example, the narrator says that McLendon and the barber "looked like men of different races" (172). Such a statement suggests the need to render the story within ideological categories at the same time that it exposes the constructedness of racial ideology by using putatively "natural" and biologically based race categories in an ideologically inappropriate setting, that is, in the context of trying to describe two "obviously" white men.

The narrator's self-representation as both inside and outside racial ideology should alert us to attend to our own assumptions

and stakes as readers. While we readily recognize the obvious
ideology that circulates in the story—the ideas that black men
rape white women, or that spinsters are desperate for attention—we are less likely to recognize our own tendency to fill in
the gaps of the narrative with silent, probably ideological,
assumptions. Yet if we leap to conclusions unawares, we are
invited by an ideological analysis of the story to notice those
leaps and ask why those conclusions. Faulkner's work is known
generally for the scenes and voices that are not represented, for
example Temple's rape in *Sanctuary* and Caddy's voice in *The
Sound and the Fury*. In "Dry September" the absences are
critical: we are never shown a scene of Will Mayes's lynching,
nor are we given a scene either of Minnie Cooper's being
accosted by a "Negro" or of her inventing a story to that effect.
Yet critics almost invariably conclude that some of these at least
are "facts." Surely this is Faulkner's last twist on ideology: he
dramatizes its power to fill in with its own story the gaps
between the lines. For many readers, that story is antiracist but
still sexist: Minnie did it, not Will Mayes. And if, instead of
leaping, we dally in the pleasures of uncertainty, we are invited
to question the structure that permits such pleasures, and the
implications and the costs of deferral. For many readers, deferral places us with the town, in the position of voyeurs. Whether
we find our pleasure in filling in the gaps of the story, or in
keeping those gaps open as questions, "Dry September" asks us
to see that our responses are already coded in the story, and to
consider their stakes and implications.

I began by recalling some of Faulkner's numerous scenes
of bodily dismemberment, and by suggesting that we might
supplement several possible ideological readings of those scenes
of dismemberment by considering an ideology of penetration
that has been particularly powerful in the South. As the men
drive towards the vats with Will Mayes, "the narrow tunnel of
the road rushed up and past. Their motion was like an extinct
furnace blast: cooler, but utterly dead" (179). This passage
suggests, in its self-contradictory imagery of a cool, dead furnace

blast, what the end of the story will make explicit—the actual powerlessness of the men. Though their own motion here is represented as penetration, then, their blasting down the narrow tunnel is already extinct, an impotent penetration, a contradiction in terms. And if we do fill in the gaps of "Dry September"—itself a form of penetration—with the assumption that Will Mayes dies stuffed into a cylindrical vat at the brick kiln, then perhaps we can venture further to read that death as a parodic penetration, a lyncher's grotesque exaggeration, as charred skin parodies blackness, of the putative crime of raping a white woman. Such a reading seems farfetched, perhaps; I hope it will seem less so as I try to convince you that penetration can be found throughout Faulkner's texts, and that his representations of penetration both invoke and call into question the multiple ideological functions of this act, an act which represents even more clearly than possession of the phallus the complicated ideological meanings of masculinity.

5. Penetrating Penetration

What then is this ideology of penetration? I imagine most of us have a pretty good idea, for it is still widely deployed. The ideology of penetration constructs masculinity not through a biological fact but through a biological act that is read as both power and pleasure.

Unlike the question of the phallus, which is associated with the young child and the Oedipal tasks, the ideology of penetration addresses its subjects as they enter adulthood. Having a penis is a necessary but not sufficient condition for manhood, it says; now it's what you do with it that counts. And there is one main thing that counts: penetration. Impotence is ideologically related to penetration, though not in exact opposition to it: a recent *American Heritage Dictionary* defines impotence as the inability to carry out sexual intercourse, that is, the failure to penetrate. Such definitions of impotence silently exclude from the field of sexual practices that might construct masculinity—

"potencies"—all that do not involve a man's penetration of another person. But failure to penetrate is not quite as humiliating as being penetrated oneself: the ideological opposite to penetration is to be penetrated.

Who is the "penetratee"? We might initially assume that she is female; certainly that would explain the gender/power equations established by the ideology of penetration—females beneath men. Furthermore, it is plausible to speculate that this ideology emerged to ensure successful reproduction, making certain the "seed" gets to the right place, neither spilled nor distracted elsewhere. Yet historically, the ideology of penetration, though it has been constant in privileging penetration over being penetrated, has not always cared about the sex of the partner, hence about reproduction. In ancient Greece, the definition of natural and unnatural sexual acts, according to John J. Winkler in *The Constraints of Desire*, had to do with the social hierarchy, not with gender. Thus "a natural sexual act was one in which a man penetrated a social inferior" and an "'unnatural' sexual act was one that did not involve any representation of the social hierarchy."[31] (Women were not socially inferior in every case.) Clearly, penetration was a sign of social dominance. Thus, in Lillian Faderman's words, "a woman penetrating another woman would have been considered unnatural because it involved neither penises that penetrate nor the articulation of relative status"; a "man penetrating another male who was his social equal was also considered 'unnatural,' certainly not because of the nature of the act in itself, but rather because it had no meaning in terms of articulating the social hierarchy."[32] A man's incest with his son, then, though "unconventional," was still natural. In *Making Sex*, Thomas Laqueur claims that in Greek homosexual practices, "the active male, the one who penetrates in anal intercourse, or the passive female, the one who is rubbed against, did not threaten the social order. It was the weak, womanly male partner who was deeply flawed, medically and morally. His very countenance proclaimed his nature: *pathicus*, the one being penetrated . . .

mollis, the passive, effeminate one. Conversely it was the *tribade*, the woman playing the role of the man, who was condemned and who, like the mollis, was said to be the victim of a wicked imagination. [Their actions] were . . . unnatural not because they violated natural heterosexuality but because they played out—literally embodied—radical, culturally unacceptable reversals of power and prestige"[33]

In Marlon Riggs's 1989 film *Tongues Untied*, two black gay men are described as arguing publicly about who is whose "bitch," a position which both angrily reject. The argument turns on who penetrates whom; the "loser" accepts his female name along with his sexual position. Clearly the sex of the partner is less important to the construction of gender here than the act of penetration, and the act of penetration is inextricable from questions of physical and social power. If, in short, sexuality is as Foucault described it, " 'an especially dense transfer point for relations of power,' " then the ideology of penetration is a focal point of that intersection.[34]

The question of sexual pleasure is likewise connected to the question of power. To enjoy being penetrated, within this ideology, it is necessary to enjoy being powerless, submissive, passive, and inferior—or to rename that position as, for example, open, giving, and receptive. When I was a teenager in the early 1960s, I remember reading the current sex manual for women, Marie Robinson's *The Power of Sexual Surrender*, whose title represents one such Orwellian effort.[35] Unless (and perhaps even if) successfully renamed, masochism then is the trajectory of being penetrated. On the other hand, to enjoy penetrating, one need only enjoy power, dominance, activity, and superiority—in a caustic mood, one might call this a complete list of the pleasures of Western patriarchy—and the pleasures inevitably merge with one another, as reports of sexual harassment repeatedly remind us.

The ideology of penetration thus harnesses the multiplicities of Foucault's "bodies and pleasures"—desire—to a single simple narrative, a narrative of entry, and a single protagonist, the one who enters. The term "penetrate" comes from the Latin for "interior of a house." The narrative tells of entering that house. The house is often, but not always, female, but the protagonist is always both biologically and culturally a man.

The ideology then loads that narrative with multiple meanings, overdetermining and thus enhancing its power. Penetration comes to mean not simply bodily pleasure, not even simply power as opposed to impotence, but also courage, for it can be risky to enter a dark house. Sometimes it means violent entry, for to penetrate also means to pierce. The military uses are legion: a successful venture will penetrate enemy ground, etc. Further, penetration constructs and means a focused, purposeful, unified identity, in contrast to an identity that is diffuse, purposeless, fragmented. In fact, one dictionary definition for "penetrate" is "to cause [an object] to be permeated or diffused."[36]

The idea of penetration thus is instrumental in the construction and buttressing of crucial Western dichotomies: outside and inside, subject and object, active and passive. Its usefulness may be a function of its high risk. For the idea of penetration locates its meaning at the very moment of these dichotomies' greatest vulnerability, the moment preceding (male) orgasm. Orgasm is conventionally represented as *loss* of control, even loss of identity itself. It is a condition when inside and outside, subject and object, active and passive no longer have such clear meanings: the moment when the dichotomies disappear. Thus penetration sets itself up in the face of the dissolution of the very dichotomies which it constructs.[37]

Finally, this overdetermined ideology of penetration begins to colonize—itself penetrates—discourses that are otherwise distinct from the discourse of sexuality. Dictionary definitions of the term itself include not only the discourse of war (another military example: "penetration" is the "depth reached by a projectile after hitting its target"), but of subjectivity (to penetrate is "to affect deeply," presumably by piercing someone's defenses), and of knowledge (to penetrate is "to grasp the inner significance of [something]"). Literary critics and teachers "know" that a "penetrating analysis" is powerful and focused; it goes deep into the text to find and bring out the truth, instead of skittering around on the surfaces.[38] Indeed, any boundary—or hole—can evoke the ideology of penetration: one could penetrate a group or a social class, an "inner circle," for example, as well.

During Faulkner's youth and adulthood, this sexual ideology was particularly powerful. The beliefs and instructions in the most widely used marriage manuals during the 1920s and 30s, manuals that were based on the work of sexologists like Havelock Ellis, depend on such an ideology. The sexual universe in which these beliefs constituted what was natural, normal, and desirable was the sexual universe Faulkner inevitably inhabited.

Joseph Blotner's study of Faulkner's library shows no volumes that can even remotely be called marriage or sex manuals, even though it does include publications on bird dogs (*Handling Your Hunting Dog*) and character building (*Character: How to Strengthen It*).[39] Yet it seems unlikely that, given his curiosity and his sensuality, Faulkner would have failed to find the occasion to read such works. These manuals were widely available, likely to be found on a bedroom shelf in many middle-class homes. The most popular, and the first to bring modern thought to bear on sexuality in marriage, was Theodore H. Van de Velde's *Ideal Marriage*. First published in 1926, it was reprinted steadily through the 1950s by Random House. But even in the unlikely event that Faulkner avoided such reading—as he claimed about his evident familiarity with Freud—it would have been nearly impossible for him to escape the ideas. For, more than Freud's, which Faulkner admitted having picked up in less studious venues than a library, the ideas in the sex manuals were "in the air." Anyone concerned about sexuality would have found it difficult to avoid them, in magazines, in films, in conversations, and in social practice, if not in books. Before looking more closely at Van de Velde's prototypical work, I will draw on the work of Jeffrey Weeks, Pat Caplan, and

Margaret Jackson to establish the intellectual background for this popularizing doctor's work.[40]

Weeks reads Krafft-Ebing as the modern source of the notion that male sexuality was so powerful a drive that it was finally out of men's control. Krafft-Ebing wrote that male sexuality is a "'natural instinct' which 'with all conquering force and might demands fulfillment.'"[41] If its demands were not met in consensual sex, they would find expression in rape—or, if still unexpressed, in the man's consequent mental illness.

Jackson locates Havelock Ellis as the first to compare male sexuality not just to animal sexuality, but to animals hunting and killing prey. This made it easy to move to the conclusion that "pain and violence were inherent" in the sexual act, and that for males to exert power over others was equally natural and unstoppable.

In this ideology, women's sexuality depended entirely on men's; there is no notion of real female sexual autonomy. For women, pleasure comes ultimately in penetration, and penetration is, it is assumed, painful; if women seem resistant and fearful, the manuals counsel, this is to be understood as their actual desire to be conquered, especially if they have had some sexual experience. According to one manual, most women "'wanted to be deeply, even savagely penetrated, even if that penetration should imply suffering.'" Women's orgasms sometimes required being beaten and brutalized.[42]

The wise woman masked her own immediate pleasure to focus on the man's: a woman was taught to "'restrain herself at passionate moments' to keep him 'eager in his pursuit.'"[43] The correct positions for intercourse were not necessarily those that gave her the greatest pleasure, but those that represented the man's active and dominant role. One manual counsels: "The only [sexual] positions which should be regularly adopted are those which allow the man 'to entirely play the active part allotted to him.'"[44] A female sex specialist, Helena Wright, called this "educating the vagina." The point for her was to teach women to enjoy "vaginal orgasm by means of penile penetration."[45] Despite his innovations in other areas of sexual ideology, Freud supported this idea, in his argument that womanhood means abandoning clitoral for "vaginal" orgasm.[46]

The sexual "problems" that were defined as such by this ideology focused predictably on male "impotence" and female "frigidity." Impotence was defined as "inability to sustain an erection adequate to full and prolonged penetration"; frigidity was defined as a woman's failure to achieve orgasm as a result of penile penetration.[47] It is evident that such definitions not only pathologize all nonheterosexual pleasure, but tend to pathologize any kind of heterosexual pleasure other than (or, more accurately, not culminating in) male penetration, thus enforcing penetration as the natural sexual act.

Normal sex, then, is defined in terms of penetration alone, and penetration is represented as an act of power, violence, and control. Interestingly, this intensification of the ideology of penetration took shape exactly as women were gaining political and economic independence after World War I, and as men were feeling the disempowerments consequent upon the war. The social and political implications of a sexual discourse that denied female sexual autonomy and enforced male sexual dominance seem inescapable, whether "intended" or not.

At the time, however, this interpretation of the manuals' ideology—the argument that these manuals denied female autonomy and rewarded male dominance—would have seemed odd at best. For what was new about the manuals was their emphasis on sex as an end in itself (within marriage), on female satisfaction, and on mutuality and equality between men and women. This new norm (for the middle class) was called "companionate marriage." Theodore Van de Velde's was the first manual to spin out the logic of such a norm, and to detail—quite remarkably—the techniques of a considerable variety of sexual possibilities in marriage.[48]

Yet even the avant-garde and very popular *Ideal Marriage* reads today as a conflicted and contradictory document. Its arguments for companionate marriage are silently subverted by its arguments for male supremacy—and vice versa. At other moments, its efforts to rhetorically marry an ideology of equality to one of dominance and submission produce a rhetoric of doubletalk, in which woman's submission becomes triumph, and man's dominance becomes sexual sensitivity. John D'Emilio and Estelle Freedman note that the twentieth century "resonated with the past even as it articulated something decidedly new and modern" about sex.[49] They cite as an example the continuity of a contrast between male focus on physical sex and female interest in "spiritual communion." Yet, they claim, over time "the disengagement of sexuality from polarized gender definitions weakened certain barriers to sexual expression in marriage."[50] Despite its apparent modernity, I find that *Ideal Marriage* instead reinforces bipolar gender. It seeks to weld the mutuality and equality of companionate marriage to the power relations (and thus polarized gender definitions) of patriarchal marriage, and the effect is a document that unravels its own premises. Interestingly, it is penetration that once again takes center stage.

The specific problem that *Ideal Marriage* implicitly tries to resolve, and that constructs what now appear to be its contradictions, is the problem of female desire. How can Van de Velde encourage and endorse the development of female desire (which he insists adds to male sexual pleasure and sense of worth) and yet retain male dominance?[51] To encourage female desire runs the risk of encouraging female autonomy, which will open Pandora's box. The solution is to teach the female to desire domination, or in Jackson's title phrase, to "eroticize women's oppression."[52]

Van de Velde acknowledges—indeed, insists angrily—that literal sexual dominance by the man is counterproductive. Brutality and insensitivity have no place in "normal" marriage. But Van de Velde shifts questions of dominance to more subtle arenas, arenas of language. Both the public discourse of sexuality to which his book gives access and the narratives of mutual pleasure he invents for his readers remain coded as exclusively the domain of men. For, like most marriage/sex manuals, his was directed to men, not women; their purpose was to show men how to teach their wives to enjoy sex. Thus men—led by a male doctor, Van de Velde—continue their control over the discursive determination of the "normal." The discourse of medicine is added to that of science, and offered on a plate to husbands. "There is a striking consensus of opinion among serious specialists . . ." he writes, "that the average woman of our time and clime, must *learn* to develop specific sexual enjoyment, and only gradually attains to the orgasm in co-itus. . . . The wife must be *taught*, not only how to behave in coitus, but, above all, how and what to feel in this unique act! . . . And the teacher is her husband."[53]

The contradictions in Van de Velde's argument deserve to be presented in some detail. On the one hand, Van de Velde insists upon the need for woman's sexual pleasure and satisfaction, defined as female orgasm. He focuses on the clitoris as a primary site for her sexual pleasure, even allowing the possibility of a clitoral orgasm. Van de Velde recognizes the existence of female masturbation, and endorses it as a way to gain sexual experience. He discusses the "instinctive" fear and reluctance of most women to be penetrated for the first time, and tells his readers that a bad experience can subsequently confirm their reluc-tance. He insists on the need for mutuality and equality in every phase of the sexual relationship, including emotional awareness and sensitivity. He even argues that the sexual position that gives women (and men) the most pleasure is the "equestrian," or woman astride, and "admits" that the sexually experienced woman is inevitably "more potent"—i.e., able to enjoy sex longer and more frequently—than the experienced man: "The sexual vigor, efficiency (and technically *tolerance*) of the healthy, erotically awakened woman is very great; decidedly greater, indeed, than the potency of the average man" (267). All these add up to an awareness and endorsement of a distinctive and powerful female sexual desire.

Yet Van de Velde in a number of ways seeks to control this

desire even as he urges equality and mutuality. First, Van de Velde uses his rhetorical power to define the "normal": he refuses to discuss or even to name the abnormal "perversions" he alludes to; and he expands the territory of the "normal" by emphasizing that every act he does discuss is entirely normal. Yet normalcy means bipolar gender. "[Man's] main interest and preoccupation [is] his work; whereas [woman's] nature, more profoundly and exclusively emotional, is dependent on personal relationships," he claims (3). Indeed, "at the supreme acme [of sex] the archetypal characteristics appear—power in the man's aspect and expression, tenderness in the woman's" (247).

At crucial points his expansion of the definitions of normal marital sex receives qualifiers based on gender polarities. Although woman astride is the most pleasurable position for both partners, for example ("the main decisive factor in the choice of this attitude must be the wish to experience the keenest possible excitement and gratification"), it should be indulged in very infrequently: "the main disadvantage in . . . frequent practice of the astride attitude lies in the complete passivity of the man and the exclusive activity of his partner. This is directly contrary to the natural relationship of the sexes, and must bring unfavorable consequences if it becomes habitual" (223). On the other hand, the "habitual" or "normal" (missionary position) attitude "expresses the man's intense unconscious urge to *feel that he both protects and possesses* his partner, and equally the *corresponding psychic needs* of the woman [to be protected and possessed] (213).

Most startlingly, Van de Velde claims that "what both man and woman, driven by obscure primitive urges, wish to feel in the sexual act, is the essential force of *maleness*, which expresses itself in a sort of violent and absolute *possession* of the woman. And so both of them can and do exult in a certain degree of male aggression and dominance—whether actual or apparent—which proclaims this essential force (158–59).[54]

This male focus helps to explain his narration of coitus. In Van de Velde's story, "the" sex act (which he calls not coitus but "communion," in keeping with his refusal to separate physical from emotional concerns) is defined entirely in terms of penetration. It begins with "immissio penis" and ends with withdrawal. "Sexual communion (coitus, copulation, the sexual act, or connection or intercourse) is the third act in the love drama. It begins with the insertion of the male penis (or *phallos* as the Greeks termed the erect and active organ) into the female vagina (*immissio penis*); and reaches culmination in the ejaculation of semen into the vagina, and in the approximately simultaneous orgasm or summit of enjoyment in both partners. Communion ends when the phallos is removed from the vagina" (172). The woman's sexual experience naturally dovetails (and—contradictorily—must be taught to dovetail) exactly with this narrative. The woman's orgasm comes naturally as a direct and immediate response to her husband's, and the flow of ejaculate offers her the highest bliss she can feel. In a very interesting if profoundly implausible appropriation of the woman's voice, Van de Velde writes that

> We must admit that only few women are at present capable of observing and recording their own sensations, and then subsequently of analyzing them; and a certain practice is necessary. In cases where it is possible to question and receive a coherent answer, we find some individual instances of orgasm in response to the gush of semen. The majority of women who can be articulate on this subject express themselves in this sense: "After the accumulated tension of the preceding contacts and stimuli has brought me to a state of intense anticipation and excitement, I feel the onset of the orgasm at the precise instant that I perceive the first convulsive contractions of the phallos in the vulva and vagina, and simultaneously the orgastic spasms of my husband's whole body. The ecstasy of this supreme moment is such that its increase by further stimuli would be impossible and beyond my power to endure. Then—I feel the liquid torrent of the ejaculate—which gives a perfectly distinct sensation—as *gloriously soothing* and refreshing at the same time. It enables me to receive unimpaired delight and benefit from the concluding rhythmic ejaculatory movements, without overstrain. These stimuli, afforded by the masculine spasms, and the soothing libations of the seminal liquid are so complete and harmonious that

my enjoyment remains at its summit, until my husband's orgasm ceases, when mine also very gradually and slowly subsides (184).

If by chance she suffers from what Van de Velde calls "infantile genitality" (supposedly a physiological as well as psychological condition for many women, having to do with inadequately developed genitalia and sexual desire), it can finally be overcome only by successful penetrative sex. In fact, "it is significant that the clitoris, in common with the rest of the female genital apparatus, only attains its full development and dimensions with regular and constant sexual intercourse" (201).

Other strategies which Van de Velde encourages—such as oral sex—are ancillary to simultaneous penetrative orgasm, and should never become the main event. He asks: "Does the habitual exaggeration of prolonged coitus by the Hindoos, Javanese, and other Orientals, *really give the woman the fullest extent of pleasure, from phallic friction in the vagina?* I am inclined to doubt it, *because such deliberate distraction of the man's attention would probably imply some degree of local passivity—or at least much less frequent and vigorous phallic motions*. And in any case it is fairly certain that *prolonged passivity in coitus* is out of the question for men of white Western races in modern civilization, on purely aesthetic grounds" (201). (Aesthetic? One hears the mystifying diction of ideology . . .) Though he claims that he deliberately omits discussion of birth control in order to discuss it in a different context, he repeatedly argues that "coitus condomatus" and coitus with a "rubber cap" (186) are unsatisfactory and deleterious for both partners. (For the woman, for example, it makes the flow of ejaculate impossible to feel.) Further, "she runs some risk in the long run . . . of local congestion and unrelieved tension, which is far from negligible whether physically or psychically, especially if there is an individual tendency to neuroses" (186). Speaking for the woman again seems to be a way of stating man's interests.

Perhaps most disturbing of all, and most suggestive, is Van

de Velde's belief that sexual attraction is all that keeps the sexes out of mortal combat: "As soon as sexual attraction is extinguished, *sexual repulsion and enmity* manifests itself" (181). Indeed, "the coital bite can be given out of *concentrated sexual hatred:* . . . Only a very superficial observer can miss the primitive repulsion and antagonism between the sexes which are as real as and more permanent than the attraction. The attraction may, and often does, prevail for a time; but the antipathy is there, and its expression is much wider and often quite as vigorous. Underneath love there always lies in wait hatred" (161). Almost in explanation, Wilhelm Stekel observed about the semiotics of "frigidity" (1926) that "to be roused by a man means acknowledging oneself as conquered."[55] The urgency of making good sex, and of Van de Velde's book that teaches how to do it, may lie ultimately in fear.

In *Ideal Marriage* then, the woman does not initiate. She responds: first to her husband's tutelage, and later to his penetration, orgasm, and ejaculation. She has nothing to teach him beyond her own preferences; she does not teach because she does not "know," as Van de Velde and his male readers do, a larger context of "information" about sexual behavior. All she "knows" is what she experiences and what her husband teaches her. Literally, of course, women did read the book. A book like this would often have been shared, and was no doubt designed for the mass market it quickly reached and steadily maintained. Yet the impact of reading a book ostensibly written for men— even with full "permission"—is to subtly disempower a woman reader, constructing her with every (non)interpellation as an interloper on the male turf of sexual discourse and hence sexual knowledge and power.

Ideal Marriage thus represents ambivalences that point to a historical moment in which differing discourses of women's sexuality were contending. One discourse still argued for her passivity and essential "anesthesia" or frigidity, at the very least for her lesser desire (arguments that Van de Velde is at pains to refute). Another, the emerging discourse that would increasingly dominate the twentieth century, argued for her sexual desire and ultimately her right to sexual (and other forms of) knowledge, initiative, power, and autonomy.

In sum, Van de Velde seeks to encourage female desire yet harness it to male knowledge and power, to masculine control, no matter how sensitive and respectful its expression. Men have exclusive access to more than personal knowledge; even knowledge that men are "less potent" than women as experienced adults is comforting and empowering to an isolated man. And the story of sexual experience—though Van de Velde encourages a variety of positions and methods, insists on female satisfaction, and reiterates the importance of both partners being alert to relational and emotional realities—is narrated exclusively in terms of the act of male penetration and ejaculation within the vagina. This not only privileges the traditional male point of view, but constructs male sexuality itself narrowly and exclusively as a narrative of entry. And that narrative of entry—into a woman, into a text, into a discourse—is primarily a narrative of the pleasures of power, the ideology of penetration. It is no wonder that "the husband of one woman declared to me that the merging and saturation of the beloved person of his wife with the product of his sexual activity, as shown by the faint tang of semen in her breath [from the total body saturation effected by vaginal ejaculation], and the reminder of the delight felt in the act, had both appealed to his imagination so strongly that he experienced a renewed transport" (33). In "penetrating" her he has "permeated" and "diffused" her as well; now he is, in effect, making love to himself.

When female desire extends beyond sexual desire, the problem becomes clearer: desire for entry into the professions, for access to public power, for freedom of movement, and for freedom to choose sexual partners will require (indeed by 1926 are already requiring) more subtle forms of masculine control. Interestingly, the only freedom for women unequivocally endorsed by the sex manuals was the freedom of marital sexual pleasure. Otherwise, one would have been forced into a radical rethinking of the meaning of power and control, and perhaps the rejection of patriarchal models. Neither Van de Velde nor Faulkner, in my opinion, is ready for that; in both writers, we see played out the crisis of ambivalence created by these conflicting discourses of female desire and male control, and the effort to resolve that ambivalence by recuperating female desire into patriarchal ideology. For Faulkner, however, as I hope to demonstrate, the conflict is complicated by his capacity and desire to locate himself in the position of the woman.

For reasons that I will suggest in a moment, the ideology of penetration seems at least to me to have been (perhaps it still is) particularly powerful in the literature of the South. Eudora Welty explores it in various ways, most directly in her story "At the Landing," for example, in which a young girl loves the boy who rapes her. Margaret Mitchell actively celebrates it in Rhett's rape of Scarlett, and in *Let Us Now Praise Famous Men* James Agee agonizes over his "entries" into the houses and minds of the male sharecroppers while at the same time representing female interiority, especially women's sexual desire for him, with no apparent misgivings. Even the New Criticism developed a literary theory based on the image of the work of art as a whole and inviolable—read impenetrable—entity, a well-wrought urn.

It makes a certain sense that Southerners would be preoccupied with penetration. Mary Douglas, in *Purity and Danger*, shows how the human body becomes a metaphor for a society, representing its vulnerability at boundaries and "orifices."[56] The South had invented itself as a separate body before the Civil War, yet it was to be penetrated by Northern troops. Within the plantation household, both before and after the war, the geographical intimacy of blacks and whites, men and women, aristocrats and working class, was enabled by an elaborate code that constructed distance, distance whose violation was most powerfully represented by the image of a black man penetrating a white woman. In short, the South (using its conventional meaning as the dominant interests in the South) had particular reasons to be concerned with questions of power and powerlessness, boundaries and penetrations, sex and sexuality. It is no wonder the ideology took on such complex and visible power there.

6. Faulkner at Last

Given the context of this rather prohibitive discourse of sexuality, the variety of sexualities Faulkner allowed himself to imagine is remarkable. Without a doubt, these issues of sexual ideology affected his personal life; Panthea Broughton and Noel Polk have written essays that explore certain literary and biographical connections that point to this conclusion.[57] Yet in Faulkner's fiction we can see perhaps a wider range of responses than was possible to him in his life, responses that both represent this ideology, frequently in its full horrors, and articulate what can be read as forms of resistance to it, of critique. Consider for example Thomas Sutpen, whose goals include penetrating the patriarchal aristocracy by penetrating a woman who can produce a son; Ike Snopes, whose one effort to penetrate his beloved ends in failure but preserves his love; or Quentin Compson, whose confusion between sexual penetration and the use of weapons structures his ideas about sex.

Faulkner, like many Southern men, but especially as a Southern male *artist*, identified with both "sides" in penetration ideology—that is, the penetrator and the penetratee. This was evidently the case when the ideology was displaced onto regional identity and aesthetic theory, so that the identification with the "female" position was unavoidable (*qua* Southerner and artist), but it appears even as an explicitly sexual set of representations. The sites and forms of resistance and other responses that were available to him, then, were multiple, because the points of interpellation by the ideology were multiple, which is another way of saying that, as for all Southerners, Faulkner's identities were many and sometimes embattled ("I *dont* hate the South"). Through his "masculinity" (as defined by the ideology of penetration) Faulkner explored the ideology's focus on successful performance, dominance, a focused sense of identity, the power of speech, and sexual autonomy; through his "femininity," he explored its emphasis on violent intrusion, submission, diffused and passive subjectivity, speechlessness, and lack of sexual autonomy. Thus he could represent, expose, endorse, and dismember the contradictions and simplifications of an ideology that claimed to make men.

Any Faulkner work could be profitably examined in terms of this ideological context. The key scene of the ideology pervades the fiction in various displacements: people enter doors and windows and houses, they hunt, they pierce other people with knives, and they do all this in frequently sexualized language. On the other "side" of the ideology is the repetitive figure of the urn, whether "still unravished" or cracked and bleeding. Like many artists, Faulkner saw himself as a (feminine) "vessel" for his art,[58] implying a sort of penetration of himself, the "down" position in the ideology. Perhaps that awareness fueled what Bleikasten called a "fierce resentment of any violation of his private self," of being penetrated against his will. At the same time he wanted, shifting to his biological gender, to "*father* an 'intact world of his own'" (my emphasis).[59] That world, the world of Yoknapatawpha and beyond, the world of art, is thus ("intact") figured as a virginal woman and a daughter, a favorite Faulknerian image of wholeness and integrity. Two of his novels, *Light in August* and *Absalom, Absalom!*, bore the same early title, "Dark House," associating them with femininity. John Irwin enters this discourse himself in his conclusion to *Doubling and Incest, Repetition and Revenge*. He writes that

> Faulkner realized that it is precisely because the novelist stands outside the dark door, wanting to enter the dark room but unable to, that he *is* a novelist, that he must imagine what takes place beyond the door. Indeed, it is just that tension toward the dark room that he cannot enter that makes that room the source of all his imaginings—the womb of art. He understood that a writer's relation to his material and to the work of art is always a loss, a separation, a

cutting off, a self-castration that transforms the masculine artist into the feminine-masculine vase of the work.[60]

By this reading, failing to penetrate is a castration that ironically (re)produces the feminine novel.

To be seen as the "corncob man" was then to be seen as the polar opposite to his preferred ideologically feminine position, the vessel out of which would come an urn. Yet inscribed on the urn itself—Keats's urn—is the ideology of penetration: "maidens loth," youths in "mad pursuit," and a "still unravished bride." And Faulkner did not hesitate to represent that ideology with what seems like endorsement. In *Sanctuary*, Ruby explains to Temple what it means to be wanted by a "real" man: "If he is just man enough to call you whore, you'll say Yes Yes and you'll crawl naked in the dirt and mire for him to call you that."[61] John Duvall points out that Ruby's father too was "man enough" to call her whore; he also beat her, as Goodwin now slaps her around.[62] Temple echoes this ideology as she screams at Popeye, "You're not even a man . . . when you cant even—When you had to bring a real man in to—." He violently grabs her jaw; later, she looks in the mirror and says "Shucks . . . it didn't leave a mark even."[63] Frequently in Faulkner it is the women who enforce, or try to enforce, the ideology; think of Drusilla in *The Unvanquished*, trying to get Bayard to take and use those pistols; then think of Ike McCaslin, who gives up his sexual life to atone for his family history of *le droit de seigneur*, and later offers the hunting horn "left him in [General Compson's] will" to Roth's black mistress;[64] or of Harry Wilbourne, the reluctant abortionist; or of the violently willful leg in "The Leg." More frequently, though, Faulkner seems to have sought a position that evaded the opposition altogether, by looking for some androgynous combination of penetrator/penetratee, or even by moving to a space "prior" to the dichotomy altogether.

In the earliest novels, Faulkner was not quite so daring as he would later become in his challenges to the ideology of penetration. The relationship between Narcissa Benbow and

Bayard Sartoris in *Flags in the Dust,* for example, repeats the ideology in numerous images. It is clear especially in Bayard's violence and Narcissa's virginal intactness. It is his violent ride on the stallion that penetrates Narcissa's psyche and attracts her to him; Byron Snopes's intrusive notes turn her on; yet her ultimately impenetrable core (read "frigid"), like a lily in a gale, returns to its "still unravished" state after Bayard leaves. Yet reading the novel alternatively as a critique of the ideology, we notice a woman who gains power and voice by resisting the desire to succumb to the pleasures of being penetrated, and a man whose violence and power fail in every sense, leaving him finally in pieces on the ground.

With Quentin in *The Sound and the Fury,* Faulkner undertook an extensive examination of the ideology of penetration. Quentin is caught on the rack of penetration's polar oppositions; he wants to be a man, but will not accept the definition his culture offers; the only alternative he can locate is feminization. In fainting during the conflict with Dalton Ames, he exposes his preference—albeit unconscious—for the feminine ideological position. In the scene with Caddy at the branch, Quentin begs her to help him pierce her with his knife, cries on her breast, and ends by dropping his knife. Earlier, in thinking of a man who "mutilated himself," Quentin says, "But that's not it. It's not not having them [male genitals presumably]. It's never to have had them then I could say O that that's Chinese I dont know Chinese."[65] Thus he exposes and rejects, though unwillingly, the violent implications of the ideology of sexual penetration. In his death, his last effort to join Caddy, he chooses the substance whose penetration entails the least violence and pain: water.

With the character of Joe Christmas, Faulkner explores the possibility of cross-gender identification as a form of resistance to the ideology of penetration. Joe is obviously uncertain about his racial identification; perhaps less obviously, he is uncertain about his gender as well. Thus he becomes obsessed with gender oppositions. The passages in *Light in August* that claim to represent Joanna's putative "nymphomania," her "masculinity," and her split self surely should be read as projections, whether from the narrator or from Joe, of an obsession with the ideology of penetration. The struggle of "two creatures," for example, which pits the "still, cold, contained figure of the first phase who . . . remained somehow impervious and impregnable" against the second one, who "strove to drown . . . that physical purity," should be understood as a struggle constructed by ideology, not biology. Similarly, the narrator's obsession with coding her behavior as masculine or feminine, as in the passage, "There was no feminine vacillation, no coyness of obvious desire and intention to succumb at last. It was as if he struggled physically with another man" is exactly duplicated by Joe's own insistence on the ideology of binary gender: "'My God,' he thought, 'it was like I was the woman and she was the man.'"[66] We do not need to take either of these voices as accurate descriptions of Joanna's interiority. Joanna's behavior, at least some of it, can be understood as the effect of her sexual initiative and autonomy; for Joe and frequently for the narrator, that effect has to be interpreted through the gender dichotomy. Thus when she is "manlike," Joe must be feminized: there are no other choices. Joe's anxiety to "take or be taken," as Bleikasten puts it,[67] his vomiting up the coil of toothpaste, can be read within this ideology as rejections of the feminized position, refusals to be penetrated.

Faulkner was well aware of the links between racism and the ideology of penetration; "Dry September," as we saw, exposes the impotence of the man of violence and power and rank, and the story "Was" exposes through humor the connections between hunting, slavery, and sexuality. Even the integrity of class is represented within Faulkner's fiction through the ideology of penetration. In *Faulkner and Modernism,* Richard Moreland locates a "primal scene" of "purifying exclusion" that Faulkner writes out in *Absalom, Absalom!* as the scene of the slave turning away the youthful Thomas Sutpen from the front door of a plantation house. Thus is he rejected by, in Moreland's

words, the "unviolated, unbroken Southern plantation tradition."[68] Faulkner repeats and revises this scene, notably in
"Barn Burning," when Ab Snopes pushes his way inside a
similar white house and smears manure on the blond rug at the
door. Moreland reads these as scenes of social exclusion; thus
he can understand Snopes's smear as a "peculiar writing style"
(what Kristeva might call a minor revolution in poetic language)
and understands this as Ab's social critique, smudging "Sarty's
and their society's mythic image of the plantation as radiant and
redeeming source of beauty, cleanliness, and moral improvement."[69] What happens if we read this repetitive scene as
overdetermined by the ideology of penetration? The text of the
story and even Moreland's critical terminology more than invite
us to do so. When Ab enters the house, for example, in "Barn
Burning," Moreland describes his entry as "pushing his way
inside."[70] Yet if we see this overdetermination, it is more
difficult to take pure pleasure in Ab's moral victory. For just as
clearly as he has challenged social hierarchy, Ab has raped and
fouled a woman. To understand this is to appreciate Sarty's
resistance to his father's revolutionary designs as in this respect
a sign of empathy and even identification with women, including
the women in his family whom his father so brutally and
repeatedly oppresses.

I have not even touched upon the possibilities of reading
penetration as a question or issue of form, except to suggest, as
so many have before me, that Faulkner saw the work of art as
itself a whole, intact, rounded, and clearly female figure. In
fact, he objected to the separation of "Old Man" from "Wild
Palms" by calling it a "dismemberment," and referred to himself
as "sole owner and proprietor" of Yoknapatawpha County. An
analysis of textual structure in terms of boundaries and intru-
sions could be quite promising. But what I hope seems plain
enough now is the permeation of images of penetration, and the
associated images of dismemberment and diffusion, through the
body of Faulkner's texts. If penetration is a sign of power—
masculine power, social power—and if being penetrated is a

sign of weakness and submission, then Faulkner explores both "positions" with enormous subtlety and a clear sense of the costs and pleasures of each. Even dismemberment itself, a sign of the origin, goal, and risk of penetration—of the feminine—takes on multiple valences, as we will see in the conclusion.

Conclusion

We have come a long way from desire and dismemberment, but perhaps they are not altogether forgotten. The dismemberments in Faulkner surely cannot all be understood in terms of this ideology of penetration. But some can: dismemberment becomes a way for the narrative to reject the penetration ideology's particular organization of desire, by showing its consequences in violence and dominance and dehumanization, with images of women perforated and bleeding—Temple after her rape, Charlotte after her abortion, Joe's urns cracked, Addie's body pierced. Yet dismemberment becomes also a way of representing the efforts of certain men, like Ike and Bayard (in *The Unvanquished*) and Quentin, who find radical alternatives to the penetration ideology, and who sacrifice their patriarchal member-ship in various ways.

Perhaps the most powerful critique of the ideology of penetration is the representation of Joe Christmas's castration. Castration, one of the worst fears of the ideology, becomes a source of ecstasy for Joe. The blood spurts orgasmically as a look of peace comes on his face, Van de Velde's man and woman in one. If the ideology of penetration locates sexual pleasure and even manhood itself only in the penetrating penis, here we have the revision of that claim in every sense.

Yet finally Faulkner recuperates the power lost in giving up penetration by taking up the pen. To succeed at moving beyond penetration (and stay alive), like Bayard in *The Unvanquished* or the narrator in "Carcassonne" or Van de Velde in *Ideal Marriage*, Faulkner's men take control of the narration—of the construction of ideology itself: they remember the story.

"What people want, and what they do, in any society, is to a large extent what they are made to want, and allowed to do. Sexuality . . . cannot escape its cultural connection." So writes Pat Caplan, in a splendid introduction to the collection of anthropological investigations called *The Cultural Construction of Sexuality*.[71] The ideology of penetration constructed desire with particular focus and intensity during the time of Faulkner's life and work; his writing can be read as efforts to explore and at certain moments to deconstruct and dismember this particular cultural construction of sexuality, to expose its costs, for men and women, and to drain away some of its power.

NOTES

1. After I delivered this paper at the 1992 Faulkner and Yoknapatawpha conference on "Faulkner and Ideology," André Bleikasten suggested that this discourse of penetration not be called an "ideology," because it is more particular than the sets of assumptions "ideology" normally refers to (such as the "unified self"). However, it seems to me, as I hope will become clear, both quite particular and very general, in that it overlaps and overdetermines several other "ideologies"—among them the unified self—while remaining itself rather precisely focused on the action of entry.

Interestingly, in his widely read 1926 sex guide, *Ideal Marriage*, T. H. Van de Velde uses "phallos" to represent the "erect and active organ," claiming this was the Greek meaning of the word. See Theodore H. Van de Velde, M.D., *Ideal Marriage: Its Physiology and Technique* (first published 1926) (New York: Random House, 1930, 1957), 172.

2. *The Cultural Construction of Sexuality*, ed. Pat Caplan (London: Tavistock, 1987).

3. William Faulkner, "Carcassonne," in *Collected Stories* (New York: Random House, 1950), 896.

4. André Bleikasten, "Terror and Nausea," *The Faulkner Journal*, 1 (Fall 1985): 28.

5. William Faulkner, *The Hamlet* (New York: Vintage, 1964), 263.

6. Bleikasten, *The Ink of Melancholy* (Bloomington: Indiana University Press, 1990), 244.

7. Carolyn Dean, "Law and Sacrifice: Bataille, Lacan, and the Critique of the Subject," *Representations* 13 (1986): 42.

8. Sigmund Freud, "Medusa's Head," *The Standard Edition of the Complete Psychological Works of Sigmund Freud*, ed. James Strachey (London: The Hogarth Press, 1955), 18: 273–74; Helen Cixous, "Castration or Decapitation?" trans. Annette Kuhn, *Signs*, 7 (Autumn 1981): 41–55; Luce Irigaray, *The Sex Which Is Not One*, trans. Catherine Porter (Ithaca: Cornell University Press, 1985).

9. Trudier Harris, *Exorcising Blackness: Historical and Literary Lynching and Burning Rituals* (Bloomington: Indiana University Press, 1984), xi.

10. Middleton. A. Harris, ed., *The Black Book* (New York: Random House, 1974), 58.

11. Trudier Harris, xi.

12. But Armistead falls back on race in the end. "The true skin . . . or *dermis* is *white in all*," he writes; only an insignificant "pigment" that lies between dermis and epidermis is responsible for color differences; hence, he writes, "racial unity is proved." W.S. Armistead, *The Negro Is a Man* (Miami: Mnemosyne, 1969), 318.

13. Lawrence Schwartz, *Creating Faulkner's Reputation: The Politics of Modern Literary Criticism* (Knoxville: University of Tennessee Press, 1988), 12, 97, 58, 27.

14. *Faulkner and Idealism: Perspectives from Paris*, ed. Michel Gresset and Patrick Samway (Jackson: University Press of Mississippi, 1983), 6–8.

15. Terry Eagleton, *Ideology: An Introduction* (London: Verso, 1991), 1.

16. James Kavanagh, "Ideology," in *Critical Terms for Literary Study*, ed. Frank Lentricchia and Thomas McLaughlin (Chicago: University of Chicago Press, 1990), 306.

17. Myra Jehlen, "Introduction: Beyond Transcendence," in *Ideology and Classic American Literature*, ed. Sacvan Bercovitch and Myra Jehlen (Cambridge: Cambridge University Press, 1986), 3.

18. Sacvan Bercovitch, "The Problem of Ideology in American Literary History," *Critical Inquiry*, 12 (Summer 1986): 635.

19. In *"The Politics of Truth" from Marx to Foucault* (Palo Alto: Stanford University Press, 1991), Michele Barrett observes that no one has actually located this popular phrase in a Marx text.

20. Jehlen, 12.

21. Bercovitch, "Afterword," in *Ideology and Classic American Literature*, 638.

22. Quoted in Barrett, 5.

23. Eagleton, 112ff.

24. W. J. Cash, *The Mind of the South* (New York: Vintage, 1969, orig. pub. 1941), 43.

25. Quoted in Barrett, 123.

26. Michel Foucault, *History of Sexuality: Volume 1, An Introduction* (New York: Pantheon, 1978), 105.

27. Ibid., 157.

28. Bleikasten, "For/Against an Ideological Reading of Faulkner's Novels," in *Faulkner and Ideology*, 39.

29. William Faulkner, "Dry September," in *Collected Stories* (New York: Random House, 1950), 172. Further references will be cited in the text.

30. Zora Neale Hurston, "The 'Pet' Negro System," in *I Love Myself When I Am Laughing . . .* , ed. Alice Walker (Old Westbury: Feminist Press, 1979), 156–62. Faulkner, *The Sound and the Fury*, Corrected Text (New York: Random House, 1984): "That was when I realised that a nigger is not a person so much as a form of behavior; a sort of obverse reflection of the white people he lives among" (86); "suddenly I saw Roskus watching me from behind all his [the Deacon's] whitefolks' claptrap of uniforms and politics and Harvard manner, diffident, secret, inarticulate and sad" (99).

31. See Lillian Faderman, *Signs: Journal of Women in Culture and Society*, 17 (1990–91), 820–21 (review).

32. Ibid.

33. Thomas Laqueur, *Making Sex: Body and Gender from the Greeks to Freud* (Cambridge: Harvard University Press, 1990), 53.

34. Quoted in Pat Caplan, "Introduction," *The Cultural Construction of Sexuality*, 7.

35. Marie Robinson, *The Power of Sexual Surrender* (New York: Signet, 1959).

36. I am not sure which sort of penetration comes "first," logically or chronologically; the sexual seems intuitively more fundamental to me than the territorial or the military, but that may be my gender speaking.

37. See Klaus Theweleit, *Male Fantasies*, Vol. I (Minneapolis: University of Minnesota Press, 1987), for extended commentary on the intense conflicts between identity and engulfment experienced by the German Freikorps.

38. It is interesting to note how penetration subtly undercuts its own power by locating the truth outside itself and inside the "object," whether person or text. Penetration thus becomes an acknowledgment of lack at the same time that it is an assertion of power, power to redress the lack; yet it must go again and again after that "truth" for it can never really remove it from the object and take it home, except as a memory, a representation.

39. Joseph Blotner, comp. and intro., *William Faulkner's Library: A Catalogue* (Charlottesville: University Press of Virginia, 1964).

40. See also Patricia J. Campbell, *Sex Education Books for Young Adults, 1892–1979* (New York: Bowker, 1979).

41. Jeffrey Weeks, "Questions of Identity," in Caplan, 35.

42. Margaret Jackson, " 'Facts of Life' or the Eroticization of Women's Oppression? Sexology and the Social Construction of Heterosexuality," Caplan, 63.

43. Ibid., 61.

44. Ibid., 63.

45. Ibid., 68.

46. Thomas Laqueur has pointed out that Freud made this claim in the face of what he must have known from the medical literature about the impossibility of vaginal orgasm, and suggests that his persistence is an indication of the power of this ideology. See *Making Sex*, 134ff.

47. Caplan, 73.

48. See John D'Emilio and Estelle B. Freedman, *Intimate Matters: A History of Sexuality in America* (New York: Harper & Row, 1988), especially 265–274.

49. Ibid., 274.

50. Ibid.

51. Nowhere does Van de Velde explicitly claim this as his task. In a volume dedicated to companionate marriage, the desire to retain male dominance could hardly be stated explicitly, perhaps not even thought consciously. I hope instead to demonstrate that the contradictions in his thinking, and the narratives of sexuality he constructs, can be adequately explained if we assume his task (conscious or not) to be to graft female desire onto patriarchal power relations.

52. Jackson, 78.

53. Van de Velde, *Ideal Marriage*, 262. Further references will be cited in the text.

54. Van de Velde, 158–9, quotes from Havelock Ellis "Love and Pain," Vol. III of *Studies in Psychology:* "We have to admit that a certain pleasure in manifesting his power over a woman by inflicting pain upon her is an outcome and survival of the primitive process of courtship, and an almost or quite normal constituent of the sexual impulse in man. . . . The physical force, the teasing and bullying, which he may be moved to exert under the stress of sexual excitement are, he usually more or less unconsciously persuades himself, not really unwelcome to the object of his love. Moreover, we have to bear in mind . . . that the normal manifestations of a woman's sexual pleasure are exceedingly like those of pain . . . a lady very truly writes that when she implores the man to desist . . . that is really the last thing that she desires." Here follows Van de Velde's passage on the essential force of maleness.

55. Quoted in Caplan, 71.

56. Caplan, "Introduction," 14.

57. Panthea Reid Broughton, "The Economy of Desire: Faulkner's Poetics, from Eroticism to Post-Impressionism," *The Faulkner Journal*, 4 (Fall 1988/Spring 1989): 159–179; Noel Polk, "The Artist as Cuckold," unpublished manuscript.

58. Letter to Joan Williams April 1953, quoted in *Faulkner and Idealism*, 3.

59. Bleikasten, "Terror and Nausea," 35, 37.

60. John T. Irwin, *Doubling and Incest, Repetition and Revenge: A Speculative Reading of Faulkner* (Baltimore: The Johns Hopkins University Press, 1975), 171.

61. William Faulkner, *Sanctuary* (New York: Vintage, 1958), 57.

62. John N. Duvall, *Faulkner's Marginal Couple: Invisible, Outlaw, and Unspeakable Communities* (Austin: University of Texas Press, 1990), 67–68.

63. Faulkner, *Sanctuary*, 224, 226.

64. Faulkner, *Go Down, Moses* (New York: Random House, 1942), 362–63.

65. Faulkner, *The Sound and the Fury*, 115–16.

66. Faulkner, *Light in August*, Corrected Text (New York: Vintage International, 1990), 235.

67. André Bleikasten, *The Ink of Melancholy*, 308.

68. Richard C. Moreland, *Faulkner and Modernism: Rereading and Rewriting* (Madison: University of Wisconsin Press, 1990), 8.

69. Ibid., 8.

70. Ibid.

71. Caplan, 25.

The Razor, the Pistol, and the Ideology
of Race Etiquette

MARTHA BANTA

I begin with a personal anecdote from the 1930s, then a reference to a book dedication of 1899: two seemingly disparate items which, over the course of this paper, I hope to bring together with other material to form a commentary upon scenes taken from Faulkner's "Fire and the Hearth" and *Light in August*—scenes that treat the way social identity is linked to one's choice of weapons of violence which, in turn, have acquired their cultural accreditation through their complicity with ideologies of race etiquette.

The anecdote is drawn from memories of being a very small child growing up in Muncie, Indiana—that place made famous (and somewhat infamous) by the Lynds' seminal sociological studies of regional mores, *Middletown* and *Middletown in Transition*.[1] Unbeknownst to me at the time, the Lynds' first book set the scene into which I was about to be born. The sequel contained my presence as a tiny blip on its statistical charts, which of course concerned me not at all. Still, I was there as an "observer," aware (although hardly "knowing") of ways by which the town made distinctions among its citizens according to cultural modes of action.

On Mondays *The Muncie Morning Star* provided a run-down of the weekend's police reports of what had taken place in and around the taverns "across the tracks"—activities that resulted in varying degrees of violence from bloodlettings to homicide. The coding used in the newspaper's accounts was clear enough: (1) when guns were involved, the participants were inevitably native Hoosiers; (2) the use of knives signaled the presence of "white trash" Kentuckians and Tennesseans—some of the many heading north during Depression times in patterns of migration parallel to those heading Westward along Highway 66; (3) whenever a razor had flashed, the *Muncie Star* named "Negro."[2]

As for the book dedication: I refer to the phrases that E. M. Woods, an Afro-American member of the faculty of the Lincoln Institute of Jefferson, Missouri, placed at the head of his text of 1899, *The Negro in Etiquette*.[3]

It is no surprise that in 1899 Woods follows convention in dedicating his book to "his sainted mother," or that he voices his hope for "the unity of the North and South." As for the final goal to which Woods directs his review of proper etiquette: is this statement what we expect to find heading the manuals of manners later compiled by Emily Post or Amy Vanderbilt—"the logical obliteration of 'lynch law and mob violence'"?

I shall take the long way around to the scene where Lucas Beauchamp and Zack Edmonds crouch on either side of Zack's bed—an episode that rises to the moment when Lucas flings his razor out the window and cries, "I dont need no razor. My nekkid hands will do. Now get the pistol under your pillow"; and to scenes from *Light in August* in which Joe Christmas's shuttling between the use of razor and pistol reflect his swervings between self-identification as "black" or "white." My intention here is to demonstrate the ways by which precise rules of etiquette were put into effect in post-Reconstruction America that directly controlled relationships between races (whites and people of color)—both in the form of Jim Crow laws that lay down codes of proper conduct and in the rituals of lynching and mob violence that sought to punish whoever broke those rules. I wish also to indicate how Northerners came to accept the authority of "Southern manners" out of their need to interpose an ideology of "civilization" between themselves and the forces of "savagery" they perceived as threatening their lives on all sides.

The ten years that span 1897 and 1907, the formative first

decade of William Faulkner's young life—the Vardaman era—is where I place my main emphasis. Many of the quotations I use, as well as the illustrations that follow, are drawn from the pages of *Life*. No, not Henry Luce's *Life* which he founded in Chicago in 1936, but the New York City weekly that flourished as America's *Punch* and a forerunner to *The New Yorker* from its beginnings in 1883 through the peak period of its popularity during the 1900s and 1910s. As a prominent Northern journal whose primary goal was to satirize an increasingly "mixed" society and the diverse strata of manners making cultural dislocations, *Life* also included "serious" editorial commentary on major political and cultural events of the day; it recorded the shifts being made in the urban Northeast toward fuller accommodation to the views held by Southern whites once *Life* discovered the "truth" that the Negro is *not* a white man with a black skin.

At issue here is not simply the fact that *Life* as an articulate arbiter of sophisticated Northeastern urban manners determined that blacks cannot be contained within the rules of etiquette that pertain among whites because of differences in race culture; more crucially (and tragically in terms of the consequences in violence), *Life* came to agree in large part that the total "otherness" of Negro conduct was a matter of biological difference. As one checks through the weekly issues appearing between 1897 and 1907, one finds an increasing willingness to state (or to intimate) that the real threat is not to niceties of drawing room decorum, but to white racial purity and the strength of the nation, if ever breaks in race etiquette permit miscegenation.

Life's call for greater control over race relationships at the cultural level confirms what Christopher Herbert's fine new study, *Culture and Anomie,* cogently singles out as "the polemically charged shift from the social-control model toward a symbolically oriented theory of 'culture' in which society is configured in a new metaphorical guise as 'an inextricable web of affinities' and as an enigmatic object of interpretation."[4]

The connections that E. M. Woods made in his 1899 dedication to *The Negro in Etiquette* between his people's anxieties over mob violence and the codes of manners established by the whites in authority was further elaborated by Bertram Doyle, Professor of Sociology at Fisk University, in his 1937 study, *The Etiquette of Race Relations in the South*. Doyle (disciple of Robert E. Park, founder of the "Chicago School" of Sociology), subtitles his book *A Study of Social Control*, as one might expect of a work coming out of the 1930s; but it is the ideology of "culture" that he addresses.[5] The cultural forms expressive of the evolving "race problem" are also examined in the more recent scholarly analyses of the post-Reconstruction era by C. Vann Woodward, August Meier, Thomas Gossett, and Joel Williamson, among others.[6]

I wish to take the matter of "cultural control" by means of "race etiquette" several steps further—prompted in part by Herbert's remarks concerning the increased authority imposed through internalized forms of control, extensions of what Adam Smith called "the man in the breast" and Freud named the Super Ego, and of what the author of an etiquette book of 1881 implied when he declared that society is run by "the Great Director" of a vast drama.[7] By the end of this paper, we shall see whether the Grand Chessman—he who propels Percy Grimm toward his dual use of pistol and knife out of Grimm's "swift, blind obedience to whatever Player moved him on the Board"—is ironically engaging Grimm as the agent to "correct" those faulty points of etiquette by which Joe Christmas conducts his "social" relations with Joanna Burden.

Let me make these other points clear before I get into particular examples. First, manners do not depend upon words. Based upon emotions, not reasoned concepts, manners are best expressed through bodily action engaged in "events" with other bodies, and the instruments put to physical use (the hat that is tipped, the door that is opened, the gun that is fired).[8] As we look at the historical merger of American mob violence at the turn of the century with the nation's aggressive moves outside

manners do not depend upon words — based on emotions & bodies

its own borders into "savage" territories, it becomes clear that the high-sounding rhetoric concerning "civilization" and "moral mission" masked the deeper concerns of the nation's white population which questioned America's new imperialism—concerns that unacceptable bodies and bloods might mingle unrestrained by the "right" codes of behavior. As we shall see when looking at an essay of 1906 titled "Southern Manners," words are equated with defeat. Only manners (one's body English) have the force to "sign" victory for the white race.

Second, ideologies of codes of violence predicated upon keeping people in their "place" inevitably involve economics and class as well as notions of "race." Faulkner's keen attention to the complex interfoldings that make up the conduct of Southern life shows us how difficult it is for "poor whites" to kill "correctly." Witness the frustration experienced by Mink Snopes when he murders Jack Houston because he lacks the money to buy a better rifle and enough ammunition; the situation is duplicated years later when Mink sets out to get revenge on Flem, unable to purchase more than a cheap pistol and three faulty shells.[9]

And lest you think that the economics of killing is an issue relegated to the imaginary lives dreamed up by novelists or to a long-ago past, consider the 1991 trial of one Alfred Lavers in Phoenix, Arizona, who unsuccessfully argued against the death penalty he received for having, with excruciating slowness, stabbed his wife and stepdaughter to death. It was Lavers's claim "that the law discriminates against poor people who cannot afford expensive guns to commit murder and therefore must rely on crude weapons that kill slowly."[10]

If manners function in relations between equals, they are most marked in the actions binding those who consider themselves to be superior to those viewed as their inferiors—persons who, in turn, follow carefully constructed codes of manners as a means of strategic survival. "Class" (determined by economic and social status) blends with matters of "caste" in which economic and social status come into play with ideologies of "race."

It is often impossible to separate the entangled reactions that result.

Third, among the many questions that arise at the junctures of such complex cultural nuances, I shall ask, then answer, the following: If—as it is commonly claimed—codes of manners first came into existence to prevent people from killing one another, can there be codes of manners that regulate who is to kill whom and according to what rules of decorum? And if codes of conduct are "historical artifacts" and "cultural constructions," what does this mean for the American South which was (in one of Faulkner's more vivid tropes) cast "outside" history?[11] Does this limit our study of Southern manners to abstractions held within an ahistorical dimension?

The answer is *yes* to the first; *no* to the second. Yes to the fact that, not only was there an active etiquette for the killing of those who broke society's taboos, many refinements were incorporated into that etiquette over the years to terrible and ironic effect. Aristocrats once impeccably followed the niceties of the *code duello,* while their inferiors addressed their grievances with cruder, less couth methods. Therefore, in both the South and the North when lynching was at its peak, much was made of the supposed fact that "the best people" in the South stood apart from the social misconduct of "the rougher element" in their community—behavior, the former claimed, they deplored but over which they had no control.

No, to the notion that manners remained an abstraction in a South wrenched from the kind of historical consciousness which the North "won" by terms of its victory in the war. Lynching as executed in the 1890s and early 1900s was quite specific to the times. As Vann Woodward and others have demonstrated, the Jim Crow codes were only then regularized *as laws*—making visible earlier, more subtle codes of relationships between blacks and whites that had been randomly in effect in uneven degree since the 1870s.[12] Lynching as both a participant and spectator "social event" was prompted by alleged transgressions of the recently "institutionalized" Jim Crow laws. These laws

were constantly affected by what was going on "in history" up
North, at the same time the North was in the process of coming
around to greater sympathy with these changes in Southern
"etiquette"—all of these shifts the consequence of the economic,
political, and cultural pressures underway throughout the nation
between 1897 and 1907.[13]

Now, the editors of *Life* were outspokenly in opposition to
the violence done against blacks, whether in the Wilmington
riots or in Evansville, Indiana. There is little cause to doubt the
authenticity of the horror they expressed over the failure of
manners to place a curb on the white man's "savagery."

In August 1897, one month before Faulkner was born, *Life*
had warned against "The Lynching Game of the Future" in
which "During Recess the Southern Schoolboys of the Next
Generation May Indulge in This Sort of Fun." [Figure 1] In
March 1904 the magazine reran this sketch together with a

THE LYNCHING GAME OF THE FUTURE.

DURING RECESS THE SOUTHERN SCHOOLBOYS OF THE NEXT GENERATION MAY
INDULGE IN THIS SORT OF FUN.

Figure 1.

note about a recent incident in Springfield, Ohio, in which schoolboys, intent upon imitating adult activities, were stopped just short of lynching a black boy.[14] Even so, *Life* perceived there were other considerations than human decency to take into account.

An editorial of September 1904 regarding the recent situation in Georgia notes that lynching results in more votes for the Republicans; it quotes Democratic Governor Terrell as asking anxiously, "Can nothing be done to make negro-burning unfashionable?"[15] And when *Life* inserts the sketch of the scorched body of a man dangling from a tree (an object of extra-legal activity), the editors use the occasion to discuss the crimes of the Standard Oil Company and to muse over the difficulty of bringing true criminals to justice within the boundaries of the nation's legal system.[16] [Figure 2] But over and above questions about procedures that affect the making and breaking of political and financial structures loomed the ideology of race fear—one that was beginning to alter the North's former objections to the less tasteful "race" practices of Southern whites.

In 1899 two editorials appear in quick succession as a result of the lynching of Sam Hose.[17] *Life* states that "In the North we have no fear of negroes" because of their relative lack of numbers, but the editors acknowledge that if Northerners ever came to "feel the race question as Georgia feels it . . . maybe our virtue would not be superior to hers." *Life* then chides Julia Ward Howe for her outmoded "Boston" views left over from Abolitionist days which do not take into account the fact that to the Southerner the Negro is a potentially dangerous force—one who "must mind his manners and keep his place." For these reasons, the editors conclude that it is not right for Northerners to censure the South out of "ignorance" and "unconscious hypocrisy."

Life accelerated the number of pointed editorial rebukes throughout 1903, 1904, and 1905, as indices of the increase in mob violence down South.[18] At the same time, *Life* stepped up its requests that Northerners abdicate their anachronistic role

Figure 2.

as arbiters of conduct over the South. It is wisest, *Life* declares, to leave the handling of race relations to "the best people" down South who will do all they can to retain "good fame" despite the behavior of the "pretty poor human stock in white skins."[19] Whatever savagery of behavior was released on the part of Southern white low-lifes would be mediated by the civilized conduct of the right kind of Southerners in order that both classes of whites could effectively keep the innate savagery of the Negroes under rigorous control.

I can only suggest here the kinds of contradictions that make the pages of *Life* the treasure-trove of contending ideologies that it is. Within a single issue it could rebuke the Secretary Beveridge of the International Military encampment of Chicago for his discourtesy in failing to invite former members of a Negro troop to a Union Army reunion *and* print the most grotesque of Sambo jokes.[20] It finds much to praise in *The Souls of Black Folk* for DuBois's "subjective view-point of the black" that "gives the book an importance which deserves the strongest emphasis."[21] It also recommends Thomas Dixon's *The Clansmen* and William Benjamin Smith's *The Color Line;* especially the latter because of the "facts" it offers about the inferiority of the Negro that stand solidly in contradistinction to mere matters of "theory" about which intelligent people can differ.[22] It supports Theodore Roosevelt's invitation to Booker T. Washington for dinner at the White House, the president's sponsorship of the black postmistress from Indianola, Mississippi, and the handling of the Brownsville incident.[23] But it also provided its readers with the following visual lampoons in 1904 and 1905.

Figure 3 projects "Harvard's football Eleven of 1909, Under President Roosevelt of Harvard."[24] Figure 4 further jibes at Roosevelt's "softness" toward blacks in defending the presence of Booker T. Washington as "my chum" against the distaste voiced by William Jennings Bryan and Senator Thomas Platt.[25] (Note the winged figure to the left; his significance will be made clear below.) Figure 5 makes clear that the "civilizing" effects aspired to by the upwardly mobile "New Negro" cannot compensate for speech-manners "bred into the bone" of a biological inferior: "A darky girl once went to Vassar./ In her studies no one could pass her./ She knew Latin and Greek, and Sanskrit could speak—/ But she always said 'massa' and 'yassir!'"[26]

Underlying *Life's* representations there is the single "truth" its editors had discovered—one that is clearly voiced in an editorial of May 1903.

The country is in so remarkably receptive a state of mind about the Southern negro as to be exceptionally inclined to pay attention to

HARVARD'S FOOTBALL ELEVEN OF 1909, UNDER PRESIDENT ROOSEVELT, OF HARVARD.

Figure 3.

instructive discourse from persons who have studied them and seem
competent to add to our knowledge about them. To many Northern
minds the idea that the negro is not a white man with a black skin
is still novel, but realization of that truth is spreading almost
too fast.[27]

By 1926 Bronislaw Malinowski would attempt (with varying
success) a new ethnography based on an "argument from manners" that was meant to mitigate the distortions of the "argument from numbers" formulated by pseudosociologists such as
William Benjamin Smith.[28] By the very nature of the kind of
periodical it was, *Life*'s arguments revolved around "manners,"
but in the early 1900s "manners" defined as cultural differences
were still inextricably entangled with "numbers" predicated on
the total otherness arising from differences of "blood." Once
this view was established as a "fact" in Northerners' minds,
the ideological distance between prevailing regional rules of
etiquette diminished rapidly; the cultural kinship between the

Life's Sunday-School Class.

PRESENT : *Teddy Roosevelt, Willie Bryan, Tommy Platt, Jacob Riis, Booker T. Washington.*

Figure 4.

white North and the white South began to outweigh previous political differences over the treatment of the blacks.

Manners keep all inferiors in their place, whatever their race.[29] The "Presidential Impossibilities" which *Life* satirized in 1904 included not only Booker T. Washington (the Negro with the docile look and the harmless, inturned palms of a pet ape) [Figure 6], but the more dangerous Carrie Nation (the female of militant bearing with a sharp-edged axe in hand).[30] Up North, at least, the New Woman was still more of a scare than an Old Negro dressed in new clothes.

Let me offer some examples from earlier issues of *Life* that indicate that the post-Reconstruction Negro had not initially been imaged as a threat to the uninitiated North; then move to later representations that demonstrate exactly where the new anxieties lay, shared by Northerners and Southerners alike—

BRED IN THE BONE.

A DARKY GIRL ONCE WENT TO VASSAR.
IN HER STUDIES NO ONE COULD PASS HER.
  SHE KNEW LATIN AND GREEK,
  AND SANSKRIT COULD SPEAK—
BUT SHE ALWAYS SAID "MASSA" AND "YASSIR!"

Figure 5.

anxieties demanding the enforcement of codes that would protect white civilization against black savagery.[31]

Figure 8 from 1887 objectifies the black servant of a Northern widow as an adjunct to her stylish wardrobe. She who has been a widow for three years says, "Atticus, I—er—intend to lighten my mourning after Lent, and I'm afraid your color is a little *too*

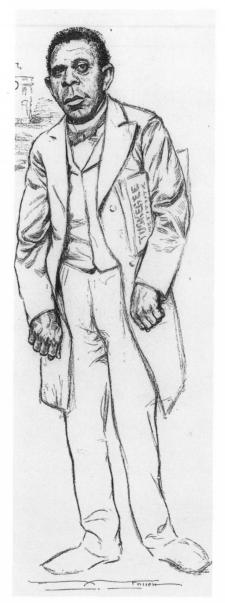

Figure 6.

Figure 7.

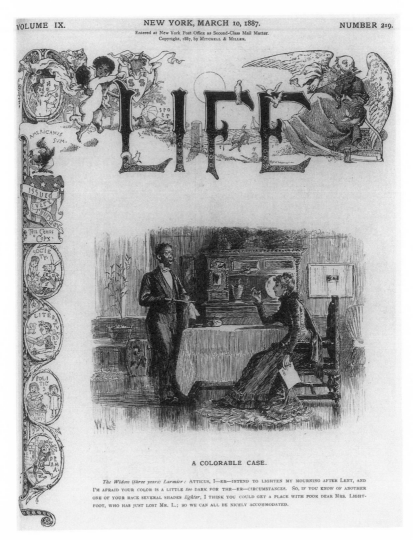

VOLUME IX.   NEW YORK, MARCH 10, 1887.   NUMBER 219.

Entered at New York Post Office as Second-Class Mail Matter.
Copyright, 1887, by MITCHELL & MILLER.

A COLORABLE CASE.

The Widow (three years) Larmier : ATTICUS, I—ER—INTEND TO LIGHTEN MY MOURNING AFTER LENT, AND
I'M AFRAID YOUR COLOR IS A LITTLE *too* DARK FOR THE—ER—CIRCUMSTANCES. SO, IF YOU KNOW OF ANOTHER
ONE OF YOUR RACE SEVERAL SHADES *lighter,* I THINK YOU COULD GET A PLACE WITH POOR DEAR MRS. LIGHT-
FOOT, WHO HAS JUST LOST MR. L.; SO WE CAN ALL BE NICELY ACCOMMODATED.

Figure 8.

dark for the—er—circumstances. So if you know of another one
of your race several shades *lighter,* I think you could get a place
with poor dear Mrs. Lightfoot, who has just lost Mr. L; so we
can all be nicely accommodated."[32]

Figure 9 from 1895 is one of the many sketches supplied by
E. W. Kemble, known in the trade as "the best coon artist"

THE CAKE WALK INTERRUPTED.

The Pastor : 'Tis with pain dat I hab to announce to my listeners dat de second prize in de cake walk, a large sugar ham, hab disappeared since de ceremonies began. I don't wish to cast aspersions on de assembly by saying who is de culprit, but I hab my 'spicions.

Figure 9.

around. Here the decorum of the "darky" social set is disrupted by the snitching of the party ham—the sort of behavior Kemble's fans expected of those he was wont to call "Coontown's Four Hundred."[33] It is noticeable that in all Kemble's cartoons his "coons" are carefully contained *inside* his fantasies of their social lives; they are not seen in interaction with the white world.

Other visual vignettes by other artists, however, set up relationships, usually that of mistress and servant, that allow little jokes to be made about blacks' sex life. Figure 10 from 1898 makes merry about interracial marriage; it can comment playfully with impunity upon the strange progeny that might result from this grotesque liaison since "the best people" are not involved.

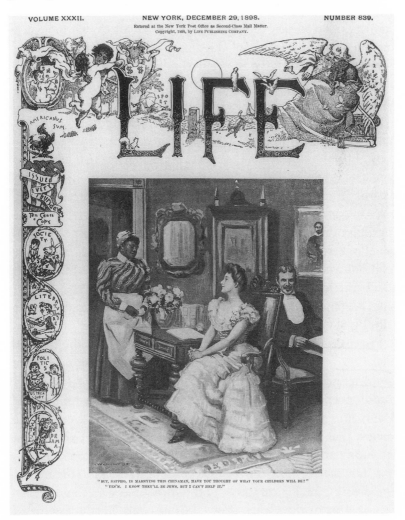

Figure 10.

"But Sappho, in marrying this Chinaman, have you thought of what your children will be?"

"Yes'm. I know they'll be Jews, but I can't help it."[34]

Up to this point in time, *Life* could have its own kind of fun making mock of the "aping" by inferiors of white middle and upper-class mores. But the Nativists realized that a dark cloud was hovering over the nation: the threat of the diminution of the Anglo-Saxon race and its codes of behavior by the biological and cultural infiltration of all those "others"—those "others" pouring into the United States from abroad, and those "others" being swept under America's sovereign rule through its imperialistic moves into new lands over seas.

Life's logo was the winged Cupid, an active little figure who jumped down off the masthead and onto many of its pages. It constantly defined itself as representing the vital impulses that connote "life": joy, romance, pleasure, fancy, and yes, carnal desire: in fact, the meanings rolled up in the German word *lust*. In his frolics, *Life*'s Cupid played hide-and-seek with the contemporary proprieties that regulated how explicit one could be about stating sexual themes, but its allegiance to sexual relations was always present. But what about the magazine's stand on "life, liberty, and the pursuit of romantic happiness" once it pointed toward the mating of strange bedfellows and the tainting of the privileged "American" racial heritage?

From the 1880s on, *Life*'s cartoons indulged in the general bigotry toward the influx of the so-called New Immigrants from Eastern and Southern Europe and Asia. In Figure 11 from 1887 Cupid prepares "A Composite Photo" of the new "Average American," in which the Negro is but one of many types.[35] The images that delineate "A Cosmopolitan Face" eight years later are more grotesque, but it is the Irish, the Chinese, and the Jew, not the Negro, who are placed under attack.[36] [Figure 12] The possible biological threat of the Afro-American seems yet to be a matter of the "freak show" business up North. Figure 13 (also from 1895) gives us the spiel of a new Barnum who presents

Figure 11.

Miss Cadwallader Hoogay, the Childish Venus of the Azores; one, if not the greatest, curiosity on the face of the earth, inasmuch as she alternates in color every year—one year being entirely white, the next year changing to decided black. This year, as you perceive, she is entirely black![37]

A COSMOPOLITAN FACE.

Figure 12.

Now, this, of course, poses a potentially dangerous situation. If "the best people" cannot "know" from a stranger's appearance just "what" he or she is biologically at any one moment, then unfortunate consequences might result once new generations spring forth from the womb of this "Venus of the Azores." It is

BARNUM REDIVIVUS.

Showman: LADIES AND GENTLEMEN, ALLOW ME TO INTRODUCE TO YOUR NOTICE
MISS CADWALLADER HOOGAY, THE CHILDISH VENUS OF THE AZORES; ONE, IF NOT
THE GREATEST, CURIOSITY ON THE FACE OF THE EARTH, INASMUCH AS SHE ALTER-
NATES IN COLOR EVERY YEAR—ONE YEAR BEING ENTIRELY WHITE, THE NEXT YEAR
CHANGING TO A DECIDED BLACK. THIS YEAR, AS YOU PERCEIVE, SHE IS ENTIRELY
BLACK!

Figure 13.

one thing for *Life* to take digs at Mormon polygamy in 1904.[38]
[Figure 14] It is far more serious when in 1907 "The Father of
His Country As Seen By His Children" places a strange brood
on view.[39] [Figure 15]

The rising tide of outre races and ethnic groups immigrating
to the United States, and of Afro-Americans migrating from
South to North, caused fears to the nation's Nativists, South and
North, over the delicate balances that must be maintained
between the etiquette of life and *lust*. A still larger threat
appeared during the crucial decade between 1897 and 1907: the

MORMON ELDER-BERRY—OUT WITH HIS SIX-YEAR-OLDS, WHO TAKE AFTER THEIR MOTHERS.

Figure 14.

threat triggered by the nation's military moves into the Carib-
bean and the Pacific. Above all other factors, contemporary
debates over America's new imperialism brought the editors of
Life Magazine, like so many of their Northern compeers, around
to the "Southern" view that the heart of "good manners" lay in
"keeping the nigger in his place."

Throughout the decade that saw the Spanish-American War,
the imbroglio in the Philippines and the South Seas, and
America's aggressive thrusts into Asia and Latin America, *Life's*
editorial policy was resolutely anti-imperialist.[40] It sincerely
abhorred the use of military force; it was scathing about the
missionaries' wish to "Christianize" the heathen; it roundly
supported Aguinaldo in his fight to gain the political independence of the Filipinos. But *Life* had other, obviously racist,
reasons for its displeasure with the nation's new global enterprises.[41] How striking is its use of visual cautionary tales about
the consequences of a national policy which promised unpleas-
ant genealogical surprises!

Uncle Sam "buys" the Philippines—imaged as an entrancing
"slave"—from her former master, while Columbia as the injured

Figure 15.

RUSSIAN   GERMAN   FRENCH

SWEDE   GREEK   TURK

JAP   FILIPINO

wife, looks on with disapproval at Sam's new concubine; or he is portrayed as an unwilling "bachelor" suddenly faced with the "savage" dependent dumped upon his doorstep by the 55th Congress.[42] [Figures 16–17] (Here, as elsewhere, the Philippines is usually represented according to "jungle" stereotypes that bear no relation to the actual "look" of Filipinos.)

Figure 16.

Figure 17.

This motif of unwanted progeny reoccurs through the early
1900s as the American eagle observes, "Whoever thought I
would have such possessions" [Figure 18],[43] but a new visualization is introduced by 1904, as anxieties mount over the bodily
corruption of the American Way. Now it is the representatives
(and representations) of the major "civilized" powers who have
debased their own heritage by taking females of inferior races as
their partners in the cakewalk.[44] [Figures 19–20] In 1864 Lincoln's policies toward the Negro had been ridiculed in adversar-
ial cartoons that imaged "miscegenation balls"; elegant social
occasions were made mock of through the coupling of black
females and white males within the European waltz-mode.
Forty years later, cartoons testify to a far more heinous degree
of cultural corruption by focusing upon the white male elite who
have crossed the color line in the opposite direction by their
participation in the savage mores of the cakewalk.[45]

The times were ripe for violence. As represented in the pages
of *Life*, Northerners continued to disapprove of the rope and
coal oil used by "white trash" down South, and on occasion,
above the Mason-Dixon line, but by the early 1900s North and

Figure 18.

South alike so feared miscegenation that the willful bending of the rules of decorum could almost be condoned. Identified as the particular menace, perhaps because the visual signs of that menace were disturbingly ambiguous, was the mulatto who raises the ultimate question that powers the "race problem": where does "white" begin and "black" end.[46]

Figure 19.

Figure 20.

In the editorial of May 14, 1903, previously touched upon in regard to the "truth" that the Negro is not a white man with black skin, *Life* featured the opinions of Alfred Stone of Mississippi. Characterized by the editors as "one of the wisest of all the students of negroes," Stone could aid Northerners in realizing the difference between the "comparatively simple proposition" of "the pure negro" and the "far more complex one" of the mulatto.

> Negroes for thousands of years, says Mr. Stone, have kept their place in society which they hold now, because they have lacked the natural capacity to rise above it. And they have been happy in that place because it fitted them, as the bulk of the Southern negroes are happy now. But mulattoes occasionally have first-rate abilities and the aspirations that would naturally go with them. Classed as negroes, which they are not, they become leaders of the negroes; powers sometimes for great good . . . but often great mischief-makers and stirrers up of unrest among their black half-brethren. Except for the mulattoes, Mr. Stone thinks, there could hardly be a negro problem, so naturally and satisfactorily would the relations of the white and black races adjust themselves.[47]

There is the mulatto who can not be contained within a specific racial or cultural code.[48] There is also he whom Ray Stannard Baker named "the floating Negro."[49] Both types are dangerous since neither keeps his appointed place, and what were the Jim Crow laws for if not to define precisely where one sits, sleeps, eats, plays, and has social intercourse?

In 1910 DuBois wrote a short piece for *The Independent* on "Marrying of Black Folk."[50] This is, he states, "a present or future problem [that] cannot be met by inhumanity, barbarism and the methods of the jungle" on the part of whites. But few whites paid DuBois much heed on that score. Violent means were justified in the minds of those who felt threatened; in turn, fear was expressed by those whose placement by race made them the ones to be feared.

The conclusion of the 1899 study of *The Negro in Etiquette* makes clear what E. M. Woods's dedication meant when he urged the obliteration of lynching and mob violence through the adoption of proper codes of etiquette on both sides of the color line. Woods's manual is filled with advice about the social niceties he hopes will be practiced by the New Negro.[51] His suggestions range from how to comport oneself in church; to not blowing on a saucer of coffee or making a scene when one finds a fly in one's soup; to getting over the old habit of saying "Thank you, Bos' [which] is more 'nigger' [than saying] 'Sir.'" But Woods saves the worst for the last.

The final chapter, titled "The Black Husband and White Wife," speaks of the problems caused when Cupid forgets that the United States has laws against "the joining of ebon and 'lily white' hands in marriage." The practical disadvantages of intermarriage are itemized: the crippling of the chance of gaining a livelihood and extreme social isolation—punishments that are either "the result of divine displeasure or the whims of society."

Woods goes even further as he brings his little etiquette book to its close. He lists the ways by which those who breech acceptable decorum will be destroyed, and the instruments used either in suicidal despair or in the white man's correction of the social impropriety of miscegenation:

> . . . a frenzied bound from the bridge, an exciting of others to use the hemp, a gulping of the deadly poison, a report of the suicidal pistol or whizzing of the murderous bullet, a fatal thrust of the knife, a throwing of one's self across the rail in front of an oncoming train. . . .

This, then, is "The Negro in Etiquette" in the recent aftermath of the *Plessy vs. Ferguson* decree of 1896 and as part of the rigor with which Jim Crow laws were being enforced, since he or she who, through interracial intercourse, "disturbs the social world, is an enemy to good society."[52]

In Woods's resumé of the weapons of choice employed by the white enforcers of race etiquette, the hemp, the pistol, and the knife are used interchangeably. Even more precise distinctions vis-a-vis codes of killing continued to appear during the years that mark the first decade of William Faulkner's life. In 1907 the movie *The Fights of Nations*, produced by Thomas Edison's Biograph Company, strings together scenes of paired males fighting according to the cultural patterns associated with their ethnic group.[53] Scots use Highland swords and Latins employ knives, while—in a sequence called "Sunny Africa, Eighth

Avenue"—two Negroes slash at each other with razors in a fight over a woman, then pause to watch a jazz dance.

And now we come to William Faulkner—to his renditions of how one's existential sense of social "placement" is expressed by the choice of weapons used at those moments when the rules of etiquette governing one party's ideology of race relationships come into conflict with another's code.

Once Lucas Beauchamp faces the fact that Zack Edmonds "had" Molly at the big house after his wife dies in childbirth, he is faced with two lines of action: to take Molly and run or to let his own "blood" "break out and run" by killing Zack—Zack, descended on the female side from old Carothers McCaslin, the man who grandfathered Lucas, the "black" cousin to the Edmonds and McCaslin clan. The answer comes quickly to Lucas: he must kill. The question remains: how to do it correctly by means of which weapon—the black man's razor or the white man's pistol?

Even before he enters Zack's house, Lucas envisions himself standing beside Zack's bed, above, "the undefended and oblivious throat, the naked razor already in his hand." Upon entering, Lucas assumes the same stance, "facing again the act which it seemed to him he had already performed." But when Zack tells Lucas to put down the razor, Lucas flings it out the window, "the naked blade whirling almost blood-colored." "I dont need no razor," he declares. "My nekkid hands will do." But if Lucas thinks to rely on his hands—that universal human weapon that bears no burden of race coding, he urges Zack to take up the white man's pistol.

Upon Zack's throwing his gun upon the bed, Lucas kneels, "facing across the bed and the pistol the man whom he had known from infancy, with whom he had lived until they were both grown almost as brothers lived." Then Lucas seizes the pistol, knowing he needs two shots—one for killing Zack, one for himself in suicide. He pulls the trigger, the pistol goes off, but misfires. In a characteristic Faulknerian time-leap, the scene closes down at precisely this moment. What matters most

is what Lucas thinks later as he examines the live cartridge that
did not go off.

> I wouldn't have used the second one, he thought. I would have
> paid. I would have waited for the rope, even the coal oil. I would
> have paid. So I reckon I aint got old Carothers' blood for nothing,
> after all.[54]

Lucas has elected to play by "the white man's rules." He
chose the pistol, not the black man's razor, as his potential
weapon of revenge, but he was ready to pay for having leapt out
of his "place" with the black man's suffering of rope and coal oil.
Lucas's race etiquette—his race pride—is here identified with
that of his white ancestor. As Alfred Stone of Mississippi would
acknowledge, Lucas is the mulatto who is classed by his society
as the Negro he is not, while acting like the white man he
believes he is.[55]

The situation is reversed in *Light in August*. Joe Christmas
eerily fits what Ray Stannard Baker describes as the most
frightening force let loose upon a Southern community: "The
Floating Negro"—the individual whom Joel Williamson notes
was called "the nigger in the woods."[56] Lawless is the way Joe
Christmas affects the folks in Jefferson from the day he appears,
insolent, sullen, silent, at the town's sawmill, but Faulkner
continually shows that Joe is the most rule-ridden of men. Rigid
codes of behavior dictate all his relations, from McEachern on.
He only turns vicious when others break those codes, forcing
him to exact retribution for their betrayal, as when he beats
almost to death the Northern whore who, by voicing her indifference to his insistence that he is a Negro, makes mock of
society's careful codes against miscegenation carried out by
black men and white women.

And so one night Joe finds himself on the road approaching
Joanna Burden's house, surprised at one point to realize he
holds a razor in his hand. Placing it back in his pocket, he
confronts Joanna who then asks him to kneel beside her in
prayer. Upon his refusal (how could he ever do such an obscene

thing as bow his head in prayer?), Joanna takes a pistol out from beneath her shawl and cocks the hammer, her eyes "calm and still as all pity and all despair and all conviction."

And then Joe is standing in the road with an upraised hand, flagging down a car, only later realizing he's been holding aloft Joanna's pistol with its two loaded chambers—one which had been fired but didn't explode, the second still to be released: "For her and for me." But the white man's way of the pistol—for murder or for suicide—is not the way Joe Christmas chooses, out of his willed race-pride as the black man on whose terms he has forged his identity since childhood.

Gavin Stevens's "race theory" about the motives for Joe's actions, as his theories often are, is inadequate to the situation. In Stevens's mind "it was the black blood which snatched up the pistol and the white blood which would not let him fire it." He should have considered that (according to Joe's own "race theory") it was Joe's belief in his blackness up to this point that would not let him fire the pistol, that drew him to take up the razor instead.[57]

In order for Faulkner to register all the diverse codes of violence sanctioned by a culture that knows better how to kill than to let live, Percy Grimm must intrude his own warped race etiquette into the sequence of events. This petty soldier-manque will blast away at the prone body of Joe Christmas with his "black, blunt, huge automatic" out of his trivial, but deadly, imitation of the war hero he could never be. But then confirming his inferior caste status, Grimm grabs up a butcher's knife and castrates the dying man, saying "Now you'll let white women alone, even in hell."[58]

White womanhood has been vindicated, despite the fact that Joanna Burden, the despised Yankee version of the female, had wished to carry out her own etiquette for death—using "the suicidal pistol" in the exact manner E. M. Woods describes at the conclusion of *The Negro in Etiquette*, using it as must the "enemy to good society" who has dreamed of "the joining of ebon and 'lily white' hands in marriage." Everyone in Faulkner's

portrayal of this tragic charade of race relationships has be-
haved—if not impeccably—at least according to the demands of
their individual ideologies of race.

Faulkner, like the editors of *Life* before him, realized the
often overpowering force of the codes of conduct by which
ideologies of race seek out appropriate cultural expression:
Faulkner at the level of high art, *Life* at the level of the mass
media; Faulkner with far more awareness than *Life* of the tragic
ironies involved in the killing games staged with exquisite nicety
by the Great Director of mores and manners; Faulkner more
ambivalent in regard to "arguments by numbers" than *Life*,
although still implicated in ideologies of biological difference;
Faulkner a master at interpreting the "Southern manners" that
lie behind all acts of violence taking place within all the texts
and subtexts of his Yoknapatawpha narratives.

In conclusion, there is a final visual image to introduce
from the decade under review; there is one last contemporary
commentary on the matter of manners to take into account.
Figure 21 is one among many that filled the advertising pages
of *Life*, that portion of the magazine that added complications
to the editorial positions held up front. *Life*'s official position
was to abhor violence. Its winged mascot representing joy, love,
and *lust* had no wish to besmirch its role as "civilizer" with any
taint of "savage" behavior. But the advertisers which helped to
support the magazine with cash revenue saw no reason to take
a strong line on benign "good manners." Indeed, the decade's
ideological biases appear here even more blatantly. "Civilization" is to be upheld by "savage" means—by the use, for
example, of "The New Savage Automatic Pistol."[59]

Figure 21 reads in part:

Is Yours An Egg shell Home?

Suppose your wife, mother or sister, left alone in the house,
should wake up to-night and find a burglar in her room. What
would she do? Suppose she were left alone and a tramp, drunk or
vicious person, should come to the house and attack her. What
could she do by way of resistance?

Is Yours An Egg shell Home?

¶ Suppose your wife, mother or sister, left alone in the house, should wake up to-night and find a burglar in her room. What would she do? Suppose she were left alone and a tramp, drunk or vicious person should come to the house and attack her. What *could* she do by way of resistance?

¶ Nothing. Absolutely nothing! She would be helpless—helpless as a little child.

¶ Get her the new "human arsenal"—the new Savage Automatic. We call it a pistol, but, in reality, it should be called a "human protector"—a human protector in the condensed form of pocket arm. It converts your home from a helpless, defenseless egg shell of a place, into an arsenal. It converts your wife, mother or sister into a human arsenal. It actually makes her able to put up a crack shot's defense, for any novice can aim it as expertly as any crack shot, and it is the quickest pocket arm ever built—gets in the first (vital) shot. Please send us the name of the retailer from whom you buy fire arms, and we'll have him show you the new Savage Automatic quick. Do it today and take your wife, mother and sister out of their defenseless egg shell and put them into an impregnable arsenal.

10 Shots Quick

¶ Loads 10 Shots at a time; shoots one at a time, as *fast* as you press the trigger, ¶ You can't realize what this rapid fire gun is until you read "Bat" Masterson's book, "The Tenderfoot's Turn." No charge for it either.

SAVAGE ARMS CO.
882 Savage Ave.,
Utica,   New York.

¶ The new SAVAGE RIFLE book is ready. Full of valuable rifle information; handsomely illustrated. Sent to sportsmen free for dealer's name on post card. With our new factory additions we can now supply high power rifles ('99 model) 303 repeater. Ask dealers to show our .22 cal. Repeater.

THE NEW SAVAGE AUTOMATIC

Figure 21.

Nothing. Absolutely nothing! She would be helpless—helpless as a little child.

Get her the new "human arsenal"—the new Savage Automatic. We call it a pistol, but, in reality, it should be called a "human protector"—a human protector in the condensed form of pocket arm. It converts your home from a helpless, defenseless egg shell of a place, into an arsenal. It converts your wife, mother or sister into a human arsenal.

America's white womanhood is menaced in the night by "the floating man." One need not label him as the Negro, since any "other" will do. The point is that the true American male of "the best" sort must practice the consumer etiquette appropriate to the times and the circumstances.

Women are unable to resort to either knife or razor—weapons which draw the assailant too close in toward vulnerable bodies and exact a physical strength beyond the capacity of feminine fragility. Thus their menfolk must prepare them to fight the "savage" with the "Savage Automatic Pistol." Forget the cultural niceties of an advanced society which leaves women unprotected

in "eggshell houses." Revert to the manners of medieval for-
tresses under siege; to pioneer days when lone women held off
bloodthirsty Indians with rifles; to the War Between the States
when (as we know from later images implanted by *Gone with
the Wind*) the female fends off lustful Yankee soldiers or drunken
Negroes with her pistol. The savagery of modern times demands
that the modern women rely on the pistol; only then might she
be safe from the razor or knife of savages that lurk in the night;
even worse, from the guns used by those with the effrontery to
play "the white man's" game.[60]

For all the "Northernness" of its crude commercialization of
fear, this advertisement is a variation of the essay written four
years earlier by a Mrs. L. H. Harris. Titled "Southern Manners," it appeared in *The Independent*—which, by the way,
originated in 1848 as a militantly Abolitionist periodical that
urged armed resistance to the Fugitive Slave Law.[61]

Striking the note reminiscent of that which DuBois voiced
three years earlier in *The Souls of Black Folk*, Mrs. Harris
speaks of the double consciousness experienced by all post-
Reconstruction Southern whites. Because Southerners are both
what they "are" and what they have "been," their system
of manners is "as difficult to interpret as it is dangerous to
misinterpret them."

The author first defines the codes—at once, charming and
dangerous—upheld by Southern white males that result from
the pride they take in "the pedigrees, morals and manners." The
"cavalier" blood which permeates the "well-bred Southerner"
affects "his conscience and consciousness more than all the
modern training he gets." The Southerner is "a social enigma,
because he is himself and his favorite forefather at the same
time." He lives with a "pose" behind which he "watches the
effect of his own mannerism with all the shrewdness of a
dramatic critic." All Southerners are good actors. "The duality
of their personal consciousness begets a remarkable facility
of expression."

How like the Southern black to the Southern white in this

regard, notwithstanding the outward differences in manners that result from this doubling of consciousness begot from each group's struggle to deny the social and political defeats that define their existence.[62]

Although blacks go unmentioned in this or any other regard, what Mrs. Harris states about Southern relationships carry their presence as a powerful subtext. Yankees, she says, are

> nothing to one another . . . and so they [have] no feelings wounded. But in the South, we are always something to one another, friend or foe, really or prospectively, and must therefore cultivate the courtesies and discourtesies of personal intercourse more than other people.[63]

Then the author makes a most telling comment. "For this reason also, we carry our sword next to our manners, not literally, but figuratively—we have been compelled to substitute much that is figurative for what was once literal in our conduct." Cut off from past codes of social behavior centered on the dueling sword, the contemporary Southern male relies on "his manner" to make it clear he is still capable of killing. "Nothing is more offensive to Southern men than to intimate that every man-jack of them is not as dangerous today as when his favorite ancestor wore . . . a sword tied in his sash." The modern "absurdity" of existence in postwar society with which Southerners must contend means the men hold "to the sword-point manner of observing their honor."[64]

Mrs. Harris does not treat of the literal ways by which males in the South ("well-bred" or not) actually express their angers and fears: no mention is made of pistol, knife, razor, hemp or fire as contemporary weapons of punishing infractions of their code. Her emphasis remains upon the symbolism of manners that stands in for the males' ability to kill. But she offers three final points of interest: (1) It is reverence for the war dead that gives "a startling sting to our manners." (2) Defeat cannot be admitted. "It cannot be done in our language. We have the words, but not that use of them. And it does not comport with our victorious manners." (3) Before the war Southern whites

manners as weapons

were divided into two classes—"those who descended from a fine ancestry and those who descended from nobody in particular." The former took their place in the big houses, the latter knew their place as "peasants" toiling in the fields. But now that both "the cavalier and peasant stock have faced a common enemy," "they become brothers, entitled to the same coat of arms and to the same manners and features."

With this closing of the class/caste ranks among whites bound by a common code of behavior based on the symbolism of the drawn weapon, Mrs. Harris ends her essay. It is for us to notice two further implications of her delineation of Southern manners whose ideology stems from reverence for the past: (1) the shared "pedigrees, morals and manners" of all Southern males merge into the pride of "victory" gained from their faith in racial supremacy; (2) the cavalier's sword is no longer used to prove how "dangerous" this code is to whoever stands outside his proper "place," but other weapons (coal oil, hemp, knife) are now available—even those (especially those) borrowed from the culture of "the peasants," now deemed "brothers" of the "aristocrats."

Leave it to mannerless Yankees to advertise the selling of pistols to Northern women forced to defend themselves against "savage" intruders. Southern males will do the defending, according to the proud codes of their own culture.[65]

Just as I, a child in the North of the 1930s, observed as a spectator the cultural mores of violence enacted before my wondering mind, William Faulkner as a child of the South in the early 1900s paid attention to the "manners" by which his people expressed their victory over the "language" of defeat. But whereas I was a creature caught, as it were, within the "culture narratives" spun by the Lynds about Muncie, Indiana (county seat of Delaware County)—the "Middletown" saga which was the Yankee sociologists' version of the life and times of other such places as Jefferson, Mississippi (county seat of the Yoknapatawpha world)[66]—Faulkner was that special person who got *to write into being* the cultural history of his own hometown.

Not only that, Faulkner went on to demonstrate, in ways beyond the power of Mrs. Harris or the editors of *Life*, those dramas that arise once carefully constructed codes for killing slice across class, caste, regional, and race lines, whenever individuals struggle to the death to define who they are in relation to the violent codes it seems to be their tragic fate to enact.

NOTES

1. Robert S. Lynd and Helen Merrell Lynd, *Middletown: A Study in Modern American Culture* (New York: Harcourt, Brace, 1929) and *Middletown in Transition, A Study of Cultural Conflict* (New York: Harcourt, Brace, 1937).

2. At the time the two "Middletown" studies were made, the black population was around 6 percent, while the native-born white population made up 92 percent of the total. Blacks, however, figured in 17 percent of all arrests during the mid-1930s, most of them labeled as "property crimes." Thefts were also categorized by type: "Negroes steal chickens, hungry men hold up small groceries . . . and boys rob coal sheds" (*Middletown in Transition*, 349). Statistics concerning the number of blacks accused of violent crimes are not given, but mention is made of the lynching of two blacks in a nearby city and of the fact that the "angry race resentments set roaring by the Klan in Middletown only ten years ago can again be made to blaze out in Middletown's South Side almost overnight" (Ibid., 465).

3. E. M. Woods. *The Negro in Etiquette: A Novelty* (St. Louis: Buxton and Skinner, 1899).

4. Christopher Herbert, *Culture and Anomie. Ethnographic Imagination in the Nineteenth Century* (Chicago: University of Chicago Press, 1991), 38.

5. Bertram Wilbur Doyle, *The Etiquette of Race Relations in the South. A Study of Social Control* (Chicago: University of Chicago Press, 1937). As do most scholars in the field of race history, Doyle observes that the codes imposed by whites were countered in part by the rules of behavior created by blacks that masked contempt for and manipulation of the white man's codes. Doyle makes distinctions between antebellum codes, those being tested during the Reconstruction, and the etiquette that evolved in the South from the 1880s onward—each phase marked by shifts in the forms used by both whites and blacks. Woodward also points out differences between antebellum codes arising from race relationships based on physical proximity and post-Reconstruction codes marked by the physical and psychological distancing through which the "exclusions" of a segregated society were put into play.

6. C. Vann Woodward, *The Strange Case of Jim Crow* (New York: Oxford University Press, 1955, 1957, 1974); August Meier, *Negro Thought in America, 1880–1915. Racial Ideologies in the Age of Booker T. Washington* (Ann Arbor: University of Michigan Press, 1963, 1966); Thomas F. Gossett, *Race: The History of an Idea in America* (New York: Schoken Books, 1965); Joel Williamson, *The Crucible of Race: Black-White Relations in the American South Since Emancipation* (New York: Oxford University Press, 1984), and *New People. Miscegenation and Mulattoes in the United States* (New York: Free Press, 1980). The observation that "the race problem" was seen to have developed once emancipation took place is made by Doyle, xxi.

7. Adam Smith in *The Theory of Moral Sentiments* and Freud in *Civilization and Its Discontents* are linked by Herbert, *Culture and Anomie*, 84. S. L. Louis remarks about society conducted as a vast drama by "the Great Director" in *Decorum. A*

Practical Treatise on Etiquette and Dress of the Best American Society (Chicago: University of Chicago Press, 1881), 335.

8. When radical Southern whites deal with blacks it was "not only a matter of choosing specific words to fall in sequence; it was also a matter of speech inflections, pauses, rises and falls in pitch and volume, of body postures and relative positions, of movements of eyes and hands. . . . It was a matter of dress and costume, of naming and titles of address, of place and setting." Each side in this ever-fluctuating cultural relationship "evolved words to say, gestures to make—a language in which individuals might negotiate interracial encounters; but each situation was unique, and the solution in each situation personal and creative" (Williamson, *Crucible of Race*, 224, 258).

9. See *The Hamlet* for Mink's nearly botched murder of Jack Houston, and *The Mansion* for the difficulties Mink faces in his killing of Flem Snopes.

10. Lavers's defense is paraphrased by Chuck Shephard in "News of the Weird," *Reader: Los Angeles's Free Weekly* 14, no.3 (November 1, 1991): 70. My thanks to William Gleason for calling this incident to my attention.

11. In the closing months of the Civil War the state of Mississippi was dispossessed, just as even earlier Mohataha had been "swept, hurled, flung" out of whatever history would be experienced by the rest of the United States. See *Requiem for a Nun* (New York: Random House, 1951), 221–22.

12. The Jim Crow laws had their greatest importance as "symbols" that helped consolidate white power and solidarity (Williamson, *Crucible of Race*, 247). Williamson tracks the legalization of segregation through three waves—(a) 1889–93; (b) 1897–1907; (c) 1913–15—each addressing relationships affected by changes in the Southern industrial situation located in factories, urban housing, and public facilities (253).

13. The Spanish-American War and the move into the Philippines gave a boost to Southern white supremacist ideology. In the view of Thomas Dixon, these events heralded "the birth of a nation" (Williamson, *Crucible Of Race*, 336).

14. *Life* (August 5, 1887): 114; rerun in March 31, 1904, 310.

15. *Life* (September 1, 1904): 206. In *Following the Color Line. American Negro Citizenship in the Progressive Era* (New York: Doubleday, Page, 1908), the Northern journalist Ray Stannard Baker observed the growing revulsion against lynching expressed by certain Southerners. They found it not only "not wholly moral," but—because of their "awakening industrial ambition"—they "realised that disorder had a tendency to frighten away capital, stop immigration, and retard development generally. Good business demands good order." With increasing frequency Baker heard the question being asked, "Can we at the South afford it [racial disorder]?" (Baker, 192).

16. *Life* (November 12, 1903): 458.

17. *Life* (June 1 and 8, 1899): 456, 482.

18. As could be expected, available statistics on the number of lynchings taking place between 1890 and into the 1900s are not wholly reliable. It is commonly contended that the peak of violence occurred during the 1890s; this seems to be the case if one looks at the total numbers of persons lynched, white and black. However, though the total drops by 1900, the proportion of blacks killed to whites increases greatly. Thomas Gossett, for one, maintains that ten times as many blacks were lynched as whites between 1906–1915. See Gossett, *Race*, 269–270. Ray Stannard Baker's research during 1904 and 1906–1908 that resulted in his report, *Following the Color Line*, also suggests the high incidence of black lynching, figures largely substantiated by later investigations carried out by the NAACP. Scholars vary, however, on the dates for the peaks in violence. For example, because of the emphasis *The Crucible of Race* places upon the moves made by the Southern Radicals, Williamson not only focuses upon the timespan between November 1898 (the Wilmington riot) and September 1906 (the Atlanta riot), he also gauges variations in the emotional temperature of Radicalism: very hot from 1889–93; cooled between 1893–97; at its most feverish between 1897–1906.

19. *Life* (February 1, 1900): 92; (April 30, 1903): 386.

20. *Life* (August 18, 1887): 92–93.

21. *Life* (May 21, 1903): 462.

22. *Life* (March 16, 1905): 308.

23. *Life* (January 22, 1903): 66; (August 18, 1904), 160; (January 10, 1907), 50.

24. *Life* (December 22, 1904): 641. In Ray Stannard Baker's articles for *McClure's* at this time, he comments that previously black athletes did well at Harvard, but that because of a recent incident at Harvard (undefined) involving a black baseball player, "there will probably never be another coloured boy on the university teams" (*Following the Color Line*, 123).

25. *Life* (April 20, 1905): 456. From left to right, the line–up includes Washington, Bryan, Roosevelt, Riis, and Platt. In the piece that accompanies this illustration, Senator Platt objects to Washington's presence, saying, "He can't come in here. He's black." When Washington asks permission to sit with the others, Bryan retorts, "Not on your life. Do you want to queer us?" Roosevelt, however, tells Washington to be seated, announcing to the others, "He's my chum," and that no one can tell him not to play "with a little black boy." At this, Riis begins to cry, saying Roosevelt "loves [Washington] more than he does me." But Roosevelt reassures him, "No, I don't, Jake. This is only a bluff."

26. *Life* (February 11, 1904): 141.

27. *Life* (May 14, 1903): 440.

28. The final chapter of William Benjamin Smith's *The Color Line: A Brief in Behalf of the Unborn* (New York: McClure, Phillips, 1905) is titled "The Argument from Numbers." However lame a piece of sociology Smith's treatise may be, it represents the struggles of the practitioners of this new discipline to achieve full legitimacy for their "science" by means of an obsessive use of statistics, here employed to "prove" biological inferiority. Bronislaw Malinowski's *Crime and Custom in Savage Society* (London: K. Paul, Trench, Trubner 1926) points in another direction (however fraught with ideological distortions of its own): the "argument by manners" pursued by ethnographers who valorized the study of social codes over the formulation of genetic tables. Two examples: (a) Frederick L. Hoffman, Social Darwinist and statistician for the Prudential Life Insurance Company, compiled *Race Traits and Tendencies*, published in 1896 by the American Economic Association; (b) by the 1920s social scientists had developed thirty specific traits for mulattoes, including thirty-three shades of skin, each with an identifying number (Gossett, *Race*, 281; Williamson, *New People*, 3).

29. When speaking of the Conservative Restoration, Williamson states that " 'Place' was the key word in the vocabulary of Conservatism, and place applied not only to blacks, but to all people and to all things" (*Crucible of Race*, 79).

30. *Life* (April 14 and 21, 1904): 360, 387.

31. Throughout the 1880s and early 1890s *Life* depicts the harmless darky, while the South lay stress upon "the menacing black male." However, by 1915, Williamson asserts, once the Radicals had given way to the Southern Conservatives, "the black beast was lost to sight, and the black as child was very much to the fore" (*Crucible of Race*, 182, 259). White paternalism was allowed to guide the use of good manners among the "children" under its care. Up to 1915, of course, Southern Radicals had handled the "menace" according to its own unfatherly codes—codes that Northerners emulated on occasion, and tried to "understand" in large part out of growing sympathy with their own race–brothers.

32. *Life* (March 10, 1887): cover.

33. *Life* (December 26, 1895): 423.

34. *Life* (December 29, 1898): cover.

35. *Life* (March 24, 1887): 167.

36. *Life* (September 26, 1895): 197.

37. *Life* (April 14, 1895): unpaginated advertising section.

38. *Life* (April 28, 1904): 404.

39. *Life* (February 21, 1907): 274–75.

40. The popular journals in favor of United States expansionism included *Harper's*, *Scribner's*, *The Century*, and *McClure's*; the anti-imperialist periodicals numbered *The Arena*, *The Dial*, and *Life* (Gossett, *Race*, 336).

41. In the *Williams vs. Mississippi* case of 1898 the Supreme Court opened the way to complete disenfranchisement. Woodward recognizes the ideological affinities between "the Mississippi plan" and the attitudes that lay behind imperialist moves into "barbaric" territories whose inhabitants the *Atlantic Monthly* characterized as the "new-caught, sullen peoples" (Woodward, 71–72, 83).

42. *Life* (December 8, 1898): cover; (February 23, 1899), 150–51.

43. *Life* (May 10, 1900): cover.

44. *Life* (March 24, 1904): 288–89; (May 24, 1900), 462–63.

45. Future developments of the material contained in this essay will look closely at the nature of the social occasions the cakewalk created, and possible cultural responses to it, advanced by James Weldon Johnson in *The Autobiography of an Ex-Coloured Man* (Boston: Sherman, French, 1912); also, the Inauguration Ball held by the "colored society" of Washington, D.C., featured in W.E.B. DuBois's novel *The Quest of the Silver Fleece* (Chicago: A. C. Clurg, 1911). *Life*'s various takes on the cakewalk will be analyzed in depth, as will E.M. Woods's rebuke to his fellow blacks for their naiveté in believing that "the most refined, educated and wealthy white folks are taking to the cake-walk fad" out of genuine appreciation for this dance mode. No, says Woods, whites perform the dance only "as a light evening amusement and burlesque," and for blacks to do the cakewalk is at "expense to the laws of ethics and refinement" (Woods, *The Negro in Etiquette*, 133).

46. "Legislatures have repeatedly attempted to define where black leaves off and white begins," especially in regard to marriage (Ray Stannard Baker, 151).

47. *Life* (May 14, 1903): 440. Alfred Holt Stone was born in 1870, graduated from the University of Mississippi in 1891, practiced law, edited the *Greenville Times* between 1900–01, and was a prominent member of the University Alumni Association: His *Studies in the American Race Problem* (New York: Doubleday, Page) was published in 1908. For further information see *History of the Alumni Association of the University of Mississippi, 1852–1985*, ed. Franklin E. Moak (University: The Alumni Association of The University of Mississippi, 1986).

48. Of particular value, Joel Williamson's book *New People: Miscegenation and Mulattoes in the United States* grounds this issue directly within the socio-historical context of the post-Reconstruction South.

49. Section on "Danger from the Floating Negro," in Baker's *Following the Color Line*.

50. DuBois "Marrying of Black Folk," *The Independent* 69 (October 13, 1910): 813.

51. Woods's manual, written in the "earnest desire to raise the social and moral standard of the Negro," deserves a full-scale study of its own, in regard to the enterprise it undertakes, the grotesque illustrations supplied by his publisher, and the conflicted nature of Woods's own attitudes toward the New Negro—they who must learn that "People of refinement don't go where they are not wanted" (Woods, 147). The following quotations are from the final chapter: 157, 159.

52. In 1971 an entirely different kind of etiquette book was published. Written by Sheila Rush and Chris Clark, *How To Get Along with Black People: A Handbook for White Folks. And Some Black Folks Too* (New York: Third Press, 1971) includes a section on "Dating and Marriage." It mentions that whites often enter mixed relationships in rebellion against their parents, while blacks will do it to get even with whites, to get power, to "show off." Different times, different cultures, different motives, different consequences.

53. See Thomas Cripps, *Slow Fade to Black: The Negro in American Film, 1900–1942* (New York: Oxford University Press, 1977).

54. Faulkner, "The Fire in the Hearth," in *Go Down, Moses* (New York, 1942), 50, 52–53, 55, 58.

55. Doyle's *The Etiquette of Race Relations in the South* includes this account from Powell Clayton's *Aftermath of the Civil War in Arkansas* (New York: Neale, 1915): "in order to make an impressive tableau," local Klansmen "killed Fed Reeves, an unoffending Negro" together with the white sheriff of the Reconstruction party. They then

"tied the white man and Negro together in the attitude of kissing and left them in the public road, where they remained for two days." In "The Fire and the Hearth" (111, 114), Henry Beauchamp and Roth Edmonds (sons respectively of Lucas and Zack) have played, eaten, and slept together as "brothers" up to a certain moment; then Henry is made to feel that the "rules" have changed between them. New rules now apply, else a form of "male miscegenation" be permitted to take place, as bad (if not worse) than intercourse between a black man and a white woman.

56. Williamson, *The Crucible of Race*, 58.

57. Williamson observes that "the 'etiquette' of race relations" necessitated "forgiveness of the avowedly contrite transgressor" whenever a break in the code took place. In contrast, violence results when the black does something that is perceived as being unforgivable: such as when he acts like a white man (Williamson, *Crucible of Race*, 258, 282). Nearly as unforgivable are the actions of "white niggers"—people who are "Negro in their behavior, attitudes, and morals" (Williamson, *New People*, 107). But then there is Joe Christmas, the man who chooses not to forgive himself for all the disruptions he causes to the social order during most of his lifetime. It must be noted, however, that Joe's death takes him beyond race categories; the burst of blood wipes out social and cultural identities based on "blood." Joanna has tried to fix Joe as a Negro, something he has allowed no one else to do for him, and so he has had to kill her. This act accomplished, he reenters the circle that sent him on the run before. But he does not return to the mark where, as a child at the orphanage, he had the label "nigger" imposed upon his small being. At the very end, he returns to a private self that effaces the social self.

58. William Faulkner, *Light in August* (New York: Random House, 1932), 267, 270, 424, 439.

59. *Life* (February 3, 1910): 224.

60. In the South, as a result of the Atlanta riot of 1906 and the rising fear among whites over "floating blacks," women were told to arm themselves. Trained to shoot guns, they were also offered $10,000 rewards for killing would-be assailants (Williamson, *Crucible of Race*, 214).

61. Mrs. L. H. Harris, "Southern Manners," *The Independent* 61 (August 9, 1906): 321–25. Note that DuBois's piece on "Marrying of Black Folk" appeared in the same journal in 1910, and that his *The Souls of Black Folk* with its famous discussion of "double consciousness" was published in 1903.

62. But major differences, as well. To Mrs. Harris, the whites' double consciousness helps them to deal with their position of powerlessness vis-a-vis the North. With DuBois, double consciousness as experienced by blacks must not be allowed to maintain the status quo exacted by white society, South or North. Bertram Doyle comments that the Southern black "moves in a world of forms" and that "he plays at the practice, as at an amusing game." Having "contempt for the white man's codes," he "has detached himself from the situation, has evaluated it critically, and needs to spend small emotional energy either in defending or decrying existing conditions" (*Etiquette of Race Relations*, 159, 168). A manipulation of the "boss's" codes that furthers political passivity was not to the liking of DuBois. Doyle observes that under DuBois's "scheme the races were not to be allowed to come to terms, and race relations were not again to be fixed in custom and formulated in codes before the Negro had fully experienced his freedom. Resistance to compromise has, then, helped to keep the racial situation in a state of flux." (162).

63. Northerners find it quaint to have it said that they have no manners because they have no relationships with one another. It is useful, however, to notice those instances in Faulkner's fiction descriptive of persons of no discernible "humanity"—possessed of no feelings to wound, no one to be something to—in regard to the difference it makes in the ways they kill. As Jay Watson of the University of Mississippi has observed, Popeye uses a silencer on his pistol; no personal relationships are involved where his murderous intent is concerned. In contrast, we see the urgency with which Mink Snopes (who could have sneaked up on his enemy Flem and killed him with an

anonymous bullet) must signal his presence; his code for killing definitely mandates *a relationship*.

64. In an editorial of May 16, 1895 (318), *Life* remarks upon "the Kentucky method"—the use of the pistol by the deceived husband who kills his wife and her lover, all "persons of high social respectability." This incident is set in contrast to the razor used by an immigrant Italian woman in New York City who slashed the throat of her lying lover. *Life* tops off this review by noticing that the native citizens of New York prosaically tend to take their grievances into the law courts. There is more than a sneaking respect for "the Kentucky method" which makes it clear that a man is a man.

65. Mrs. Harris remarks upon the lack of "literal" relations between white Southern women and men. Since the males idealize their womenfolk, they exist only as symbols; thus it is for the sake of such symbols that the men stand ready to "kill," even if only symbolically (324).

66. There are far more similarities than differences in method between the "Middletown" accounts and Faulkner's chronicles of "Jefferson." Neither of the Lynds received formal training as sociologists, and they fell into their assignment to interpret the mores of an "average" mid-western community more by chance than by calculation. The particular genius that sets their study apart lies in the narratives they incorporate. Charts and statistics are dutifully present, but the series' real energy results from the voices of the townspeople and the strange tales they tell about their often confused, wistful, heart-felt negotiations within ever-changing patterns of cultural conduct.

Realism, Naturalism, Modernism: Residual, Dominant, and Emergent Ideologies in *As I Lay Dying*

JAMES M. MELLARD

No one, these days, would reasonably dispute that William Faulkner is a "modernist" author—however we may take the meaning of that loaded word. Nor would anyone question whether *As I Lay Dying* is a modernist novel. Typical of this assumption is Donald Kartiganer's recent essay in *Mississippi Quarterly* and the most comprehensive study of the novel yet, André Bleikasten's book-length reading published almost twenty years ago.[1] "If by subject matter," says Bleikasten, "*As I Lay Dying* belongs to the oral and literary tradition of folktales and tall stories, the novelist's approach to his art is definitely modern" (3). But in 1930, as an aesthetic mode or ideology, modernism was still emergent rather than residual or dominant, in the terms supplied by Marxist critic Raymond Williams.[2] Williams's terms are very useful in literary analysis because the set—dominant, residual, emergent—provides a persuasive description of what most of us believe we see going on in our culture at any given moment. Our "natural" sense of things suggests that indeed things do change, that what's up at this moment will be down at a later moment, that what's in now will be out then. We do see values come and go, ways of doing things evolve into other ways of doing things. We may feel, in fact, that those things we associate with the ideological— fashions, assumptions of value, orientations toward modes of thought—come and go like the young Eula Varner's lovers:

there may be one in the porch-swing, but there's another who's just left, and a third waiting in the wings to displace the one swinging in the swing right now.

What I want to argue is that in *As I Lay Dying* one of the elements that make it both so troubling and so fascinating to ordinary and specialist readers alike is the tension among the three aesthetic ideologies it was then subjected to—its then-culturally dominant naturalism, its residual realism, and its emergent modernism. The first two terms—naturalism and realism—are not so frequently set off against each other today, but if today's critics and scholars ignore the differences between the terms because of what they construe as their superior historical perspective, their doing so puts at risk their very historicism. For when we conflate naturalism, as we often do, into realism as *just* another realism, we deny the power of those concepts in their own historical context. In fact, these three concepts—realism, naturalism, and modernism—locate rather precisely where all of Faulkner's early novels were placed in the critical debate at the time of their production. Consequently, I want to examine some of the elements of that critical debate as it primarily surrounds *As I Lay Dying*.

1

First, I need to examine those terms—residual, dominant, and emergent—introduced by Raymond Williams. Williams's terms help us by their admitting process into what may look like a merely static system. Williams develops the notions residual, dominant, and emergent to get away from some of the traditional Marxist notions of "totality" that, regarding social and cultural life, suggest an unchanging and unchangeable monolith that experience teaches none of us quite to believe in. But while we may not believe in some uniform cultural monolith, we do readily believe there is a "dominant," if not totally determining, modality of cultural existence. Thus Williams adopts Antonio Gramsci's concept of "hegemony" in place of "totality" to suggest the variable relations of social practices. "The theoretical model which I have been trying to work with is this," says Williams. "I would say first that in any society, in any particular period, there is a central system of practices, meanings and values, [that] we can properly call dominant and effective" (38). But there are as well other systems of practices that do not have quite the same cultural status or power or the same historical genealogy. He calls the one that is displaced by the dominant the "residual" and the one that in turn shall displace the dominant the "emergent." "By 'residual,'" Williams says, "I mean that some experiences, meanings and values, which cannot be verified or cannot be expressed in terms of the dominant culture, are nevertheless lived and practised on the basis of the residue—cultural as well as social—of some previous social formation" (40). "By 'emergent,'" says Williams, "I mean, first, that new meanings and values, new practices, new significances and experiences, are continually being created" and, sometimes, being incorporated into the hegemonic, reigning, "dominant" culture (41). For Williams, then, these terms and the process of interaction their productive relations may take defines a historical paradigm and potentialities that may occur in time, time being the dimension required for any perspective from which to determine the relations. The hardest to see at any given moment, of course, is the emergent; consequently in our discussion of Faulkner that is the one that will perhaps be the hardest to isolate within the historical context of 1930.

I now need to proceed to my main goal, to suggest how the elements of realism, naturalism, and modernism—as aesthetic practices carrying an ideological burden—interact in Faulkner's novel. First, I need to speak of "realism." There are at least two senses of realism I must mention. One is the sense that whatever is *dominant* will represent our notion of "realism" at any given time. This is the sense one employs when thinking that one is not expressing ideology at all, but is merely being natural or commonsensical or—in a word—realistic. But this sort of thinking is still ideological. The second sense of realism I advert to—and the more important one for my purposes—is its use as a label for what is regarded as the most traditional method or system of aesthetic practices characterizing the novel-as-a-genre. From the perspective of the historically innocent, realism in this sense cannot be distinguished from the first sense, for this methodological realism is taken simply to be the way things are supposed to be done in fiction. That these practices exemplify an ideology is generally taken as a fact by critics and literary historians these days, although the standard explanation of the ideology underlying the epistemology of the novel—Ian Watt's *The Rise of the Novel*—would not use the term. Instead, Watt himself, because he regards realism as somehow "natural" to the novel, remains rather blind to the ideological elements inscribed in the techniques of realism, even though what he identifies is to us precisely the ideological. We may say, then, reading Watt through the lens of almost any contemporary Marxist critic, that the novel-as-genre not only has come into being, but has brought along with its form all the ideological baggage originating when Defoe and Richardson and Fielding put into practice the narrative procedures of formal realism.[3]

So to the extent that *As I Lay Dying* employs the epistemological devices of realism, that is, the techniques of the mode of realist production, Faulkner's novel is indeed ideological within an ideological convention. But is Faulkner's use of the conventions of realism residual or dominant? Before addressing that question directly I want first to consider two other questions. The two questions are these: how much does Faulkner use the devices of realism? And, equally important from a contextualized ideological perspective, how much did the readers in its time of production assume a realistic basis for *As I Lay Dying*? Let's take the first question first. It is fairly plain, from the beginning of the novel, that Faulkner is at least laying down a realistic base. We see that in the paragraphs that open the novel:

> Jewel and I come up from the field, following the path in single file. Although I am fifteen feet ahead of him, anyone watching us

from the cottonhouse can see Jewel's frayed and broken straw hat a full head above my own.

The path runs straight as a plumb-line, worn smooth by feet and baked brick-hard by July, between the green rows of laidby cotton, to the cottonhouse in the center of the field, where it turns and circles the cottonhouse at four soft right angles and goes on across the field again, worn so by feet in fading precision.[4]

No passage in any novel is likely to fit Watt's requirements for realist practices or what he also calls its formal realism better than this one. Though the features Watt enumerates include the repudiation of traditional plots, it is too early yet to determine whether that will turn out to be the case (it is, but the plot *is* traditional in another sense—that of the oral epical tradition of quest or journey). But the other features Watt names are immediately recognizable: we see Faulkner eschewing figurative eloquence; we see the particularization of character and background; we see the use of naming, the invocation of temporality, the reliance on causation, and the precise evocation of a physical environment. Thus, we see virtually all the traits of formal realism that suggest *the* novel—the novel-as-genre—is properly "referential." The opening of *As I Lay Dying*, in short, names characters, moves them through time, and presumes an external world available to representation through description, nominalization, and spatial extension.

Now for that second question regarding readers. How, for example, did the readers—reviewers and historians alike—at first locate Faulkner and, whenever it is mentioned, *As I Lay Dying* in the terms of our triad of ideologies? Essentially, they focused on the residual realism and the dominant naturalism. In a history of American literature published in 1932, A. C. Ward assumes the authority of realism. Referring to *The Sound and the Fury*, Ward writes, "[H]owever much we wish for reasonable freedom for the novelist in choice of subject and method, there must be limits of sanity beyond which literary experimentation can hope to produce only pathological documents with no significance as works of art. Art must always have some at least implicit standard of reference, but imbeciles and madmen could conceivably use completely incoherent language which, if embodied in a novel, might be held up as a masterpiece of absolute realism."[5] But, Ward concludes, Faulkner here never achieves art because he never achieves the referentiality necessary to realism. While I regard realism as the residual aesthetic, Ward—who writes from a British perspective—assumes realism is dominant, naturalism merely aberrant somehow. But American literary historians, with their different sense of things, regarded naturalism as dominant, and thus felt they were locating writers such as Hemingway and Faulkner with the more powerful agenda when they could identify naturalistic elements in their works.

An American literary historian who illustrates my point is John Herbert Nelson. In the introduction to the last volume of a prestigious five-volume anthology of American literature published in 1933, Nelson speaks of Hemingway and Faulkner among several others (Dos Passos, Evelyn Scott, Elizabeth Madox Roberts). Nelson concludes that though these writers are less interested in "sociological diagnosis" than, say, Dreiser or Lewis or Anderson, it is, says Nelson, "most important of all [that] practically every one of them discloses a bent toward naturalism. The success of Hemingway after 1926, as that more recently of Faulkner, strongly indicates that naturalistic fiction holds its own in America, despite reactions against it, and despite the critical efforts made to discredit the assumptions on which it relies for support."[6] We may wonder why it is so important to Nelson that the best young novelists be regarded as naturalists, but the answer seems plain: it saves them from whatever ideology lies beyond. That ideology, as yet unnamed, but identified, metonymically, by the company it kept—James Joyce, Marcel Proust, Gertrude Stein, and Virginia Woolf— seemed too interested in technique, experiment, and human pathology. Whatever it was, it was not conventionally representational. The failure of traditional mimesis makes it easy to understand the dismay of Marxist critics of the time. Historically, Marxists have been almost exclusively interested in realism and naturalism. Thus one could predict the response of, say, Granville Hicks to Faulkner. Mimesis, not affect, is his concern. In 1933, Hicks says of *As I Lay Dying*, "The wild meditations of Darl and the childish hallucinations of Vardaman do very little to help us understand the Bundren family, but they intensify, even more effectively than the introduction of loathsome physical details, the horror that Faulkner wishes to arouse in the reader of *As I Lay Dying*. An enormous ingenuity has gone into the construction of Faulkner's novels, but it has not been devoted, as James's ingenuity was devoted, to discovering 'the way that most presents the subject and presents most of it'; but rather to discovering the way that creates in the reader the most violent loathing."[7]

Ward, Nelson, and Hicks represent entrenched positions and yield responses we might readily predict. What of someone who does not represent the entrenched and who, moreover, became invested in the emergent ideology of modernism itself? How might such a critic regard Faulkner in the terms of our triad? Among the earliest of a new generation to appreciate Faulkner's talents was Robert Penn Warren. Warren feels conflict over the issues, whereas Ward, Nelson, and Hicks have everything already figured out. Moreover, his stake is in the new, but he simply has not yet determined how to name it apart from the reigning credos. New credos interested Warren, who had taken his stand with eleven other Agrarians in their manifesto of 1930, the same year *As I Lay Dying* had appeared. Warren's first reports on Faulkner appear a bit later, in an omnibus-review including *These Thirteen* published in early 1932; later, he made mention of *A Green Bough* in an omnibus review published in early 1934. But Warren's most important early comments occurred in his second reference to Faulkner. In 1933 he published an important essay that discusses residual and dominant aesthetic ideologies in ways germane to any understanding of how modernism was constituted as an ideology basic to American fiction at this time, the late 1920s and early 1930s. Interestingly, Warren's essay is not on Faulkner, however. It is on T. S. Stribling, whom he calls a "paragraph in the history of critical realism."[8] But in the final couple of pages of this long essay Warren not only speaks of Faulkner, but also speaks of him and *As I Lay Dying* explicitly in the terms of two elements of the triad—realism and naturalism. Although modernism as such does not seem to cross his consciousness, Warren both speaks of Faulkner expressly in the context of the dichotomy of realism and naturalism, and, eventually, puts himself on the side of the then-dominant naturalism. In these early comments, Warren is important precisely because he works within the terms of a dominant and a residual ideology, but is not at all explicit—however much we identify Warren himself with the emergence of modernism—on the emergent itself.

Warren's views on the earlier two are quite conventional. Both realism and naturalism, Warren insists, are dependent upon the sort of attitude or perspective derived from science. Both ideologies are marked by forms of objectivity. But whereas naturalism depends upon its ideological relation to the natural sciences—biology and bio-chemistry—realism depends upon its ideological relation to what Warren calls a pseudoscience, sociology. Though Warren seems to imply that realism *could* be kept uncorrupted, in practice it is usually perverted by something in that pseudoscience upon which it models itself. That something is an interest in values rather than fact, in changing society rather than simply describing it. As Warren says, the naturalistic novelist uses a "transcriptive" method "interested in fact, not value" (464). Because of its ideological roots in sociology, however, realism is readily corrupted into what Warren disparages as "critical realism." Apparently to be distinguished from the traditional, uncorrupted realism found earlier in, say, Howells or James, the critical realist, claims Warren, "like the sociologist, professes a scientific objectivity in dealing with his materials, that is, in making his surveys" (464). The origin of realism in sociology, says Warren, virtually demands an orientation to *values*. And lurking values give the realist-cum-critical realist "a prescriptive, as well as a descriptive, aspect"

(464). To the extent that the naturalistic novel imitates the rigorous objectivity of the biologist, the naturalist avoids the fault lurking in realism. But the realist is easily corrupted into the critical realist by an almost intrinsic need of the sociological perspective to change things. In the hierarchy of modes Warren establishes, therefore, realism degenerates into critical realism, apparently before it is retrieved in the purer form offered in naturalism. In his argument, moreover, Stribling is not a realist or a naturalist. He is a *critical* realist in novels such as *The Forge* (1931) and *The Store* (1932; for which Stribling won a Pulitzer Prize).

But is Faulkner a realist or a naturalist for Warren? It appears that, like John Herbert Nelson, Warren regards him as a naturalist. But because Warren is more conflicted on the issue than Nelson, we have to read between Warren's lines to conclude that. Though Warren seems clearest on realism because he wants to attack Stribling's perversion of the purer form of that mode, he plainly valorizes naturalism. We find that valorization in Warren's admiration of scientific detachment, the scientist's focus on fact, not value. Therefore, we conclude that he finds Faulkner a naturalist because his work exhibits the objectivity of the scientist. Warren uses this element to attack Stribling. He suggests that his critique of Stribling may become clearer if we compare him to Faulkner and other novelists who have represented the same Southern socioeconomic material. "Take the 'poor whites' of Faulkner's *As I Lay Dying* as compared with those of *Teeftallow* or *The Store*," Warren instructs us. In Faulkner we will not find the overt political program. "As a citizen, in his practical and public role," says Warren, "Faulkner may want to see a broadened way of life possible for the back-country people of Mississippi; but he is too much of an artist to commit himself to the easy satire of the reformer or aesthete" (483). It is plain that Warren makes Faulkner an objective observer who simply presents his material and leaves the reader to be the judge or to make political associations. Faulkner's superior objectivity is also represented in *Light in*

August, says Warren, and has the same effect there as in the
earlier novel: it makes the "problem" Joe Christmas exhibits an
intrinsic feature of his character rather than a "piece of legerde-
main to point a moral" as, for instance, Warren finds the
lynching of one of Stribling's characters in *The Store*.

Though it is important that Warren see Faulkner as a naturalist, more important to me is another set of conclusions we may
derive from Warren's argument. Examined closely, Warren's
essay suggests how the residual, dominant, and emergent ideologies of realism, naturalism, and modernism, respectively, reveal themselves in the interplay of Stribling's and Faulkner's
texts. I believe Warren's—and my—more-than-a-paragraph on
Stribling reveals all three ideologies at work in precisely the
terms I have wanted to exhibit. By this late point in the essay,
though Warren seems to have entirely forgotten realism, critical
or otherwise, and naturalism, his essay not only provides a
touchstone for both realist and naturalist concerns, but also
provides a bridge into the concerns of modernism and how it
was constructed as an ideological abstraction. We may see all
these elements if we examine not his argument so much as the
implications of his language. Since the historical moment is
rather complex, my argument is going to be complex as well. As
I have said, the implications of his original enfigurations—of
naturalism in the dispassionate objectivity of the scientist, of
critical realism in the involved perspective of the sociologist—
suggest that Faulkner is indeed some sort of naturalist, though
if we are misreading Warren on this point, then at the least he
sees Faulkner as a realist in the good sense Warren mentions at
the start of his discussion of Stribling. But there is more in
Warren's commentary, for, although only dimly, we begin to
see coming into focus elements of the modernism yet to emerge
except for reviewers' frequent remarks about Faulkner's interest
in form or experimentalism or his corruption of representational
content by his peculiar interest in technique for its own sake.
Warren's language suggests a distancing that in naturalism is a
function of the authorial perspective. Though Warren is not yet

totally clear on what the pivotal issue is, his language suggests the distancing has been transformed in Faulkner into a function of the aesthetic object itself, and so represents a break with conventional naturalism as such and a movement toward modernism.

In naturalism, objectivity is assumed to be an aspect of the observer or author—as the analogies between scientist and author suggest. In modernism, objectivity begins to be attributed to the work as an intrinsic feature of the art object itself. Warren writes that whereas the problem with *Stribling* is that his "work approaches allegory," the strength of a Faulkner and other younger Southern novelists is that they "conceive of the novel as *itself* the communication. They are interested in putting, so far as their powers permit, the question about the destiny of certain obscure individuals, their characters, so that the question will remain alive. Perhaps the questions, or some of them, are unanswerable. But that sort of passionate, *yet disinterested and patient, contemplation* is, presumably, the business of art, even the art of the novelist. *It is a contemplation rooted in the poetic attitude*" (485–86; my emphasis). By his transferring objectivity to the aesthetic object, Warren is also beginning to reveal the objectivist, but *formalist*, underpinnings of an emergent New Criticism, precisely the critical ideology associated with a likewise emergent modernism. The ideology of modernism in fiction is finally most clearly evident in Warren's now ascribing to fiction writers the aesthetic, largely formalist, powers of the poet.

If we look ahead to Warren's next reference to Faulkner, a review of *The Hamlet*, we will see that, indeed, Warren's values are those of the modernist, even if he has not yet taken the name. Of that largely traditional novel of 1940, Warren says, "It might be argued that for the present purpose the form is adequate, but I hope that the author will not cease to concern himself with the formal problems which have apparently engaged him in earlier work and which, sometimes, he has so brilliantly solved."[9] Thus, as we traverse Warren's comments on Faulkner, we see in one guise or another all three ideologies—realism, naturalism, and modernism. We see them, moreover, in the relations identified in Raymond Williams's terms. Realism is residual, naturalism is dominant, and modernism is emergent. And, finally, though without the name, modernism for Warren has become the aesthetic of choice at a time when New Criticism is about to take over the critical establishment.

2

Faulkner's use in *As I Lay Dying* within an apparently dominant social practice (within, that is, the realistic or naturalistic novel) of the stylistic techniques of traditional oral storytellers (such as we find in Twain) from a residual culture *and* within the context of an emergent modernist ideology may be the most important of the novel's subversive or alienating devices. Where Faulkner employs traditional realist or naturalist devices—take your pick—of objectivity and descriptive representation, he does so largely to subvert them, to distance us from them, to alienate us from them, in short, to defamiliarize them by virtue of their extremity or their subtle (or sometimes blatant) violations of the representational norms of realism and naturalism. In the tension between hegemonic dominant, on the one hand, and, on the other, either the waning residual or the emergent oppositional, the familiar becomes unfamiliar. Though the Russian Formalists speak of defamiliarization ordinarily as the defamiliarization of a content, we might take it equally to mean the defamiliarization of a constructive technique or a set of techniques such as those found in the aesthetic ideologies—realism, naturalism, modernism. *As I Lay Dying* defamiliarizes realist and naturalist techniques by giving us an ostensibly representational context that seduces us by its very familiarity.[10]

We see the effect of defamiliarization where Faulkner uses the more conventional elements of the ideology of realism in this novel. These elements include the use of standard "realistic" narration and description such as that we saw in the distinctly "objective" two-paragraph sequence that opens the novel. But immediately upon those paragraphs comes another that undermines those very conventions. When Darl and Jewel reach the cottonhouse, says Darl,

> I turn and follow the path which circles the house. Jewel, fifteen feet behind me, looking straight ahead, steps in a single stride through the window. Still staring straight ahead, his pale eyes like wood set into his wooden face, he crosses the floor in four strides with the rigid gravity of a cigar store Indian dressed in patched overalls and endued with life from the hips down, and steps in a single stride through the opposite window into the path again just as I come around the corner. In single file and five feet apart and Jewel now in front, we go on up the path toward the foot of the bluff. (4)

Here, however, Faulkner does not yet violently transgress the tradition's conventions of realistic perspective. This passage, while only subtly amiss, is amiss. To see the transgression, we must recall again the original paragraphs.

As our doorway into the novel, those first paragraphs I quoted earlier seem entirely proper, for the medium—apparently conventional realism or naturalism—fits the message: the traditional content of American fiction we easily identify as the young man from the provinces or the protagonist situated in a rural or pastoral landscape. In its suggestion of a bonded pair of youths— one of whom even evokes an Indian—the passage suggests as well perhaps the great myth of American fiction: the American Adam or Leatherstocking and the Last Mohican.[11] But it does not take much examination of the next passage to make Faulkner's prose look like one of those puzzles accompanied by the caption, "What's wrong with this picture?" What's wrong, so far as the conventions of realism and naturalism go, is that Darl here cannot "see" all that he describes for us. The traditions of realism allow for both the objective/perceptual and the subjective/projective report, but traditional mimesis typically keeps them carefully separated and clearly identified. Here, they are not separated. While the objective content of what Darl reports would of course be available to a typical omniscient narrator or even to a first person narrator situated differently from Darl, it is not available to him in his position fifteen feet ahead of Jewel or on the outside of the cottonhouse as Jewel strides across it. Thus from the very start, Faulkner undercuts, questions, or challenges the epistemological assumptions of realism in various ways and on several levels.

Any ideology, aesthetic or otherwise, brings an epistemology. To subvert the traditional ideology of mimesis, Faulkner must subvert its epistemology. Since conventional theory of communication focuses on the objective content of any representation, Faulkner finds ways to subjectivize the conventionally objective. He thereby often questions the possibility and conditions of knowledge and representation themselves as they must occur in language. On a minor level, Faulkner raises questions by representing as different what, objectively, *ought* to be the same, and as the same what, subjectively, *ought* to be different. For example, we see the *differences*, comically, in *As I Lay Dying* in the "speech" of Cash's adze. To one of the brothers, the adze says "Chuck. Chuck. Chuck" (5). But to another it says "one lick less" (15). While one of these is clearly more subjective than the other, their contrast, within realistic conventions, undercuts ordinary mimetic representation. We must wonder, Is one representation or "vocabulary" more "true" or "real" or "natural" than the other? Faulkner likewise questions traditional epistemological assumptions in the strange *similarities* of representation where similarity should not occur. In my experience of this novel, the most interesting such occurrences are the representations of Anse not only in relation to a steer, but also of the steer in relation to a pond. In one place, Dewey Dell sees Anse "like a steer that's been kneeling in a pond and you run at it" (61). Tull also sees Anse as "like he was a steer standing knee deep in a pond and somebody come by and set the pond up on edge and he aint missed it yet" (72). Someone may argue that Faulkner means to make nothing of these similarities and even expects readers to ignore them. But another sequence suggests not only that he expects us to see them, but that we are also to recognize his playfulness. This sequence involves Cash's saw. Peabody says, "Cash's saw snores" (46). Then Darl says "the saw begins to snore" (50) and, again, "The sound of the saw snores steadily into the room" (52). Finally, in a passage that requires us to recall the other two, Vardaman says, "The saw sounds like it is asleep" (66), a remark that, metonymically, compels us to leap from saw and sleep all the way back to the earlier descriptions of snoring. We may indeed, as some readers have done, account for such parallels by assuming a traditional "omniscience," but if we do not assume omniscience we can only begin to question conceptions of objectivity and subjectivity. Objective reality may be sharable, but we question whether subjectivity is ever as sharable as seems represented here.

3

It is to the confluence of the oral tradition of the storyteller and the modernist—perhaps even postmodernist—challenge to representation that I now want to turn in order to conclude my discussion of Faulkner's emergent modernism. Most who comment on the ways the novel challenges ordinary mimesis focus on Darl. But I like Tull. He is funnier. He also exhibits the same challenges, though in his own ways. The passage I want to turn to is that in which Tull attempts to narrate his part in the fearful crossing of the rickety bridge over the flooded river. The passage, more than anything else, represents the *problem* of representation. It makes some of the essential features of oral narration itself an object of contemplation and critical analysis. But it is not merely the reader who analyzes; Tull himself becomes analyst as he struggles mightily to represent what, clearly, for him is unrepresentable. Faulkner makes us see this struggle by foregrounding the main feature of oral narration. That feature is the simile, often the outrageous simile or comparative figure. Previously this feature, like the "folk" itself, had appeared largely as content, as a feature marking the "character" of the folk and its speech as print culture assimilated the American tradition of oral storytelling.

In that tradition, however outrageous it may become, the simile remains an aspect of representation, both as something to be represented and as the means of representation. In the modernist cooptation we find in Faulkner, the representational feature gets lost. Moreover, in Tull's account of the bridge crossing we see a whole series of figures beginning with *like* that eventually break down representation. They evacuate, rather than fulfill, the traditional means of ordinary mimesis, even as they provide a representative content. To see this process in action, we have to look at long strings of Tull's words as he builds his similes and destroys representationality and with it our feeling that things *can* be represented truly. The section opens, innocently enough, with just one, more or less representational, simile:

> *like* he thought maybe, once he was outen the wagon, the whole thing would kind of blow up and he would find himself back yonder in the field again and her laying up there in the house, waiting to die and it to do all over again. (137, my emphasis in this and succeeding quotations)

Next, however, we find a string of Tull's similes in which the very profusion begins to work against representation:

> [T]he bridge [was] shaking and swaying under us, going down into the moiling water
>
> *like* it went clean through to the other side of the earth, and the other end coming up outen the water
>
> like it wasn't the same bridge a-tall and that them that would walk up outen the water on that side must come from the bottom of the earth. But . . . it didn't look like the other end swagged at all: just
>
> *like* the other trees and the bank yonder were swinging back and forth slow
>
> *like* on a big clock. (137–38)

Though the first passage may seem representational, the second seems less so. But of both we may prefer to say that since Tull's real purpose is indeed to represent reality, he merely employs unusual verbal measures to capture a reality somewhat out of kilter. Moreover, since there is something comic about those measures, we may still feel comfortable with their conventionality since local color realism and compilations of folk lore often turn the verbal resources of the folk—again, as content—to comic ends.

But in the next passage we must begin to feel that the unrepresentability of reality becomes the issue. Though Addie might articulate that theme *as* a theme since her view of language as representing a lack is precisely what is at stake here, Tull cannot. Instead, Faulkner has Tull "show" instead of tell. Tull demonstrates the inadequacy of language to representation by attempting to explain the most impossible thing he knows: he himself thought to have performed a courageous act. "It was," he says,

> *like* when we was across, up out of the water again and the hard earth under us, that I was surprised. It was
>
> *like* we hadn't expected the bridge to end up on the other bank, on something tame
>
> *like* the hard earth again that we had tromped on before this time and knowed well.
>
> *Like* it couldn't be me here, because I'd have had better sense than to done what I just done. And when I looked back and saw the other bank and saw my mule standing there where I used to be and knew that I'd have to get back there someway, I knew it couldn't be, because I just couldn't think of anything that could make me cross that bridge ever even once. Yet here I was, and the fellow that could make himself cross it twice, couldn't be me, not even if Cora told him to. (138–39)

From this point on, Tull's enfigurations through simile drift further and further from any sense of what we might construe as "truth" or "reality." The words do something else. They begin to take on a life of their own and to form their own reality. In that respect, his words begin to represent the main feature of the "creative" artist. "I be durn," he says, "if it wasn't *like* he [Vardaman] come back and got me;

like he was saying They wont nothing hurt you.

Like he was saying about a fine place he knowed where Christmas come twice with Thanksgiving and lasts on through the winter and the spring and the summer, and if I just stayed with him I'd be all right too.

When I looked back at my mule it was *like* he was one of these here spy-glasses and I could look at him standing there and see all the broad land and my house sweated outen it

like it was the more the sweat, the broader the land; the more the sweat, the tighter the house because it would take a tight house for Cora, to hold Cora

like a jar of milk in the spring: you've got to have a tight jar or you'll need a powerful spring, so if you have a big spring, why then you have the incentive to have tight, wellmade jars, because it is your milk, sour or not, because you would rather have milk that will sour than to have milk that wont, because you are a man. (139)

It seems to me that what Faulkner does here is project the simple oral simile into the epic or Homeric conceit. Clearly, the "content" of this episode is epical enough, as Tull himself refers, at the end of his account, to the Bundrens' risking "fire and the earth and the water" just to go to town "to eat a sack of bananas" (140). Just as clearly, however, the "technique" of the simile, once presumed to represent and to be a means of representation, here *displaces* representational content and becomes the very content we are, finally, compelled to examine. It is not merely that the passage is comic. It is. Nor is it merely that the passage characterizes Tull as the very paradigm of the uxorious anti-hero. It does that too. Nor is it merely that the passage represents the oral storyteller in all his verbal pyrotechnics. Yes, it does that in spades. Above all, though, the passage challenges the norms and presuppositions of representability on which not only the epic is based, but of course the novel as well. The traditional novel, whether realistic or naturalistic, has required a presumption of a tie, a link, between words and some putative reality, but it is precisely that tie, despite the folk content and colloquial concreteness of vocabulary, that disappears here, as Tull drifts into what, in a grander historical context, Richard Poirier has called "a world elsewhere."[12]

4

Though it is clear that Faulkner adverts to the techniques of traditional fictional mimesis and so participates in its ideological implications, I think the main importance of *As I Lay Dying* is the way it interrogates the conventional—realistic *or* naturalistic—genre's modes of representation. Here Faulkner's modernism is largely emergent and oppositional. While in retrospect we may say that this novel is modernist, as indeed I would, we are entitled to say that because, in the history *we* now understand, modernism moved from the emergent to the dominant, from the subversive to the hegemonic, displacing both ideologies—realism and naturalism—that were founded on traditional principles of mimesis. But as I have been at pains to show in my discussion of Warren's response to Stribling and Faulkner, modernism was not dominant yet in 1930, however much from our perspective it might appear to have been. We always read retrospectively and we write history retrospectively, doing both always in the terms of what we already know. Warren, the reviewers, and the literary historians of the early 1930s *knew* realism and naturalism. But some—Warren and a few others—were beginning to construct a new ground from which literature could be observed. In some sense that ground remains the one that we ourselves stand on today, since most of us remain more implicated in a dominant modernism than in the emerging ideology of the postmodern. Someday I suspect someone will analyze an essay like mine as I have analyzed Warren's in order to demonstrate that while I thought I was reading modernism in Faulkner's text, I was really reading postmodernism and just did not yet know what it was.[13]

NOTES

1. See Donald Kartiganer, "The Farm and the Journey: Ways of Mourning and Meaning in *As I Lay Dying*," *Mississippi Quarterly*, 43 (Summer 1990): 281–303, and

André Bleikasten, *Faulkner's "As I Lay Dying,"* trans. Roger Little and André Bleikasten (Bloomington: Indiana University Press, 1973). Other studies that argue for or merely assume Faulkner's modernism include Virginia V. Hlavsa's "The Mirror, the Lamp, and the Bed: Faulkner and the Modernists," *American Literature*, 57 (March 1985): 23–43, Hlavsa's book that makes the same argument as the article, *Faulkner and the Thoroughly Modern Novel* (Charlottesville: University Press of Virginia, 1991), Richard C. Moreland's *Faulkner and Modernism: Rereading and Rewriting* (Madison: University of Wisconsin Press, 1990), and, in its relating Faulkner to modernist art, John Tucker's "William Faulkner's *As I Lay Dying*: Working out the Cubistic Bugs," *Texas Studies in Literature and Language*, 26 (Winter 1984): 388–404. See also Dorothy J. Hale's "*As I Lay Dying*'s Heterogeneous Discourse," *Novel*, 23 (Fall 1989): 5–23, and my own *The Exploded Form: The Modernist Novel in America* (Urbana: University of Illinois Press, 1980), which has a chapter that assumes Faulkner's role as modernist, though, consistent with my argument in this essay, as "naive" or prescient modernist rather than "critical" or one fully aware of his modernity.

2. See Raymond Williams, "Base and Superstructure in Marxist Cultural Theory," in *Problems in Materialism and Culture* (London: Verso, 1980), 31–49. Because of space demands and a concern about redundancy, the text of my essay is relatively silent about the concept of ideology. But the main sources for my sense of its uses include three books by Terry Eagleton: *The Ideology of the Aesthetic* (Oxford: Basil Blackwell, 1990), *Ideology: An Introduction* (New York: Verso, 1991), and *Literary Theory: An Introduction* (Minneapolis: University of Minnesota Press, 1983). Other important sources I have used include Michael Ferber, "The Ideology of *The Merchant of Venice*," *English Literary Renaissance*, 20 (Autumn 1990): 431–64, David Forgacs, "Marxist Literary Theories," in *Modern Literary Theory: A Comparative Introduction*, ed. Ann Jefferson and David Robey (London: Batsford Academic, 1982), 134–69, and James H. Kavanagh, "Ideology," in *Critical Terms for Literary Study*, ed. Frank Lentricchia and Thomas McLaughlin (Chicago: University of Chicago Press, 1990), 306–20. I have also found helpful Georg Lukács's *Realism in Our Time: Literature and the Class Struggle* [1957] (New York: Harper & Row, 1964), especially the chapter "The Ideology of Modernism."

3. See Ian Watt, *The Rise of the Novel: Studies in Defoe, Richardson, and Fielding* [1954] (Berkeley: University of California Press, 1974). Perhaps the greatest challenge to Watt's basic thesis is Michael McKeon's *The Origins of the English Novel 1600–1740* (Baltimore: Johns Hopkins University Press, 1987), but McKeon still concedes Watt's essential importance even while recasting his ideas into a more ideological critique that relies heavily on Marxist notions of dialectic. McKeon sees a much more particular "reflection" of a socioeconomic base not only in the superstructural creations we call novels, but those called romances as well, since that genre is critical to McKeon's sense of the dialectical development of the novel-as-genre. The novel, like the romance or any other genre, both reflects the ideological conflicts of a culture and mediates problems within it. Indeed, the mediation accounts for its origin and survival. "Genres," says McKeon, "provide a conceptual framework for the mediation (if not the 'solution') of intractable problems, a method for rendering such problems intelligible. The ideological status of genre, like that of all conceptual categories, lies in its explanatory and problem-'solving' capacities. . . . Genres fill a need for which no adequate alternative method exists. And when they change, it is as part of a change both in the need they exist to fill and in the means that exist for its fulfillment" (20). The best source-book on both realism and naturalism remains *Documents of Modern Literary Realism*, ed. George Becker (Princeton: Princeton University Press, 1963). Though of limited use for my purposes, one might also see Charles C. Walcutt's *American Literary Naturalism: A Divided Stream* (Minneapolis: University of Minnesota Press, 1956) and Donald Pizer's *Twentieth-Century American Literary Naturalism* (Carbondale: Southern Illinois University Press, 1982). Material on modernism abounds. See, for example, *Modernism 1890–1930*, ed. Malcolm Bradbury and James McFarlane (New York: Penguin, 1976). The dates in this book's title would seem to contradict my basic argument, but that the book does

not include an essay on *American* modernist fiction actually helps make one point—that modernist fiction came much later in America than in Europe. See also *Critical Essays on American Modernism*, eds. Michael J. Hoffman and Patrick D. Murphy (Boston: G. K. Hall, 1992).

4. William Faulkner, *As I Lay Dying* [1930], *The Corrected Text* (New York: Vintage International, 1990), 3. Further references will be cited in the text.

5. A. C. Ward, *American Literature 1880–1930* [1932] (New York: Cooper Square, 1975), 155.

6. John Herbert Nelson, ed., *Contemporary Trends: American Literature since 1914*, vol. 5, *American Literature*, ed. Oscar Cargill et. al. (New York: Macmillan, 1933), 11–12. Faulkner's entry in Nelson's anthology is "A Rose for Emily."

7. Granville Hicks, *The Great Tradition: An Interpretation of American Literature since the Civil War* (New York: Macmillan, 1933), 267. Ward, Nelson, and Hicks represent merely the tip of the iceberg. For a survey of the responses to Faulkner during this period, see also O. B. Emerson, *Faulkner's Early Literary Reputation in America* (Ann Arbor: UMI Research Press, 1984). Overwhelmingly, the responses to the early works valorized realism and naturalism; those traits we would identify with modernism—formalism, objectivity, interiority—were almost universally assailed because they displaced attention from the "proper" or "natural" or "artistic" elements associated with traditional theories of reference, that is, realism and naturalism.

8. The three pieces referred to here are "Not Local Color," *Virginia Quarterly Review*, 8 (January 1932), 153–60, "Twelve Poets," *The American Review* 3 (May 1934): 212–18, and "T. S. Stribling: A Paragraph in the History of Critical Realism," *American Review*, 2 (November 1933–March 1934): 463–86. Further references to the last essay will be cited in the text.

9. Robert Penn Warren, "The Snopes World," *Kenyon Review* 3 (Spring 1941): 257. Warren reviewed *Requiem for a Nun* in 1951, but the remaining truly important entry in Warren's list of writings on Faulkner is the review of Malcolm Cowley's edition of *The Portable Faulkner*. That review appeared in *The New Republic* in two issues in August of 1946; the essay "William Faulkner" that came from it and whose ideas resurfaced in one guise or another ever after in Warren's commentaries on Faulkner appears in *A Robert Penn Warren Reader* (New York: Random House, 1987), 207–23. For the full listing of Warren's pieces on Faulkner, consult James A. Grimshaw, *Robert Penn Warren: A Descriptive Bibliography, 1922–1979* (Charlottesville: University of Virginia Press, 1981).

10. See Viktor Shklovsky, "Art as Technique" (1917) and "Sterne's *Tristram Shandy*: Stylistic Commentary" (1921), in *Russian Formalist Criticism: Four Essays*, trans. and ed. Lee T. Lemon and Marion J. Reis (Lincoln: University of Nebraska Press, 1965). The concept of defamiliarization has been quite fruitful in Marxist criticism. For some of the uses of the term, see McKeon's *The Origins of the English Novel 1600–1740*, 425 n. 17.

11. My allusions here, of course, are to R. W. B. Lewis, *The American Adam: Innocence, Tragedy, and Tradition in the Nineteenth Century* (Chicago: University of Chicago Press, 1955) and to Leslie Fiedler, *Love and Death in the American Novel* [1960] (New York: Meridian, 1964).

12. See Richard Poirier, *A World Elsewhere: The Place of Style in American Literature* (New York: Oxford University Press, 1966).

13. Yes, I am aware that many assume we are already well into a postmodernist age. Lately, it seems as if half the books published on literature have postmodern or some version of the word in their titles. But the debate over postmodernism has not resolved yet just what it is, though the debate seems to have clarified better than ever what *modernism* is or might have been. I have a bibliography of some thirty *books* with postmodern or some variation of the word in their titles; see, for just one example, Fredric Jameson, *Postmodernism: Or the Cultural Logic of Late Capitalism* (Durham: Duke University Press, 1991).

Reading Faulkner's Compson Appendix: Writing History from the Margins

THADIOUS M. DAVIS

I have always found "Appendix/The Compsons/1699–1945" disturbing, and curiously seductive. Its elevation of an aggressively white masculine heraldry with a concomitant erasure of all traces of female lineage has the overtures of high, yet failed romance. Its debasing of Caddy Compson into an icon of evil and its lauding of Jason Compson as a rational philosopher appear contradictory to their representation in *The Sound and the Fury* (1929). Its tortured inclusion of Ikkemotubbe as a "dispossessed American king," its extended referencing of Andrew Jackson as "Great White Father" embroiled in defending his hapless wife against charges of bigamy, and its brief deprecation of black males seem gratuitous. The included references to black, urban, and female dissipation, the deleted negative references to Jews, and the allusion to the male Compsons' right to aspiration through property and ownership all reside in historical and cultural ideologies contributing to my discomfort with the text. Few of the critical discourses on the Appendix have made it more palatable. The exoticizing of lineage, race, and gender taken together makes the Appendix unsettling reading for me as a female and a person of color. My project here is to read the Compson Appendix without dismissing my instinctive reactions but with an awareness of Faulkner's writing it as self-reflexive history from the margins.

The Appendix to *The Sound and the Fury* is a well-known document completed in October, 1945, specifically for Malcolm Cowley's collection for The Viking Press, *The Portable Faulkner*

(1946), a thematic anthology that revitalized Faulkner's career. Subsequently, however, the renamed "Appendix/Compson, 1699–1945" appeared with new editions of the novel. Produced ostensibly to concretize the history of the Compson family dispersed throughout the novel, it follows a chronological structure, but the internal organization is more impressionistic than logical. The historicizing process blurs the distinction between fiction and biography by accommodating the period between 1929, the publication of *The Sound and the Fury*, and 1945, the production of the Appendix. Spanning centuries, the site of narrative reality is the social and cultural contexts for the reinvented, reconceptualized subject. Its most obsessive concern is ownership, property, and masculine enterprises of competitive exchange.[1] At once an act of memory, the recollection of the novel, and an act of invention, the extension of the novel proper, the Appendix interacts with the past project, *The Sound and the Fury*, and with the author's present historical moment.

As a white masculinist construction of history, the Appendix enacts a repositioning of the author himself from the margins to the center. The encoding of ownership and the concomitant creation of law as a protection of property may be one residue of Faulkner's writing of *Go Down, Moses* (1942). In recognizing the marginalization of himself as a white Southern author, Faulkner rewrote not simply the conclusion of his novel, but the implications of the lives of his characters and their positions in or out of history.

Though today we seldom think of white males as marginal, in the period of the 1920s when the novel was written and again in the period of the 1940s when the Appendix was written, a white Southern male, despite his position of power and authority within his cultural matrix of a caste and class-bound Southern society, was a marginalized figure, relative to the majority culture of the larger nation. While it would be a mistake to over-emphasize the importance of H. L. Mencken's essay "The Sahara of the Bozarts" (1917),[2] it is no mistake to extrapolate from that essay at least one negative published attitude toward Southern writers living within the South.

Faulkner's youthful masquerades—RAF hero, for instance— and his disguises—hard-drinking creative genius in New Orleans during the 1920s, for example—may be read as attempts on his part to disassociate himself from the actuality of being who he was, a working-class Mississippian on the downward curve of social significance. The romantic implications of his masking his identity and assuming false identities are numerous, but the practical implications are specifically that he distanced himself from the relatively powerless position that the larger world, in particular the literary world, perceived a white male Southerner, Mississippian in particular, to occupy. Faulkner perhaps himself recognized as much in 1942 when he stated about his consignment to Mississippi: "I have been buried here for three years now for lack of money and I am stale. Even a military job will dig me up and out for a while."[3]

His own life and career were in as much of a shambles as Europe, with Hitler changing its surface. He concluded in August, 1945, when he was feeling "bad, depressed, dreadful sense of wasting time . . . of some kind of blow-up or collapse. . . . My books have never sold, are out of print; the labor (the creation of my aprocryphal country) of my life, even if I have a few things yet to add to it, will never make a living for me" (SL, 199). Unable to participate in the Second World War, and deprived of service in the First, Faulkner constructed a means of getting even in the Appendix. As he wrote to Harold Ober in 1944, "I am 47 . . . I am like an aging mare. . . ." (SL, 187). His self-deceptive attempts to receive an Air Force or Naval commission occupy a series of letters from 1942 to the mid-1940s,[4] though beginning as early as 1940 he was already contemplating participation in the war and trying on his old uniform: "I can button it, even after twenty-two years; the wings look as brave as they ever did. I swore then when I took it off in '19, that I would never wear another. . . . But now I don't know. . . . But my feeling now is better so; that what will be left after this one will certainly not be worth living for" (SL, 125).

The patriarchal symbolic order of the Compson clan signifies Faulkner's patriotic desire to participate in war as an enactment of masculinity. "This world is bitched proper this time," he complained of the war in 1942. "I'd like to be dictator now. I'd take all these congressmen who refused to make military appropriations and I'd send them to the Philippines" (SL, 148). Beyond inclusion in a masculine enactment of patriotism, the patriarchal order of the Compson men is also connected to Faulkner's personal desire to escape the influence of women: "But if I can get some money, I can get away for a while—either in service, or out of it. Incidentally, I believe I have discovered the reason inherent in human nature why warfare will never be abolished; it's the only condition under which a man who is not a scoundrel can escape for a while from his female kin" (SL, 153).

The creation of second stories for women and for blacks, and the invention of an uninterrupted history for men in the Appendix represents both a continuation of the fiction of the novel and an invention of a new fiction for the author. In his exchange of letters with Malcolm Cowley, Faulkner identified himself as the "Garter King-at-Arms,"[5] his meaning being that he had the power of final arbiter and that he controlled his creation. Cowley, however, understood the term to mean that "the Garter King-of-Arms presides over the Heralds' College, or College of Arms, which rules on questions having to do with armorial bearings and pedigrees" (FC, 45). While Cowley read the identification as Faulkner's artistic and aesthetic license allowing for the lack of agreement between "Appendix/The Compsons" and The Sound and the Fury, he did not perceive that the label also renegotiated Faulkner's own place as creator and inventor. The result of his renegotiation is perhaps projected into A Fable (1954) which, though already in process while Faulkner was writing the Appendix, proceeds from the implied concerns with warring over lands, morality, and his own recognition, all complicated by the various crosses the individual bears. He implied as much in 1944: "It's too bad I lived now though. Still too young to be unmoved by the old insidious succubae of trumpets, too old either to make one among them or to be impervious, and therefore too old to write, to have the remaining time to spend waiting for the trumpets and the lightning strokes of glory to have done. I have a considerable talent, perhaps as good as any coeval. But I am 46 now. So what I will mean soon by 'have' is 'had' (SL 181).

Faulkner's erasure from significance in the historical moment during which he recreated the Compsons is inscribed in his positioning himself differently in the discourse. The Appendix reflects an awareness of multiple historical moments, but what Faulkner did not quite succeed in conveying to Cowley is that the empirical materials from *The Sound and the Fury,* to which Cowley kept returning, were largely secondary to his project in the Appendix. That project is not simply discursive. Faulkner's power over issues of progeny, gender, race, and history in the Appendix renders his knowledge of the specific characters and events of the novel less important. The sexism and racism (and even the anti-Semitism that Cowley persuaded him to omit)[6] stem from the material conditions and the social/cultural practices of the 1940s, which allowed Faulkner to practice a self-consciousness as male, as white, as Southerner, as well as in relational roles as son, husband, father.

Cowley's literalistic reading fastened on contradictions within the text, the discrepancies between the two texts, as he said: "The more I admired his Appendix, the more I found that some of the changes raised perplexing questions" (FC, 41). Cowley's more literal imagination did not allow him to read the main correspondence functioning in the space between the two texts—that is, Faulkner himself. The divergences between the novel and the Appendix are marks of Faulkner's attempt to define his own privileged condition at a point when his condition was more accurately marked by relative obscurity and lack of privilege. In the shaping of the Appendix, he both legitimates and valorizes himself as creator, as author. In situating himself in relationship to what Fredric Jameson calls "the political unconscious" of dominant cultural discourses and their underlying "master narratives," Faulkner asserted his place in a literary continuum that had flowed on without him, or perhaps bypassed him in Mississippi.[7] In retextualizing *The Sound and the Fury*, as a hallmark of high modernism, and reinscribing the cultural narratives specific to the South and to Mississippi already embedded within *The Sound and the Fury*, Faulkner arched his control over a new text, over the capacity to create that text, and over his own paradigmatic place within the literary history of American modernism.

His pleasure in the completed Appendix is unmistakable: "When you reprint THE SOUND AND THE FURY," he wrote to Robert Linscott in 1946, "I have a new section to go with it. I should have written this new section when I wrote the book itself. . . . When you read it, you will see how it is the key to the whole book, and after reading it, the 4 sections as they stand now fall into clarity and place" (SL, 220). And as he wrote to Cowley: "The job is splendid. Damn you to hell anyway. But even if I had beat you to the idea, mine wouldn't have been this good. By God, I didn't know myself what I had tried to do, and how much I had succeeded" (FC, 90–91).

To read the Appendix is to read a history that is a mythologizing of a fantasy, a constructed past, that somehow bears the insignia of fact, not fiction. It is history designed to reinterpret characters in the context of a present moment, which by Faulkner's own account was fraught with the debilitations of war and despotism. Cinematic in its sweep, the Appendix is a visualization of *The Sound and the Fury* and a retextualization of the cultural narrative always already present in the novel. Not a common cultural perspective, but highly idiosyncratic, it is a self-enclosed, self-referential inscription of the author as inventor, film maker, screen writer and cinematographer: a conscious manipulation of Faulkner's exposure to the technologies of Hollywood.

The visual sweep intensifies the dominance of the Compson

men. The Appendix privileges the fathers in action storyboards and erases the mothers. It names the males and frees them from domesticity. They participate as cross-cultural forces little differentiated from one another by name or deed. From Scotland to Georgia to Kentucky to Mississippi, the different cultures and historical moments are melded into a similar patriarchal code with scant variation in social forms, but with consistent attention to ocular spectating.

Yet it is Jason IV who is constructed as both quietly desperate and successful. With his bourgeois existence of minimal material consumption (he lives in an apartment above his business) and his not quite domesticated weekends spent with a woman ("big, plain, friendly, brazen-haired pleasantfaced . . . no longer very young"),[8] imported by bus from Memphis on weekends only, Jason lives an ideal life, if such a life can be ascribed to a male's being undomesticated by women and controlling his own fortune and devoid of familial responsibilities: "He was emancipated now. He was free" (718). And Faulkner implicates his own otherwise inexpressible desires in his signification of Jason's freedom.

If Quentin is the flawed hero of the novel, then Jason is the differently flawed hero of the Appendix. Although Faulkner insisted that he had not rewritten Jason's character, even a novice reader and clearly a discerning one such as Cowley can decode the veiled celebratory attention paid to the entrepreneur, the sane bachelor who satisfied his sexual appetites on weekends and attended to his major expression of masculinity, his business enterprise, undisturbed and unencumbered on weekdays. Faulkner identified Jason of the Appendix as "the new South . . . the one Compson and Sartoris who met Snopes on his own ground and . . . held his own" (FC, 25). The identification and the trope of freedom are the subtexts of an experiential core fantasized in application to Faulkner's own material reality. In eschewing property as land for property as money, Jason is the lone Compson to redefine the balance between property, acquisition, and ownership. His business is himself and he owns the business free and clear, without any interference from women and blacks: " 'In 1865,' he would say, 'Abe Lincoln freed the niggers from the Compsons. In 1933, Jason Compson freed the Compsons from the niggers' " (718).

Both females and blacks, however, bear the weight of the changed and destructive material world of the 1940s. Writing and creating from an alternative ideological and cultural base, Faulkner replaced his biases of the 1920s with a different set of biases, in which both females and blacks could be dismissed from history. Thus, the discursive act of invention in and of itself is value laden. The text strains toward the production of a completeness, a self-containment, that is not strictly the Compson family geneology.[9] Faulkner later objected to the title, suggesting instead "Compson/ 1699–1945," because "it's really an obituary, not a segregation" (SL, 237). Yet while the Appendix extends the available historical information about the Compsons and might be envisioned as an obituary because of its measured funereal cadence, it destablizes its referential text *The Sound and the Fury* by proceeding at several angles of difference in which females and blacks become the oppositional other to the white, Southern male subjects.

Caddy Compson remains the central, othered presence. Her continuing story is the longest of the chronicles, though length is not the only marker of her centrality. She is the first female included, and her daughter Quentin is the only other female given a place in the family history. Faulkner's gaze is on Caddy and on her relationship to a history which would have been unimaginable in the 1920s. Still transgressing boundaries culturally mandated for females, Caddy is imagined now in Europe, now with a German officer, now with another car, this time foreign-made, all of which project her transgression onto a wide cultural space and re-embody her as a different Southern female.[10]

Caddy's precarious position in the 1940s, an Eva Braun-like figure prostituting herself with evil, speaks to Faulkner's latent sense of the moral corruption of Southern white females. Unable to deal openly with his hostilities toward women (especially the females in his family who, he complained, were dependent upon him for everything including Kotex and toilet paper),[11] Faulkner deflected his rage and justified his hostility by reincarnating Caddy as spectacle—the cold, beautiful face of corruption and evil: "ageless and beautiful, cold serene and damned" (713). The gap between the social and the cultural domain, between the textuality of the novel's discourse and the sexuality of the female's body, figures the absence of purpose for a woman such as Caddy in any ideology construed as Southern by the 1940s.

Caddy is only real within sexual relations with men, but her actuality is always a function of Faulkner's desire for her. Her body is envisioned as a sexual commodity for the pleasure of a man, and yet as a fiction, a textualization, she is always denied Faulkner. Contained within a libidinal economy, as Minrose Gwin points out,[12] Caddy is excluded from participation in any female-based relational activities, and thus she cannot be granted self-consciousness. She must be externally positioned as object to satisfy the male, but only potentially so. That the specific male is a "German staffgeneral" (713) speaks to her lack of morals, but more significantly to her lack of historical consciousness. Ultimately, Caddy remains icon, a visual symbol of masculine desire and longing, of male need and loss. In part, the iconography resonates with the author's sense of his own perceived, diminished ability to participate in contemporary history. In standing beside a machine, "an open powerful expensive chromium-trimmed sports car" (712-13), and a German officer, Caddy is appended to both the mechanistic world of power and to the militaristic world of power seeking race and class dominance. Her stance is a reiteration of the disruptiveness marking her presence in and absence from the novel proper. In the Appendix, however, she is no longer the disruptive feminine voice that Gwin identifies in the novel proper.[13] Although Melissa Meek, "the mouse-sized mouse-colored spinster" (713) who is described in direct relation to her lack of value in a sexual marketplace, would want to ascribe to Caddy a voice crying for help, for salvation, she cannot restore Caddy's language or recover her physicality. Caddy is rendered static and voiceless in the very reproduction of the photograph that Melissa Meek covets and protects in her symbolic function as librarian, a preserver of texts and history and ideology. Caddy exists as a commodity of exchange between Faulkner and the German staffgeneral, and in a sense, she serves as Faulkner's entrance to the war.

The photograph, unseen by a reader of the text and unseen by the aged Dilsey, is the visualization of the would-be-possible, a concretizing of damnation and doom which begins the Appendix in the representation of Ikkemotubbe, whose name Faulkner insisted was Doom.

Quentin, the last Compson treated in the Appendix, is positioned in relation to doom and biological determinism: "QUENTIN. The last. Candace's daughter. Fatherless nine months before her birth, nameless at birth and already doomed to be unwed from the instant the dividing egg determined its sex" (719). Despite the reference to procreation, Faulkner dooms Quentin not only "to be unwed," but to be barren: "The last." Significantly, if she cannot fulfill the procreative function of the female and cannot inspire the creative function of the male—Faulkner the author—then Quentin's femaleness is threatening and unpredictable, and more dangerous than her mother's. In implicating the mother ("Candace's daughter") rather than the father ("Fatherless nine months before her birth") in the formation of Quentin's subjectivity, Faulkner indicts the maternal influence as biological not social. The negative maternal imprint survives separation and rupture that is the history of Quentin's and Caddy's interaction, and ascribes to Caddy as mother and shaper of her daughter the power of the female as witch.

Quentin cannot recuperate Caddy and thus is exiled from both attachment and herself. Theft from her male uncle, Jason, of the money sent for her support cannot overcome the physical loss of her mother, and she is represented without access to her desires or to speech. She can only grasp the symbolic materiality of the money, because Faulkner can only represent her in separation from sex and language.[14]

Cowley concludes that "nothing in [Quentin's] subsequent career . . . touched [Faulkner's] imagination" (FC, 41); however, there is another way to read Faulkner's dismissal of Quentin. The product of his infatuation with Caddy is textual production. Quentin, on the other hand, is biological reproduction and as such she siphons away the sexual energy that Faulkner explodes into first the novel and then the Appendix. Her very existence is a threat to male domination, just as Faulkner represents her threat to Jason as both economic and legal. Quentin threatens Jason's ownership and his freedom, but her existence is also a threat to Faulkner's own domination not simply of Caddy but of the text and potential texts that she engenders. Writing Quentin out of history dismisses all but the textual progeny of Caddy and of Faulkner's diverted sexual desire. Dismissed from the discourse of desire that envelops and creates her mother, Quentin is not lost, like Caddy, but rather is exiled from the text and the language of future possibility.

With the vanishing of Quentin from the Appendix, after a prediction of her unglamorous maturity ("And so vanished; whatever occupation overtook her would have arrived in no chromium Mercedes; whatever snapshot would have contained no general of staff" (721), the chronicle might well have ended there, but it continues. "And that was all. These others were not Compsons. They were black" (721). The "all" already over, finalized or erased, the text begins anew. The project announced as a negative, "not Compsons," can only proceed from the negation of the "others." The othering of those who "were black" is thus achieved in a few lines of text enclosing the Compson chronicle with its marginal opposite—the four black members of the Gibson family: TP, Frony, Luster, and Dilsey. Racial subjects, like female subjects, result from both representations and discursive practices, but the configuration of power and inequity is more striking in the representation of the blacks because, less antagonistic than the representation of the two white Compson women, it patronizingly asserts a rigid hierarchy from which the powerless and unequal other is already excluded.

Without a stated history, the four race-defined characters are reduced to their relational status to a present delimited by various subjugations. TP, commodified and clothed by "the owners of Chicago and New York sweatshops," exists as a brightly colored figure attracted to the cheap surface glitter of a market economy. Luster, "A man, aged 14," is locked into both a childhood and a servitude to "an idiot twice his age," though by 1945 Benjamin has been in the State Asylum for twelve years. Frony, "married to a pullman porter," is nonetheless denied either agency or autonomy because her life can only be envisioned in terms of her mother's refusal "to go further" than Memphis, and in her subjugation to the family matriarch who is also always the Compson's, and Faulkner's, mammy. For, as Lee Jenkins concludes about Faulkner's creation of Dilsey in the novel: "One sees the arrogant self-indulgence of Faulkner's application of the dicta of his private obsessions, as revealed in his creation of Dilsey, in honorable commendation of the life of Mammy Caroline and as the pronouncement of a suitable benediction upon it."[15]

The slippage in the Appendix is Faulkner's determination to empower Dilsey within the black family though he disempowers her within the ideological position of a white Southern society; that is, she cannot impact upon either the world at war or Caddy in Europe or Melissa Meek in Jefferson. And in the Appendix Dilsey herself, unimaginable beyond her former place within the white Compson household, does not receive a textual marker. Her name stands alone, creating an image and an icon of the maternal, the caretaker, the caregiver, the undifferentiated other, whose name melds into a "they": "They endured."

And "They endured," as an oblique reference to Dilsey, may be read as a refusal to re-engage with her character at all. "They endured" signals a pluralistic dismissal of her individual subjectivity, and the collapsing of all of her into all of her primarily male progeny. Her function always already served within the novel, her positioning in the Appendix is coda and denouement, not an extension or a clarification or a reflection.[16] Yet, ironically, it is she who in the novel saw the first and the last, and she, in the Appendix, who refuses to see any remnants of the Compsons at all. She does not gaze upon Caddy, does not turn her gaze toward the clipping of the reproduced photograph that Melissa Meek brings to her. Whether the photograph is of Caddy or not, her eyes will not see, will not speculate. Perhaps it is out of this sightlessness, this myopic vision turned now elsewhere to a space that Faulkner cannot occupy or invade, that Dilsey, in the constructed collectivity of a black race, endured. Read as a racial epitaph, the words "They endured," function discursively to ascribe to a subsequent generation the traits and the proclivities of *a* Dilsey, but not necessarily *the* Dilsey of *The Sound and the Fury*.

Faulkner's revisioning of the black male Gibsons signifies a fear of the movement of Southern black men out of their traditional places in the rural South. The character Butch Beauchamp, from the last chapter of *Go Down, Moses* (1942), is an earlier development of Faulkner's construction of the racialized, flawed male attracted by the lure of the urban, of the easy life, of the city vices. TP's brief representation is an extension of Butch. From his specific clothing ("the fine bright cheap intransigent clothes") to his implicit behavior (prowling Memphis's Beale Street), TP, and by extension the black males of his generation, are purged from the traditional economic landscape of Faulkner's representative South, punished for their deviance, and left to the fluctuations of fate.

Black males, then, are only real within obligatory material relations. Represented in conjunction with greed, lust, and entertainment, they signify the baser male vices that are appended to racial instincts. They are expressive of male appetites, desires, and needs that are not sanctioned within the domestic, marital sphere, yet are public demonstrations of a particular

kind of masculinity which is objectified under cultural domination.

The ideologies of right and power and control and tradition
inform the Appendix. Theoretically, the constructions of race
and gender function together as a mask for the construction of a
writerly self and autonomy and authority. The subterfuge is
conscious. The result is not, as Cowley would have us believe,
that Faulkner regarded his creation with "a mixture of horror
and unwilling affection" (FC, 41), but rather that by means of
his creation he reflected on his own position in a material world
over which he exercised little control. As he had written to
Malcolm Franklin in 1943: "[P]erhaps the time of the older men
will come, the ones like me who are articulate in the national
voice, who are too old to be soldiers, but are old enough and
have been vocal long enough to be listened to, yet are not so
old that we too have become another batch of decrepit old men
looking stubbornly backward at a point 25 or 50 years in the
past." (SL, 166). His obsessions figure what was to come: the
ridiculing of women in his texts of the 1950s, the complicated
immersions in historical narratives of war, the dismissal of blacks
from all but the most visually benign texts (*Intruder in the Dust*
and *The Reivers*).

In positioning his Compsons and Gibsons differently in the
Appendix, Faulkner assumes both their different relation to one
another (racial and gendered) and to the text already written.
But more, he positions them differently in relation to the
private and public spheres that the new text seeks to collapse.
Faulkner's complicity with hierarchies and divisions he abhorred in foreign ideologues is apparent in his creation of
historical objects and subjects governed and predicated upon
actual social events and economic relationships. The intercon-
nected sets of personal relationships all are contingent upon the
signature of a specific middle-aged, frustrated Faulkner making
a calculated attempt at fixity, at a removal of chaos from his own
writerly and personal life, at an assertion of the significance and
stability of his own place in history; or so, in my own middle

age, I think in reading "Appendix/ The Compsons/ 1699–1945" as emblem of artistic and social redirection at the expense of not a few metaphoric, expendable little old ladies.

NOTES

1. Luce Irigaray deploys these terms in her description of texts with male signatures in "This Sex Which Is Not One," in *Feminisms: An Anthology of Literary Theory and Criticism*, ed. Robyn R. Warhol and Diane Price Herndl, (New Brunswick: Rutgers University Press, 1991), 350–56.

2. The essay first appeared in the *New York Evening Mail* (November 13, 1917) and was collected in *Prejudices, Second Series* (New York: Alfred A. Knopf, 1920).

3. *Selected Letters of William Faulkner*, ed. Joseph Blotner (New York: Random House, 1977), 153. Further references will be cited in the text as SL.

4. See, for example, Faulkner to Robert K. Haas (received March 27, 1942): "I am going before a Navy board and Medical for a commission, N.R. I will go to the Bureau of Aeronautics, Washington, for a job. I am to get full Lieut. and 3200.00 per year, and I hope a pilot's rating to wear the wings. I dont like this desk job particularly, but I think better to get the commission first and then try to get a little nearer the gunfire, which I intend to try to do. . . . This in confidence . . ." (SL, 149–50). See also Faulkner to Harold Ober, March 1942, and Faulkner to Bennett Cerf, June 1942 (SL, 150, 152).

5. Malcolm Cowley, *The Faulkner–Cowley File: Letters and Memories, 1944–1962* (New York: The Viking Press, 1966), 44. Further references will be cited in the text as FC.

6. See Cowley on Faulkner's use of "Jew owners of New York and Chicago sweatshops": "In these present days, I'd drop out the word 'Jew'. . . . with all that's going on I'd rather not see a false argument over anti-Semitism injected into the reviews" (FC, 60).

7. See Fredric Jameson, *The Political Unconscious: Narrative as a Socially Symbolic Act* (Ithaca: Cornell University Press, 1981).

8. *The Portable Faulkner*, ed. Malcolm Cowley (New York: Viking Penguin, 1946, rev. ed. 1967), 718. Further references will be cited in the text.

9. See, for example, the inclusions of Andrew Jackson and the Gibson family.

10. The contrast in the Appendix is specifically to Melissa Meek, the librarian whose life is bounded by Jefferson, whose work is protecting the morals of the young from the corrupting influence of textuality.

11. See Faulkner to Robert K. Haas (May 3, 1940, SL, 122). See also Anne Goodwin Jones, " 'The Kotex Age': Women, Popular Culture, and *The Wild Palms*," in *Faulkner and Popular Culture: Faulkner and Yoknapatawpha, 1988*, ed. Doreen Fowler and Ann J. Abadie (Jackson: University Press of Mississippi, 1990), 142–62.

12. *The Feminine and Faulkner: Reading (Beyond) Sexual Difference* (Knoxville: The University of Tennessee Press, 1990), 47.

13. Ibid., 61.

14. This representation would appear to be the case, despite Faulkner's portrayal of Quentin's promiscuity in the novel proper. I am indebted here to Luce Irigaray's response, in "Women's Exile," to whether in a relationship with a man a woman discovers her mother. See *The Feminist Critique of Language*, ed. Deborah Cameron (London: Routledge, 1990), 80–91.

15. *Faulkner and Black–White Relations: A Psychoanalytic Approach* (New York: Columbia University Press, 1981), 165.

16. I have examined Dilsey at length in *Faulkner's "Negro": Art and the Southern Context* (Baton Rouge: Louisiana State University Press, 1983), 102–118. See also Jenkins on the irony of Dilsey's position within the Compson household (171–76).

Ideology and Topography in Faulkner's
Absalom, Absalom!

J. HILLIS MILLER

Does any feature of Faulkner's *Absalom, Absalom!* escape from ideology or is every bit of it, from one end to the other, ideological through and through? How would one recognize the right answer to that question or verify it? What difference would it make if we gave a yes or a no answer to the question? Would we like the novel better or worse if some aspect of it could be shown to be not ideological?

In order to begin to answer these questions a definition of ideology is necessary. "Ideology" is an odd word. In the English language, it has a complex and to some degree contradictory history, though not a long one. The earliest example in the OED is from 1796. The OED defines ideology either as meaning "The science of ideas; that department of psychology which deals with the origin and nature of ideas," especially as "applied to the system of the French philosopher Condillac, according to which all ideas are derived from sensations," or as meaning, by 1813, "ideal or abstract speculation; in a depreciatory sense, unpractical or visionary theorizing or speculation." The word originally came into English as a borrowing from the French word "idéologie." "Idéologues" was the name given to Condillac, Destutt de Tracy, and other empiricists who, following Locke, believed in the material or sensationalist origin of ideas. The contradiction inherent in the word today is already present in the earliest uses. On the one hand ideology is the science of ideas, a mode of clear and distinct knowledge. On the other hand ideology is visionary error, a lack of clear and distinct knowledge. In one case the origin of ideas in sensation is known. In the other case ideas are freed from their material origin and taken in error as an independently valid realm.

The word "ideology" is used in many conflicting ways today. The word is a battleground fought over by conflicting ideologies. But in all its uses it bears the marks of its appropriation and transformation by Marx and Marxism. It also still retains some version of the contradiction inherent in the word from the start. In the People's Republic of China or in the now defunct Soviet Union "ideology" is (or was) a set of beliefs and practices consciously promulgated by the state. In the United States or Western Europe, by contrast, the word tends to suggest something bad, a set of prejudices and valuations, for example racial or gender prejudice, taken so much for granted that the victims of ideology are not aware that their prejudices are imaginary, not real. But the latter definition is already present in Marx. In *The German Ideology* Marx sees the Germans as living in a dream world cut off from the material determinants of their lives. As Louis Althusser puts this in his influential essay "Ideology and Ideological State Apparatuses (Notes towards an Investigation)":

> Ideology, then, is for Marx an imaginary assemblage (*bricolage*), a pure dream, empty and vain, constituted by the "day's residues" from the only full and positive reality, that of the concrete history of concrete material individuals materially producing their existence.[1]

Whether or not Althusser is being entirely fair to Marx here is a complex question. It would require a detailed analysis of *The German Ideology* and other works to answer this question. It can also easily be seen that the words "concrete" and "material" in Althusser's formulations are problematic, to say the least. What Marx says in *The German Ideology* about language can be shown to anticipate what Althusser regards as his way of going beyond Marx. Althusser conceives his crucial modification of Marx to be seeing ideologies as historical and as materially embodied in everyday practices and in what Althusser calls, in his quaint Marxist language, "ideological state apparatuses" such as church, school, and mass media. Such apparatuses are opposed to "repressive state apparatuses" like the police. Ideological state apparatuses determine the way we see and evaluate people and things around us. Ideology distorts and screens from our knowledge the real material conditions of our lives. Far from being a pure dream, as for Marx in Althusser's view of him, ideologies for Althusser have a solid reality in radios, television sets, newspapers, school buildings, textbooks, and even in works of high culture like Faulkner's *Absalom, Absalom!* On the one hand, says Althusser, "Ideology is a 'representation' of the imaginary relationship of individuals to their real conditions of existence" (162). The word "relationship" is important here. Ideology is not a self-enclosed dream world. It is a way of representing the relation between the individual and his or her material existence. On the other hand, for Althusser "an ideology always exists in an apparatus, and its practice, or practices. This existence is material" (166). For Althusser this materially embodied ideology interpellates individuals as subjects. Subjectivity, consciousness, is not a natural given but is called into being by various ideological state apparatuses such as family, school, the media: "all ideology has the function (which defines it) of 'constituting' concrete individuals as subjects" (171). Applying this to *Absalom, Absalom!* one would say that Sutpen, Henry, Charles, Judith, Miss Rosa, and the rest are not born what they are. They come to be what they are as the result of the impingement on them of various ideological forces. These call them into being as what they are. Whether Faulkner's own presentation agrees with that formulation remains to be seen.

One form of the material existence taken by ideologies is language or, more concretely, some specific text or other, for example the text of *Absalom, Absalom!* It is this form of material existence that Paul de Man stresses in the definition of ideology he gives in *The Resistance to Theory*. De Man's definition of ideology is close to Althusser's or Marx's, unexpectedly close given their radically different intellectual heritages. For all three ideology is an erroneous relation between consciousness and material reality. For de Man this mistake goes by way of a linguistic confusion. De Man's definition of ideology is one of the few places where he appeals directly to Marx, specifically to a way of reading *The German Ideology*, as a means of defending literary theory from those critics on the left who accuse it of neglecting social and historical reality:

> It would be unfortunate, for example, to confuse the materiality of the signifier with the materiality of what it signifies. This may seem obvious enough on the level of sight and sound, but it is less so with regard to the more general phenomenality of space, time or especially of the self; no one in his right mind will try to grow grapes by the luminosity of the word "day," but it is very difficult not to conceive the pattern of one's past and future existence as in accordance with temporal and spatial schemes that belong to fictional narratives and not to the world. This does not mean that fictional narratives are not part of the world and of reality; their impact upon the world may well be all too strong for comfort. What we call ideology is precisely the confusion of linguistic with natural reality, of reference with phenomenalism. It follows that, more than any other mode of inquiry, including economics, the linguistics of literariness is a powerful and indispensable tool in the unmasking of ideological aberrations, as well as a determining factor in accounting for their occurrence. Those who reproach literary theory for being oblivious to social and historical (that is to say ideological) reality are merely stating their fear at having their own ideological mystifications exposed by the tool they are trying to discredit. They are, in short, very poor readers of Marx's *German Ideology*.[2]

For Marx, Althusser, and de Man, though in a different way in each case, ideology is falsehood, error, aberration. It is not entirely clear, however, whether the notion of falsehood and error in question for any of the three is the reciprocal of any notion of attainable truth. It may be that, according to de Man's concept of ideology, Althusser's, or Marx's, we can at best replace one ideology with another. We cannot help confusing linguistic with material realities in one way or another, so we can at best replace one error with a different error. We cannot help living our lives according to unconscious assumptions that are replaced, when they are brought into the clear light of consciousness, by new unconscious assumptions that just as successfully hide the real material conditions of our lives. For Marx and Althusser even a radical change in the material conditions of production, distribution, and exchange might still leave us subject to the interpellations of ideology that bring the subject into existence. De Man sees study of "the linguistics of literariness," by which he means "rhetorical reading," the study of figurative language in texts, as a powerful tool for unmasking ideological aberrations. Elsewhere, however, for example at the end of this same essay, he sees even this as leading only to the replacement of illusion by illusion. Behind each mask there is only another mask, not the real face of reality. Theory itself, says de Man, is the resistance to theory, that is to say resistance to the clear seeing and correct reading that would unmask ideological aberrations: "To tne extent that they are theory, that is to say teachable, generalizable and highly responsive to systematization, rhetorical readings, like the other kinds, still avoid and resist the reading they advocate. Nothing can overcome the resistance to theory since theory is itself this resistance" (19). Is there any possible escape from these sad scenarios of our domination by ideology? Or, to ask the question more concretely, does Faulkner's *Absalom, Absalom!* have any aspect that might be said to escape from ideology? Does reading *Absalom, Absalom!* free us from ideology or only imbed us more inextricably within it?

It is far easier to identify the features of *Absalom, Absalom!* that *are* ideological than to find anything in it that escapes ideology. Nor is it all that easy to defend a claim that by dramatizing the suffering caused by Southern ideology Faulkner unmasks that ideology. Too many of the ideological aberrations are asserted by the primary narrator as opposed to the various characters who narrate. Moreover, the image of unmasking presupposes a true face behind. The unmasking of ideology should be a revelation of the truth as well as a showing that aberrations are aberrations. Exactly what true face beyond ideological masking does Faulkner reveal?

No careful reader can doubt that *Absalom, Absalom!* is a magnificent dramatization of the various assumptions about race, gender, and class that make up what might be called "Southern ideology." As is characteristic of Faulkner, this dramatization is made by way of a story that is told with what might be called, in a scarcely excessive oxymoron, hallucinatory realism. Faulkner excels at presenting human consciousness as suspended in amazed outrage at its own situation, poised immobile and at the same time in terrific motion. Emblems of this are Lucas Burch in *Light in August* hanging momentarily in the air as he leaps out of the boxcar to run once more from Lena Grove, or Miss Rosa sitting bolt upright in her chair with her feet not quite touching the floor imposing with implacable intensity her obsessions about the Civil War and about the Sutpen story on Quentin Compson.

Like all great novelists, Faulkner embodies a larger historical and social context in a family narrative that might be said to represent it allegorically. I say "allegorically" because the analogies between the one and the other are by no means transparent or literal. An effort of interpretation is required to get from one to the other, to read one as the expression of the other. In this case the parallels between the Civil War as experienced by the South and the Sutpen story are complex and not altogether straightforward. The retrospective contemplation of the two in their intertwining generate the amazement and outrage in the various characters. Rosa's telling is a voice inhabited by Sutpen's ghost "by outraged recapitulation evoked,"[3] just as, much later, Sutpen's own telling of his life story of Quentin's grandfather is described as "patient amazed recapitulation" (263). This amazement and outrage might be expressed as two related questions. The first: Why did the South lose the war? or, as Shreve poses his question to Quentin at the end of the novel: "Why do you hate the South?" (378). The second: Why did the Sutpen family story have to come out the way it did, or, as Thomas Sutpen puts it to Mr. Compson, "You see, I had a design in my mind. Whether it was a good or a bad design is beside the point; the question is, Where did I make the mistake in it, what did I do or misdo in it, whom or what injure by it to the extent which this would indicate. I had a design" (263).

If the characters of *Absalom, Absalom!* spend their lives going over and over the events of their personal and historical pasts trying to understand them and so free themselves from those pasts, Faulkner's way of telling the story (or the primary narrator's way) matches the recapitulative obsessions of the characters. The "time shifts" that repeatedly violate chronological time are related to the brooding recapitulation that characterizes all the narrators, including the primary one. To Faulkner's way of storytelling in *Absalom, Absalom!* applies perfectly that splendid description by Henry James of Conrad's method of narration in *Chance*. James described Conrad's narrative as "the prolonged hovering flight of consciousness over the outstretched ground of the case supposed." No doubt Faulkner learned much from Conrad in this regard. It is as though all the events of *Absalom, Absalom!*, covering more than a century in time, were going on occurring over and over all at once somewhere in a kind of simultaneous spatial array, so that the primary narrator and each of the narrating characters—Miss Rosa, Mr. Compson, Sutpen, Quentin, and Shreve—can move back and forth across time as though it were a landscape. The narrators anticipate events, withhold facts from the reader, for example the fact that Charles Bon has African-American blood. They put the story together in the way that will have the most powerful performative effect on the reader.

The compulsion to patient amazed recapitulation that characterizes human consciousness for Faulkner may be defined as subjection to a set of ideological assumptions not seen to be ideological. These assumptions are taken as natural. They are a confusion of linguistic with material or phenomenal reality. Though it may not be easy to decide what Faulkner thinks or what the novel thinks, it is clear that the characters think, mistakenly, that they have been victimized by some malign fate or perhaps by some meaningless mischance or trivial mistake. Their erroneous assumptions about race, gender, and class have prevented them from understanding the real material conditions of their lives and have brought on their suffering.

Worst of all, these ideological errors are shown in a series of eloquent formulations to be passed from generation to generation, from person to person, by that most ineradicable of human habits: storytelling. We think that if we can just go over the story once more, in outraged recapitulation, explaining it carefully to another person, putting all the ingredients carefully and clearly together, we shall succeed in understanding why it happened as it did and so freeing ourselves from it. But in retelling the story we succeed only in passing on to others the ideological mistakes that we have not been able to understand and are perhaps in principle doomed never to be able to understand. Quentin broods over the way a story that involves his part of the country and his fellow townspeople but only tangentially his own family nevertheless is determining not only his own life but even the lives of those he knows, like Shreve, his roommate at Harvard. Such people are entirely outsiders to the Sutpen story and come from a different part of the world. For them the story should be no more than a story, but just hearing it infects the hearer with its obsessions: *"Am I going to have to hear it all again* he thought *I am going to have to hear it all over again I am already hearing it all over again I am listening to it all over again I shall have to never listen to anything else but this again forever so apparently not only a man never outlives his father but not even his friends and acquaintances do"* (277). In another passage Quentin invents a splendid image to express this compulsion to a repetition that is like that biblical belief, alluded to obscurely in the title of the novel, that the sins of the fathers are visited on the sons, generation after generation. The biblical allusion in the title is a powerful reinforcement of the concept of repetition the novel dramatizes, since the story of Sutpen, Henry, Charles, and Judith repeats with many differences the story in 2 Samuel of David, Absalom, Amnon, and Tamar, though no character, not even the primary narrator, is shown to be aware of this. In Quentin's case, his incestuous desire for his sister Caddy, the central motif of *The Sound and the Fury,* repeats (proleptically, since *The Sound and the Fury* was published first), as if by an implacable fatality, the incest motif in *Absalom, Absalom!,* though not the motif of miscegenation. This kind of repetition seems to Quentin like the duplication in one pool of the perturbations in another.

> *Maybe nothing ever happens once and is finished. Maybe happen is never once but like ripples maybe on water after the pebble sinks, the ripples moving on, spreading, the pool attached by a narrow umbilical water-cord to the next pool which the first pool feeds, has fed, did feed, let this second pool contain a different temperature of water, a different molecularity of having seen, felt, remembered, reflect in a different tone the infinite unchanging sky, it doesn't matter: that pebble's watery echo whose fall it did not even see moves across its surface too at the original ripple-space, to the old inerradicable rhythm . . ."* (261)

Whether or not this belief in an inescapable repetition is itself an ideological construct may be difficult to decide, though nothing more urgently needs deciding. As readers of the novel we are in the situation of Quentin listening to Miss Rosa or Quentin's grandfather listening to Supten or Shreve listening to Quentin. If the novel is right in what it says about the power of storytelling, then we as readers of *Absalom, Absalom!* can never be in the situation of detached indifferent readers simply learning about Faulkner or about the South or about narrative technique. To read the novel is to subject ourselves to the effects of a speech act. Reading is a performative rather than a constative event. Far from achieving a liberating understanding, we readers submit ourselves, willynilly, to the pattern of the story. We will be forced in one way or another to repeat that pattern again in our own lives. In order to learn enough of this disquieting fact to try to avoid it we must read the novel. By then it is too late. In seeking knowledge, for example knowledge about Southern ideology, we have unwittingly and without wishing to do so subjected ourselves already to its performative power. Does the novel offer no possibility of an escape from this fate? That this is no light matter is indicated by the fact that Quentin's obsession with his Southern heritage contributed to his suicide in 1910, a short time after the "now" of Quentin's reconstruction with Shreve of the story of Sutpen, Henry, Charles, and Judith. This is true, that is, if it is legitimate to link this novel to *The Sound and the Fury*, published several years earlier.

Just what are the ideological errors that cause all this grief and why do they have such power to cause suffering? I have mentioned the Three Fates of contemporary cultural studies: race, gender, and class. Ideological assumptions about all three are materially embodied in the characters of *Absalom, Absalom!* Ideology is also embodied in the characters' way of life, in the concrete material conditions of their existence, in their houses, roads, institutions, in what they have done to the landscape. These assumptions determine what happens in *Absalom, Absalom!* If these assumptions were not so inalterably in place the story could not have happened as it did. Sutpen is never shown for one instant suspecting that he may be living his life as the mystified victim of ideological delusions, nor is he shown for one instant suspecting that it might be possible to think otherwise about these things. He is convinced that he has just made some "mistake" that has defeated his project.

First, class ideology: Sutpen's "design" is generated spontaneously in response to the episode in his childhood that labelled (Althusser would say "interpellated") him poor white trash. The house servant in the big plantation who turns him away from the front door and orders him around to the back brings him into existence as a subject. From then on he belongs to the class of poor whites. This new sense of himself does not lead him to want to transform the class structure. *That* he never questions. It generates rather a fierce and unremitting desire to put himself in the place of the white plantation owner. He wants to treat those beneath him, black and white alike, as he has been treated. This desire motivates everything he does until the moment of his death. It even lies behind his final attempt to father a son on poor Milly Jones. His fanatical pursuit of his goal makes his story a hyperbolic Southern version of the American dream. Fitzgerald's Jay Gatsby is also a victim of that dream. It is the belief that though you may be born in a log cabin you can end up in the White House: "I had a design. To accomplish it I should require money, a house, a plantation, slaves, a family— incidentally of course, a wife. I set out to acquire these, asking no favor of any man" (263). No doubt Sutpen's refusal to recognize Charles Bon as his son is motivated primarily by racial prejudice. It also has an element of class prejudice. Just as he was fifty years before turned away by the slave servant from the plantation owner's door, so when he has become a slave-owning plantation owner himself he does to another, in this case his own son, what has been done to him. He treats Charles as he had been treated. In doing so he perpetuates by what seems a fateful repetition the class as well as racial prejudice that has been imposed on him. The "fate" in this case, however, is his inability to free himself from the ideology that has called him into existence as the subject he is. The connection is made explicit in Quentin's imagination of what must have happened when Henry brought his college friend Charles Bon home for Christmas and Sutpen recognized that it was his son by his first marriage to the daughter of the West Indian planter:

> . . . he stood there at his own door, just as he had imagined, planned, designed, and sure enough and after fifty years the forlorn nameless and homeless lost child came to knock at it and no monkey-dressed nigger anywhere under the sun to come to the door and order the child away; and Father said that even then, even though he knew that Bon and Judith had never laid eyes on one another, he must have felt and heard the design—house, position, posterity and all—come down like it had been built out of smoke, making no sound, creating no rush of displaced air and not even leaving any debris. (267)

Second, gender ideology: If Sutpen's "design" is determined by class assumptions, his way of carrying it out is determined by assumptions about gender. Sutpen himself is the embodiment of certain presuppositions about male nature and power. The mythologized memory of Confederate bravery and suffering during the Civil War is the broader social concomitant of this. Sutpen's self-contained silence, his indomitable stubborn bravery in carrying out his design against all odds, his prowess as a hunter, his naked battles with one or another of his slaves while his male neighbors look on as audience—all these make him a hyperbolic version of the stereotypical strong silent American frontier male.

Absalom, Absalom! is also permeated by certain ideological presuppositions about the "nature" of women. These are not only expressed by characters like Mr. Compson, Quentin, or Shreve. They are also expressed by the primary narrator. Not just Sutpen but all Yoknapatawpha society shares some version of these presuppositions. The features of the Southern gender ideology about women make a complex and not entirely coherent whole. The lack of coherence makes this set of preconceptions all the more able to motivate actions that seem to be based on material reality, the supposed "nature" of women, but are in fact motivated, as de Man puts it, by a confusion of linguistic with phenomenal reality.

One element in this intertwined set of what might be called "ideologemes" sees women as unfathomably mysterious and strong. They are strong both in love and in hate. This is expressed succinctly in a thought Shreve imagines Charles Bon as having about his mother: ". . . maybe he knew now that his mother didn't know and never would know what she wanted, and so he couldn't beat her (maybe he learned from the octoroon [his mistress before he meets Judith] that you cant beat women anyhow and that if you are wise or dislike trouble and uproar you dont even try to)" (310). Women have motivations that remain impossible for men to understand, that men should primarily respect and fear. Examples are Miss Rosa's implacable hatred of Sutpen, or Ellen Coldfield's incomprehensible dream world, or Judith's inscrutable faithfulness to Charles Bon and her stoic silence after his death, or Sutpen's Haitian wife's prolonged implacable revenge, her willingness to sacrifice her son to get even with Sutpen for having repudiated her. These women are presented more or less from the outside, from the male perspective, for example in what Quentin says to himself about Rosa Coldfield: *"Beautiful lives women live—women do. In very breathing they draw meat and drink from some beautiful attenuation of unreality in which the shades and shapes of facts—of birth and bereavement, of suffering and bewilderment and despair—move with the substanceless decorum of lawn party charades, perfect in gesture and without significance or any ability to hurt"* (211). Such women are incomprehensible to men, however hard they may try to understand them. Nevertheless, one thing is sure. Faulkner's women are presented as just as obsessed, just as mad as the men are, just as much caught up in the prolonged recapitulation of some decisive event of the past that has frozen them in the terrific immobility of a backward look. The past event that obsesses them is almost always some wrong done them by men: Sutpen's first wife's outrage at Sutpen's repudiation of her; Judith's mourning as a widowed virgin after the death of Charles Bon, slain by her other brother; Miss Rosa's decades-long obsession with the insult Sutpen dealt her.

Another Southern ideologeme sees women as valuable only so long as they remain absolutely pure, innocent, virginal, white as snow. This facet of Southern gender ideology may help to explain Faulkner's fascination with the theme of brother-sister incest. He is said to have suggested more than once to crews of script-writers with whom he collaborated in Hollywood that when you get stuck with a script the solution is to introduce incest. Just as for the Egyptian Pharoahs or for that French nobleman Duke John of Lorraine (to whom Henry Sutpen appeals in his mind as a justification for the marriage of his sister Judith and his half brother Charles Bon), so for Henry in

Absalom, Absalom! or for Quentin Compson in *The Sound and the Fury*, the only way to preserve a sister's purity is, paradoxically, to marry her yourself. In Henry's case, the strategy is to marry his sister vicariously by way of her marriage to that half brother whom he loves with an abject homosexual adoration and identification. If he can join together Judith and Charles he can join himself to both of them in a hetero-homosexual triangle that is the only thing capable of satisfying his secret desires.

The complex of contradictory ideologemes about women includes, finally, the assumption that the real purpose of women is to bear children, to carry on the male line. In order to make certain this happens without any contamination women must be kept absolutely innocent and pure before marriage. Men are permitted to visit brothels, to father children on their slaves, or to keep mistresses without any stain on their honor or blemish on their right to marry pure women and father sons to carry on their names. The novel ascribes to Sutpen an ugly analogy to express this conviction that women are valuable only as a means of producing sons. When he insults Miss Rosa, who would eagerly have married him, by suggesting that they mate first and then marry if she produces a son, this is described by Miss Rosa as *"the bald outrageous words* [spoken] *exactly as if he were consulting with Jones or with some other man about a bitch dog or a cow or a mare"* (168). Later Sutpen is killed by Wash Jones because he repeats the same insult in what he says to Wash's granddaughter Milly just after she has borne Sutpen a daughter on the same day his mare has foaled to his black stallion: "Well, Milly; too bad you're not a mare too. Then I could give you a decent stall in the stable" (286).

Third ideological motif, race: Of the three motifs, class, gender, and race, race is without doubt the most important by far. Southern society was built on slavery and on the ideological assumptions about race that accompanied slavery: the radical differences between blacks and whites, the inferiority of African-Americans to European-Americans, the ineradicable contamination that even a drop of black blood causes in a white man or woman, the assumption that it is all right for a white man to father children on a black woman, though he has no responsibility to accept such children as his own, while the mating of a black man with a white woman is an abomination. The ugly word "nigger" echoes through *Absalom, Absalom!* as the invidious name that holds in a single sound all those ideological assumptions, as when Charles Bon at a climactic moment in the novel says to his half brother Henry: *"So it's the miscegenation, not the incest, which you cant bear . . . I'm the nigger that's going to sleep with your sister. Unless you stop me, Henry"* (356, 358).

All the decisive events of *Absalom, Absalom!* are the result of racial ideologemes. The Civil War was fought, at least in part, to protect the institution of slavery and in the name of all the ideological assumptions that went with slavery. The fact that Sutpen is turned away from the plantation owner's door by a black servant is an important part of his humiliation in the primal scene that calls him into being as what he is. He repudiates his first wife when he discovers she has black blood. He refuses to accept his son by that marriage as his own for the same reason, though if he had given Charles Bon the least sign of recognition Charles would have been satisfied and his murder at Henry's hand would not have occurred. The building of Sutpen's Hundred depends on slavery and on those twenty "wild blacks" Sutpen brings to help him build his plantation, just as the colonialism in Haiti where Sutpen meets his first wife is built on slavery. If the reader tries to imagine *Absalom, Absalom!* for a moment without those racial ideologemes (it is not easy to do so) the whole novel vanishes in smoke just as instantly as Sutpen's design vanished when he saw that the friend Henry was bringing home from college was his son by the first "tainted" marriage. Everything that happens in *Absalom, Absalom!* depends on the ideology of racism and would be impossible without it.

Whatever Sutpen does, every move in his life is in response

to the call on him of one or another of the set of assumptions
making up Southern ideology. If he is the blind victim of
that ideology, his mystifications cause him to inflict prolonged
unremitting suffering on all those around him: Eulalia Bon,
Ellen Coldfield, Henry, Judith, Charles Bon, Clytie, Miss Rosa.
They too share his ideological assumptions and are victims of
them as much as he is. Does the novel offer the reader no
possible escape from being the momentary last in the line of
those called to act somnambulistically according to the patterns
of judgment and decision Southern ideology determines?

It is by no means easy to answer that question. On the one
hand, it could be argued that the hyperbolic presentation in
Absalom, Absalom! of Southern ideology in all its complexity,
along with the dramatization of the savage retribution of suffering brought on those who live their lives according to that
ideology, make of the novel a critique of ideology, an exposure
of its mystifications. Shreve the Canadian is the reader's representative. He is the outsider who wants to understand the South
and who, so the Genealogy at the end tells the reader, lived on
to become a practicing surgeon in Edmonton, Alberta. His
survival is evidence that it is possible to know about Southern
ideology and not be destroyed by it. On the other hand, the
novel shows Shreve joining with Quentin in the imaginary
reconstruction of the events of the novel. Shreve becomes, like
Quentin, identified with Henry and Charles as they ride together toward that moment when Henry will turn on his horse
to shoot his brother, kill him "dead as a beef" (133). Moreover,
as I have already shown, the novel constantly reinforces the
notion that patterns of belief and action ineluctably perpetuate
themselves from generation to generation in blind repetitions.
These repetitions are like the way the characters in *Absalom,
Absalom!* repeat the biblical story of David, Amnon, Tamar,
and Absalom without being shown even to be aware of it. Since
ideology is by definition unconscious, how could we be sure
that reading *Absalom, Absalom!*, or perhaps not even reading
it, just hearing about it, or just living in the same nation in

which it could be written, might lead us unwittingly to repeat in our own lives something like Sutpen's unwillingness to recognize Charles Bon as his son or the blind submission of Ellen and Rosa Coldfield to Sutpen's command (not really proposal) that they marry him, the one acceptance duplicating the first many years after? On the one hand, the novel may give knowledge about ideology that might help liberate us from it. On the other hand, the novel may have an irresistible performative effect that goes against that knowledge. The epistemological and performative dimensions of the novel may go in different directions. It might be difficult if not impossible to decide which one would win out in a given case, for example in my recent rereading of *Absalom, Absalom!* in order to write this essay.

Without trying to mitigate the difficulties or the urgencies of this need to decide, I turn back to the novel for a look at several elements not yet identified. These might tip the balance toward saying that *Absalom, Absalom!*, if it is read with vigilance, may not so much free the reader from ideology as put him or her in a new position where a decision about it may be made, must be made. The knowledge reading the novel provides is performative in the sense that it puts the reader in a new situation. Reading *Absalom, Absalom!* imposes on the reader a new responsibility and makes necessary a new decision. The novel itself gives the reader the terms in which this might be understood.

Reading the novel puts the reader in a situation different from that of any of the characters. We see the whole novel, hear the stories all the characters tell, benefit in addition both from the narrator's commentary and from Faulkner's careful organization of the various blocks of narration so they have the effect created by these juxtapositions. Reading the novel is not just a passive act of absorption. It is an active intervention. Reading *Absalom, Absalom!* requires the reader to make energetic efforts. He or she must put two and two together, emphasizing this or that passage, filling in gaps. For the results of these acts of reading the reader must take responsibility. If the reader repeats the ideology the novel gives knowledge of, this is something for which the reader can be blamed, even though what happens in reading happens, willynilly. Two passages in the novel articulate the way the activity that might be called "reading" in an extended sense is not an automatic passing on of a certain pattern but a violently neutral transition space, like that "terrific immobility" of consciousness as Faulkner defines it. What passes through that space, the space of decision, comes out different on the other side. For that difference the reader must be held liable.

The first passage is the great speech Judith makes when she gives Charles Bon's letter to Quentin's grandmother. This is the same letter that Quentin's father gives him to read, to make of what he will. Having said that life is "like trying to, having to, move your arms and legs with strings only the same strings are hitched to all the other arms and legs and the others all trying and they dont know why either except that the strings are all in one another's way like five or six people all trying to make a rug on the same loom only each one wants to weave his own pattern into the rug" (127), Judith goes on to assert that in any case the endpoint of each life is "a block of stone with scratches on it provided there was someone to remember to have the marble scratched and set up or had time to, and it rains on it and the sun shines on it and after a while they dont even remember the name and what the scratches were trying to tell, and it doesn't matter" (127). The conclusion she draws from this and the decision she makes for action is a strange non sequitur from the grim darkness of this view of human life. She says the thing to do is to pass something on that will make a mark or scratch not on dead stone but on a living person. Though this is obviously an image of our own activity as readers of the novel, allowing ourselves to be marked by the text, Judith emphasizes not the legibility of the scratch but its materiality and the fact that it is inscribed not on a block of stone but on living mortal flesh, flesh that is living because it can die:

And so maybe if you could go to someone, the stranger the better, and give them something—a scrap of paper—something, anything, it not to mean anything in itself and them not even to read it or keep it, not even bother to throw it away or destroy it, at least it would be something just because it would have happened, be remembered even if only from passing from one hand to another, one mind to another, and it would be at least a scratch, something, something that might make a mark on something that *was* once for the reason that it can die someday, while the block of stone cant be *is* because it never can become *was* because it cant ever die or perish . . . (127–128)

Judith distinguishes between two kind of marks or scratches. The distinction is not, as might have been expected, between random, meaningless marks, on the one hand, and significant marks like letters on the other. No, from the perspective of the distinction she is making both kinds of marks work in exactly the same way. The distinction is rather between marks of any kind made on stone and those made on flesh. Scratches made on stone, for example the inscriptions on those Sutpen tombstones Quentin visits with his father in the cedar grove, are not happenings. They are not events because they are made on something that cannot die, that is outside time. Only living flesh, flesh that is mortal, is within time, has a history, and can remember. Therefore only a mark made on living flesh is an event in the present. Such a mark is an *is* because it can become *was*, whereas a tombstone has no *is* because it cannot become *was*. Just as Miss Rosa, as Quentin realizes, tells Quentin about Sutpen because "she wants it told" (10) to others so her anger, hatred, and shame will be perpetuated, so Judith takes Bon's letter to Quentin's grandmother not so she can read it but just so it can make an impression on her flesh and so be given a kind of immortality as it is passed on to Quentin's father, then to Quentin, and then to us as readers. This concept of a memory that is material rather than legible escapes ideology. It is not only an explanation of the way ideological elements are passed from generation to generation, but it also shows that in the moment of passing the recipient is liberated from being the blind repetition of a previous pattern. The person receiving the mark is given freedom and the responsibility to decide. This freedom is inserted in that interval between seeing the marks as mere scratches and seeing them as legible. The one who is marked has to decide how to read them and what to make of them.

Judith's notion of a memory that is primarily material, only secondarily articulated and readable, links this passage with the topographical motifs in the novel. Like Hardy or Trollope, Faulkner has a strongly topographical imagination. The events of his novels take place within an elaborately mapped mental or textual landscape in which characters are associated with places. The configuration of houses, roads, fields, rivers, swamps carries a considerable part of the meaning of the novel. Like Trollope and Hardy, Faulkner made a map of the landscape within which his novels take place. That map is reproduced at the end of *Absalom, Absalom!* The legend identifies it as "Jefferson, Yoknapatawpha Co., Mississippi, William Faulkner, Sole Owner and Proprietor." On that map the reader can see the location of Sutpen's Hundred, of Miss Rosa Coldfield's house, of the "Church which Thomas Sutpen rode fast to," and of the "Fishing Camp where Wash Jones killed Sutpen." Even without the map the reader produces a mental map of the landscape as she or he reads. The reader understands the novel in terms of the movements of the characters across it, the changes they make in it. Examples are that slow movement of Sutpen's family when he is a child back from the West Virginia cabin to the Tidewater plantation where he is refused entrance at the front door, or Faulkner's presentation of the later stages of the Civil War as the constant movement of retreat by the Confederate Army, or Sutpen's physical embodiment of his design in the making of Sutpen's Hundred:

> Immobile, bearded and hand palm-lifted the horseman sat; behind him the wild blacks and the captive architect huddled quietly, carrying in bloodless paradox the shovels and picks and axes of peaceful conquest. Then in the long unamaze Quentin seemed to

watch them overrun suddenly the hundred square miles of tranquil
and astonished earth and drag house and formal gardens violently
out of the soundless Nothing and clap them down like cards upon a
table beneath the up-palm immobile and pontific, creating the
Sutpen's Hundred, the *Be Sutpen's Hundred* like the oldentime *Be
Light*. (8–9)

For Faulkner as for Althusser and for Marx ideology is not
something abstract and dreamlike, the impalpable confusion of
linguistic with material reality. That confusion is embodied. It
is marked on the bodies of the human beings who are mystified
by the ideology. It is embodied in another way in all the
material changes men and women have made on the "tranquil
and astonished earth," turning that earth into a landscape, a
topography. That remade earth becomes the scene in which
the evil done by ideological aberrations can work itself out.
Subjectivity, including all the subject's ideological presumptions, is inseparable from his or her body. Not just the minds
but the bodies too of Sutpen, Rosa, Judith, Clytie, and the rest
are the incarnations of their *"stubborn and amazed outrage"*
(174).

Subjectivity, including its ideological presumptions, is also
diffused into the landscape. It is not just projected there but
incarnated there. Sutpen, in Rosa's sense of him when he
returns to his ruined plantation after the war, is

*absent only from the room, and that because he had to be elsewhere,
a part of him encompassing each ruined field and fallen fence and
crumbling wall of cabin or cotton house or crib; himself diffused
and in solution held by that electric furious immobile urgency and
awareness of short time and the need for haste . . . not . . .
anywhere near the house at all but miles away and invisible
somewhere among his hundred square miles which they had not
troubled to begin to take away from him yet, perhaps not even at
this point or at that point but diffused (not attenuated to thinness
but enlarged, magnified, encompassing as though in a prolonged
and unbroken instant of tremendous effort embracing and holding
intact that ten-mile square while he faced from the brink of disaster,
invincible and unafraid, what he must have known would be the
final defeat)"* (160, 162–63).

If the earth, like a stone, cannot have a history, cannot be *is* because it can never be *was,* nevertheless for Faulkner the earth turned into topography is essential to the making material of human history. This is analogous to the way Judith's love for Bon and his for her is carried from generation to generation by way of its material embodiment in that letter. The bare earth made topography, like Bon's letter to Judith, is an essential medium of communication between one person and another, one generation and another. Faulkner articulates this in a passage explaining that the fact that Shreve too came from the Mississippi trough helps explain why he is able to understand as well as he does Quentin's heritage of family and regional history: "both born within the same year: the one in Alberta, the other in Mississippi; born half a continent apart yet joined, connected after a fashion in a sort of geographical transubstantiation by that Continental Trough, that River which runs not only through the physical land of which it is the geologic umbilical, not only runs through the spiritual lives of the beings within its scope, but is very Environment itself which laughs at degrees of latitude and temperature . . ." (258). Faulkner's insight into the role of landscape in making ideology concrete is another nonideological element in the novel, like Judith's distinction between marks on flesh and marks on stone.

This insight is reinforced in one of the crucial passages in the novel, the one describing the imaginative recreation of the lives of Sutpen, Henry, Judith, Bon, and Rosa in the collective recapitulation by Quentin and Shreve. When a mark making history is tranferred from one topographical locale to another it is made material in a new way and in a new situation. The role of material surroundings in making possible a new start, not just a passive repetition, is signalled in the vivid emphasis the novel makes on the way the ice-cold Harvard dormitory room where Quentin and Shreve sit up long after midnight is so different from the wisteria and cigar smoke-scented porch where Quentin's father had passed the story on to him. The recreation of the story by Quentin and Shreve is a free (and yet bound) response made to a demand for narration inherent in the facts as Quentin knows them. Quentin and Shreve go beyond the data, as has Faulkner in his writing of a great novel about the South. All three have created new stories with their own coherence and meaning. For this new coherence and meaning, as well as the effects this may have on those who hear it, Quentin, Shreve, and Faulkner can be held liable. This is the case even though the new version of the story is a result of the marks made on them by the events and even though the effects on us as readers are irresistible, since what happens in reading happens as it happens.

This remaking and reembodiment is defined by Faulkner, in a brilliant phrase, as an "overpassing to love." The love in question is first that of Judith, Henry, and Bon for one another. But the imaginative recreation of the past is also an overpassing to love. The love reached by "overpassing" is not just the love between Judith, Henry, and Bon, seen as something positive and a going beyond the situation that has been imposed on them by their father. It is also the love between Shreve and Quentin and their love for Judith, Henry, and Bon. These new loves repeat the old ones and are the result of a joint act of recreation. In a similar way our relation as readers to the characters in the novel is also a kind of love. Love here is the name for a relation to history and to other people that may transform ideology and provide the glimpse of an escape from it:

> . . . all that had gone before [had been] just so much that had to be overpassed and none else present to overpass it but them, as someone always has to rake the leaves up before you can have the bonfire. That was why it did not matter to either of them which one did the talking, since it was not the talking alone which did it, performed and accomplished the overpassing, but some happy marriage of speaking and hearing wherein each before the demand, the requirement, forgave condoned and forgot the faulting of the other—faultings both in the creating of this shade whom they discussed (rather, existed in) and in the hearing and sifting and discarding the false and conserving what seemed true, or fit the preconceived—in order to overpass to love, where there might be paradox and inconsistency but nothing fault nor false. (316)

Ideological presuppositions have a stubborn recalcitrance. They tend to form themselves again even when we think they have been abolished. Nevertheless, *Absalom, Absalom!* gives the reader a momentary free space in which he or she might go beyond ideology—if he or she chooses to do so. It does this not so much in its exposure of Southern ideology and its malign effects, as in its demonstration of how those malign effects are determined by the embodiment of the ideology in topography and in the bodies of those subject to it. Understanding here is a possible means of liberation. This will happen if the right action occurs in response to "the demand, the requirement," in this case changes in the material conditions that supported Southern ideology in the first place. This does not mean that knowledge guarantees right action. Knowledge never determines decision nor the effects that follow action. An incommensurability between knowledge and action remains the human condition. Nor does knowledge of the past give foreknowledge of what will happen in the future if we follow a certain course of action. But it does change our relation to the past. That change provides a new space within which decision and action are possible.

NOTES

1. Louis Althusser, *Lenin and Philosophy and Other Essays*, trans. Ben Brewster (New York: Monthly Review Press, 1971), 160. Further references will be cited in the text.

2. Paul de Man, *The Resistance to Theory* (Minneapolis: University of Minnesota Press, 1986), 11. Further references will be cited in the text.

3. William Faulkner, *Absalom, Absalom!* (New York: Vintage Books, 1972), 8. Further references will be cited in the text.

Molly's Vision: Lost Cause Ideology and Genesis in Faulkner's *Go Down, Moses*

Glenn Meeter

When Molly Beauchamp, a "little old negro woman with a shrunken, incredibly old face beneath a white headcloth and a black straw hat which would have fitted a child," steps into the office of Gavin Stevens, county attorney in Jefferson, Mississippi, in the last and title story of *Go Down, Moses*, she presents him with what can only be called a vision.[1] The vision is a product of the second sight by which Molly is able to divine that her missing grandson, Butch Beauchamp, from whom she has not heard in five years, is in some sort of trouble. Stevens does not doubt this divinatory power of hers; in fact we are told that he would not be surprised if "she had also been able to divine where the boy was and what his trouble was" (373), and he seems to associate his own success at finding these answers with this same power of Molly's.

We as readers are not surprised either, for we have seen Molly in "The Fire and the Hearth" warning her husband Lucas not to disturb buried treasure because it has God's curse upon it (102, 122); and we have seen Lucas experience a foretaste of that curse in the avalanche he brings upon himself when digging near the old Indian mound, "a sort of . . . admonitory pat from the spirit of darkness and solitude, the old earth, perhaps the old ancestors themselves" (38). So we know that Molly is both Orphic and Delphic, able to speak for the gods of both earth and heaven. She is evidently something of a soothsayer and a prophet. When she first presents her vision to Stevens in his office, Faulkner tells us "she began to chant" (371); when she repeats the chant later, in Miss Worsham's house, aided by her brother and his wife, Stevens hears it as "strophe and antistrophe," and Molly sways back and forth in her chair, neither seeing Stevens nor hearing him as he tries to interrupt her, for her senses are attuned to an inner vision (380–381). The chant makes Stevens profoundly uncomfortable, and he rushes outside to get his breath.

This vision of Molly's, as we glimpse it in her repeated chant, makes subtle, rich, and daring connections between the stories of the McCaslin family and McCaslin land in *Go Down, Moses* and the stories of the patriarchs and the promised land of Canaan in the biblical book of Genesis. " 'Roth Edmonds sold my Benjamin. Sold him in Egypt. Pharaoh got him—' " (371). It is a vision worth attending to, for although *Go Down, Moses* makes use of many themes and motifs from the book of Genesis (genealogy, land, birthright, and inheritance are among them), it differs from its biblical prototype in two ways. First, it is a story of origins which ends in the fictional *present*, not the still distant past, so that it is the origin of the fictional future we are reading about; and second, there is no editorial or authorial voice telling us the divine plan and purpose for this family and this land. We are therefore in the position of the characters, not the readers, of Genesis: we have to evaluate the claims, for example, of Ike, Roth, and Lucas without clues from history or theology—unless we can get them from a visionary like Molly.

We should not be put off by the fact that Molly's vision is presented in an oracle and that its biblical elements furnish "no chain of one-to-one correspondences" with the story of *Go Down, Moses*.[2] We must remember that Molly is a prophetess, not a biblical pedant like Stevens, the Heidelberg Ph.D. who busies himself translating the Old Testament "back into classic Greek" (371), not an exegete like Cass Edmonds and Ike McCaslin, who make claims about how Scripture was written and should be interpreted (259–261), and not a purveyor of popular analogies like Fonsiba's husband, who tosses off an allusion to the post-war South as " 'the new Canaan' " (279). Molly speaks as one having authority and not as the scribes. The reason for Faulkner's spelling Molly's name one way in "The Fire and the Hearth" and another in "Go Down, Moses" (Mollie) may lie in the dual spelling's suggestion of Molly's preliterate condition, a condition helpful in attaining the prophetic state; or it may lie in the connection between Molly and Faulkner (born Falkner) himself. As it has been said of Faulkner, in regard to the biblical resonances of *Absalom, Absalom!*, that he has "the uncanny power to immerse us in a reading process appropriate to but not simply imitative of his sources," so it must be said of Molly.[3] In her visionary chant in Stevens's office she manages to juxtapose and condense several biblical stories just as earlier she has been known to conflate the three generations of Edmondses, Cass, Zack, and Roth, in "The Fire and the Hearth" (100, 122).

1. Selling Benjamin

The first of these conflated stories are those of Joseph and Benjamin. Benjamin was the last child of the patriarch Jacob, the child of his old age, and so it is fitting that Molly refer to the grandson she brought up as her "Benjamin." But Benjamin in the Bible is only *threatened* with being lost into Egypt; it is of course Joseph whom his half brothers actually sell into Egypt as a slave.[4] So in uniting "Benjamin" and "sold in Egypt" Molly evokes both stories at once. Further, in making Roth Edmonds play the role of the threatening or betraying brothers in both instances she evokes several stories as well in Faulkner's novel. From the title story itself we know that in a literal way all Roth has done to Butch Beauchamp has been to order him off the McCaslin property after catching him breaking into the commissary store (373); this incident, given to us through the memory of Stevens, may make us think as he does that Molly's indictment, "sold him in Egypt," is a bit overdone (380). But we may remember also that in "The Fire and the Hearth" Roth has referred to Molly not once but three times as "the only mother he ever knew" (100, 110, 117); that reference makes him and Butch brothers, since Molly stands *in loco parentis* to them both. And their relatedness is certainly literal as well, since both claim McCaslin blood; this together with their metaphorical brotherhood makes Molly's accusation considerably more pertinent. We may remember also the poignant episode in which Roth separates himself, at age seven, from Henry, Molly and Lucas's son, whom he thinks of as his "foster brother," in order to enter "his heritage," the white landowner's heritage, and eat "its bitter fruit" (111–114). Finally, we may think of the incident in "Delta Autumn" in which Roth plays the role of betraying kinsman not to a brother but to the woman who has been his lover and to their son—both of them descendants, as he is, of the founding McCaslin patriarch. In all these stories Roth plays the role of the unkindly kinsman, thus bearing out Molly's prophetic evaluation of his character; and in thus "predicting" the events of "Delta Autumn," which follows "Go Down, Moses" chronologically though narratively it precedes it, Molly's accusation of Roth becomes prophetic in another sense as well.

All these stories in their turn allude to others from Genesis, and with each such allusion comes an implied moral evaluation. Roth's eating the "bitter fruit" of his heritage makes us think of the garden of Eden—and foreshadows Ike McCaslin's opinion, in "The Bear," that land ownership itself is what has dispossessed us of Eden (256–258). Roth's self-imposed separation from his foster brother Henry reminds us of his father Zack's earlier conflict with Lucas (45–59) and of a series of biblical brothers in conflict regarding a heritage: Cain and Abel, Isaac and Ishmael, Jacob and Esau, Joseph and his brothers. The biblical stories themselves may remind us, even though we read them through many overlays of interpretation, that it is not always easy to separate the good brother from the bad, the true inheritor of the blessing and birthright from the pretender and usurper. To mention only two of Genesis' surprises in this regard, it is the "good" brother Joseph who is sold into Egypt and the "good" brother Jacob who must flee for his life; it is the bad or threatening brothers in each case who remain on the patriarchal property.

In Faulkner's novel, it is Roth who holds title to the McCaslin land; but both Henry and Butch Beauchamp have more McCaslin blood in their veins than he does, and so do the woman and the child in "Delta Autumn."[5] After his separation from Henry, the young Roth is shocked to hear his father, Zack, refer to the Edmonds line as "usurpers" (114). Is he a "usurper" also in regard to the woman and child he sends away in "Delta Autumn"? In biblical terms, is he acting out the role of Abraham in sending away Hagar and her son Ishmael—though here there is no question of a "legitimate" wife and son—or is he replaying the role of Judah toward his daughter-in-law, Tamar, toward whom he has acted shamefully and about whom he eventually must confess, as he reunites her with his family, "She hath been more righteous than I" (Genesis 38:26)? Only time will tell. But for now, Molly's " 'Roth Edmonds sold my Benjamin' " makes her instinctive evaluation clear: Roth, though counted among her children, has acted in the role of the bad brother(s). It should be clear as well that Molly's vision, in casting Molly herself in the role of the patriarch Jacob, makes a claim quite radical for its time and place: it is she and Lucas and their children who represent the line of the birthright, and Roth's claim to the promised land, that is, the McCaslin land, comes to him through her, his foster mother.

2. Egypt and Israel; Canaan and Eden

Does Molly, with her second sight, indeed see the McCaslin land as the promised land of Genesis? So Gavin Stevens seems to think, for after remembering what Molly has said about Roth Edmonds selling her Benjamin in Egypt, he remembers what she "had meant"; he remembers that Roth after catching Butch breaking into the commissary store "had ordered him off the place and had forbidden him ever to return" (373). And we also know that the net effect of Roth's other actions implied in

Molly's indictment is that his other black relatives—Henry, and the woman and child in "Delta Autumn"—are also "off the place." Since Molly speaks from the standpoint of the grieving Jacob, she must conceive of the McCaslin "place" as the promised land even as "off the place" is Egypt. And if the McCaslin place, then by extension the whole South for which it stands synecdochically: we remember Ike's comment, in "The Bear," that the commissary ledgers and the record they contain represent "a whole land in miniature" (293).

That this indeed is a true reading of Molly's vision—the South as the promised land of Genesis—is borne out in her vision's practical result, which is to bring back the body of her grandson for burial in Yoknapatawpha County, just as at the end of Genesis Jacob's body is brought back out of Egypt for burial in Canaan, and just as Joseph charges his brothers to do for his body at the time of the Exodus (Genesis 50). Earlier, in "Pantaloon in Black," the only story in the book that does not involve a member of the McCaslin family, though it is set on the McCaslin land, Faulkner has prepared us for this funeral. In that story about the grief of Rider, the black protagonist, for his dead wife—a grief so extreme that he seeks to join her in death by getting himself lynched for the murder of a white man who has cheated at dice—he gives us another version of the South as sacred soil, sacred even to the black man who in burying his wife there sets his claim upon it, in the description of the graveyard marked off by "shards of pottery and broken bottles and old brick and other objects insignificant to sight but actually of a profound meaning and fatal to touch, which no white man could have read" (135).

Here if anywhere the biblical elements of Molly's vision do form "one-to-one correspondences" with her own situation in Faulkner's novel: she is the grieving Jacob, the McCaslin land is Canaan, "off the place" is Egypt. There are two major reasons that we resist this interpretation, however. One of these, mainly extrinsic to the book, is our discomfort at seeing Molly made what might seem a too convenient mouthpiece of the Southern establishment. The other, more intrinsic, is Ike McCaslin's strong repudiation of what Molly's vision seems to accept.

To see the South as a reincarnation of ancient Israel was a commonplace of Lost Cause ideology and a staple in the oratory of Southern preachers from the collapse of the Confederacy well into the twentieth century. In the words of a 1909 memorial sermon, " 'God is in our history as truly as He was in the history of Israel.' "[6] In making use of what Charles Reagan Wilson, in his study of "the religion of the Lost Cause, 1865–1920," calls "the ubiquitous Old Testament analogy," Southern preachers compared the South to Israel during many stages of its history. The South was like Israel wandering in the wilderness, like Israel led into captivity by heathen conquerors, like Israel purified by fire, like Israel renewed through the endurance of a saving remnant and eventually triumphant, like Israel the suffering servant whose sufferings would bring "a blessing to all people" though they were harsh as the trials of Job. The analogy is extended to New Israel, the Church: the South is compared to Christ on the cross and Paul in his prison cell and the woman in Revelation who flees from the cruel beast (65, 71, 75). In this ideology, the lesson of 1865 is that defeat in a "holy war" is not at all the end of God's favor, for "God's chosen people did not give up that chosen status when defeated" (77).

In Faulkner's novels we see this ideology at work even after 1920 in the mingling of religious and sectional-patriotic themes in the sermons of the Reverend Gail Hightower in *Light in August;* and we see an earlier version of it in *The Unvanquished,* when Granny Millard during the Civil War prays for those who have given their sons to a " 'holy cause, even though You have seen fit to make it a lost cause,' " and when her helper, Brother Fortinbride, preaches that "victory without God is mockery and delusion, but . . . defeat with God is not defeat."[7] Faulkner himself becomes a part of this analogical tradition in his use of Davidic parallels in portraying the South in the Civil War and Reconstruction periods in both *The Unvanquished* and *Absalom,*

Absalom!—though to be sure with subtleties and depths that challenge and transcend the ideology of which the analogy was an expression.[8]

But the question of how far he was able to challenge and transcend that ideology is important for Molly and *Go Down, Moses* precisely because in it there was small room for blacks. The ideology as Wilson outlines it became segregationist and white supremacist under the influence of the Ku Klux Klan, but even in its most benign phase it included the slaves and their descendants within the chosen nation only as loyal black Confederates, the " 'dear old mammys and faithful servants' " to whom a memorial monument was proposed by the United Daughters of the Confederacy—a monument finally raised at Harper's Ferry, against opposition from both whites and blacks, after an effort extending from 1896 to 1937. One proposed statue was described, by a Methodist cleric in 1904, as " 'a trinity of figures . . . consisting of the courtly old planter; the plantation 'uncle,' the counterpart in ebony of the master so loyally served and imitated; and the broad-bosomed black 'mammy,' with varicolored turban, spotless apron, and beaming face, the friend and helper of every living thing in cabin or mansion' " (Wilson, 105–106).

Is this the tradition to which Molly subscribes when she imagines her grandson sold into "Egypt" because he has been sent away from the ancestral plantation? Faulkner's dedicati of *Go Down, Moses* to Caroline Barr begins with the words "To Mammy," and its fine tribute is repeated with only minc variations by Roth, in "The Fire and the Hearth," and applied to Molly (117). There is another possible echo of the notion of the loyal black Confederate in Roth's shocked recognition of the face of Molly's husband, Lucas, as a "composite of a whole generation of fierce and undefeated young Confederate soldiers, embalmed and slightly mummified" (118)—though of course Roth's exasperation here and the Egyptian allusions, as well as the context of the whole novel, including the McCaslin genealogy, all make the passage complex rather than sentimental. In the figure of Ringo, Bayard Sartoris's playmate, friend, and servant in *The Unvanquished*. Faulkner has given us an example of the slave so completely identified with his white family as to cut himself off from his fellow black Southerners (128–129). And readers of *The Sound and the Fury* have sometimes found it hard to feel toward Dilsey, another character modelled on Caroline Barr, the unreserved admiration that the book seems to ask for because to do so seems to them tantamount to subscribing to a tradition of black subservience.

There is, then, a disturbing suggestion of the racial sellout in Molly's identification of the South with the promised land— especially so because the biblical metaphor that traditionally *opposes* the Lost Cause identification of the South and biblical Israel, the South as an Egypt of racial bondage, is ready to hand in the very title of the book. That Faulkner is aware of this opposed biblical metaphor is obvious not only from his allusion to the Negro spiritual but in his portrayal of a "black Exodus," as it has been called, in *The Unvanquished*.[9] And within *Go Down, Moses* itself there are allusions to the metaphor of the South as Egypt that the spiritual implies. The words that form the spiritual's chorus, "Let my people go" (Exodus 5:1), are echoed by Ike in "The Old People" when he says to Cass about Sam Fathers, his spiritual mentor of mixed racial heritage, " 'let him go!' "—a plea echoed by Sam himself in "The Bear," when he asks to go back to his cabin to die: " 'Let me out, master. . . . let me go home' " (167, 245). Later, in his effort to find and provide for Fonsiba, his black cousin, Ike strenuously resists her feckless husband's calling the South a " 'new Canaan' " (279); and in his discussion of the meaning of history with Cass, Ike seems to picture John Brown as a kind of Moses of black liberation (285)—a failed Moses, since Ike sees black bondage in the South continuing at least a hundred years after "a bloody civil war" (255). By the time of "Delta Autumn," the "delta" of whose title contains its own suggestion of Egyptian bondage in the land of Goshen, Ike as an old man seems ready to continue this period of bondage for another *"thousand or two thousand years*" (361). In that story he advises his young, "almost white" kinswoman, who has borne Roth Edmonds' son, " 'Go back North. . . . That's the only salvation for you' " (363).

In answer to these reservations about Molly's vision of the South as the promised land of Genesis it must be said, first, that Faulkner's putting the anti-Lost Cause metaphor of the South as Egypt into the mouth of Ike McCaslin tends to undercut that metaphor. In his mouth, the admonition "go back North" to a black woman who is his relative seems self-serving and cruel—as indeed it would outside the story; for by the 1940s the Negro spiritual's picture of the South as the Egypt of racial bondage could easily be associated with the view, held alike by black nationalists and white racists, that the descendants of the slaves should go back to Africa. If the South as chosen nation (but mainly for whites) is the biblical metaphor favored by Lost Cause ideology, Faulkner's novel makes clear that the opposed metaphor, the South as Egypt of racial bondage, is only its mirror image; neither has room for black inheritance in the South.

Most importantly, it must be insisted that Molly envisions the South not as the defeated but still chosen Israel of Lost Cause ideology but as the promised land of Canaan in Genesis. The difference is great; and it should be noted that Wilson's survey of the extensive use of "the Israelite comparison" (67) and the "ubiquitous Old Testament analogy" (71) by preachers of the Lost Cause includes no reference to the book of Genesis. In Molly's vision there is no room for white supremacy or for segregation; for the children of the patriarchs and matriarchs may be white or black, Edmonds or Beauchamp. In her vision there is room for black inheritance and possession, even though long delayed, for the "bad" brother is an Edmonds and the "good" brother who has been "sold," like Joseph, is a Beauchamp. The South is not an Egypt from which her children must make an exodus, it is the promised land to which they must return in order to claim their inheritance. And in her Genesis vision there is room, finally, for racial reconciliation, since the "bad" brother is not after all Pharaoh but is still Roth, her son, who may yet be forgiven as were Joseph's half brothers after the burial of Jacob.

Far from the "faithful black mammy" of Lost Cause ideology, then, Faulkner makes Molly a matriarch like Sarah, Rebekah, and Rachel. In giving us Molly's Genesis vision at the end of *Go Down, Moses* he changes our reading of the book: now we must retrospectively read "Was," for example, as an "origins" story of the Beauchamps, a story of how Tomey's Turl found his bride, Tenny Beauchamp—and how Tenny was protected from the potential threat of her master, Hubert, much as Sarah and Rebekah were protected from "the princes of Pharaoh" (Genesis 12:11–20) and the "king of the Philistines" (Genesis 26:6–11). That this threat to the matriarch is a real one we may gather from Hubert's later activities with the " 'new cook' " in "The Bear" (302–303). We see in the conflict between Zack and Lucas (45–59) another instance of this Genesis theme, with Zack in this reading playing the role not only of the rivalrous brother but also of the threat to the matriarch, Molly herself (45–59).

And Faulkner changes our reading of the South. No longer a chosen nation of whites, forged in the crucible of a holy war, nor yet a land of Egypt out of which blacks must go to be saved, it is instead pictured in Molly's prophetic vision as a land promised to the founder's children of both races, whose inheritors may turn out to be surprising to those not privy to God's purposes, and whose history as a chosen nation lies not in the past but in the future.

If Molly accepts the McCaslin inheritance, though on markedly different terms from the acceptance of Southern inheritance proposed by Lost Cause apologists, Ike McCaslin repudiates that inheritance altogether. His repudiation is hinted at in the first page of "Was" and alluded to in "The Fire and the Hearth" before we ever see Ike himself as a character in "The Old People," "The Bear," and "Delta Autumn." It is what he is known for, it is his life's work, his *raison d'etre;* and his long defense of that repudiation to Cass Edmonds in the fourth section of "The Bear" forms the climax of the book.

The heritage Ike repudiates is represented by the commissary ledgers and, above all, the history of slavery that they contain. It is a representative history in that it records both the worst of slavery as an institution, in the founding McCaslin's incest with his own slave-born daughter, and the best, in the "amelioration and restitution" (261) that resulted from the plan of the second-generation McCaslins, Buddy and Buck, for the gradual manu-mission of the slaves. Ike sees slavery as a curse, one that was brought upon the South by whites and is only to be lifted by whites (259, 278), and one that God has tried to ameliorate through men like Buck and Buddy and even Ike himself (259, 283) and also to destroy, both through the "suffering" caused by the Civil War (286) and the "enduring" of the descendants of the slaves (294).

But the "curse" that the ledgers record is larger than slavery; it has to do with ownership of the land and even with "taming" it, that is, clearing, plowing, and planting it. Ike repudiates

> the tamed land which was to have been his heritage, the land which old Carothers McCaslin his grandfather had bought with white man's money from the wild men whose grandfathers without guns hunted it, and tamed and ordered or believed he had tamed and ordered it for the reason that the human beings he held in bondage and in the power of life and death had removed the forest from it and in their sweat scratched the surface of it to a depth of perhaps fourteen inches in order to grow something out of it which had not been there before. (254)

In biblical terms Ike sees the South not as (or not only as) the Egypt of bondage, like the Negro spiritual, not as the chosen nation of Lost Cause apologetic, certainly not as the promised land envisioned by Molly's Genesis metaphor; he sees it as a fallen Eden, fallen because of Man's original sin of trying to own and tame the land, a sin of which slavery forms only a part. That is why it is appropriate that on the last day of the life of Old Ben, the primordial bear who represents the wilderness, Major de Spain leads a hunting party "almost as strong . . . as some he had led in the last darkening days of '64 and '65" (236). Killing the bear and the wilderness he represents is for Ike the same "Cause" as the war to perpetuate slavery. And the destruction of Ben and the wilderness has the same quality of doom and fatality about it as the fighting in those "last darkening days." For Ike, the land in its unfallen state is held "mutual and intact in the communal anonymity of brotherhood" (257), a condition that sounds like the Marxist's primitive communism; his way of ritually recreating this primitive paradise is the hunt, where one can pretend that the wilderness is still unowned (or, as Ike sees it, can escape the pretense that it *is* owned) and can pretend that one lives in communal anonymity of brotherhood where there are only men, "not white nor black nor red but men, hunters" (191).

Ike's notion of land ownership may owe something to Henry George and through him to the Bible.[10] But its appeal to us as readers is based less on its evoking those Scriptural texts that Henry George liked to cite (for example, "The earth is the LORD'S," Psalm 24.1)—which in any case do not prohibit ownership, much less agriculture—than on its romantic back-to-nature theme and on its contemporary ecological, environmentalist, green-party ring. It reawakens in us the millenia-old suspicion that as a human race we have paid too high a price for leaving the hunting and gathering stage. It reawakens also the particularly American belief in an American Adam and Eden, whether Adam is Thoreau on Walden Pond, Rip Van Winkle in the Catskills, Melville in the South Seas, Huck on the Mississippi, Nick Adams up in Michigan, or John Muir in Yosemite. Finally, though, its appeal comes from the fact that Ike's experience of the wilderness in both "The Old People" and "The Bear" is so vividly and powerfully presented. Ike is by no means a stick figure in an allegorical argument; if Molly is a prophet, so is Ike in his own way. Among the many Genesis motifs in *Go Down, Moses* are the book's convincing evocations of the numinous, including not only Molly's second sight but Rider's vision of his dead wife in "Pantaloon in Black." But among these Ike's experiences of the supernatural in both "The Old People" and "The Bear" are the most impressive of all.

If Ike sees the South as a fallen Eden, his view of Southern history and his (or Faulkner's) conception of his own place in it are also based on Genesis. The War and Reconstruction periods are not nation forging experiences, for him; rather he sees them in terms of the "Flood," a bygone period following which the land has been divided among "three separate peoples," white, black, and alien, like the races of Japheth, Ham, and Shem that people the earth after the biblical flood (289; Genesis 10). Ike sees his own role, somewhat jocularly, as that of " 'an Isaac . . . repudiating immolation,' " meaning repudiating, paradoxically, his heritage, " 'because maybe this time the exasperated Hand might not supply the kid' " (283). Later he flirts with a comparison of himself and "the Nazarene" (309–10); but of course "repudiating immolation" and "declining the altar" (283) have already barred him from fulfilling the role of either Isaac or Christ. His acceptance of the word "escape" (283) for what he is doing means that he knows that his apparent self-sacrifice is really self-service.

It has been persuasively argued that Ike finds a "surrogate" heritage in the spiritual legacy of Sam Fathers, and that Sam—a great hunter, son of a bondwoman, who finds his own heritage in the wilderness—has the biblical Ishmael as his prototype.[11] This is the more persuasive in that the patriarchal history in Genesis contains a series of stories of brotherly conflict: Isaac-Ishmael, Jacob-Esau, Joseph and his brothers. And just as Molly's vision alludes to the last of these, and the Ishmael resonances in Sam Fathers to the first, so Ike in his repudiation evokes the figure of Esau in the second. For Esau is a "hunter," like the "archer" Ishmael (Genesis 21:20, 25:27), and he is the only one of the brothers in the patriarchal series to voluntarily give up or "despise" his birthright, selling it to his brother Jacob for a dish of "pottage" (Genesis 25:34). It is appropriate to see in Hubert Beauchamp's spurious legacy—the silver cup full of gold that by Ike's twenty-first birthday becomes a tin pot full of I.O.U.'s (300–308)—the "pottage" for which Ike sells his birthright, inasmuch as Ike in repudiating the McCaslin land has *not* repudiated his other heritage which he thinks of in capital letters as "a Legacy, a Thing, possessing weight to the hand and bulk to eye and even audible" (301)—a phrasing that must owe something to Eve's temptation scene, when she sees "that the tree was good for food, and that it was pleasant to the eyes, and a tree to be desired to make one wise . . ." (Genesis 3:6). No wonder Ike does not want to kill the bear, for it and the wilderness are now the only heritage he has left. As for the substitutionary animal sacrifice, *that* has already been supplied for Ike in the opening pages of "The Old People," in the death of the deer and the smearing of its "hot smoking blood" across Ike's face (164). It is this sacrifice that at once initiates him into the way of Ishmael and Esau—the hunters living apart from the promised land—and serves as the "scapegoat" in place of his own sacrifice in accepting his father's heritage.[12]

Ike's repudiation is more complete than that of Esau, even as Sam's aloneness is more extreme than that of Ishmael; while their biblical prototypes both found nations, Sam and Ike remain childless and landless. And Ike's repudiation of Lost Cause ideology is in one way more complete than that of Molly, since he repudiates all human "progress" since the stone age. In that perspective the human bondage in Egypt is less important than Man's self-inflicted loss of Eden. But Ike's vision of the South is more race-bound than hers, seeing miscegenation as a kind of vengeance imposed by the dying wilderness. Here too Ike is true to his Genesis metaphor, since he sees the South at the end of "Delta Autumn" as a Babel of racial mixture.

It is the ritual of the hunt that recreates for Ike the illusion of the primitive communism of unowned, untamed Eden. We know that the ritual by the time of "Delta Autumn" has become a kind of lifeless ritualism. Already in "The Bear" we know that the wilderness is doomed and that the hunt itself does *not* recreate that Edenic state of brotherhood that Ike imagines,

where men are "not white nor black nor red but men, hunters";
we know that except for Sam as a guide without a gun and the
hilariously incompetent marksmen Boon and Ash there are no
red or black hunters at all; the hunts are already "fallen." But
the fact that there are no women on the hunt marks another
kind of incompleteness in the ritual—not for any egalitarian
reasons but in terms of the book's substratum of Genesis allusions. For Genesis is a book of origins, of generation and
genealogy, and *Go Down, Moses* is as well. Consequently the
importance of the matriarchs in both. As Tomey's Turl says to
the young Cass in the book's opening story: "anytime you wants
to get something done, from hoeing out a crop to getting
married, just get the womenfolks to working at it" (13). This is
the story that includes the implied triumphs of two matriarchs,
Sophonsiba and Tennie. From that perspective, the three hunting stories focusing on Ike, as powerful as they are, nevertheless
take on something of the farcical quality of the hunting/gaming
ritual in "Was," and Ike appears to deserve the harsh comment
about him in "Delta Autumn." For all the nobility of his
identification with the wilderness, and despite his own adulation
of the act of sex as divine (as with D. H. Lawrence, sex itself
seems to have become the last wilderness for him)—for all this,
he has forgotten the power of love (348, 363).

Throughout *Go Down, Moses*, then, there are two Genesis
metaphors for the South that stand in opposition to the chosen
nation metaphor favored by Lost Cause ideology: Ike's and
Molly's. Though Ike's is vividly and powerfully presented, it is
Molly's that is given the last word; and in the tension between
them lies much of the meaning of the book.

3. The Funeral

If there is a "Moses" in the title story of *Go Down, Moses* it
must be Gavin Stevens. He it is whose "serious vocation," we
are told, is a "twenty-two-year-old unfinished translation of the
Old Testament back into classic Greek," and if he is thus

associated with the writing of the Bible he is also associated, by Molly, with "the Law" (371). Molly clearly expects him to get her grandson out of "Egypt" and away from "Pharaoh." How then can she imagine him as part of that Genesis story she seems to be telling in which she is Jacob/Rachel, her grandson is Benjamin/Joseph, and Roth is the brother who has sold him?

The charge that Molly gives to Stevens, to bring her grandson's body home for burial, is the charge that Joseph at the end of Genesis gives to his brothers regarding his own body: "ye shall carry up my bones from hence" (Genesis 50:25). That charge is fulfilled by Moses during the Exodus (Exodus 13:19), and Joseph is eventually buried in Canaan (Joshua 24:32). And the charge given by Molly to Stevens, strongly seconded by Miss Worsham, is fulfilled by Stevens. It is he, aided by the local newspaper editor, who determines where the grandson's body is and arranges to have it brought back for burial. In fact he arranges a highly public funeral procession, with onlookers and participants from all segments of the community, rich and poor, black and white.

Once again, moreover, Molly and Faulkner have juxtaposed and condensed several biblical stories. The Bible gives no details concerning Joseph's burial except that it took place in Canaan. But the last chapter of Genesis records an elaborate funeral procession for the patriarch Jacob. It is a procession from Egypt back to Canaan that ends with Jacob's burial in the ancestral burial plot, the cave of Machpelah (Genesis 23:19, 25:9, 49:31). It is Joseph, in this case, who receives permission for the event from Pharaoh; and the funeral procession involves contributions from the Egyptians, wonderment on the part of onlooking Canaanites—both of these groups better known as enemies of the Israelites—and, finally, the reconciliation of Joseph and his brothers. In the same way the funeral of Butch Beauchamp involves at least momentary reconciliation of the rival McCaslin lines, Beauchamp and Edmonds, for both Lucas and Roth are contributors to the proceedings (only Ike McCaslin's name is conspicuously missing); and it involves onlookers from both Negroes and whites. As the funeral procession for Jacob includes chariots, horsemen, and "all the elders of the land of Egypt," so Faulkner's procession for Molly's grandson includes Stevens' car and the editor's car, bearing Molly and Miss Worsham and the editor and Stevens, "the designated paladin of justice and truth and right, the Heidelberg Ph.D.," along with the Negro undertaker's hearse, all moving across the town square, around the Confederate monument and the courthouse and on to the burying place on the McCaslin land seventeen miles away (Genesis 50:4–13, 382).

Stevens is correct, then, in thinking of Molly that she *wanted that casket and those flowers and the hearse and she wanted to ride through town behind it in a car*—not because Molly is a simple-hearted old woman who loves pageantry but because she sees in the pageant a fulfillment of her family's Genesis story. Throughout the book of Genesis there are burials that serve as opportunities for reconciliation: Isaac and Ishmael unite to bury Abraham (25:9) and Esau and Jacob unite to bury Isaac (35:29) just as Joseph and his brothers unite at the end. The other function that the burials serve, however, is the establishing of a claim to the land, for the promised land is the place where the bones of the ancestors lie. The Indian mound in "The Fire and the Hearth" constitutes a claim; the grave of Mannie in "Pantaloon in Black" constitutes a claim; the grave of Sam Fathers in "The Bear" constitutes a claim. And so the grave, the burial, and the funeral of Butch Beauchamp form part of Molly's claim to the McCaslin "promised land."

There would seem to be tremendous ironies in this "claim." One could hardly imagine a more ironic avatar of either Jacob or Joseph than what Faulkner calls "the slain wolf," the dead murderer (382). Nevertheless in calling Butch Beauchamp "the slain wolf" Faulkner sets his own seal of approval upon Molly's patriarchal claim. In Genesis 49, Jacob's last words to his twelve sons, which comprise both a deathbed blessing and a predictive history of each of the twelve tribes, conclude with this comment to the youngest: "Benjamin shall ravin as a wolf: in the morning he shall devour the prey, and at night he shall divide the spoil" (49:27). Thus Faulkner's apparently demeaning epithet itself confirms both Molly's claim of matriarchal status and Butch's role as her "Benjamin." And it is Benjamin, as we have seen, whose story Molly and Faulkner conflate with that of Joseph. Butch as Benjamin is the slain wolf; but as Joseph in "Egypt" he is able to give his occupation to the Chicago reporter as " 'Getting rich too fast' " (370). Further, he plays both Joseph and Jacob in that his body is brought back to the land of promise.

Molly's role for herself, in the reworking of Genesis motifs that informs her future-oriented vision, a vision whose earliest stages she herself brings to pass, is that of Rachel, favored spouse of the eponymous patriarch—and a Rachel who not only weeps for her children but establishes their claim to a future in their land. In Molly, then, Faulkner has turned the favorite biblical metaphor of Lost Cause ideology on its head. The "Mammy" of his dedication of the novel to Caroline Barr, like the " 'dear old mammy and faithful servant' " envisioned for the Harper's Ferry monument, has become the black matriarch of a chosen Southern nation of the future.

Molly lives in the mythic present; for her the McCaslin place is *the* promised land, not merely a version of the biblical one. She is able to juxtapose and condense past, present, and future even more successfully than the young Ike, about whom it was said: "gradually . . . these old times would cease to be old times and would become a part of the . . . present. . . . And more: as if some of them had not happened yet but would occur tomorrow . . ." (171). As a prophetess Molly perhaps sees further into the future than readers in 1942, or in the present, can see. Though it may take a long time, as Ike would have it, eventually the Beauchamp inheritors—Henry, Fonsiba, Roth's unnamed son and his mother, or their descendants both direct and, like Rider and Mannie, collateral—will return to claim the land of their fathers.

NOTES

1. William Faulkner, *Go Down, Moses* (New York: Random House, 1942), 371. Further references will be cited in the text.

2. Dirk Kuyk, Jr., *Threads Cable-strong: William Faulkner's Go Down, Moses* (Lewisburg: Bucknell University Press, 1983), 185. I am indebted to Kuyk's discussion of "juxtaposing and condensing" in *Go Down, Moses* and to his thoughtful discussion of the whole book.

3. Stephen M. Ross, "Faulkner's *Absalom, Absalom!* and the David Story: A Speculative Contemplation," in *The David Myth in Western Literature*, Raymond-Jean Frontain and Jan Wojcik, eds. (West Lafayette: Purdue University Press, 1980), 148.

4. See Genesis 42:36, 37:36, 45:4; Acts 7:9. All Scripture quotations in the text are from the King James version.

5. See the helpful genealogies in John Kenny Crane, *The Yoknapatawpha Chronicles of Gavin Stevens* (Selinsgrove: Susquehanna University Press, 1988), 281, 287, 291.

6. Charles Reagan Wilson, *Baptized in Blood: The Religion of the Lost Cause, 1865–1920* (Athens: University of Georgia Press, 1980), 76. Further references will be cited in the text.

7. William Faulkner, *Light in August* (New York: Random House, 1932), 56–60; *The Unvanquished* (New York: Random House, 1938), 155, 167. Further references will be cited in the text.

8. For *Absalom, Absalom!* see Ross, *op. cit.*

9. George W. Van Devender, "William Faulkner's Black Exodus: Multiple Narration in *The Unvanquished*," *South Central Bulletin*, 42 (1982), 144–148.

10. Dale G. Breaden, "William Faulkner and the Land," in *Bear, Man, and God: Seven Approaches to William Faulkner's "The Bear,"* Francis Lee Utley, Lynn Z. Bloom, and Arthur F. Kinney, eds. (New York: Random House, 1964), 273–278.

11. Stanley Sultan, "Call Me Ishmael: The Hagiography of Isaac McCaslin," *Texas Studies in Language and Literature* 3 (Spring 1961), 66.

12. For a helpful psychological and anthropological approach to the patriarchal narratives of Genesis, see Devora Steinmetz, *From Father to Son: Kinship, Conflict, and Continuity in Genesis* (Louisville: Westminster/John Knox Press, 1991), especially her discussion of the importance of animal sacrifice on pages 40–44.

"Polysyllabic and Verbless Patriotic Nonsense": Faulkner at Midcentury—His and Ours

NOEL POLK

For Jim Hinkle

There's a wonderful moment in the 1952 *Omnibus* television program on Faulkner. In one of the early scenes, Phil "Moon" Mullen, Faulkner's old friend and a former associate editor of the Oxford *Eagle,* comes to Rowan Oak to tell Faulkner that he's won the Nobel Prize. The *Omnibus* camera stationed in the Rowan Oak living room watches from behind Faulkner as he answers Mullen's knock at the front door; Faulkner is neatly dressed in a coat and a tie. He greets Mullen: "So you're the one the trouble begins with?" "Who did you want it to begin with?" Mullen responds, as they move together into the living room, sit down and chat. Faulkner says, "Look, Phil. I don't see what my private life, the inside of my house, or my family have to do with my writing." Mullen insists that somebody will do the story, and he wants to be the one. "All right," Faulkner relents: "Do your story. But no pictures." Mullen remonstrates: "But you let the Oxford High School paper print your picture, by golly." Faulkner, smiling genially and with a sense of complicity, closes the conversation: "Yes, but my daughter was the editor of that paper, by golly." Cut, end of scene, move to Stockholm and the Nobel Prize.

The scene is cleverly written and staged, even pretty well acted by the players. But I am always stopped short at the image of the smiling author looking into the camera and saying "No pictures." That smiling face, that beatific halo of graying hair, that well-cut coat, all reek of immortality: of wisdom, of

297

comfort, contentment, serenity, and security. And not just of success, but of success hard won; hard won indeed, if you consider his struggles of the previous decade. Despite the "No pictures," there's anything but defiance in his face; no matter what sounds his mouth is making, his face says Welcome; I may be eccentric, but I am friendly. Thus the tableau is virtually iconic: he's everybody's Platonic image of Grandfather, if not of God, standing in the very sanctuary of the castle whose privacy he had become notorious for defending; he's looking into the TV camera that stands on the other side of that living room bastion, sitting comfortably in an easy chair throne, and saying: "No pictures" to the tens of thousands of people watching that very picture.

It's an interesting and in some ways delicious biographical moment, in a film whose very existence is an extended series of such moments. One wonders what ironies smirk behind those twinkling eyes, what congeries of satisfactions and secret plea-sures gather there giggling or laughing out loud. One also wonders whether any sense of how terrifically the scene contra-dicts itself weighs, and how heavily, on his conscience or his soul.

There's a mildly dark underbelly to the film, of course: those who know anything about Faulkner's relationship with Phil Stone during this period will perhaps find their teeth set on edge a bit by Stone's performance, and those who know any-thing about the Faulkners' home life during the 1940s and 1950s may find some jarring discrepancies between the biographical reality and the film's iconic depiction of Faulkner as home-centered family man, devoted husband and father, and as man about town. He is eccentric in the film, to be sure, but the center of the image is *Citoyen Faulkner*, a man who except for being a literary genius is not so different from you and me: husband, father, neighbor, responsible involved citizen. "Faulk-ner is a farmer," summarizes the narrator in the film's closing line, "who looks deep into the heart of life, and writes what he sees there."

What makes the film a curiosity, and of interest to us here at this conference, almost exactly forty years later, is its very successful effort to edit Faulkner, to normalize him: the film rather consciously *mainstreams* him into, makes him acceptable to, a culture and a world whose Chamber of Commerce values he had subjected to the intense scrutiny of his critical eye, and which he would continue to reject in his fiction and his personal life, even if not in his public pronouncements and postures. He's a farmer who looks deep into the heart of life, writes about it, and doesn't want his picture taken.

A small caveat before I proceed: the evidence of the entire film suggests that he was enjoying himself immensely, and perhaps the most reasonable way to think about the film is to assume that he's perfectly aware of what he's doing, and getting a big laugh out of it. I do not, in other words, think it necessary to be judgmental, as we have traditionally been, about what we might consider his betrayal of his former artistic behavior in going so public during the 1950s—by God, we like our artists to *suffer*, not to be successful—or to discern in his life as a public figure a kind of simplemindedness and hypocrisy which in some important ways pandered to and used the Great American Publicity Machine for his own benefit on the one hand, while on the other condemning it, as Louis J. Budd suggested from this platform in 1988. It's far more complex than that, I think. Budd was absolutely correct, of course, in arguing that the most interesting thing about the apparent disparities between the public and the private Faulkner of the 1950s lies in the ways we as readers and students have reacted to them, and that as his readers we have mostly failed to confront the Faulkner of this period in all his complexity. In doing things so differently in the 1950s, Faulkner may have been responding to the chastening experiences of his personal and professional hardships of the previous decade; he may simply have been bored, and seeking new avenues of expression. In thinking about his life during these very complicated times, we should never forget that he continued a *very* active writing and publishing life, a highly

visible literary life, an active and vigorous social life in Charlottesville and elsewhere, and a highly energetic engagement in
the media with social and political issues of his day; nor should
we forget that he was still capable of being very funny, of
discussing his work with students, and of taking great pleasure
in his grandchildren. We have only to look at the photographs
of him in the fifties to see that at some level he did indeed enjoy
his celebrity, and we should not begrudge him pleasure in his
success, whatever of consistency it costs us. Finally, I don't
believe we have to think of him as either duplicitous or simple-
minded because we have no more right to expect a seamless,
contradictionless life from him than we do from ourselves or,
say, Emerson, who very well contradicted himself.

Nevertheless, the scene at Rowan Oak in the *Omnibus* film is
the nub of a very complicated issue in Faulkner studies, out of
which one can see spiraling in double helixes an increasingly
complex series of biographical issues which have been turned
into critical issues. And I'd like to digress here for a moment to
reflect on the ideological mainstreaming of Faulkner and upon
the consequences of that mainstreaming for Faulkner as writer
and for us as readers.

So far as I am aware, we were not given a chance to vote on
which Faulkner we'd prefer to have on our stamps. But the
terms of the debate about the Elvis stamp vote[1] are very
interesting indeed, and analogous to what might have occurred
in a debate over the Faulkner stamp.

Given a choice, which Faulkner—which *image* of Faulkner—
would we have preferred on our stamps, which one enshrined
in our official memories? The genial grandfatherly Faulkner of
the *Omnibus* portrait, in less than a decade to become the
image on the stamp: the wise and compassionate, the certifiably
Immortal and Successful Faulkner, Faulkner the visionary, the
very nearly transcendent being so bathed in light as to seem to
be the source of light itself, whose very few public statements
about enduring and prevailing allow us not just to endure and
prevail but also to believe in a reformed, a domesticated, a tame

and *safe* Faulkner, one congenial to our own moral and ethical systems, our own cultural and ideological codes?

Or would we prefer the young, hard-gutted, demon-driven, frequently rude and arrogant Faulkner of the early years, the one who revolutionized American fiction, who wrote about decay, disaster, the horrific, who looked unflinchingly at all that is nightmarish and threatening in our lives and culture, all that we keep buried? This Faulkner's most well-known image is J. R. Cofield's photo, taken about the time of *Sanctuary*. In this photo Faulkner is full of a different kind of self-confidence, his head slightly tilted, his dark hair unkempt above deep dark eyes that stare straight at you, not even taking the trouble to be defiant but just bemused that you'd have the effrontery to look; he is tieless, casual, in a tweed sport coat, his arms folded tightly across his chest; he's self-sufficient and complete, and his right hand, *his writing hand,* holds a lighted cigarette that looks like a fuse. It's a closeup: Faulkner fills the frame, and the blurred forearm of that selfsame writing hand at the front edge threatens to spill over it; he's standing against a darkened curtain or wall that shuts out social context. He's young, lean, hard, anything but benign; the set of his mouth suggests he may be about to break out into laughter, but probably not at anything funny: as he wrote of Pete in *Requiem for a Nun,* you don't know what he's going to do, and you hope he's not going to do it this time. He's cocky, insolent, slightly menacing, almost threatening, sinister. Looked at abstractly, the portrait makes of him a chiaroscuro of darkness and light, of shadows in which a large part of him always lurks, simmering and brooding, the better to see into the light. He's not saying "No pictures" to *this* camera, neither welcoming nor avoiding its gaze: he's staring it down, daring it to do its worst. There's no fitter emblem for the works of that period, which are also youthful, cocky, insolent, and in some ways very threatening indeed, if we extrapolate from them (as we regularly do) a world view and a view of human nature that is almost unrelievedly bleak and problematic.

Like the Post Office, we have mostly chosen the older, benign

Faulkner as our icon of the man and his career, while at the
same time actually preferring the work of the lean, mean,
writing machine. In certain important ways, we as a profession
have grabbed and clung tenaciously to the rhetoric, fictional
and nonfictional, of certain of Faulkner's public "hopeful" or
"reformed" or "positive" assessments of human nature, even
though they form a very small part of his published work, and
have made them central to our understanding of his life and
work. Most curiously, and paradoxically, as I say, we don't
generally care very much for the fictional works of *this* Faulkner,
precisely because we do take them to be moralistic. So we can
have it both ways: on the one hand we can be responsible,
serious New Critical critics, and dismiss as inferior the fiction of
the post-Nobel period because we know that moralizing fiction
is bad fiction. At the same time, from the vantage of the benign
author's pronouncements, we can look backward into the early
fiction, the fiction that we *do* like and, at last, see redeeming
social and spiritual values that save those works from the nihilism and despair that *seemed* so inevictably lodged in them prior
to the period of the late forties, when Faulkner's resurrection
was getting a head of steam.[2] As Cheryl Lester has demonstrated, in editing *The Portable Faulkner* in the mid-'40s,
Malcolm Cowley believed that Faulkner's strengths lay not in
the individual stories and novels but in the larger pattern
or design of the creation of Yoknapatawpha County.[3] Cowley
assumed that one could more readily see that design, and
therefore more completely grasp Faulkner's claim on our attention, by emphasizing chronology. The result of this, Lester
argues, is that chronology and location in north Mississippi
became, willy-nilly, Cowley's principal critical agenda as, for
years, following him, it became ours: fiction like *Pylon* or *The
Wild Palms,* which did not fit a geographical or chronological
grid, Cowley simply dismissed as inferior.

Likewise, we have permitted the two-Faulkner theory to
control the way we read his fiction: we neuter the early and
mostly dismiss the later, by reading the early through the filter

of the later, and by using the early as a club to beat the later up with. I'd argue that the most deleterious ideological construct of the Faulkner field right now is that which has the notion of "the great books" or "the major phase" at the center. You may have noticed over the years here at the Faulkner and Yoknapatawpha Conference that no matter what the topic— Faulkner and Race, Faulkner and Religion, Faulkner and Women—we seem to examine and to cite not only the same set of books but to a large extent the same passages within those "great" books. To say this is by no means to criticize in any way the selection of papers for the conference; it is rather simply a description of Faulkner studies at the present, which right now is mostly structured around such a hierarchy of books and passages. We talk about Faulkner's "great books" in ways which make it unnecessary to take the late works, especially *A Fable*, seriously. I do it myself, in evangelizing for *Requiem for a Nun* and *A Fable*, when I have tried to argue that these novels too are "great" and *therefore* worth our attention, rather than that they are worth our attention because they are interesting and by an author whom we admire. Thus we tame those early, disturbing works, dismiss the later ones, and make them all serve the purposes of our own ideologies.

The question, *Which Faulkner?*, then, although I pose it whimsically, is not really an idle one, and the answer—the variety of possible answers—may allow us to think for a few moments about the ideology of Yoknapatawpha or, more generally, about what we bring to and take away from our reading of Faulkner: *why*, perhaps, we read literature, what expectations we have of the works themselves *as well as* what expectations we have of the authors whose works we read and admire, what expectations we perhaps have about any author's moral responsibilities to his or her works. That is, we perhaps assume that there is a direct and mutually validating relationship between an author's life and works, that the life must be in some measure the moral equivalent of the moralities of human behavior, tragic or comic, contained in the work. After all, at

some level, most of us look to literature for some understanding
of our lives, for some insight into our own behavior and that of
others that will help us, in Walker Percy's phrase, to make it
through a Thursday afternoon. What does it signify if an author's
work is somehow at ideological odds with her or his private life?

Faulkner's on-camera refusal to have his picture taken, then,
invites some speculation, about the extent to which in the film
he is acting out the public rituals of individuality, of privacy,
under the auspices of the very elements that had invaded his
privacy. The scene stands there in Faulkner's life, memorialized
on film, pristine in its paradoxicality, all the more so because
Faulkner did not own, and would not have, a television in his
house, refusing to make one of the two-thirds of American
households that by 1952 owned at least one.[4] Biographers have
treated the episode of the film as part of a rather seamless series
of incidents in Faulkner's life, one among many things in which
he was involved in the years following his investiture as a Knight
of the Nobel Prize. But it strikes me as something of a pretty
large blip on the screen of his life, even during this very volatile
period of his life when he teetered on the brink of the abyss far
more unsteadily than in the years of his early struggle. So the
scene, and the film, stand for me as something of an emblem of
Faulkner's private and professional lives during the years following the prize and his public acclaim. The *Omnibus* film is a
pristine example of what Roland Barthes calls "the proletarian-
ization of the writer."[5]

It is, at the very least, one of the most curious episodes in
Faulkner's life, and from certain points of view it's one of the
most astonishing—that he would have agreed to the idea of the
program in the first place, much less been *in* the durned thing.
He had spent a lifetime generally protecting his right to be a
private individual; specifically, he had for over a year steadfastly
refused to cooperate with *Life* magazine reporter Robert Coughlan, who wanted to do a profile on him: he refused to cooperate
and, when Coughlan did the piece anyway and later published
it as a book,[6] Faulkner wrote an extended essay about the

episode called "On Privacy" (written October 1954) as part of a planned series of essays under the general title "The American Dream: What Happened to It?" Less than a year later, when Random House asked him to cooperate with *Time* magazine for a story to publicize *A Fable*, he again refused, telling Bennett Cerf to calculate how much his refusal would cost the firm, and he would pay it.[7]

Other contradictions rag and tatter at the edges of his life during this period. In April of 1952, for example, he wrote to Else Jonsson that he was going to accept the invitation of the French Government to participate in Paris's festival of 20th century works, but that he was not going as a "delegate": "the words 'delegate' and 'freedom' in the same sentence are, to me, not only incongruous," he wrote, "but terrifying too."[8] But before the end of the lustrum he was travelling for the U.S. State Department around the world as a "delegate" for American values, though of course these trips seem to have been problematized by some sort of internal resistance to what he was doing, so that he was constantly on the edge of shooting himself in the diplomatic foot. His local State Department hosts were constantly fearful that he would embarrass them and the United States by his excessive drinking, though in all cases he finally did behave and perform admirably. He spent a good deal of time and energy in the mid-50s speaking out against racial injustice in the South, but practically destroyed all his good efforts with one short statement—probably made while he was drinking, but almost certainly *made*—that if he had to kill Negroes in the street to defend Mississippi against federal intervention, he'd do it.[9] In public speeches in Stockholm, Oxford, Pine Manor, and later at the University of Virginia, he insisted that human beings had the capacity to endure, to prevail, to complete an incomplete world, to rid the world of tyrants by simply refusing to yield to the forces of oppression, by refusing to be afraid of the bomb, and by lifting their voices for justice and compassion. Privately, he expressed quite contrary opinions: "human beings are terrible," he wrote Else

Jonsson in 1955. "One must believe well in man to endure him, wait out his folly and savagery and inhumanity" (SL, 382). Early in the decade he wrote Joan Williams that she had to give up her enchainment to middle-class values in order to be a writer; by mid-decade, he was a Cold War warrior wittily writing to other writers that one way to end the Cold War was to bring 10,000 communists a year to this country for a year, let them buy automobiles on the installment plan, get jobs in our plants and factories, experience collective bargaining, say what they wanted to say, and so see for themselves how good and satisfying a middle-class American life could be (SL, 404); but by 1957 he was dressing in jodhpurs and foxhunting with the haute bourgeoisie of Charlottesville. At the same time that he was railing against such Depression issues as farm subsidies, he was travelling as a representative of the government that was giving the subsidies. At the same time he was delivering speeches extolling the value of home and family and *normalcy* (Pine Manor), he was perfectly aware of how far short of even normal, let alone ideal, his own family situation was.

Publicly, Faulkner was at the pinnacle of a career to be dreamed about; privately, his life was a singular hell, for reasons he didn't seem to understand. He suffered excruciatingly from a bad back; he was in and out of hospitals here and abroad; he drank heavily and, in 1952, entered a New York hospital where he had psychiatric care and may have been administered electric shock treatments.[10] Even an amateur Freudian might want to see some form of self-punishment in his continued insistence on riding horses that frequently threw him and reinjured his back, and in his refusal to have the operation that might have relieved some of his back pain. This was, then, a *highly* troubled period in Faulkner's life, a period characterized by a kind of restlessness that was entirely new to him.[11]

I don't want to trivialize the issues that I'm engaging here by suggesting that he, *even he*, was undergoing a belated midlife crisis, but in fact just about every one of his fictional and private utterances of the period is eyeball deep in the symptoms of midlife crises that find emptiness in the very success one has worked so hard to achieve. I would bet there's something very personal in Faulkner's portrait of Flem Snopes in *The Mansion*, the bank president, the pillar of the community, who after years of pursuing his own version of the American Dream finds less fulfillment at the peak of his success than at the beginning of his quest, sitting alone in his bigger house and chewing not even tobacco or gum but merely air. "I seem to have lost heart for working," Faulkner wrote his agent Harold Ober on August 20, 1952. "I cant find anything to work, write, *for*" (SL, 339).

One of the most interesting and revealing of the letters he wrote to Joan Williams was this one, on April 29, 1953:

> And now, at last, I have some perspective on all I have done. I mean, the work apart from me, the work which I did, apart from what I am. . . . And now I realise for the first time what an amazing gift I had: uneducated in every formal sense, without even very literate, let alone literary, companions, yet to have made the things I made. I dont know where it came from. I dont know why God or gods or whoever it was, selected me to be the vessel. Believe me, this is not humility, false modesty: it is simply amazement. I wonder if you have ever had that thought about the work and the country man whom you know as Bill Faulkner—what little connection there seems to be between them. . . . [SL, 348]

This letter rings with authenticity; it emerges tenderly, naively, from some amazed recognition of his gift, almost as an epiphany, producing a helpless sense of awe at how radically that gift had set him apart from ordinary people. There's no trace of megalomania, it seems to me, but just a bewildered astonishment at what he'd made of himself. It is as though he is looking at some such image of himself as we see in the *Omnibus* film, trying to find in the icon, the Nobel laureate, some semblance of himself that he can recognize.

This was by no means of course the first time he was conscious of the difference between himself and his background, of how paradoxical and outrageous he was. James Meriwether has long held that in his famous description of Eula Varner as a

Frenchman's Bend product, he was probably also talking about himself as a product of a "little lost village, nameless, without grace, forsaken, yet which wombed once by chance and accident one blind seed of the spendthrift Olympian ejaculation and did not even know it."[12] Faulkner had echoed this in a description of Oxford in a letter of August 3, 1951, to Bob Haas at Random House about his refusal to cooperate with *Life* magazine: "I have deliberately buried myself in this little lost almost illiterate town, to keep out of the way so that news people wont notice and remember me" (SL, 319). One of the characteristics of his work during this period is its tendency to incorporate his created world, and himself, into it. As Michel Gresset and others have shown, Faulkner's work throughout his career is full of autobiographical elements and of demonstrable self-portraits.

Three quasi-autobiographical pieces that he wrote within six weeks of each other in February and March of 1953, hard on the heels of the *Omnibus* filming in November and of its airing in December, and only a few weeks before that letter to Joan Williams, may be relevant here. The slightest of these is "A Note on Sherwood Anderson," which he wrote as an introduction for a proposed edition of Anderson's letters that never happened. Published in the *Atlantic* in June of 1953, it is a warm memoir of Anderson, whom Faulkner credits with having taught him that one place is as good as another to write about, that the single requirement of being a writer is to remember what you were, no matter where you start from: "You're a country boy," he says Anderson told him: "all you know is that little patch up there in Mississippi where you started from. But that's all right too. It's America too." To Anderson he attributes mentorship both in his example as a working writer and in his straightforward advice about the dishonesty of glibness: "You've got too much talent," Faulkner says Anderson told him: "You can do it too easy, in too many different ways. If you're not careful, you'll never write anything." I think it's fair to wonder whether Anderson did in fact say these things to Faulkner or whether Faulkner simply attributes them to Anderson in

acknowledgment of the older writer's significance in his career—
his looming giantism. The memoir recounts their friendship,
their life in New Orleans, and their falling out over the satire of
Anderson's style in *Sherwood Anderson and Other Famous
Creoles* in terms that praise Anderson's hard work and his
dedication to his craft, especially to his style—"the exactitude
of purity or the purity of exactitude"—long after style was all he
had left, and which he in effect hid behind to protect the writer
who knew that there was no content left. The essay resonates
with so many things that seem to be on Faulkner's mind
throughout this period that it is tempting to think that he is
mostly talking about himself, especially in the recognition of the
virtuosity of his talent and of his responsibility to discipline that
gift strictly. His fatigue and his difficulties completing *A Fable*
certainly were major concerns that he expressed to others,
privately, as a fear that he had scraped the bottom of the barrel
and had no more to write. He may also have been thinking of
himself, even if not consciously or deliberately, when he described Anderson as "a giant in an earth populated to a great—
too great—extent by pygmies."[13]

The second piece is a short story that he sent to his agent on
February 19, three days before he finished the appreciation of
Anderson. "Mr. Acarius" is demonstrably autobiographical, at
least in its origins in the time Faulkner spent in a private
hospital in the Bronx, where he may or may not have had
electric shock treatments, in December of 1952 during the
interim between the filming and the airing of the *Omnibus*
feature. He began working on "Mr. Acarius" on January 16,
while the details of his stay there were fresh on his mind.
Briefly, Mr. Acarius is a wealthy man who is nevertheless very
unhappy, whose money and Picassos and the other accoutre-
ments of success don't bring him any sense of permanence, any
conviction that there is any part of himself that, after the bomb,
will have "left any smudge or stain" on the world.[14] He wants to
do something to give his life meaning and he undertakes to
"experience man, the human race" (436) by getting drunk and

debasing himself, even if not on skid row but rather in an expensive alcoholic's hospital. His reason for doing this is primarily to punish himself for being different, somehow to atone for that difference by finding a common sty to wallow in with humanity:

> I'm not just no better than the people on skid row. I'm not even as good, for the reason that I'm richer. Because I'm richer, I not only don't have anything to escape from, driving me to try to escape from it, but as another cypher in the abacus of mankind, I am not even high enough in value to alter any equation by being subtracted from it. But at least I can go along for the ride, like the flyspeck on the handle of the computer, even if it can't change the addition. At least I can experience, participate in, the physical degradation of escaping . . . the surrender, the relinquishment to and into the opium of escaping, knowing in advance the inevitable tomorrow's inevitable physical agony; to have lost nothing of anguish but instead only to have gained it; to have merely compounded yesterday's spirit's and soul's laceration with tomorrow's hangover. . . . Mankind. People. Man. I shall be one with man, victim of his own base appetites and now struggling to extricate himself from that debasement. Maybe it's even my fault that I'm incapable of anything but Scotch, and so our bullpen will be a Scotch one where for a little expense we can have peace, quiet for the lacerated and screaming nerves, sympathy, understanding . . . and maybe what my fellow inmates are trying to escape from—the too many mistresses or wives or the too much money or responsibility or whatever else it is that drives into escape the sort of people who can afford to pay fifty dollars a day for the privilege of escaping—will not bear mention in the same breath with that which drives one who can afford no better, even to canned heat. But at least we will be together in having failed to escape and in knowing that in the last analysis there is no escape, that you can never escape and, whether you will or not, you must reenter the world and bear yourself in it and its lacerations and all its anguish of breathing, to support and comfort one another in that knowledge and that attempt (436–38)

It's not terribly difficult to hear Faulkner's voice in Mr. Acarius's explanation—his prose could certainly be taken as a parody of Faulkner's style—nor to see in Mr. Acarius's argument perhaps some of Faulkner's explanations for or rationalizations of his similar behavior, and his self-lacerations and his pure bewilderment at not knowing what he needs to escape *from*. Doubtless Mr. Acarius—whose curious name is a form of a word naming a genus of "minute spider–like animals," a mite, one of the smallest of vermin, whose sole function in life seems to be to cause skin disease—doubtless Mr. Acarius's speech echoes Faulkner's agony in trying to understand why he of all people should be so unhappy.

Mr. Acarius's desire to enter humanity is precisely Faust's desire, stated almost in Faust's own language, in Goethe's great poem:

> Frenzy I choose, most agonizing lust,
> Enamored enmity, restorative disgust.
> Henceforth my soul, for knowledge sick no more,
> Against no kind of suffering shall be cautioned,
> And what to all of mankind is apportioned
> I mean to savor in my own self's core,
> Grasp with my mind both highest and most low,
> Weigh down my spirit with their weal and woe,
> And thus my selfhood to their own distend,
> And be, as they are, shattered in the end.[15]

This is not the Faustus of legend who sells his soul to the devil to gain all knowledge and power, but rather that Faust who has already *gained* all knowledge and power, has drunk its lees and found it wanting, and who asks Mephistopheles's dark powers to help rid himself of the burden of his superiority. Faulkner's evocation of Faust here is, I believe, deliberate, and the autobiographical nature of the allusion speaks for itself.

Mr. Acarius doesn't find a humanity that he can share anything with. He is appalled at what he finds in the expensive hospital among the humanity who can afford to be there, much less what he would find in a Manhattan skid row gutter. They are shattered indeed, but he is not, and so returning home, unlike Faulkner, who goes home and writes about it, Mr.

Acarius smashes all his bottles in the bathtub and swears off drink: "So you entered mankind, and found the place already occupied," his doctor taunts him. "Yes," Mr. Acarius says, cries, in an apparent non sequitur that echoes the runner's cry at the end of *A Fable:* "You can't beat him. You cannot. You never will. Never" (448).

"Mr. Acarius" and "A Note on Sherwood Anderson"—one fiction, one nonfiction—are, then, only thinly veiled autobiographical explorations of his sense of his differences from other people. "Mississippi," which he wrote in March of 1953, is a *sui generis* combination of fiction and nonfiction, which he overlays with the deliberately autobiographical. In "Mississippi," Faulkner negotiates for his central autobiographical character a reconciliation with his native land and its citizens. He does not appear as a writer or artist but instead as a fully contextualized citizen, like the character in the *Omnibus* portrait. Unnamed, he could be Everymississippian; we know him only by his ages, as the boy, the young man, the middleaging, the gray-haired. In "Mississippi," then, Faulkner eloquently claims the full kinship, the commonality, with fellow human beings that he had sought in "Mr. Acarius" and "A Note on Sherwood Anderson."

I suppose what I'm moving toward is some agreement with Michael Grimwood that Faulkner became increasingly aware of the extreme distance between what he wrote and the capacity of the people he wrote about, and so putatively *for*, to understand anything he wrote, and so derive some benefit from it.[16] Grimwood does not deal with the post-Nobel Faulkner who, for him, was so far gone in decline by 1942 that his career was virtually over. Nevertheless, from this vantage it becomes possible to see Faulkner's willingness to engage political and ideological issues publicly—to travel to universities in Oregon and Washington to deliver "On Privacy" as an address, to spend time at the University of Virginia discussing his work with students and faculty, as well as his sustained efforts in behalf of racial justice in the mid-'50s, his numerous expeditions around the world in behalf of the State Department, and even his *Omnibus* portrait—as a necessary and inevitable extension of a growing conviction that artists don't have to be, don't even have a right to be, alien to or alienated from the world in which they have to live. This view would help us understand why he would accept commissions from such decidedly blue-collar publications as *Sports Illustrated* to do pieces on the Kentucky Derby and on an ice hockey game.

But I certainly don't agree with critics of the late Faulkner who implicitly side with Phil Stone's comment that Faulkner got "Nobelitis in the head,"[17] and that his public life in the fifties is a direct expression of an inflated and preening sense of himself as having been certified Wise and so competent to speak on all things. There's simply too much pain and doubt in his life during these years to allow me to accept that. More to the point, there's simply too much disillusionment with the common run of humanity he has allied himself with: like Mr. Acarius, he joins humanity to atone for his superiority and finds not atonement but chaos, death, and disillusionment.[18] More particularly like the runner in *A Fable*, he wants to join the ranks of the common soldier, to give up his pip, the sign of his superiority. The officer from whom he asks this boon assumes "[y]ou love man so well you must sleep in the same mud he sleeps in"; the runner argues that it's not at all that he loves humanity, but quite the reverse: "It's just backward," he says. "I hate man so. Hear him? . . . Smell him, too":

> When I, knowing what I have been, and am now, and will continue to be . . . can, by the simple coincidence of wearing this little badge on my coat, have not only the power, with a whole militarised government to back me up, to tell vast herds of man what to do, but the impunitive right to shoot him with my own hand when he doesn't do it, then I realise how worthy of any fear and abhorrence and hatred he is. . . . So I must get back into the muck with him. Then maybe I'll be free.

"Free of what?" his company commander asks, and he responds: "I dont know either. Maybe of having to perform forever at inescapable intervals that sort of masturbation about the human

race people call hoping. That would be enough."[19] For all his
public testimony to humanity's capacity to renew itself, to
endure and prevail, etc., there is no evidence whatsoever to
indicate that Faulkner really believed it, and quite a bit of
evidence to suggest the opposite.

Thus whatever glaring contradictions one wants to find in
Faulkner's career during the 1950s, the ones that don't glare
publicly are the most problematic for him as a person and
artist—and for us as admirers. These contradictions represent
the absolute schism between his public pronouncements and
his private convictions; given that schism, there are certainly
ways in which we can call his appearance in the *Omnibus* film
and his other public appearances at worst a gross hypocrisy, at
best a moral preening, a pandering for attention.

But those who would criticize Faulkner for performing these
charades might well think again. As Morse Peckham has reminded us, the three speeches most often cited as *proving*
Faulkner's new-found celebration of human dignity—the Nobel
Prize address, and his addresses to the Oxford High School
graduates and the graduating class at Pine Manor Junior College—were occasional utterances, written for specific audiences,
all three of which included his own daughter, and delivered
under circumstances which made some form of optimism mandatory.[20] What should the gloomy tragedian say to a group of
high school graduates on the verge of their lives?—
*Congratulations on making it this far. You've been lucky. I'm
sorry to have to tell you now, however, that life is all sound
and fury, signifying nothing. Breathing is a sight draft dated
yesterday. Between grief and nothing always take grief, but
don't count on much more. Go forth and await your doom.
Thank you very much?* Or how should he have addressed the
younger aspirants to the Nobel Prize on the futility of it all when
he, standing so successfully on that pinnacle in Stockholm,
would himself have been the denial of his own nihilism? Could
he discourage younger writers from their life's work by forecast-
ing meaninglessness and doom? Manners, if nothing else, dic-

tated that he could not,[21] and so he found himself participating in, acting out, literally and figuratively, the ideological rituals of his culture, formally endorsing them even though he himself did not find them fulfilling.

On its darkest side, one may find in this participation disturbing resonances with Arthur Koestler's novel of the Stalinist show trials of the 1930s, *Darkness at Noon,* whose protagonist, completely innocent of the political crimes with which he is charged and for which he is going to die in any event, at first adamantly resists his counsellor's request that he confess publicly anyway, and accept his punishment, and then finally accedes to the idea that the Party, the ideological structure, is more important than any of the individuals within the structure; he dies in the name of the structure. On the slightly less somber side, there are ways in which Faulkner resembles Miguel de Unamuno's memorable priest, "San Manuel Bueno, Martyr," who long after his own faith is gone continues to minister to his rural flock in the terms of that faith's rituals, and so to sustain in them the hope of salvation (perhaps it's the hope of meaning, significance) that he himself has lost. In sustaining their faith, he asserts the value of the very ideology he has given up, sacrificing himself in its name but for their sake. In the Compson Appendix, Faulkner described Andrew Jackson's defense of his wife's honor as having nothing to do with her honor in and of itself but with "the principle that honor must be defended whether it was or not because defended it was whether or not."[22] Like Jackson, Faulkner seems in the fifties to be defending certain values, whether they are or not, and by doing so asserting their value, if not their validity: hope, like grief, being better than nothing, certainly better than chaos.

Of course he could have refused to take part, he could have refused the Nobel Prize, as Jean-Paul Sartre did, on Sartre's grounds that he didn't want to accept the compromises that he felt such recognition would necessarily entail. But Faulkner didn't refuse the recognition or the prizes, nor did he refuse the compromises, although he may have seen them not as compromises but as opportunities for expansion. In any case, act out those rituals he did, perhaps quite simply out of a refusal to extrapolate from his individual experience a universal declaration that success had to be empty for everybody, a refusal to believe that because he was not happy at home, nobody could be. Perhaps Unamuno's and Koestler's heroes are not so far apart in the practical effects of their sacrifices, but Koestler's hero sacrifices himself for the system, Unamuno's—and Faulkner—for the people within the system. San Manuel learned, as Faulkner would, how essential to people are the illusions that their ideologies provide.

During the mid-50s, then, I'd propose that Faulkner tried his hand at the political *engagement* for which the French existentialists argued. He attempted to give the masses a sign they could understand and respond to, in a language and in a medium they did have access to rather than in the language of his high art: to see if he could somehow persuade them if not to individuality, then at least to their personal *and* collective best interests. For example, he argued the race question first on the moral grounds that racial inequality was wrong, then on the practical grounds that if Southerners didn't change the situation themselves, some other, outside, agency would force change upon them. Then as now, neither argument worked because of the mass mind that clung so tenaciously to the "mouth-sounds" of their allegiance to the ringing rhetoric of liberty and justice for all,[23] while clinging equally tenaciously to racist and nationalist ideologies that denied equality, and would brook no suggestion that the mouth-sounds flatly contradicted one another.

There is on occasion a kind of shrillness in Faulkner's ministry that doubtless emerges from his increasing frustration with a humanity that insisted on acting in the mass, that acted out of mindless subservience to blatantly political ideological aggression and manipulation. It is, in short, a frustrated confrontation with humanity's refusal to be free, its fear of freedom, and its humiliating and debilitating *need* to move en masse, in the ideological safety of numbers. His funniest and most trenchant treatment of this sort of behavior erupts—no: *explodes*—out of nowhere as the final paragraph of his January 24, 1955, *Sports Illustrated* piece called "An Innocent at Rinkside," in which he reported on his first visit to an ice hockey match:

> Only he . . . did wonder just what a professional hockey-match, whose purpose is to make a decent and reasonable profit for its owners, had to do with our National Anthem. What are we afraid of? Is it our national character of which we are so in doubt, so fearful that it might not hold up in the clutch, that we not only dare not open a professional athletic contest or a beauty-pageant or a real-estate auction, but we must even use a Chamber of Commerce race for Miss Sewage Disposal or a wildcat land-sale, to remind us that that liberty gained without honor and sacrifice and held without constant vigilance and undiminished honor and complete willing-ness to sacrifice again at need, was not worth having to begin with? Or, by blaring or chanting it at outselves every time ten or twelve or eighteen or twenty-two young men engage formally for the possession of a puck or a ball, or just one young woman walks across a lighted platform in a bathing-suit, do we hope to so dull and eviscerate the words and tune with repetition, that when we do hear it we will not be disturbed from that dream-like state in which 'honor' is a break and 'truth' an angle?[24]

Faulkner indeed became a Cold War warrior, but he opposed Joe McCarthy and voted for Eisenhower in 1952 because he feared that another "liberal" president would lead to a backlash that would put a McCarthy in the White House. And, critical as he was of his own country, he did indeed support the notion that America, with all its problems, offered better alternatives for individual achievement than the Soviet Union. But he did not take the real problem to be a simple struggle between two contending ideologies, as he wrote in "On Fear":

> Because it makes a glib and simple picture, we like to think of the world situation today as a precarious and explosive balance of two irreconcilable ideologies confronting each other: which precarious balance, once it totters, will drag the whole universe into the abyss along with it. That's not so. Only one of the opposed forces is an ideology. The other one is that simple fact of Man. . . .[25]

The first paragraphs of "On Privacy" even more explicitly define
the American Dream itself as a

> sanctuary . . . for individual man: a condition in which he could be
> free not only of the old established closed-corporation hierarchies of
> arbitrary power which had oppressed him as a mass, but free of that
> mass into which the hierarchies of church and state had compressed
> and held him individually thralled and individually impotent.[26]

The nations of the old world "existed as nations not on citizenship but subjectship, which endured only on the premise of size
and docility of the subject mass."[27]

Thus Faulkner conceived the ideological problem of the fifties
not as a horizontal one, in which two contending economic and
social philosophies vied for world dominance, but rather as a
vertical one which in blood-chilling fact found Capitalism and
Communism actually united with each other and standing in a
deadly hierarchical opposition to the very people, the citizens
of both persuasions, whom by their rhetoric they claimed to
serve—but which rhetoric in fact made them servile, by holding
out both numerical security and hope: precisely the condition
that makes them contemptible to Mr. Acarius and to the runner
of *A Fable*. What happened to the American Dream was not
merely a problem of temporal political and economic concerns,
but rather a structural problem, systemic and, as Faulkner
may have come to believe, given human nature, probably
ineradicable.

Throughout this period, Faulkner's continued work on *A
Fable* forms a steady ground bass for all his other activities,
public and private. It provides tempo and key for all the themes
and variations, all the jazz riffs, going on in the upper and more
visible registers, and, like the ground bass, is always at the root
of the chord. Like Mr. Acarius, the runner in *A Fable* wants to
leave the empyrean realms of officerhood and rejoin the human
race, to lose himself in that moiling mass, so that he can quit
hoping *for them*. Like Mr. Acarius, and for the same reasons,
the runner is also at least partly an autobiographical—or autometaphorical, at any rate—figure, in some ways more specifi-

cally than Mr. Acarius is. When the runner leaves the front lines and returns to his old Paris neighborhood, specifically to seek his lost dead youth, he seeks it by retracing "the perimeter of his dead life when he had not only hoped but believed" (148). In Paris, he passes through the Luxembourg Gardens, past the stained queens, and down the rue Vaugirard, already "looking ahead to discern the narrow crevice which would be the rue Servandoni and the garret which he had called home (perhaps Monsieur and Madame Gargne, *patron* and *patronne,* would still be there to greet him)" (148–49). The rue Servandoni, of course, was the address of Faulkner's own little garret during his time in Paris in 1926, and I'd bet Luster a quarter that Monsieur and Madame Gargne were Faulkner's own landlord and landlady.

If in going to Paris to find his lost dead youth the runner is indeed an autometaphorical figure, he is also an artist figure, an artist like Faulkner, whose goal has become an impossibly romantic one—nothing less than to save the world through art—and who is ruthless in advancing his idealism. He believes that if he can just find the right secret sign, even if he has to steal one from the Masons, even if he doesn't fully understand its meaning, and even if he has to kill somebody in order to put himself in a position to show it, he can inspire the world toward pity and compassion, toward peace; he is searingly scarred in the attempt; and, at the end of the novel, for all his idealism, he remains always the needy child in a Pietà, sucking at the empowering and delimiting breast of the political institution which alone can provide him nourishment and comfort, and screaming in echo of Mr. Acarius, "I'm not going to die. Never" (437)—though he is of course here one of *us* instead of one of *them*.

*   *   *

In *A Fable,* a Christ-like corporal leads the troops on both sides of the line simply to stop fighting; the novel is about the efforts of the Allied military elite to work in concert with their German counterparts to prevent the soldiers from destroying the military structures—here symbolizing the world's political and ideological structures—which are, the novel seems to demonstrate, essential to their lives. Without those structures, without the symbolical walls of the city of Chaulnesmont to hold and contain them, they flow, shapeless and impotent, into the plains surrounding the city. The officers on opposing sides of the war speak to each other in each other's language—that is, they speak to each other in ways the soldiers cannot; they have a common language not of nationality or geographical boundary, that the soldiers do not have: the language of class and power. The novel thus specifically evokes the class tensions of Jean Renoir's great 1937 film *Grand Illusion,* in which the enemy officers demonstrate their own class solidarity by holding their most important conversations in English, which the French prisoners and the German guards cannot understand. I'm not prepared to defend any proposition that the language of that novel is as vivid or as rich in ecstatic or supple rhythms or in that vital allusive and implicative quality of the prose we generally understand, at its best, to be "Faulknerian," but I do claim that the prose is deliberate, as consciously a part of the novel's structure and meanings as it is in his other novels. The prose in some ways actually presents fewer problems than others of Faulkner's novels. There is, I think, less of the destabilization of meaning caused by ambiguous pronominal references, for example, and fewer of the deliberate narrative gaps, as in *Absalom, Absalom!* or *Go Down, Moses* or *The Hamlet,* where Faulkner frequently refuses to tell us *what happened,* preferring instead to allow narrator-characters to fill in those gaps themselves through their own reconstruction, reconstitution, and interpretation of the very few factual givens they have to work with—and, indeed, making of those attempts to reconstruct, reconstitute, and interpret the substance of the works, the essence of the fictional enterprise itself.

There are very few such gaps, even historical ones, in *A*

Fable. What *happens* in *A Fable,* or even in the world created for *A Fable,* is seldom at issue. Indeed, the entire military establishment is committed precisely to avoiding those historical and factual gaps: the military has a "metabolism which does everything to a man but lose him, which learns nothing and forgets nothing and loses nothing at all whatever and forever—no scrap of paper, no unfinished record or uncompleted memorandum no matter how inconsequential or trivial" (240). In fact, the completeness, the intactness of the record of Europe's past is very much a part of the "ponderable shadow" of the Roman citadel (343) that looms over the martial headquarters city of Chaulnesmont, very much the "stone weight" (342) of that citadel, of that specifically military history, which seems to "lean down and rest upon" (343) the actors in this drama. It is not, then, the corporal's reinterpretation of history or any effort to understand it, but simply his straightforward intervention in the people's blind and sheeplike allegiance to their history that rouses their ire, forcing the top-ranking generals of the Allies and those of their historical enemies, the Germans, to confederate, to heal the rupture the corporal has caused not just in the historical record, but in the very structure of the way things are, which is itself a product of that history.

If we accept John T. Matthews's formulation that central to Faulkner's understanding of language is the conviction that "any form of representation, any sequence of signifying gestures, behaves like a language," we may be persuaded as well that whatever the effect of the prose of *A Fable,* that novel is no less concerned with language than any of his other novels, and that it accepts the idea of language as a "sequence of signifying gestures" perhaps more directly and intensely than any of the other books do. Matthews suggests that Faulkner's novels "regularly center their crises on the capacity or failure of characters to interpret, explain, master—in a word, to articulate—the common predicaments of loss, change, or desire."[28] This does not hold strictly true for all the characters of *A Fable,* however; none of them seems to have any problems with articulation,

much less an experience of articulation as a crisis, though
each of the main characters does indeed face the "common
predicaments of loss, change, or desire" in varying degrees. Yet
the book as a whole is very much concerned with problems of
articulation, with the whole problem of fictional meaning and
the ways in which fictional meaning is conveyed. In the most
often quoted passage from *A Fable's* climactic interview between general father and corporal son, this powerful father
defines for his idealistic son, and the reader, precisely what the
issues in their relationship are. They are not "two . . . peasants
swapping a horse," he notes, but rather "two articulations"
(347), not "representatives" or "symbols," but specifically "articulations" of two opposing but complexly related views of life:
power, structure, pragmatics, disillusion if not cynicism on the
one hand; weakness, idealism, hope, and need on the other.
Put this way, the issues are the same we have seen constantly
at work in his other fiction, but in reverse relief. The old general
and the corporal are not, then, as the general reminds us,
representations of ordinary, "real" people engaged in quotidian
economic and social intercourse, and verisimilitude is no part of
the problem: the old general admits, in ways I'm not sure occur
elsewhere in Faulkner, that they are characters in a novel,
signs, if you will, which are part of the language of fictional
discourse. *A Fable* is a semiotician's dream.

They are, then, two "articulations"; it is, for a number of
reasons, a significant term, for if the corporal and the old general
are equally articulations of their respective positions, they are
by no means equally articulate of those positions. Indeed,
though their confrontation has been compared to the dramatic
discussion between Isaac and Cass in *Go Down, Moses*, theirs
in no sense resembles a dialogue, since the old general does all
the talking; the corporal hardly says anything at all, much less,
like Isaac McCaslin, put forth anything resembling a coherent
philosophical justification for what he does or thinks, here or
anywhere else in the novel. There are sufficient reasons for this.

I have argued in another place at greater length that what

Roland Barthes has to say about the nature of myth and of mythical language in his *Mythologies* seems to me particularly useful in thinking about *A Fable,* for *A Fable* is also precisely about the nature of myth, as Barthes defines it, and of its language.[29] The two books are roughly contemporary—*A Fable* was published in 1954, but Faulkner had conceived and begun working on it in 1943; *Mythologies,* published in 1957, was written between 1954 and 1956—and both books are at least partly their authors' responses to the postwar ideological scramble in which the cold war, the mass media, and modern technology combined in ways that drove the wedge between the powerful and the powerless, the individual and the masses, the illusioned and the disillusioned, even more deeply than the war had. Though Faulkner doubtless would not have stated his own motives in the same way, a paragraph in Barthes' preface may well also stand as Faulkner's animus: the starting point of Barthes' reflections was usually a feeling of impatience at the sight of the

'naturalness' with which newspapers, art and common sense constantly dress up a reality which, even though it is the one we live in, is undoubtedly determined by history. In short, in the account given of our contemporary circumstances, I resented seeing Nature and History confused at every turn, and I wanted to track down, in the decorative display of *what-goes-without-saying,* the ideological abuse which, in my view, is hidden there.[30]

In a general sense one may say that much of Faulkner's fiction has been devoted to finding a language for saying *what-goes-without-saying.* Many of the issues in his work may be seen as a confrontation between the *what is* and the *what ought to be* or *what might have been if things could have been different.* What separates *A Fable* from the rest of the canon most strikingly is that it is most concerned with the *what is:* specifically, it is an analysis of the forces that create and perpetuate the *what-goes-without-saying.* All of Faulkner's other works are written from the point of view of the powerless, the have-nots, those who are disenfranchised in one way or another, who butt up against

the *what-is* of culture, economy, society, family, tradition—all
various names for the all-powerful father—and spend their
lives and their voices trying, unsuccessfully, to articulate their
estrangement from the historical processes that have created
the terms of their ideological grasps of the world—their myths—
and so perhaps to reconstitute themselves in history. Faulkner's
work is filled with characters who confront the myths of their
culture—Horace Benbow, for example, and the myth of justice;
Quentin Compson and that of virginity; Thomas Sutpen and
Flem Snopes and that of bourgeois power and respectability. In
general, those who *act*, like Flem and Sutpen, make more of a
mark on history, for good or, more likely, for ill, than those who
merely talk. Horace and Quentin are destroyed by their inability
to force reality to conform to their myths. But what Flem and
Sutpen want most to do is not at all, like the corporal, to destroy
or expose that myth, even though they die in the process, but
rather to join forces with it, to become its willing, even self-
sacrificial allies; and whatever their degree of success, they are
no less betrayed by those bourgeois myths than Horace and
Quentin, than Levine, the Quarter-master General, and the
priest—all of whom, like Koestler's and Unamuno's heroes,
destroy themselves rather than admit the failure of the ideological structures they have invested in.[31]

If the other novels can be said to be about the effects of the
bourgeois myths on the characters, *A Fable* may be said to be
about the established forces that perpetuate and maintain those
myths, those who benefit by them, and those who know not
only how to manipulate them to their own advantage but how
to keep the swarming, incoherent, inarticulate masses believing
that those myths operate in their own best interests. The old
general and Flem Snopes understand, more perceptively than
any of Faulkner's other characters, the ways that myths work in
people's lives, and know how to exploit those myths to their
own advantage: they know that people with illusions are ripe for
exploitation. Unlike Flem, though, the old general has no
illusions himself, except the major one that allows him to assume

that he is where he is by virtue of who he is, instead of by virtue of the several accidents of history; at the top of the historical heap, he doesn't *need* them. Flem, starting from the opposite end of the political and social spectrum from the old general, believes that he can find happiness in the American Dream, and the trilogy traces his rise from the obscurity of the Yoknapatawpha backwoods to become, in *The Mansion,* "a pillar, rock-fixed, of things as they are"—exactly what the old general is.[32] The trilogy's human scale, its intimacy, make Flem's discovery of the emptiness of bourgeois life, and the passive form of suicide he commits, a very personal thing, and perhaps finally cathartic in its effect: few have felt pity or fear or empathy in thinking about Flem, but I find him terrifying.[33]

A *Fable's* epic scale, the magnitude of the general's power over the lives of all western Europe, makes intimacy impossible, and we are confronted on page after page with an old general who really believes that he manipulates the belief systems of "the people" not for personal aggrandizement, either in the pleasure of exercising power or for any kind of personal gain, but simply because *they need it,* because they *need* some political or religious credo to provide coherence to their lives. The novel's portrait of *the people*—a portrait of sheep, helpless, inarticulate, contemptible and barely able even to feed themselves without the military's help—seems to justify the old general's paternalism. Indeed, one of the deeply disturbing aspects of the novel is how frantically the masses run from the freedom the corporal offers. They love the foul-mouthed cockney groom who cynically manipulates their fear of death, who literally sells them a reason to live by betting that they won't; they blindly follow to their deaths the runner who shows them a sign, without once asking what the sign means or who is flashing it or why. They are eager to be sheep, to live or die *for something they can believe in,* though they die gloriously in the air or ingloriously in the mud; they will eagerly die, babbling the "polysyllabic and verbless patriotic nonsense" (354) that the old general describes in articulating himself to his son. They are savagely angry at the corporal, their putative savior, because he forces upon them a challenge to the Fatherland and Motherland totems of their political belief systems.

So the old general's—Power's—absolutely inescapable bind is that it *must* sustain the masses in one illusion or another simply to maintain order, so that they don't trample each other to death: in the bleakest reaches of A *Fable's* themes, there is no alternative to the ideological manipulation of people's minds. The old general's pragmatic brilliance is precisely in co-opting the corporal's self-sacrifice, in making of him a martyr who will confirm them again in those political myths, and soothe them back into a war which is destroying them, but which they think they can understand: anything but freedom. He can make of the corporal what the corporal cannot make of himself—a sign, the sign they would see and believe in—and so give them what the corporal cannot: hope.

The old general believes that no ideological structures have validity, and that all of them have value only as they are co-opted and *used* by a political/power system that itself has no illusions. The old general, who in his small size and the delicacy of his features also makes one with other Faulknerian self-portraits, has enough of character and conscience, not to say of wealth and power, to be fully aware of all these considerations and to entertain, without illusions about them, a profound compassion for their moiling lives, their minimal needs: their capacity to endure and prevail even when their only sustenance is hope.

*   *   *

Having joined the human race in the ideological trenches, joining the battle for its soul, and being beaten over and over by its intractable and inexhaustible commitment to its own ideological prisons, during the middle part of the decade Faulkner gave up. He tried his best to engage people on their own terms, using the methods of logical argument and the media they understood, to show them where their ideological commitments were leading everybody, the nation and the world, and he failed to change one damned thing. After 1956 there's a noticeable slowdown of his public activities, a renewed and even mellow commitment to his fiction first and to a social life with Charlottesville family and friends next.

And so in fact we may not have very much to choose between the early Faulkner and the one of the mid-50s: the differences may lie more in the color of the hair and the set of the lip than in anything going on under the surface, where there is great continuity between that early tragic vision and what is arguably a profoundly darker vision in the late work, especially in *A Fable*—a darkness more visible than Milton's even, if we know how to see it, because it is systemic. It does not derive from ambition, greed, or any of the psychic or criminal compulsions, as in Faulkner's early works, but from humanity's enslavement to its ideological illusions—a humanity that will not be free because it insists on hope.

NOTES

1. Perhaps many of you also noted that while all our national attention was diverted into voting upon which Elvis we should memorialize (the old establishment figure or the young revolutionary), the Post Office, quite without any public discussion, issued first class stamps assuring us that we all supported Desert Storm!

2. See Lawrence H. Schwartz, *Creating Faulkner's Reputation: The Politics of Modern Literary Criticism* (Knoxville: The University of Tennessee Press, 1988).

3. Cheryl Lester, "To Market, To Market: *The Portable Faulkner*," *Criticism,* 29 (Summer 1987), 371–92.

4. See Charles Sellers, Henry May, and Neil R. McMillen, *A Synopsis of American History,* 7th ed. (Chicago: Dee, 1992), 402.

5. Roland Barthes, *Mythologies,* trans. Annette Lavers (New York: Noonday Press, 1975), 29.

6. Robert Coughlan, "The Private World of William Faulkner," *Life* (September 18, 1953); see *The Private World of William Faulkner: The Man, the Legend, the Writer* (New York: Harper, 1954).

7. See Joseph Blotner, *Faulkner: A Biography* (New York: Random House, 1984), 586–7.

8. *Selected Letters of William Faulkner,* ed. Joseph Blotner (New York: Random House, 1977), 330–31. Further references will be cited in the text as SL.

9. See Noel Polk, "Man in the Middle: Faulkner and the Southern White Moderate," *Faulkner and Race,* ed. Doreen Fowler and Ann J. Abadie (Jackson: University Press of Mississippi, 1987), 130–51.

10. See Blotner, 563–64.

11. See Michel Gresset, "A Public Man's Private Voice: Faulkner's Letters to Else

Jonsson," *Faulkner: After the Nobel Prize*, ed. Michel Gresset & Kenzaburo Ohashi (Tokyo: Yamaguchi Publishing House, 1987), 61–73.

12. Faulkner, *The Hamlet*, The Corrected Text (New York: Vintage International, 1991), 164.

13. Faulkner, *Essays, Speeches, and Public Letters*, ed. James B. Meriwether (New York: Random House, 1966), 6–10.

14. Faulkner, "Mr. Acarius," in *Uncollected Stories of William Faulkner*, ed. Joseph Blotner (New York: Random House, 1979), 435. Further references will be cited in the text.

15. Goethe, *Faust*, trans. Walter Arndt, ed. Cyrus Hamlin (New York: W. W. Norton & Co., 1976), 42 (ll. 1766–75).

16. Grimwood, *Heart in Conflict: Faulkner's Struggles with Vocation* (Athens: The University of Georgia Press, 1987).

17. Blotner, 562.

18. See James B. Carothers, *William Faulkner's Short Stories* (Ann Arbor: UMI Research Press, 1985), 26, 57, 105–6.

19. Faulkner, *A Fable* (New York: Random House, 1954), 61–62. Further references will be cited in the text.

20. Peckham, "The Place of Sex in the Work of William Faulkner," *Studies in the Twentieth Century*, no. 14 (Fall 1974): 1–20.

21. See Noel Polk, "Enduring *A Fable* and Prevailing," *Faulkner: After the Nobel Prize*, 110–26.

22. Faulkner, *The Sound and the Fury*, The Corrected Text (New York: Random House, Modern Library, 1992), 330.

23. Faulkner, "On Fear," *Essays, Speeches, and Public Letters*, 92–106.

24. Faulkner, *Essays, Speeches, and Public Letters*, 51.

25. Faulkner, Ibid., 102.

26. Faulkner, Ibid., 62.

27. Faulkner, Ibid.

28. Matthews, *The Play of Faulkner's Language* (Ithaca: Cornell University Press, 1982), 17.

29. See Polk, "Roland Barthes Reads *A Fable*," in *Faulkner's Discourse: An International Symposium*, ed. Lothar Hönnighausen (Tubingen: Max Niemeyer Verlag, 1989), 109–16.

30. Barthes, *Mythologies*, 11.

31. We may understand what the old general and the corporal are "articulations" of, I think, and get some sense of what is at stake in their confrontation by noting the structural similarities between *A Fable* and its closest structural cousin, *Absalom, Absalom!* Both have at their centers a confrontation between a powerful father and an abandoned son from a distant past whose untimely reappearance threatens to destroy the structures upon which the fathers' lives are built—as I went to type "lives" in that sentence, I first typed "lies," which is of course a truer word, truer to the extent that their lives are built upon assumptions which force them—and allow them—to ignore history. Both sons are children of foreign women, conceived on foreign soil, and so half foreign themselves; both fathers are pursued by women who hate them for their pasts; both fathers have the stories of their lives narrated by women who believe they have reason to hate them. But while Sutpen rises from a white trash beginning, spends his life in a frustrated and doomed effort to become a part of, and then to maintain himself in, the social and political and economic power structure of the American South, the old general, quite to the contrary, is born directly at the very top of those power structures of western civilization. No more than Sutpen, however, can he escape the entailed consequences of his birthright; and no more than Sutpen can he, finally, escape history.

32. Faulkner, *The Mansion* (New York: Random House, 1959), 222.

33. See Polk, "Idealism in *The Mansion*," *Faulkner and Idealism: Perspectives from Paris*, ed. Michel Gresset and Patrick Samway (Jackson: University Press of Mississippi, 1983), 112–26.

William Faulkner: Why, the Very *Idea!*

LOUIS D. RUBIN, JR.

I wish to begin this discourse about, or in any event making use of, a novel by William C. Faulkner of Oxford, Mississippi, with a quotation from, of all things, Abraham Lincoln's House Divided speech of 1858:

> If we could first know *where* we are, and *whither* we are tending, we could better judge *what* to do, and *how* to do it.

Lincoln, who was getting ready to run for the Senate, proceeded to develop a rather far-fetched conspiracy theory indicting Stephen A. Douglas, the outgoing and incoming Presidents of the United States, and the Chief Justice of the U.S. Supreme Court, all of whom were Democrats, for plotting to expand chattel slavery into the free states. Not being a billionaire, I am not planning to run for office this summer myself, and have no conspiracies to expose, whether political or literary. All the same, on the occasion of what I think makes my fourth involvement in the Faulkner and Yoknapatawpha Conference, I thought it might be interesting to try to step back and have a look at the whole enterprise—not just the conference itself, or my own participation in it, but what it is that we are about, or *think* we are about, in this particular kind of activity, and why. Doing so might perhaps tell us something about Faulkner and the nature and understanding of the literary imagination. And Abraham Lincoln's prescription for how to go about it seems a good way to begin.

If we could first know *where* we are . . .

We are in Oxford, Mississippi, of course, at the University of

Mississippi, holding a conference, the 19th annual as I count them, on the life and work of William Faulkner. We are here because Faulkner lived in this community for most of his life, and wrote his books here, and attended irregularly and worked briefly in the post office and power plant of this university. So if anyone is going to hold an annual conference on William Faulkner, certainly this is the place to hold it.

As participants, mostly we are academics, teachers of literature at colleges and universities, though our ranks also include, and over the years have included, persons who knew William Faulkner, members of his family, editors, other novelists, journalists, and—in the audience—persons who have read Faulkner's novels and become interested in them and in the author who wrote them.

We are here, I think, for various reasons. Some are practical, involving such things as academic standing and advancement, tenure, the availability of summer grants, getting published, earning a livelihood, and so on; and also the desire to pleasure ourselves, to see old friends and make new ones, to be part of an intellectual and social enterprise, to experience the satisfaction of being able to sound off, to be heard doing it, to be paid honoraria for doing it, etc. Nobody present, I assume, is here under duress; nobody got drafted into being present at a Faulkner conference.

We are also *here,* rather than somewhere else at which presumably the kinds of practical motives for our presence just cited might be equally furthered, because a man who lived in this town from the 1900s until the early 1960s wrote several dozen works of fiction some few of which, among the tens and even hundreds of thousands of works of fiction written during his lifetime and afterward, stand out as being more imaginatively interesting, compelling, and enjoyable to read than those of almost any other American author of his day. We want to know more about how the novels got written, about the life and times of the man who wrote them, about the relationship of the books to that life and those times, about the connections between the various books themselves, and their relationship to books by other authors.

What it comes down to is that reading those novels and stories has constituted an imaginative experience for us of sufficient emotional intensity to impel us to want to extend that experience and to understand it better. So, if it is an explanation for this particular enterprise, which is to say, the reading and study of the work of William Faulkner, that is at issue, that reading experience is where we must look; and it is therefore where the balance of these remarks will be centered.

Very well. So here we are. **Whither, then, are we tending?**

We are tending in all sorts of directions, depending on who we are and what our needs and our motives are, whether literary, social, political, psychological, biological, economic, or whatever. Each of us has opinions. Generally we will leave this place by the same gates through which we entered. Like the man who wrote the novels, we too inhabit a time and a place, and as readers (and critics) we not only evaluate our reading of Faulkner's fiction (and every other experience we have) in terms of what we know, think and feel about our time and place, but we also seek to adapt our interest in that fiction to what we should like our time and place to be, and not be, for us. We try to *use* the fiction for our own purposes.

Since for no two readers is the human involvement in our time and place identical, in no instance can what we seek to do about it be precisely the same, and neither for that matter can any of us read the fiction in exactly the same way. Still, although none of us can share *everything* with someone else, no small amount of common, shared experience is possible; in most important respects we are more *like* than *unlike* others of our species. If this were not so, then not only the reading of novels, but all communication between humans, would be impossible. When in his Nobel Prize address (delivered in American English with a Southern accent to an audience primarily composed of Swedes) William Faulkner speaks of "the old verities and truths of the heart, the old universal truths lacking which any story is ephemeral and doomed," and proceeds to enumerate them,[1] we all know what he is talking about, although the particular applications we may make can and do differ.

Faulkner once remarked about the French, in an interview I think, that as a people they tended to take ideas too seriously. Whether or not that is so, it is in our nature as human beings to attempt to sort out and organize our experience, including the experience of reading fiction, into schematic categories, and to fit each new experience into the overall ideological scheme. As noted, we read Faulkner's fiction, and then we attempt to *use* it. Abstraction is inescapable.

I was thinking the other day about some of the ideological purposes to which we have sought to put the fiction of William Faulkner over the years. Let me cite only a few.

- To demonstrate that nobody can know anything about anything real.
- To advocate social change, reform, amelioration.
- To argue that nobody can ever ameliorate or improve on any-thing—to hold back change.
- To eradicate what we perceive as being evil.
- To sidestep it or explain it away.
- To demonstrate that every idea also signifies precisely the oppo-site: $a = -a$, or *non-a*.
- To prove that the New Criticism is an "elitist" plot against the democratic way of life.
- To defend the white South, including the racial attitudes of the pre-*Brown v. Board of Education* South.
- To attack the white South and denounce its racial attitudes.
- To show that Mississippi and the South were ignorant, backward, and prone to violence.
- To show that the Old South was Classical and spiritual in outlook and that the North was Romantic and materialistic.
- To justify the theology of the Anglican and Roman Catholic churches (so far as I can tell, none of the other churches or religions seem to care about literature one way or the other).
- To show that membership in the Anglican and Roman Catholic churches is a conspiracy against the Declaration of Independence, the Bill of Rights, and the Third World.
- To attack males, whites, blacks, Protestants, silent majorities,

noisy minorities, communism, fascism, capitalism, city dwellers in general and dwellers in New York City in particular, aristocracy, the middle class, rednecks, Hollywood, television, the New Deal, the Fair Deal, sharecropping, labor unions, deconstruction, psychoanalysis, Ronald Reagan, Thomas Jefferson, Abraham Lincoln, Henry Ford, Ernest Hemingway, the internal combustion engine, the Supreme Court, the state of Mississippi, organized religion, fundamentalism, cultural pluralism, Ph.Ds, bankers, the American Legion, Wall Street, conservationists, the Modern Language Association, the National Rifle Association, capital punishment, poets, James Joyce, Allen Tate, the *Sewanee Review,* the nuclear family, supermarkets, semiotics, William Tecumseh Sherman, Harvard and Yale Universities, and several other things.

- To defend all of the above—except perhaps Harvard and Ronald Reagan.

My point here is certainly not that all such endeavors are equal in value, or equally relevant, or irrelevant; nor is it that there are not legitimate uses to be made of Faulkner's fiction for real-life purposes. It is rather that what we do here can have reverberations that go far beyond the reading of fiction as such, and also that the ways in which we read Faulkner's fiction are shaped by the real life that we take to it. What we bring to the fiction can enrich our experience in reading it, or it can impoverish it. As one very acute reader of Faulkner's fiction, Robert Penn Warren, remarked about the reading of fiction in general on another occasion,

> The materials that go into [a writer's] work come from the rough-textured life around him, made up of beliefs and facts and attitudes of all kinds. A bigoted Catholic can't read Milton, and a bigoted Protestant can't read Dante, but a civilized Catholic can read Milton with joy. There's a point, though, where one's commitment to basic ideas and basic materials, by reason of bigotry or something else, makes one incapable of accepting the total vision of an art—of a novel or a poem, or whatever. Let's face this fact. The autonomy of the art is always subject to the recalcitrance of the materials and to your own lack of self-understanding.[2]

Now the fact is—and we tend sometimes to forget this—that there are certain very definite self-limitations to what we are engaged in doing when we study the fiction of William Faulkner. First of all, who are "we"? No small number of us, I think, are teachers of literature, or ex-teachers of literature, or teachers of composition, perhaps, who hope to become teachers of literature. This is not to be deplored, or condescended to; for the plain truth is that if it were not for the so-called "academy" of which we are part, William Faulkner's fiction would be all but unknown today. Mainly it is we who keep reading it, and set our students to reading it. *Absalom, Absalom!* and *Gone with the Wind* were both published in the year 1936; both are "about" the Civil War; there are numerous other similarities. But for every person who reads Faulkner's novel, a hundred read Margaret Mitchell's. *Absalom, Absalom!* is in print today, and will I trust be in print a century from now, because of the academic audience—because of college and university English departments.

I mention this because it amuses me sometimes to read what some of our colleagues write when they inveigh against "elitism" in literary study; not only this conference but the reading and study of William Faulkner's fiction is almost totally an "elitist" operation, and for my part I say Thank Goodness for it, and for English departments and what they do. When we elect to teach *Absalom, Absalom!* instead of *Gone with the Wind* or the novels of John Jakes, and we require our students to read Faulkner's great novel, we have made an "elitist" judgment; we say that one person's taste in literature is *not* as good as another's, that there is such a thing as an informed and cultivated taste in literature, which is the product of a college education and an acquaintance with a large body of literary work that most persons have never read and never will read. We may object to some of the social, political, and economic assumptions that historically have accompanied the existence of that educated audience and the formation of that taste, but we cannot very well deny the fact that most of us, in our participation in this conference today and in what we do to earn a living, are engaged in an activity that is "elitist" all the way.

There are, even so, liabilities to the kind of academic sponsorship that William Faulkner's fiction enjoys. In part they have to do with the very nature of literary study itself. Now Faulkner's fiction, like all literary work, is "about" so-called real life; if it were not, we should not be interested in reading it. To draw on currently popular terminology, it is a simulacrum. None of us can know real life perfectly, since in order to understand it we have to translate its impact into words; but we all know that life exists out there beyond us and outside as well as within us, and it is precisely in the tension between real life and our effort to apprehend it through language that works of imaginative literature (and other things as well) have their being and their place under the sun.

When, however, we as scholars and teachers of literature set out to teach and to talk and write about novels and poems, we labor under a disadvantage (it is also a unique advantage, which I will point out presently.) For if, say, *Absalom, Absalom!* is "about" real life, a simulacrum of it with meanings added, then in dealing with and thinking about Faulkner's novel we are involving ourselves in real life only by second hand (or, if our common human reliance upon language itself to deal with real life makes all human experience a second-hand affair, then by third-hand). In writing and discoursing upon a work of literature, which is at one remove from the life it images and shapes, we are thus positioned at two removes from it. "This is a watchbird watching a watcher; this is a watchbird watching you."

Now depending upon one's temperament, this can be more or less frustrating. Most of our professional colleagues—historians, say, or political scientists, or sociologists, or philosophers, or atomic physicists—can believe that in their classes and in what they write they are dealing with real life itself (I will not get into the metaphysical dimensions of all this; I will simply assert that they at any rate assume that is what they are doing). A historian writing about the South and the Civil War believes that he is writing directly about the war as an historical entity. We, however, as literary critics—"mere litterateurs," as I remember a reviewer in the *Journal of Southern History* once describing the late Vernon Louis Parrington in contradistinction to Charles A. Beard and, I believe, Frederick Jackson Turner—cannot write directly about the Civil War; instead, we have to write about the way that William Faulkner portrays the Civil War; we have to discuss *Absalom, Absalom!*

This can make some of us, at least, extremely uncomfortable. We feel ourselves secondary, marginal; instead of teaching and writing about the actual war itself, we must spend our lives discoursing upon somebody's novel. (And perhaps our attitude toward what we do is not helped by the knowledge that many if not most of us started out, back in grammar school or high school or college, with the intention of being novelists or poets ourselves, instead of teachers and critics.) Added to this is the fact that most people in the non-academic world in which we dwell tend to share that estimate of what we do; as the late Mayor Jimmy Walker of New York is said to have declared once about a book censorship case, "no lady ever lost her virtue from reading a book." (That is not, I think, true.)

What often happens, therefore, is that we tend to spend a large portion of our time and ingenuity attempting to finesse that imaginative barrier between second-hand and direct involvement in the world of power, politics, getting and spending. We strain to place our professional activity, the study of literature, in first-hand contact with real life itself, which is to say, the subject matter of the literary work, and we use ideas and theories drawn from non-literary controversy to sort out and evaluate the worthiness and authenticity of novels and poems. We become Marxist critics, psychoanalytical critics, Agrarian critics, gender critics, existentialist critics, historical critics, anthropological critics, Afro-American critics, myth critics, liberal critics, conservative critics, Catholic critics, or what have you. We yearn for an ideological scheme, a theoretical absolute to anchor our all-too diffuse traffic with the literary imagination, and when we find one we surrender our literary doubts and equivocations to the categorical demands of the cause—and to justify our doing so, we announce that anyone who doesn't also approach literary study from a conscious and formulated ideological stance is therefore a covert believer in and defender of the *status quo ante Oliver Cromwell*. In accordance with a working principle of Marxist (and primitive Christian) doctrine, we assert that whoever is not with us is *per se* against us.

Now again, if literature were not about real life it would hold no interest for us; and I am far from denying that we have every right to explore the involvement of the literary works that we teach and write about in every aspect of the human experience that they image. Nor do I overlook the fact that an engrossment in ideology is by no means restricted to literary scholars— although I do think we tend to be especially good at it. Yet it is important, I think, not to lose sight of the fact that if we are not teachers and critics—which is to say, readers—of *literature,* then professionally we are nothing. It is the engagement with literature that brings us here rather than to somewhere else. And to choose literature as a profession entails certain responsibilities as well as opportunities.

To suggest what they are, so that we may "**better judge** *what* **to do,**" in Lincoln's formulation, I want now (and it is about time, most of you are undoubtedly thinking) to turn to William Faulkner's fiction itself.

The most famous passage in all of Faulkner's work, I think— more notable even than the description of the slaying of Old Ben in "The Bear," or the horse's advent at Mrs. Littlejohn's boardinghouse in *The Hamlet,* or Benjy's ride around the Square in *The Sound and the Fury*—is the "I dont hate it!" episode that concludes *Absalom, Absalom!* I need scarcely do more than summarize the situation here. At the very end of the novel, after Quentin Compson and Shreve McCannon have at last figured out why it was that Henry Sutpen shot to death his closest friend, Charles Bon, Shreve, who is a Canadian, makes a prediction that ultimately all of North America, including the South, will be a miscegenated society. He then asks Quentin, a Mississippian, a question. " 'Now I want you to tell me just one thing more. Why do you hate the South?' "

> "I dont hate it," Quentin said, quickly, at once, immediately; "I dont hate it," he said. *I dont hate it,* he thought, panting in the cold air, the iron New England dark; *I dont. I dont! I dont hate it! I dont hate it!*[3]

Because it so aptly encapsulates the love-hate relationship that so many of us who grew up and lived in the racially segregated South of the pre-1960s had with our native community, this extraordinary conclusion to an extraordinary novel has been quoted frequently and even interminably by literary critics and historians of the South alike (including the present writer). Coming as it does and when it does, its ramifications, of course, are multifold. Let me cite only a few of them.

The relevance to the South, and by implication to racial injustice there, is obvious. As Charles Bon himself puts it (or is imagined by Quentin and Shreve as having put it), he is not Henry Sutpen's brother, but "the nigger that's going to sleep with your sister" (358). It is the intensity of the northern Mississippi community's social mores, instilled within him, that forces Henry to do his father's bidding and shoot his friend to prevent his marriage to his sister, who is also Charles's half sister. Henry's dilemma is by inference Quentin's, for Quentin too is a member of that community, albeit nearly a half century after the murder. Quentin can imagine himself in Henry's place, and although one assumes that in his time he would not have felt similarly compelled to maintain family racial inviolability by murdering someone, nonetheless he can understand the pull of the community standards, and even feel a certain contempt for his own weakness of character, as he perceives it, in being unable to take decisive action—as in the episode with Dalton Ames in *The Sound and the Fury*. Henry Sutpen, in Quentin's eyes, may have been wrong, but he was not too spineless to act on his convictions.

What the last paragraph does is to focus the ultimate meaning of the novel upon Quentin, and in several ways. It is Quentin who in the winter of 1910–1911 (or 1909–1910, if we are to take into account the chronology of *The Sound and the Fury*) has been telling the story of Thomas Sutpen and his family to his roommate. He is the one upon whom the events that take place between the late 1810s and the 1860s and 1870s have their emotional impact. The young man we encountered in the opening pages as he listened, with indifference and even boredom, to an old woman telling him a story of doings that happened decades earlier, has by the close of the story experienced pity and terror through remembering, retelling, and coming to understand the meaning of those events. That the racial and social attitudes of his community could have made possible not only the murder of Charles Bon by Henry Sutpen but the very rise and fall of Thomas Sutpen himself is appalling for Quentin Compson to contemplate, and when Shreve concludes by asking his question, Quentin is staggered by the complexity of the moral and ethical dilemma forced upon him by dint of his birthright.

Odi et amo. But if it is Quentin who is caught up in the question, it is Faulkner who writes so intensely and passionately about it—and lest we fail to make the connection, Faulkner tells us, very early on, that, as Miss Rosa Coldfield put it, Quentin may want to "enter the literary profession as so many Southern gentlemen and gentlewomen too are doing now"(9). Any student of Southern literature can identify, in the progression of Southern fiction from the days of William Gilmore Simms through those of Thomas Nelson Page and Joel Chandler Harris and on to those of Faulkner's generation, just such a process of exploration and discovery, including self-discovery, as takes place in *Absalom, Absalom!* concerning what finally is acknowledged to lie behind the actions of Henry Sutpen. Nor did that process of self-discovery cease in 1936, the year that Faulkner's great novel appeared.

It is not only race, and community attitudes toward race, that are involved in Quentin's agony. He is both awed by and dismayed at the force and enormity of Thomas Sutpen's ambition; he recognizes the urgency of Sutpen's quest for plantation grandeur, perceives the human, including the social, motives that drove this youth of poor white origins along his upward path to status within the community, comprehends the heroic dimensions of Sutpen's courage and iron will, and is appalled by the price that is exacted on those men and women who are made adjuncts to one man's monstrous design.

"I dont. I dont! I dont hate it! I dont hate it!" What that last paragraph tells us, too, is the inadequacy of language, of words, to articulate the complexity of Quentin Compson's emotional experience. As if the single abstract verb proposed by Shreve McCannon could possibly comprehend the intensity and complication of Quentin's response to the process of discovery and recognition that he has just completed! (Yet it is through language that we are enabled to understand this; for we are reading a novel.)

Absalom, Absalom! is a tricky affair; we might even call it, as has been suggested about fiction in a different context, a labyrinth, a verbal maze. If so, Ariadne's ball of thread that will lead us to the Minotaur and safely back again is certainly the consciousness of Quentin Compson. That the route there and back is a devious path indeed, with many cunning corridors, contrivances, and turns, can scarcely be denied. And just as there is a dispute over just how Theseus killed the monster, so there has been much argument concerning how Quentin found out that Charles Bon was Thomas Sutpen's son, and also that he was part black in ancestry—*if* he was.

It is an interesting controversy. My assumption has always been that when he went out to Sutpen's Hundred with Miss Rosa Coldfield to see the dying Henry Sutpen, Quentin also saw Clytie, Sutpen's daughter by a slave woman, and, recognizing in her African physiognomy the family resemblance to the white Henry Sutpen, he deduced what the missing ingredient in the mystery of Charles Bon's murder was.

In one of the short stories from which the novel evolved, "Evangeline," a newspaperman goes out to Sutpen's Hundred, is shown a tintype of Charles Bon, and recognizes the Sutpen cast of the face.[4] But this would not do for the novel. Not only is it insufficiently rich in underlying significance and reverberation, but it would not enable the story to be what it became: a novel about a young Mississippian's discovery of the meaning of his heritage; surely the final paragraph of the novel would not have been possible had the solution to the mystery been as matter-of-fact and as specific as that. What Quentin must come to realize, through the events of the novel as they are uncovered, is that the only plausible and convincing explanation for Henry Sutpen's killing of Charles Bon, in and for that time and that place, *had* to be race: the dread of miscegenation. Nothing else could adequately account emotionally for what happened.

Quentin must come to understand this through what he has found out about the Sutpen family from Rosa Coldfield; from his father and his father's memory of what his own father, Sutpen's friend, told him; from the lore of the place in which the events took place and which has been passed on to him as a member of the community; and from his own visit to the scene of the crime. The young man who in the opening pages can see little relevance in the Sutpen story to his own time and place must learn that what is in the story lies at the very center of his identity as a member of that community, and that it is not to be set aside by going off to college at Harvard a thousand miles away.

Yet learning the answer to the question of why Henry killed Charles is not the whole story, either. Quentin makes a point of telling Shreve that it was from himself, following his nighttime visit to Sutpen's Hundred with Miss Rosa, that his father received "an awful lot of delayed information awful quick," as Shreve puts it. One assumes that among the things that he would surely have told his father was his assumption that Charles Bon was part black—hence the critical controversy over how he could have found that out. But knowing that crucial fact, and even thereby understanding why it caused Henry to kill Charles to prevent him from marrying Judith, was not sufficient. What Quentin needed to understand in order to grasp the relevance of the Sutpen story for himself—and what William Faulkner needed to understand in order to write the novel—was the full human dimension of the rise and fall of Thomas Sutpen and its impact upon his family and descendants as well as the other persons affected by Sutpen's quest to found a dynasty in northern Mississippi.

No small amount of critical discourse has taken place on the subject of whether Thomas Sutpen was a "representative" antebellum planter, whether the story of *Absalom, Absalom!* constitutes a Faulknerian allegory of the rise and fall of the Old South, and so on. I have had my say about this.[5] Glib misreadings of the matter, and corrections to such misreadings, however, do not obviate the fact that the Sutpen story has been deeply grounded by the author in the history of the Deep South, and that in developing Quentin Compson's exploration of the rise and fall of the Sutpen family, William Faulkner was engaged in exploring his own community's history, and in full awareness that the social and ethical problems thereby posed were still very much alive and in need of solution.

Shreve McCannon is in the novel to help with that exploration; a detached viewpoint was needed to complement Quentin's intense emotional immersion in the story. Faulkner placed him there for that purpose, and it is important to keep in mind that not only Quentin Compson of Jefferson, Mississippi, but Shrevelin McCannon of Edmonton, Alberta, Canada, are equally creations of and voices for the author's imagination. The last words of the novel, *"I dont hate it!,"* and the emotional revelation they contain, are Quentin's—Quentin is arguing with himself, trying to convince himself that his retort to what in his first reflexive response he takes as an accusation is indeed true, that he does not at bottom hate his homeland, but the question is Shreve's, and both are embodied in the act of developing narrative consciousness in language that *Absalom, Absalom!* is.

If we fail to give due weight to that dimension of the novel, but instead interpret the story simplistically, we will impoverish our own experience by declining to take into account the full measure of what we have been involved in when we read Faulkner's narrative. "Why do you hate the South?" A young Canadian college freshman at Harvard is asking a young Mississippi freshman at Harvard that question. A Mississippi novelist, writing his novel a quarter-century after the dialogue between Quentin and Shreve is made to take place and when the novelist is twice the age that Quentin was at the time of the dialogue, makes Shreve ask the question, and Quentin respond to it. The incident comes at the conclusion of a narrative in which first Quentin, then Quentin and his father, and thereafter Quentin and Shreve seek to unravel a labyrinthine story of the rise and fall of the Sutpen family.

The story we have read has been told to us in chronological form—but not in the order in which events happened to the Sutpens; rather, the chronological order is closer to that of Quentin's experience in learning the story and attempting to understand what was happening. Note, however, the words *closer to;* for it is by no means arranged in the strict order of Quentin's history from the time that Miss Rosa Coldfield summoned him to her house in Jefferson to tell him about Thomas Sutpen until he and Shreve have completed their reconstruction of the events. Not until very late in the narrative are we told about Quentin's visit to Sutpen's Hundred with Miss Rosa to see Henry Sutpen, which took place on the evening following Quentin's conversation with Miss Rosa and before Quentin left Jefferson, Mississippi, to attend the college at Harvard.

Bear in mind, too, the modes of discourse in which the story has been told. There has been dialogue—between Quentin and Shreve, between Quentin and his father and Miss Rosa Coldfield (mainly monologue by the last named, to be sure), between the various members of the Sutpen family and others. There has also been narration by the (implied) author, often about what Quentin is thinking and feeling. The language used, though it can be colloquial and matter-of-fact, frequently turns intensely formal and rhetorical, and moreover what may start out as realistic colloquial dialogue often becomes high-style pronouncement. The viewpoint switches back and forth, as does the time frame; there are lengthy episodes set in italic type that is generally, though not always, used to indicate not only a time shift but the fact that what is being presented as happening is in actuality Quentin's imaginative reconstruction, or Quentin's and Shreve's. (But of course it has *all* been imagined as having happened, by William Faulkner, and as readers by us.) And there is this additional complication: lest anyone overlook the presence of the shifting modes of language, or the way that what begins as dialogue becomes formal rhetoric, or that what is conjecture in one episode can become fact in the next, or that scenes are taking place and conversations described that by realistic point of view logic couldn't possibly be reported to us, the author makes sure to call our attention to these things, almost as if little finger-pointer dingbats were being inserted in the text.

The result of all this, as I see it, is that from the outset we are being passionately directed toward the presence of a storytelling personality at work, a perspective of *consciousness* through which the events over a period of time are being allowed to happen, and that, whether as readers we knowingly accept its implications or not, importantly shapes our involvement in the story. Now there is a sense in which something like this is true of any narrative, regardless of how told; we are reading discourse, not taking part in real life. But in *Absalom, Absalom!* what in most fiction is merely an inherent property of prose narration becomes part of the story that is being told; it too is an event, subject matter, an aspect of meaning. *Absalom, Absalom!* is, when all is said and done, very much a story about consciousness itself.

Whose consciousness? Quentin's? Shreve's? The implied storyteller's? William Faulkner's? The reader's? At this juncture

the business of the watcher watching the watchbird watching
you becomes too intricately complex to fathom and sort out; I
content myself with saying that if I wanted to read a book about
what makes a Southern writer Southern, and a young person
into a writer, this is the book I would read. But the point I want
to make here is that the episode that ends *Absalom, Absalom!*,
Shreve's question and Quentin's response to it, is not merely a
little tacked-on irony meant to give the book another and last
authorial turn of the screw, so to speak, but the culminating
event of a central narrative development, and absolutely necessary to the working out of the story.

This fictional construction that we call a novel by William
Faulkner, then, is "about" real life, and draws its resonance and
its power from its recreation, through language, of problems
that have vexed and continue to vex our country's history—and
not ours alone, but the entire globe's as well. We are drawn to
the novel, and persist in introducing our students to it and
trying to understand it, because of its unique capacity for
recreating the presence and emotional nature of those problems.
The ideas in it, when isolated from the text and identified *as*
abstract ideas, are in no way new or original; the uniqueness
lies in the way in which they are incarnated for us, through the
use of words, as emotions. This is the province of literature.
The emotions and the ideas are made indissoluble; no other
form of discourse, not even film, can embody them with just
the subtlety, complexity, and urgency that are possible when
they are shaped into a work of fiction by the imagination of a
master storyteller. And it is the very fact that they are *not* real
life, raw experience, but are drawn from it by the literary
imagination and recreated as a story, that makes them available
to us in their human clarity and emotional authenticity.

Isn't it obvious, therefore, that as persons who by dint of our
aptitude, training, and interests are able to help make this novel
and other literary works more thoroughly available to others,
we need not apologize for doing so, or feel ourselves marginal
or secondary because we have chosen to do that rather than

something else? Why on earth, then, should we wish to finesse the imaginative boundary between literature and life, when it is precisely the existence of that imaginative boundary that gives us so stunning an access to the emotional identity and nature of that life? Who else, among all our academic colleagues and their fields of activity, can do what we do for our students? Who else can help make accessible to others the *kind* of emotional knowledge—for that is what it is—that *Absalom, Absalom!* offers?

That, then, is what we can do about it.

Finally, *"how to do it."* I have said that in *Absalom, Absalom!* Quentin Compson's consciousness is the thread—the yarn, I might even say—to lead us into the labyrinth, confront the monster (shall we call him Thomas Sutpen, or John C. Calhoun, or Satan, or perhaps The Ambitious Capitalist?), and return safely outside. What seems plain is that here is a document set very specifically in a particular time and place, which yet has resonance and relevance for earlier and later times and places, and that can be made to speak perceptively and profoundly about many human problems and quandaries. Yet to make use of it in any meaningful way we must first follow the thread all the way in, and then all the way back out; which is to say, we must read this novel from beginning to end, and seek to understand what is happening in all of it, not just part of it.

We do not read in a vacuum, and there are many tools that are available to us, in the form of our own real life experience, what we have been taught, methods and techniques and ideas and precedents and insights. Some of the tools are more useful than others; it is not my business today to make recommendations about which ones to adapt, or to adjudicate among rival claims to usefulness. I will say only that those theories are best which allow us to take greatest advantage of what we can do best, that put us in closest and richest contact with those literary works that are our special province.

From all that I can tell, no theory, no system for sorting out the component elements of the experience of reading, possesses a monopoly on the ability to provide access to literature—including those ways that, as the product of a particular time and place, I have been taught to go about it myself. *Autres temps, autres moeurs,* as the Japanese say. Besides, at bottom it is the critic, not the method, that matters.

What I do insist, however, is that if, as we must do, we seek to use stories, and poems, to understand our experience, then *they* are where we must look, and there can be no substitute for access to them. We cannot finesse the text of the novel or the poem; we must make it our own (which, I would point out, is a very different matter from substituting our text for the author's). Thus any ideology, way of reading and thinking, system or whatever that purports to make available *Absalom, Absalom!* to us without helping us to identify and explore the role of the consciousness of Quentin Compson, whatever the terminology we may choose to designate or refer to the activity of that consciousness, is to my way of thinking inadequate, because it denies us too much of what the novel has to offer, and distorts what it does use. To be sure, *all* methods and systems are inadequate for comprehending a literary work; but it is by the access that they offer us in our individual engagements with novels and poems that their usefulness must be judged.

As one might suspect, I have always felt just about as uncomfortable as Faulkner did about any tendency toward excessive reliance upon conceptual schematizations. These have been present in literary study at least since Plato, and without a way of organizing our experience of reading that will permit grouping and comparing, we should be helpless to think to any purpose. Moreover, it is also true that in order to *do* anything, it is necessary to formulate an approach—before the atom could be split, someone had to write $e = mc^2$; so the claim that those who resist the imposition of any kind of ideological ordering upon experience may be defenders, whether intentionally or not, of the *status quo* is not without validity.

Yet here we face a paradox. For it is precisely the complexity of the literary work, its ability to fuse idea, data, and emotion into an image, that constitutes its unique virtue. Nowhere is this more vividly dramatized than in the closing paragraph of *Absalom, Absalom!* Does Quentin hate the South, as Shreve McCannon proposes? Quentin denies it, "quickly, at once, immediately" (378). He is a Mississippian, away at college in cold New England, conversing with a Canadian; he will not countenance such a statement. He denies it to Shreve, and then he denies it to himself. "*I dont hate it.*" But he isn't sure; in an effort to convince himself, he repeats his denial four times; what began as an assertion ends as an exclamation. To understand what is going on with Quentin at that moment, one must take into account what has happened in *Absalom, Absalom!* up until then, which is to say, the developing consciousness of Quentin Compson. So that any effort on our part to fit Quentin's response into a formula, in order to bear out a preconceived theoretical schematization, comes up against the recalcitrance of the literary image itself, a recalcitrance that constitutes the source of its strength and authenticity. Using literature piecemeal or through synopsis is difficult to do well.

I do not say that it cannot be done. Indeed, if literature is to be of any use to us in understanding human experience, it *must* be done. But it cannot be done crudely, or clumsily, or glibly. The keenest critical intelligence is required.

What disturbs me about so many ideological movements, or systems for pursuing literary study in order to develop social, political, theological, aesthetic, or whatever kinds of argument, is that they lend themselves so readily to oversimplification. In effect they would use chunks and facets of *Absalom, Absalom!* piecemeal, as evidence, without bothering with Quentin Compson's consciousness, when it is the development of that consciousness in order to tell the story of the Sutpen family that gives the assorted scenes, relationships, and episodes their power and clarity.

I have to say that not a few precedures for theoretical schematization remind me in their workings of those operations for producing scrap metal out of used cars. First the automobile is gutted of upholstery, plastic, rubber, wood, glass and whatever; then it is placed in a huge press, and squeezed into something resembling a slab, and the slab is in turn stacked atop other such slabs and the whole mashed down even further. We see a flatbed truck driving down a highway bearing large bundles of these pressed-together slabs; there is enough of the original paint to remind us that what we are seeing was once somebody's Ford Mustang and Chrysler Imperial and Pontiac Grand Prix and Volkswagen Kharman Ghia and so on, painted maroon, blue, ochre, black, tangerine, and off-white, sedans and convertibles and vans and pickup trucks, when new gladdening the hearts of their assorted owners and thereafter keeping repair shop mechanics prosperous. Now they will be dumped into a smelter, their remaining individual impurities boiled away, and rendered into identically shaped ingots. Presumably the metal will be used to build new cars. The junkyard operator, the scrap metal dealer, and the proprietor of the steel mill are alike uninterested in the automobiles as automobiles; whether the stripped car is a Lincoln Continental or a Ford Escort is of no concern or value to them; all they are after is the scrap metal content.

With worn-out and discarded automobiles I do not object to this. But the literary ideologist, whatever the particular ideology and cause in view, who is unconcerned with the difference between *Absalom, Absalom!* and *Gone with the Wind*, or between either and the *Lords of the Ring*, because all he or she is after are the political, or economic, or thematic, or gender, or racial, or psychoanalytical, or whatever kind of relationships, would strip novels of their very reason for existence and their source of authenticity and authority. In the effort to reduce the literary imagination into evidence for ideological concepts, we are not only deprived of a unique access to understanding our experience, but the evidence itself will be falsified. We will get Quentin without his consciousness, which is something like ordering an ice-cream cone and getting ice and cream instead of ice cream.

As I've noted, we can't do without ideas, and to use literary works to develop and illustrate conceptual thought is both desirable and inevitable. But to do so without due and proper regard for the integrity of the novel or the poem is corrupt critical practice, and to the extent that any theory, any system for schematic ordering, leads us to such falsification of evidence, whether via distortion or oversimplification, that theory or system is intellectually dishonest. We can try to rationalize it all we will, cite causes and movements and whatever, invent special vocabularies to give new names to old truisms and slogans, but what gives us our reason for being and alone justifies our professional existence is a vested interest in the integrity and authenticity of the novel and the poem; they are in our hands. We do not, finally, study civil rights as such, or the American Civil War, or caste and class in the Old and New South, or the structure of prose narrative, or gender issues in Southern fiction, or the development of the American novel, or the Southern Literary Renascence, or the family romance, or doubling and incest in the Southern novel—we study them because they are, whether implicitly or explicitly, among the numerous components of a complex work of literary imagination entitled *Absalom, Absalom!* To the extent that we become so enamored of any particular theory or ideology that we get that process turned around in our minds, and begin trying to manhandle the novel so that it will fit more tidily into an intellectual schematization, we deny the very premises upon which our professional engagement is founded.

If this sounds like a truism, I am sorry for it; but I say it out of what is now close to a half-century of my own professional involvement. I have seen the ideologies and the theories come and go, and some have been more plausible and useful than others, but what remains constant (for all our individual ways of reading and thinking) are the words on the printed page as written by William Faulkner.

Let me close with a proposal. Quentin Compson, who as character and focal point of consciousness is central to the telling and the meaning of *Absalom, Absalom!*, was an unhappy young man, for reasons that are apparent both in that novel and in *The Sound and the Fury*. His intentions were good, but as we know from reading *The Sound and the Fury*, he was deficient in backbone; when his sister Candace needed his love and understanding, he was unable to provide them. Whatever his failure of nerve, however, it must be said that he paid the price for it. He was a decent young man, and he was, to the limits of his ability, responsible.

I like Quentin, as did William Faulkner; and I feel sorry for him. It is his intellectual and emotional honesty that I admire most; when he encountered cant and dishonesty and shabby dealing, he did his best, however Quixotically, to stand up to them. He has been dead these eighty-two (or eighty-three) years now, and it is high time, it seems to me, that those of us who read and teach and study the fiction in which he so memorably figures do something in his honor.

I propose, therefore, the formation of the Quentin Compson Society for Honesty in Literary Scholarship. Its motto should be, *"I dont. I dont! I dont hate it!"* Its purpose, and reason for being, should be the identification and labeling of cant, willful oversimplification, and sneaky manipulation in literary study wherever found.

Whenever a member of the Quentin Compson Society encounters an especially flagrant example of phony or slipshod practice in literary scholarship printed in a book or a periodical, he or she must go into action. Let a member come upon a passage which is obviously ideologically motivated nonsense, and straightaway he or she whips out a rubber stamp and brands it as such in the margin, thus alerting others to the presence of critical hokum.

To accomplish this objective the Society would need a trademark, or monogram or whatever, that could be made into a rubber stamp, which each member of the Society would receive along with membership card and ink-pad upon payment of dues. The obvious choice for such a trademark or monogram would be Quentin's initials: **QC.**

But here I hesitate. Quentin was a modest young man, embarrassed by all outward display or ostentation, and I am sure that he would have preferred that another symbol or set of initials be used rather than his own. In deference to Quentin's sensibilities, therefore, I propose that the initials of some other and less fastidious character in Faulkner's fiction be adopted for this purpose. Instead of **QC,** let us draw upon Faulkner's other and lesser Civil War novel, and stamp, in the margin alongside each and every oversimplifying, cant-bound critical passage we encounter, the initials of Bayard Sartoris.

NOTES

1. William Faulkner, "Upon Receiving the Nobel Prize for Literature," *Essays, Speeches, and Public Letters,* ed. James B. Meriwether (New York: Random House, 1965), 120.

2. Ralph Ellison, William Styron, Robert Penn Warren, C. Vann Woodward, moderator, "The Uses of History in Fiction," *Southern Literary Journal,* 1 (Spring 1969): 71.

3. Faulkner, *Absalom, Absalom!* (New York: Random House, 1936), 378. Further references are to this edition and will be cited in the text.

4. Faulkner, "Evangeline," *Uncollected Stories of William Faulkner,* ed. Joseph Blotner (New York: Random House, 1979), 610–19.

5. Louis D. Rubin, "Scarlett O'Hara and the Two Quentin Compsons," *A Gallery of Southerners* (Baton Rouge: Louisiana State University Press, 1982), 26–48.

Contributors

Martha Banta is professor of American Literature at the University of California, Los Angeles. Among her publications are *Failure and Success in America: A Literary Debate, Imaging American Women: Idea and Ideals in Cultural History*, and *Taylored Lives*. She is associate editor of *The Columbia Literary History of the United States* and a past president of the American Studies Association.

André Bleikasten, professor of English at the University of Strasbourg, has published numerous works on Faulkner in French and in English. Among the latter are *The Ink of Melancholy: Faulkner's Novels from "The Sound and the Fury" to "Light in August"* and "For/Against an Ideological Reading of Faulkner's Novels." Professor Bleikasten is, along with François Pitavy, in charge of the continuation of the French edition of Faulkner in the Gallimard *Pléiade* series.

Robert H. Brinkmeyer, Jr., is professor of American Literature and Southern Studies at the University of Mississippi. He is the author of *Three Catholic Writers of the Modern South, The Art and Vision of Flannery O'Connor, The Artistic Development of Katherine Anne Porter,* and numerous essays and book reviews. He is currently writing a book on fascism and the Southern writer.

Thadious M. Davis, professor of English at Brown University, has published widely on Southern and African American writers. Among her many contributions to Faulkner scholarship are "From Jazz Syncopation to Blues Elegy: Faulkner's Development of Black Characterization," "Wright, Faulkner, and Mississippi as Racial Memory," and *Faulkner's "Negro": Art and* *the Southern Context*. She is also the author of *Nella Larsen, Novelist of the Harlem Renaissance*.

Richard Gray is a professor in the Department of Literature at the University of Essex. Among his publications are *The Literature of Memory: Modern Writers of the American South*, *Writing the South: Ideas of an American Region*, and an edited work, *American Fiction: New Readings*, which contains the essay "From Oxford: The Novels of William Faulkner." Professor Gray is currently writing a book-length study of Faulkner.

Anne Goodwyn Jones is associate professor of English at the University of Florida. She won the Jules F. Landry Award for *Tomorrow Is Another Day: The Woman Writer in the South, 1859–1936*, a book that combines biography, social history, feminist criticism, and textual analysis. Her current book project is "Faulkner's Daughters," a study of women writers of the Southern Renaissance.

Richard H. King has been a reader in American Studies at the University of Nottingham since 1983 and was a visiting professor at the University of Mississippi during the 1989–90 academic year. A specialist in American thought and culture, he is the author of *The Party of Eros: Radical Social Thought and the Realm of Freedom*, *A Southern Renaissance: The Cultural Awakening of the American South, 1930–1955*, and *Civil Rights and the Idea of Freedom*.

Glenn Meeter is professor of English at Northern Illinois University, where he served as chair from 1984 until 1990. His publications include a novel and short stories as well as essays on religion and literature. At the 1989 Faulkner and Yoknapatawpha Conference he presented "Quentin as Redactor: Biblical Analogy in Faulkner's *Absalom, Absalom!*

James M. Mellard, professor of English at Northern Illinois University, is the author of *The Exploded Form: The Modernist Novel in America, Doing Tropology: Analysis of Narrative*

Discourse, and *Using Lacan, Reading Fiction.* He has also published more than forty essays, including *"The Sound and the Fury:* Quentin Compson and Faulkner's Tragedy of Passion" and "Lacan and Faulkner: A Post-Freudian Analysis of Humor in the Fiction."

Ted Ownby is associate professor of History and Southern Studies at the University of Mississippi. He is the author of *Subduing Satan: Religion, Recreation, and Manhood in the Rural South, 1865–1920* and is currently writing a book on the history of consumer culture in north Mississippi, drawing on such varied sources as literature, newspapers, general store account books, demographics, and census records.

J. Hillis Miller is Distinguished Professor at the University of California, Irvine. In addition to having published more than a hundred essays in journals and collections, he is the author or editor of more than twenty books on American and English literature, including *The Ethics of Reading* and *The Linguistic Moment: From Wordsworth to Stevens.* His most recent book is *Topographies.* He is a past president of the Modern Language Association.

Noel Polk is professor of English at the University of Southern Mississippi. He is the author of numerous publications on Faulkner, including *William Faulkner's* Requiem for a Nun: A Critical Study, and has edited *The Marionettes, Sanctuary: The Original Text,* and many other Faulkner works. He is also series editor of the Garland Faulkner Casebooks, a member of the editorial team for Garland's *William Faulkner Manuscripts* project, and on the editorial board of the *Faulkner Journal.*

Louis D. Rubin, Jr., is University Distinguished Professor of English at the University of North Carolina and founder and president of Algonquin Books of Chapel Hill. He is the author and editor of more than forty books, among them *The Faraway Country: Writers of the Modern South, A Gallery of Southerners,* and *The History of Southern Literature.*

Index